School of History

University of
St Andrews

Awarded to

Oliver Savage

for performance in

MO1008 - 2015/2016

The Travelers' World

 EUROPE TO THE PACIFIC

HARRY LIEBERSOHN

HARVARD UNIVERSITY PRESS
CAMBRIDGE, MASSACHUSETTS, AND LONDON, ENGLAND

First Harvard University Press paperback edition, 2008

Library of Congress Cataloging-in-Publication Data

Liebersohn, Harry.
The travelers' world : Europe to the Pacific / Harry Liebersohn.
p.   cm.
Includes bibliographical references (p.) and index.
ISBN 978-0-674-02185-3 (cloth : alk. paper)
ISBN 978-0-674-02747-3 (pbk.)
1. Oceania—Description and travel.   2. Travelers—Europe.
3. Cosmopolitanism—Europe.   4. Europeans—Travel—History.
5. Travelers' writings, European—History and criticism.
6. Europe—Intellectual life—18th century.
7. Europe—Intellectual life—19th century.   I. Title.

DU20.L54 2006
919.504092'24—dc22   2005052733

Designed by Gwen Nefsky Frankfeldt

 *Contents*

Acknowledgments   *ix*

Map: The Pacific Ocean   *xiv*

Map: Europe in 1815, after the Congress of Vienna   *xvi*

Introduction   *1*
Travelers as Ethnographers—Histories—Dimensions of a World

1   *Travelers*   *15*
Philibert Commerson—George Forster—Adelbert von Chamisso

2   *Patrons*   *77*
France—Great Britain—Russia—Germany

3   *Collaborators*   *139*
Ahutoru—Tupaia, Mai, Mahine—Elliot de Castro, Marin, Kadu—
Ali'i and Kings—Kingship in Tahiti: The Pomares—Kingship in
Hawaii: Kamehameha

4   *Philosophers*   *186*
Diderot and the Shock of Tahiti—Kant and George Forster—
Wilhelm von Humboldt on Linguistic Diversity

5   *Missions*   225
Dumont d'Urville and the Triumph of Racial Science—Sex, Speech,
and Prophecy in Tahiti—Native Missionaries, New Englanders, and
Kapus in Hawaii—Science and Religion in Conflict

6   *Darwin, Melville, and the End of a World*   273
Darwin and the "More Cheerful View"—Melville and the Casket Ships

Conclusion   298
Travelers as Interpreters—Travelers as Mediators

Chronology   307
Notes   315
Selected Bibliography   359
Illustration Credits   369
Index   373

Illustrations

A Pacific paradise, 1797   *3*

A Linnaean idealization of nature   *16*

The naturalists at work: George and J. R. Forster   *47*

The Romantic artist: Louis Choris   *65*

Europe enlightens the world   *89*

The gouty patron: Sir Joseph Banks   *102*

The patron as international benefactor:
    Count Nikolai P. Rumiantsev   *117*

William Mariner in native Tongan dress   *143*

Kadu in European dress   *159*

The folkloric North: an Aleut man and woman   *179*

Native monarchy: Kamehameha I   *184*

Popular derision of Hawaiian visitors to England   *187*

Aleut skulls for phrenological analysis   *210*

The master race: Rangui, a chief from New Zealand   *229*

Hero of the American mission to Hawaii: Henry Opukahaia   *250*

Queen Ka'ahumanu   *255*

Darwin's lowest grade on the human hierarchy: a Fuegian at Portrait
    Cove   *278*

Acknowledgments

Itineraries matter for the formation of ideas. That is one of the messages of this book, and it is incidentally borne out by the travels that have shaped it since its inception in Southern California during the late 1980s. It was my good fortune there to teach two courses in the history of anthropology with Daniel Segal, who turned my attention to intellectual horizons that led beyond my training in European history and, eventually, to the terrain—or better stated, the islands and oceans—of this book. I left for the Midwest in 1990 still an intellectual historian of Europe, but with the ambition of exploring the travel accounts of Europe's new worlds in North America and the Pacific. After my move I became aware that my new program as I had first envisaged it was too large, and the histories of North American and Pacific encounters were too different, for me to encompass them in one book as I had originally planned. Instead I first wrote a study of European–North American encounters. Only after completing it in 1998 did I turn my full attention back to the Pacific. I am glad that it was so, for this detour gave me time for a more leisurely exploration of the travelers' world than I would otherwise have undertaken. Past histories, like foreign countries, only slowly yield up their peculiarities to outsiders.

Many colleagues and friends have sharpened my understanding of the naturalist voyagers. For their comments, criticisms, and encouragement I particularly wish to thank Vanessa Agnew, Jonathan Allen, Tony Ballantyne, Hans Erich Bödeker, James Boon, Marie-Noëlle Bourguet, Peter Brown, D. Graham Burnett, Natalie Zemon Davis, Philippe Despoix, Peter Fritzsche, Michael Geyer, Tony Grafton, Thomas Head, Karin Knorr, Catarina Krizancic, Alf Lüdtke, Mark Micale, Jürgen Osterhammel, Kapil Raj, Carl Schorske, Vanessa Smith, Michael Steinberg, and Adam Sutcliffe. Although John Gascoigne and I did not talk directly about this project, I have benefited greatly from his studies of Joseph Banks.

Like the travelers studied in this book, I have been the beneficiary of a network of knowledge—one extending beyond personal acquaintances and involving labors that exceed what any individual could possibly hope to achieve in a lifetime. I am grateful to editors and compilers I have never met such as Warren G. Dawson, Michael Hoare, and others whose editions of letters and travel accounts have done so much to bring about a new history of travel. One book deserves special mention: Bernard Smith's *European Vision and the South Pacific.* Its publication in 1960 marked a fresh starting point for the history of cultural encounters, and I have not ceased to learn from it since I first discovered it in the late 1980s. Nicholas Thomas and Diane Losche generously invited me to a conference in honor of Bernard Smith, held in August 1996 in Canberra, which deepened my appreciation of his scholarship and of the community of scholars who have been interlocutors with his work.

I have been blessed with friends who were frank readers, and I can only hope to have responded adequately, if incompletely, to their criticisms. My special thanks to Lionel Gossman for going through an entire draft of the manuscript that was completed in 2002. Sue Marchand commented on a later version and Fred Hoxie criticized the introduction. My frequent lunches at the Red Herring with Chip Burkhardt have been an informal history of science colloquium of many years' running, complemented by his scrutiny of the completed manuscript. My wife, Dorothee, has for some time turned my attention to the history of migration, which I can see in retrospect has shaped the subject of this book; and at the very end she cheerfully read and re-read the passages that still needed an audience.

Several leaves from teaching gave me the chance to explore different dimensions of eighteenth and early-nineteenth-century voyaging. At the University of Illinois I was granted leaves with fellowships by the Center for Values and Ethics in spring 1993, the Campus Research Board (Humanities Release Time) in spring 2000, and the Center for Advanced Study in spring 2002. In addition the Campus Research Board provided research grants in 1991 and 1992. A stay as guest at the Max Planck Institute for History in Göttingen in May–June 2003 gave me an opportunity to work in the Göttingen library collection that was of unique importance for the eighteenth-century German travelers who are central to my subject. I also feel an indirect yet important institutional debt to my colleagues of the past four years on the University of Illinois's Campus Research Board, whose deliberations have aided my understanding of research across the sciences and convinced me that now as in the eighteenth century, there are not "two cultures," but only a shared pursuit of scientific knowledge that communicates fluidly across disciplines.

Many libraries and archives have aided my work during this book's long gestation. For their hospitality during my visits I am grateful to the staffs of the National Library of Australia, Canberra; the State Library of New South Wales, Sydney; the Bibliothèque Centrale du Muséum National d'Histoire Naturelle, Paris; the Bibliothèque Ste. Geneviève, Paris; the Département des Cartes et Plans, Bibliothèque Nationale de France, Paris; the Bayerische Staatsbibliothek, Munich;

Humboldt University library, Berlin; the Geheimes Staatsarchiv Preussischer Kulturbesitz in Berlin-Dahlem and its former repository in Merseburg; Niedersächsische Staats- und Universitätsbibliothek, Göttingen; the Staatsbibliothek zu Berlin; the University of Heidelberg library; Firestone Library, Princeton University; Honnold/Mudd Library of the Claremont Colleges; Houghton Library, Harvard University; the John Carter Brown Library of Brown University; Mission Houses Museum Library, Honolulu; the Phillips Library, Peabody-Essex Museum, Salem, Massachusetts; Sutro Library, California State Library, San Francisco. I am also indebted to the Beinecke Rare Book and Manuscript Library, Yale University; the National Archives, Tartu, Estonia; the National Portrait Gallery, London; the Royal Botanic Gardens, Kew, England; and the Pitt-Rivers Museum, University of Oxford, England, for sending me reproductions of written and visual materials. My home away from home during the writing of this book has been the University of Illinois library, whose staff members have generously aided my use of its collections, especially rich in sources for the history of travel. As in the past I am especially indebted to Mary Stuart for making the History and Philosophy Library an especially valuable resource.

The publication of materials from the American Board of Commissioners for Foreign Missions archive is made by permission of the Houghton Library, Harvard University, and the Executive Minister, Wider Church Ministries, United Church of Christ.

The quotations from *A Voyage around the World with the Romanzov Exploring Expedition in the Years 1815–1818 in the Brig Rurik, Captain Otto von Kotzebue* by Adelbert von Chamisso are used by kind permission of Professor Henry Kratz. *A Voyage around the World,* translated from the German and edited by Henry Kratz, was published by the University of Hawaii Press in 1986.

At Harvard University Press, Kathleen McDermott's practical wisdom and dedication to the book helped me through the final year of revisions; Kathi Drummy took care of day-to-day business with unflappable efficiency; and Elizabeth Gilbert was an ideal manuscript editor, catching errors and making stylistic improvements in the text from beginning to end.

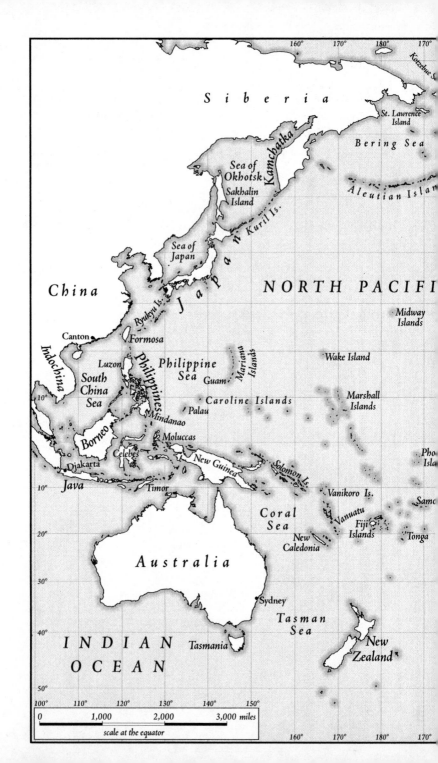

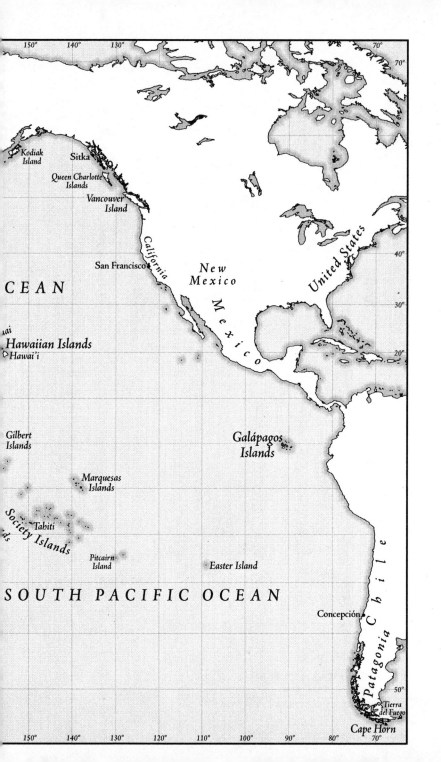

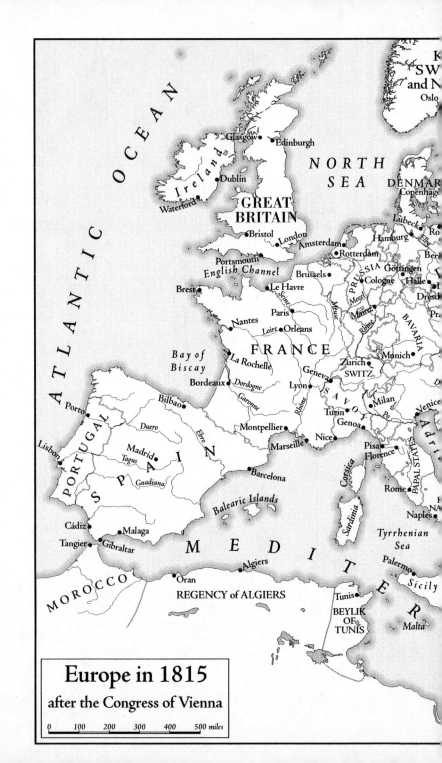

Europe in 1815

after the Congress of Vienna

0   100   200   300   400   500 miles

The Travelers' World

Introduction

This book is about travelers in a new world. From the time of Captain Cook to the time of Charles Darwin, they joined expeditions that took them to the farthest islands of the Pacific. Before the mid-eighteenth century, places like Hawaii and Tahiti were unknown or little known to Europeans; over the next hundred years, scientific voyages systematically surveyed and studied the vast Pacific portion of the earth. The travelers were at the center of this accumulation of scientific knowledge.

Travelers were intensely interested in the human societies they encountered, as were their audiences at home. It was an era first of critique of European society, then beginning in 1789 of revolution, and after 1815 of restoration of order for Europe's ruling classes. Travelers' reports from the Pacific powerfully shaped the era's debates about the nature of human society, sometimes reinforcing the old order, sometimes giving credence to utopias. This book studies how travelers mediated between home and distant places to expand European conceptions of humanity.

Three world voyagers are the book's main characters. Philibert Commerson was a naturalist aboard Louis de Bougainville's world voyage of 1766–1769; George Forster accompanied his father on Cook's second voyage of 1772–1775; and Adelbert von Chamisso served as naturalist on the Russian *Rurik* voyage of 1815–1818, captained by Otto von Kotzebue. They were influential and insightful ethnographers: Commerson wrote a letter on Tahiti that sealed its status as a Pacific paradise; Forster wrote an epic voyage narrative—with captivating chapters on Tahiti—that made him famous throughout Europe; Chamisso wrote about Hawaii and other islands with a sensitivity and accuracy still admired among anthropologists.

These three travelers were cosmopolitans. They and their voyages take in a broad swath of Europe as well as the wider world: Commerson was French; Forster, German-born, sailed on a British voyage; Chamisso came from Prussia, sailed for Russia, and wrote with the sensibility of a refugee from revolutionary France. They also cover three generations of historical experience: Commerson lived and died in the old regime; George Forster died in revolutionary Paris; Chamisso takes us into the postrevolutionary era. Their voyages serve as an armature around which tales from other voyages are wound. Readers will be able to follow a manageable cast of voyages and characters throughout this book, but will also get a more comprehensive view of the period's explorations and encounters.

Travel accounts were among the best-sellers of the late eighteenth and early nineteenth centuries. Successful ones attracted debate, translations, and fame. Their audience turned to them above all for their news of foreign peoples. This book will do the same, concentrating on travelers' descriptions of the human beings they met and their challenges to prevailing European beliefs about human nature. To be sure, naturalists wrote about much more than just humans: in the age of Ben Franklin they were scientific Jacks-of-all-trades, with all of nature their field of study, and their books were like an eclectic hobbyist's warehouse, stuffed with observations on everything from

A Pacific paradise, 1797. From Jean-François de La Pérouse, *Voyage de La Pérouse autour du monde, Atlas.*

the depths of the sea to the peaks of the mountains. Their technical observations, however, ended up in specialized publications for the learned world; for the broad educated public they concentrated on the drama of their meetings with newly encountered peoples.

Travelers as Ethnographers

There was no established discipline of anthropology before the mid-nineteenth century. Travelers had no formally established scientific paradigm, no museum authorities or university professors in anthropology departments to dispute. Nevertheless they entered into a discourse of sharply formulated controversies: previous travel writers and leading thinkers of the age made assertions about "natural man" that had revolutionary—or conservative—implications for European society. They could confirm or correct existing opinion and thereby undermine or strengthen its political, religious, and moral authority.

These anthropological discussions may not have been part of an institutionalized science, but they were centuries-old and combative. The Spanish conquests in the Americas stimulated intense debate over the capacity of the indigenous peoples for knowledge, religious instruction, and political organization; the horrific sixteenth-century French wars of religion sensitized Michel de Montaigne to the humanity of New World peoples. Travelers like Baron de Lahontan, a soldier in late-seventeenth-century New France, and Jean-François Lafitau, an early-eighteenth-century missionary among the Iroquois, wrote intimately and knowledgeably about the civility, bravery, and debating skills of North American Indians, while other European visitors described them as demonic or depraved. These conflicting reports entered into the writings of Enlightenment thinkers like Voltaire and Diderot, who turned to American Indians as natural egalitarians and used them to make their arguments about privilege and hierarchy in European society.

When the new wave of expeditions to the Pacific began in the late eighteenth century it led to new surprises. Travelers went with the confidence that Europeans had already seen and absorbed a great deal; that they knew what it meant to cross beyond the bounds of the known; and that if Europeans had already once encountered "natural" societies in America, they could expect to find something similar in the Pacific. What they encountered defied their expectations. They met with sophisticated societies, physical beauty, sexual freedoms, tattoos, and ships and nautical skills that were different from anything they had known before. They were also exposed to ferocious island politics, exploitative native elites, and disruptive consequences of their own visits that called into question the naive assumption of fraternity with native peoples.

Travelers and their public paid particular attention to Polynesia, the cultural and ethnic area stretching across the Pacific from New Zealand in the west and Easter Island in the east to the Hawaiian Islands in the north. Within that vast triangle Tahiti and Hawaii became the "new world" of the late eighteenth and early nineteenth centuries with a special significance for intellectuals arguing about human nature and social change. The inhabitants of these islands *were* new to Europeans, they were fresh, they were exciting, they were "discoveries"; they provoked the imagination of philosophes in search of a normative state of nature and Romantics in search of humanity's strange and fantastic extremes. Tahiti was initially the preferred site of European stopovers in the South Pacific, but it was soon supplanted by Hawaii, far to the north and east, as the hub of Pacific commerce and ethnographic discussion. Politics, sex, and religion on Tahiti and Hawaii set off round after round of public discussion as the first European visitors published sensational reports and subsequent voyagers returned with conflicting opinions and new revelations. Pacific travelers encountered the full spectrum of political orders from the egalitarian to the hierarchical; in Tahiti and Hawaii they came up against social hierarchies that confounded America-derived notions of natural equality and challenged them to rethink prejudices about European social or moral superiority. The sexual freedom of Polynesian societies caused scandal, astonishment, and glee from the moment Cook and Bougainville returned; Enlightenment thinkers were fascinated by societies that lacked anything like Christian sexual morality, Evangelicals in Britain and America were outraged by the travelers' frank reporting on island sexual practices, Romantics yearned for the aesthetic attractions of island cultures, and missionaries were determined to reform them. The differences over sexuality overlapped with debates over whether native religion was harmless, an anchor to the stability of marvelously peaceful societies, or Satan's workshop. The arguments and counterarguments that began in the late eighteenth century were if anything more inflamed when Darwin and Melville visited Polynesian islands in the 1830s and 1840s. Through a century of changing European politics and culture, from an age of privilege and Enlightenment to one of incipient democracy and Romanticism, reporting from the far side of the world fed public controversies.

Histories

In recent decades historians, especially historians of science, have re-discovered the history of scientific travel. Some have worked from a metropolitan perspective to show how science was inseparable from power, uniting the accumulation of knowledge with the interests of state sponsors. From its home in places like Paris, London, Madrid, and St. Petersburg, overseas scientific travel was an outlier of the En-lightenment, an application of European scientific methods to ever-farther global reaches. The Enlightenment emerges in this historical interpretation as an ambivalent epoch that provided tools for global domination even as it announced universal ideals of human dignity. The principles of scientific travel could undergo revision and change, but they appeared to further Europe's steady advance toward intel-lectual mastery of the world. In the rhetoric of one official voyage ac-count after another, explorers risked their lives and brought precious species and records back to Europe in the service of humanity. Re-cent histories have pointed out how state promoters of voyages, per-ceiving clear benefits to their governments, outfitted scientific expe-ditions with money, organization, and prestige. New trade routes, new stopping points for ships on long voyages, new fur empires abroad and seeds for cash crops at home were among the prizes for Britain, France, and their lesser rivals. The voyages they sponsored were eminently political events in the service of global empires.[1]

Other scholars—literary historians and ethnohistorians prominent among them—have shifted attention away from the Columbuses and Cooks and to the peoples they encountered in the Americas and other parts of the world. This reorientation burst into public view during the commemorations and exhibitions surrounding the Columbus Quincentennial, when controversies about Columbus, hero or villain, spilled over from academic specialists into public debate. These Atlantic encounters have their counterparts in Pacific studies. To cite two well-known examples, Greg Dening has analyzed the beach as a stage for European–Polynesian encounters, while Marshall Sahlins has illuminated the fatal confrontation of Captain Cook and Hawaiian islanders.[2] These and other scholars have multiplied our count of the number of histories simultaneously under way and made us imaginary witnesses to the dramas of islander–voyager encounters. Researchers have, then, gone far toward refreshing our understanding of global travel at the extremes of European metropolis and extra-European sites of encounter.

I have concentrated on the less explored role of travelers as links between metropolitan histories and overseas encounters. To retrace their wandering obliges us to rethink the meaning of "point of view," for they were dislodged from any single resting place. These scientific travelers of the late eighteenth and early nineteenth centuries exemplify the cosmopolitanism of world wanderers. The naturalists were the chief representatives of this viewpoint-in-motion, but not the only ones. They had companions on board the ship who shared in their work, including captains, officers, voyage artists, and physicians. And they had island counterparts, Polynesian travelers who went on board with their own thirst for knowledge, power, and prestige.

By placing the travelers at the center of my story, I have also tried to emphasize a certain set of issues that goes along with them, having to do with the formation of ideas through spatial movement. Theirs was a world of networks. Their conceptions took shape not at any one point on the globe, but at multiple nodes. Travel writing played an important part in the communications network of scholars within Europe. This intra-European network overlapped with a global system of knowledge as continental travelers and overseas correspondents fed the hunger of friends, family, learned acquaintances, academies, and government bureaucracies for accurate information about the non-European world. The travelers of the period 1750–1850 inhabited a peculiarly structured network of communications: they worked back and forth from patrons at home to collaborators (including native informants, traders, and beachcombers) abroad, and endured the authority of captains on the passage out and back; they contended with their patrons on their return and tried in one form or another to convey their findings to a European public. Their published travel accounts are not so much the work of a single author as they are the outcome of a system reaching across the globe, conveying them back and forth, squeezing from them information to satisfy state ministers, the scientific community, and public opinion. We comprehend them most fully when we view them not as isolated authors with full control over their written words but as actors in a global system of intellectual production.[3]

"Networks" implies a certain affinity with our own time, when information technology has created electronic conversations and forms of social organization. There is a danger here of imagining the travelers as inhabiting a world of global communication similar to our own electronic networks. Travelers during the Cook-to-Darwin era obviously had a different technology, a different world of knowledge, and different political preoccupations. Nonetheless to think of their world as a network clarifies some of its defining features. Their "knowledge" had to be transmitted from place to place; it was at one end of the globe and had to be brought to another. At the geographic extremes of Oceania there was at first little in the way of European settlements to ease the labor of acquiring, preserving, and conveying objects. Information had to be constructed and reconstructed at every station along the way. This process of construction was particularly necessary for the knowledge of foreign human beings and societies—the anthropology—that will be our special concern. The travelers as mediators offer a point of entry for observing transformations from person to person and place to place, a totality best understood as the sum of each of its parts, which the historian, starting from the printed travel account, must reconstruct step by step.

Dimensions of a World

If we seek to define the travelers' world, one answer comes from the frequent title of their books: voyage around the world. It signified their membership in the club of travelers who had rounded Cape Horn and been through the extremes of polar cold and equatorial heat; it suggested the European ambition of comprehensiveness, of seeing all there was to see and recording it with ever greater accuracy and completeness. The actual course of their voyages, however, was a narrow route, and this route had a starting point that anchored it in the history of a particular place. The planning of voyages occurred in one polity, one center of power. State histories defined the travelers' relationship to the rest of the world; only in a state setting can one understand the strategies of policymakers and the patronage relationships that permitted travelers to go abroad and made or broke their careers on their return.

But too exclusive a focus on individual state histories inhibits our understanding of an international movement. This book includes a great deal about British and French travelers, but it also attempts to redress the emphasis on their exploits to the neglect of almost everyone else. The expeditions of the era were part of a scientific and imperial competition that had its core in western European capitals but already encompassed Washington and St. Petersburg. Cook is too often treated as the embodiment of an isolated British genius for world mastery; yet it was Britain's French archrivals who excelled many decades before Cook in the scientific organization of expeditions. A few years before Cook or Bougainville, the Danish monarchy, in cooperation with German professors at the University of Göttingen, planned and carried out a scientific expedition to the biblical lands. Long before the brilliant days of either French or English exploration, Spanish, Portuguese, and Dutch explorers combined scientific interests with commercial and political forays across the seas. The French and British may have been the dominant imperial rivals of the late eighteenth and early nineteenth centuries, but for decades they had to contend with an ambitious Russian program of Pacific exploration, trade, and colonization. Lewis and Clark are often treated in isolation as American national heroes, yet Jefferson commissioned their expedition with a worried eye to British and Russian ambitions on the west coast of North America. La Pérouse and Bougainville have long been honored as the nearest French counterparts to Cook; only recently has Anglophone scholarship paid adequate attention to the Spanish expedition of the Italian-born Malaspina. Limited to a single state, histories of exploration may end up looking like provincial histories on a global scale instead of adventures that thrived on exchanges between European scientific and naval establishments. I have, in the end, written less about the Mediterranean, Dutch, United States, and Danish role in scientific exploration than I would have liked, but I have tried at least to point to a wider Europe than just its North Atlantic corridor.

While far from comprehensive on a European scale, I hope that my account draws sufficient attention to the special significance of German travelers in the history of ethnography. The Forsters were arguably the outstanding ethnographers of the late Enlightenment, as was Chamisso for the early nineteenth century. Alexander von Humboldt hovers like the spirit over the waters of nineteenth-century travel; his famous voyage of 1799–1804 to the Americas, unending production of books from his journey, and breadth of knowledge made his European-wide influence pervasive after the first decade of the nineteenth century. He was also an unabashed polyglot, living for years at a time in Paris and writing his travel narratives in French. He and other German travelers were participants in a cosmopolitan history of exploration, although theirs is only a fragment of a larger epic that would daunt the ambition even of a Melville.

Two features defined the era at its mid-eighteenth-century beginning. The first was its systematic application of scientific knowledge to the practical problems of overseas travel. It was this achievement that explains the appeal to contemporaries of Captain Cook's first circumnavigation of 1768–1771. Cook had many predecessors in England and abroad, yet there was a sweeping success to his voyage that captured the imagination and made his methods paradigmatic for all voyagers to come. He demonstrated how new instruments and mathematical calculations could be successfully employed on a voyage for the precise plotting of longitude, transforming the Pacific from a place of uncertain knowledge into a vast but manageable zone. With the creation of newly accurate maps, subsequent travelers could visit the islands of the Pacific again and again, steadily accumulating information on the foundation provided by Cook. Moreover Cook and the Admiralty created the model for running a ship: in matters of discipline, diet, scientific entourage, and itinerary they set the example for all others to follow.

A second defining feature of the era was the creation of a broadened public sphere for travel writing. This too was part of the scientific spirit of the era, for it turned travel reports into shared knowledge subject to critical scrutiny. As contemporaries were aware, much of the intelligence gathered on Iberian and Dutch voyages in earlier centuries ended up in state archives or in the private papers of the Spanish or Portuguese monarchy or the Dutch East Indies merchant company rather than in published books and public discussion. Much of the information disappeared or stayed hidden from view, to be forgotten even by the servants of the crown or company who had access to it. The contrast between early modern and modern travel was not absolute. On the one hand the achievements of early modern explorers were only partially hidden from public view; on the other hand northern European states did not release all their plans or information, but continued to distinguish between publicly shared knowledge and confidential intelligence. The era of free exchange of voyage histories, however, had a different quality: ethnographic information flooded bookstores and widely read journals by the end of the eighteenth century. Knowledge of foreign peoples became cumulative and comparative.[4]

These were the principles that shaped a new era of scientific travel by the mid-eighteenth century. By the mid-nineteenth century the naturalist's passion for collecting natural species, the gentleman's culture of robust hiking, and the ambition of journeying to ever farther "unknown" tropical, mountain, and extreme zones of the globe had percolated down to a broad middle class that enjoyed imitating the high-status activities once reserved for a tiny elite. "Travel" became a hobby for members of upwardly mobile middle classes, just as did once-aristocratic activities such as hunting and fencing. At the other end of the era, scientific voyaging never wholly ceased. Naturalist voyages continued into the twentieth century, with lavish expeditions, naturalists aboard naval ships, and polar exploration. Since the late twentieth century expeditions into outer space have been the successors to oceanic voyages.

Nonetheless there are good reasons for ending the story of travelers as ethnographers sometime in the 1830s or 1840s. Circumnavigations until then did not belong to a globalized world with a highly integrated economy, industrial techniques of transport and communication, and modernized nation-states. If anything, they were closer to the world of early modern travelers: they used sailing vessels as their predecessors had; despite their firepower they were deeply dependent on islanders when they traveled as far as the Pacific. They arrived in need of water, fruit, vegetables, hogs, sex, and navigational information. Again and again—somewhat camouflaged by the voyagers' language of friendship and civility in their written accounts— one can observe how effectively islanders could put overweening Europeans in their place by threatening to withhold one or another of these goods. A shift in the balance of power slowly took place: European crossings became more frequent, epidemic disease disrupted and demoralized island polities, European commerce became more invasive, and European states became bolder and surer in their global reach. Even in the late nineteenth century, that reach was anything but secure, as the Samoans demonstrated to the Europeans who tried to subdue them; but nonetheless a real contrast between the age of royal courts, merchant commerce, and sails and the later moment of nation-states, industrial capitalism, and steamships is evident. Simultaneously the European discourse about non-Europeans shifted, becoming ever more racialized in response to the widening imbalance of power. By the 1850s, Europeans and islanders had made the transition to a qualitatively different age of high imperialism.

🐾 Travelers, patrons, collaborators, philosophers back home—all were members interacting in a multifaceted network. By the early nineteenth century the world of the travelers looked like a scientific success, steadily accumulating knowledge for its European public. Yet just when it seemed triumphant, it confronted another world. Around 1800 missionaries began streaming to the Pacific, where Tahiti was their first stop. They developed their own, rival network of knowledge; they amassed their own ethnographies and claimed to be better informed than their scientific predecessors; instead of modernizing Tahitian and Hawaiian cultures, as the scientists proposed to do, their missions sought to eradicate them. The conflict between scientists and missionaries was a critical event in European intellectual history of the first half of the nineteenth century. Parties to both sides were convinced of the truth of their position and the bad faith of their opponents. In the end the great missionary controversy had the unintended effect of undermining the idea of definitive knowledge of another culture. By reconstructing the travelers' world, we can grasp some of the deep structural conditions that made their knowledge so frustratingly imperfect—and that make us no less erring travelers in our own world.

 CHAPTER 1

Travelers

One of the travelers' main jobs was to collect plants for scientific use at home. Their chief botanical guide was Linnaeus, who became a European-wide celebrity just as the age of scientific expeditions took off. His election in 1762 to the Paris Academy was a triumph over his French rival, Georges-Louis Leclerc, Comte de Buffon, powerful director of the Royal Garden of Paris. British botanists were slow to take up Linnaeus's system of binomial nomenclature despite his visit to England in 1736; but by the 1760s they too turned to the famous Swedish naturalist. The inclusion of his student Daniel Solander on Cook's first voyage of exploration in 1768 and the voyage naturalist Joseph Banks's devotion to the Linnaean method signaled its established place in the work of scientific expeditions.[1]

For the travelers in their role as ethnographers, Linnaeus had little in the way of direct guidance to offer. He was more important as a model of naturalness: a traveler through the Sami country or Lappland of Northern Sweden who praised its harsh simplicity, a self-conscious primitive who toured western Europe dressed in a Sami costume, a stylist who discarded rhetorical artifice in favor of direct speech.[2]

More important as a teacher and an embodiment of a widespread mood was Jean-Jacques Rousseau. His *Discourse on Inequality,* published in 1755, so searchingly exposed the artificiality of a society organized around legal inequality that, as his biographer Maurice Cranston has noted, it has been called the cause of the French Revo-

A Linnaean idealization of nature. This engraving, *Flora attired by the elements,* appeared as the frontispiece to Erasmus Darwin's *The Botanic Garden* in 1791.

lution and the founding work of modern social science. Rousseau tried to imagine what human beings would be like if one stripped away all their layers of culture, a reductive method that aimed at working back to the most fundamental structures of human society. In addition to this mental experiment, he looked at travel reports for hints of how "savages" lived in a state closer to nature. Rousseau imagined the original state of nature as an anarchic condition prior to language or social organization; his evolutionary model placed the indigenous peoples of his time in an intermediary stage between this original state and modern civilization. They were far enough removed from modern Europeans to aid a reconstruction of a more egalitarian past and provide a critical perspective on the present.[3]

In an aside to the reader Rousseau complained about the unreliability of travelers, who were such careless observers that they did not even bother to establish which creatures were human. In Africa, for example, hairy monsters called pongos were said to inhabit the forests. They looked almost like human beings except that they had no calves on their legs. They slept in trees, where they made a kind of roof for themselves. After natives left the fires they had burned during the night, the pongos would come and warm themselves by the embers. They covered their dead. Yet the traveler who reported this declared that they must not be human because they did not have enough sense to add more wood to the fire! Rousseau sympathized with the pongos. Of course they would get bored and go somewhere else, especially since they were vegetarians and had a lot of foraging to do. Humans were lazy, as well, and would not put more logs on a fire if they did not have to. Future investigators would have to do more careful research to determine the simple facts about pongos, not to speak of the more complicated issues surrounding what it meant to be human.[4]

Frustrated by the errors and half-truths of sailors, merchants, soldiers, and missionaries, Rousseau made a proposal to his enlightened contemporaries. Why not send out a real scientist—someone of the stature of a Montesquieu or a Diderot—on a voyage? "Suppose," he continued, "that these new Hercules, on their return from these memorable journeys, then wrote at leisure the natural, moral and political history of what they had seen, we ourselves would see a new world spring from under their pens, and we should learn thereby to know our own world." Travelers had already made long voyages to add to Europe's store of natural scientific knowledge, but the time had come, he wrote, to comprehend humanity in all its global diversity.[5]

Rousseau's discourse set out a double task for the traveler. Factually accurate reporting was one requirement: travelers had to have the education, freedom from ulterior motives, and honesty to bring back empirically accurate information. Rousseau's traveler was more, however, than just a reporter: the philosophe's discourse, with its stage theory of civilization and analysis of the material conditions of social organization, implied a need to understand social structures. Rousseau's expectation was that gathering information about indigenous societies would bring European philosophers closer to the fundamental and lasting principles of social organization.[6]

Travelers widely shared Rousseau's confidence that educated observers could return with accurate knowledge of little-known places. Their approach was more strongly shaped, however, by their experience of European society. They were born into a world of mutual dependencies that reached from aristocrats to peasants. In an unsettled era, when social resentments and utopian schemes bubbled beneath or burst onto the political surface, Pacific islands were laboratories for social observation, places for comparing European hierarchies with diverse alternatives.

The sailing ship was the travelers' immediate comparison with island societies. It was a closed society in its own right, where over the course of a voyage observers on board could view human nature at its best and worst. A traveler's place within this world was insecure. His ship was a place of work, and a naturalist or specialist scientist or gentleman traveler could be a nuisance. In his early days he might not be aware that the quarter-deck was off limits; his instruments and bottles and stores of paper got in the way of men with a heavy burden of work; he made unreasonable demands to stop or to stay on shore longer than was desirable; he claimed gentlemanly status, yet might have no money or powerful connections to back him up. Teen-age midshipmen from gentlemanly families had a much greater claim to sailors' respect and the captain's solicitude than the odd bodies who collected birds, words, and insects. The society of the ship, like society at home, was based on rank and order; the intensification of command on military vessels, and the uncertainty of the travelers' place within this order, turned travelers into acute observers of authority en route to native societies.[7]

Even though their relationship to authority was uncomfortable, naturalists were a good match for the ship's aggressively masculine character. World voyages created a segregated society of men crammed together for months or years at a time. It was not exclusively male; women were sometimes permitted to travel with their husbands, and females occasionally passed as male sailors, whether because they wanted to journey to a distant point or because they needed the work. These women did not noticeably change the male composition of the ship, however, but fit into it and demonstrated that belonging to it was a feat of personal and cultural adaptation.[8] The masculine ethos on board was an oceanic equivalent to the warrior code of fighting men on land. The sailing life required putting aside private feeling and taking part in the common hardships that began in the precarious navigation of the ship out of its home port, settled into the everyday discomforts of wet clothes and dreary diet, heightened amid the gales of Cape Horn and the epidemics of Batavia (Djakarta), and only ended with the final return to harbor.

The rigors of voyaging were not wholly out of keeping with what travelers knew from their own experience. A serious student of nature had done rough walking or riding before boarding. When Charles Darwin crossed the pampas of Argentina on horseback or walked along perilous mountain paths in Tahiti, he did so with the self-assurance of an experienced rider and hunter; Commerson had long hikes in the Pyrenees and Alps to prepare him for his voyage. Once under way, a naturalist had to be ready for every kind of hardship, from the dangers of Humboldt's tropical rain forests in South America to the disorienting plains and blazing deserts that Duke Paul of Württemberg, one of the legendary travelers of the early nineteenth century, crossed in North America, not to speak of the bandits who might prey on foreigners in any part of the world from Mexico to India or North Africa. Many naturalist travelers did not survive their voyages; survivors went out as young men and came back prematurely aged. While naturalists as sea travelers might lack a clear place in the society of the ship, they shared in the madness of voyages that were lonely, dangerous, and sometimes fatal.

Travelers endured this harsh regime with dreams of fame and honor on their return. They were keen for curiosities of every kind, none more than the customs of strange peoples that could turn a travel account into a best-seller. Tropical islands held out the promise of precious, profitable news.

Philibert Commerson

Philibert Commerson, the official naturalist on Louis de Bougainville's voyage around the world from 1766 to 1769, came close to fulfilling Rousseau's call for a scientific world traveler.

If anyone was ever a naturalist by inner calling, it was Commerson. His father, a prosperous French notary, wanted him to study law. He instead persuaded his father to let him study medicine in Montpellier, where he received his degree in 1755. In the same year he began a wide botanizing tour, hiking through Savoy, Burgundy, and the Bourbonnais region; three years later he returned to his home town of Châtillon-les-Dombes, where he developed a botanical garden. He shared his passion for plants with a university friend, Louis Gérard, who became a prominent physician and respected botanist in his own right, compiling a guide to the plants of Provence. Together they were admirers of Linnaeus at a time when the Swedish scientist's system was controversial in France. "I am going there," wrote Commerson in 1757 of a visit to Paris, "to be the champion of that author, and I don't know if I'll be creating a nice predicament for myself." He promised to be fearless: "Whatever may be I've broken more than one lance in honor of that illustrious botanist whom I consider to be my sole and real master." He certainly was shameless, pushing Gérard to bring his botanical exploits to Linnaeus's personal attention: "I'm sure he would single me out among his admirers if he knew how sincerely I'm attached to him, and disinterestedly so, which not many others can say." Later in life he would bring the same uncritical enthusiasm to his ethnographic observations.[9]

Commerson continued his march toward a career in Paris even though domestic troubles complicated his professional aspirations. In 1760 he married; two years later his wife died in childbirth, leaving behind an infant son. An episode then began that scholarly detective work has only recently reconstructed. Joseph de Lalande, a childhood friend, had already made a brilliant name for himself in Paris as a mathematician. He urged Commerson to join him in the capital and put him in touch with Bernard de Jussieu, a prominent and well-connected Parisian botanist who for decades had defended Linnaeus's system of classification. When Commerson took up his friend's offer in 1764, he did not come alone, but was accompanied by Jeanne Barret, a woman from a modest family; she had served as governess to his infant son and was now pregnant with his child. In December a son was born; he was put out with a wet nurse and died a few months later. Meanwhile Commerson's son from his marriage stayed behind in the care of his brother-in-law, one Curé Beau. Less than two years later, on October 20, 1766, Commerson had remarkable news for his brother-in-law: he had been asked to join a world voyage and had only a few days to make his decision. Traveling on a royal vessel, the voyagers would scout out new sites to make up for the loss of France's North American colonies. The commander was Louis de Bougainville, "whose name and talents are so well known . . . The commander is one of the most likable lords of the court, who loves men of learning, knows himself, and is motivated by an abundance of the enthusiasm that such a fine commission can inspire." Commerson had begged for time at least to visit his home, saying he had a four-year-old son to consider; all his objections were waved away in the face of the grandeur of the undertaking and his duty to his king.[10]

The prospect of discoveries in new countries and glory upon his return was irresistible. On November 17, 1766, Commerson announced that he would be leaving to serve as royal botanist and naturalist on the voyage. The title of royal botanist automatically carried the right to practice medicine in Paris on his return and probably would lead to a stipend, too; as for the title of royal naturalist, no one had ever previously received this distinction. On December 23 he reported that he had arrived in Rochefort (barely, after his drunken driver overturned his carriage en route), where officers and civil servants feted each other while waiting for the ship to leave.[11] On February 1, 1767, he departed on the *Étoile*. Bougainville had already left from Nantes in command of the *Boudeuse* on November 15 of the previous year, and the two ships were supposed to meet on the other side of the Atlantic.

Jeanne Barret, disguised as his valet, joined Commerson on the ship and shared his berth. She also became his assistant for his naturalist labors, carrying out her tasks and sharing the hardships of the icy passage through the Straits of Magellan without attracting special notice from any of their shipmates. The deception ended only when they arrived at Tahiti in April 1768 and the islanders insisted that she was a woman. Commerson feigned ignorance; Bougainville accepted this fiction and simply separated them without further reprisal.[12] Whether or not Bougainville was aware of the arrangement in advance, the European rules governing relations between the sexes were a source of misery to Commerson; he had good reason to be sensitive to the different rules of the Polynesian society he now encountered.

It had been a hard voyage that exposed Commerson to the vices of European colonial society as well as the rigors of a sailing voyage. From their first stop in Montevideo, he wrote to Beau that the Spanish rode their horses to death and killed three or four thousand cattle a day for their leather. "Having depopulated this part of South America, they have filled it with cattle and horses, and they dominate them as tyrannically as they once treated the people who lived here." Buenos Aires was worse. The ship's chaplain was assassinated, and the sailors and servants were insulted. Even Bougainville himself was almost arrested by the viceroy, for memories of an earlier French expedition that had pillaged the town at the beginning of the eighteenth century made the current administrator suspicious of the voyagers' intentions. Instead of wintering there, as they had originally planned, they departed after one month. Not that the society on the ships was much better. "The gorgeous voyage! As people tell me from every direction! What glory to have made it! Yes, no doubt, but who can imagine the cost of making it?" he wrote later to his brother Georges-

Marie. The rats, famine, shortage of water, scurvy, dysentery—these were all bad enough; but the saddest thing about the expedition had been "a state of defiance and of internal war setting us against one another; such are the shadows of this great showpiece of history." When it came to assessing the virtues and vices of non-European peoples, Commerson had oppressive examples of European behavior to season his judgment.[13]

The voyage was far from a complete disappointment. He took satisfaction in new places sighted, advances in hydrography, and gains for natural history. Above all there was Tahiti, where he arrived April 6, 1768, and stayed for nine days: it was a place, he wrote to his brother, where "the golden age celebrated in vain by the poets seems to exist." Commerson believed that they were the first Europeans ever to visit the island. He and his companions were not aware that a British ship commanded by Samuel Wallis had stumbled on Tahiti a few months earlier and, after getting a hostile reception, bloodied the islanders with European cannon fire.[14] When the French arrived, the islanders tried a different strategy. Women swam out to meet the European ship, and the islanders welcomed them to shore with chants of friendship. The peaceable welcome was deceptive, for Tahiti was riven with power struggles, both internecine and with neighboring islands. After months of hardship at sea, however, the voyagers were not inclined to question their luck; they quickly warmed to Tahiti's natural beauty, the climate, the good food, and the hospitality of their hosts. Even when sailors shot several "Indians" and the islanders suddenly vanished from sight, the travelers were not alarmed; on the contrary they were satisfied to see that by putting their own miscreants in chains they could quickly restore good relations. Nor was Bougainville, an unusually patient and firm commander, alarmed by the Tahitians' skillful and persistent thieving. The French did not realize that the Tahitians were calibrating their responses to their visitors, who depended on them for food.

Commerson wrote up his initial impressions in a journal entry entitled "description of the island of New Cythera." His remarks were matter-of-fact as well as favorable to the Tahitians and their island. He began with "Men. The savages of this island are all white . . . The sun and the water give a very deep tan to the savages, almost all handsome men. [They have] a handsome figure and that of the older men is quite impressive. They are very strong and very adept, especially at stealing." As for "women and girls" he wrote: "[They] can be compared to the most beautiful European brunettes except that they are not quite so white . . . It seems to us that as soon as a girl is married or at least remains attached by common consent to one man, she is faithful to him and does not try to have relations with others, for they say there is the death penalty for adulterers. The girls, on the contrary, as long as they remain thus, are very free to do whatever they wish, for premarital jealousy is unknown." He also noted the power of the chiefs and thought that the Tahitians lived in a state of perfect peace with one another. The fertility of the island, its different species of fruit, its pigs, its ducks and other aquatic birds, all attracted his attention, and he thought that different kinds of grain could grow in Tahitian soil "as in France." This journal record had the tone of a government servant's report, designed to make a favorable impression on authorities at home in search of colonies and friendly ports of call.[15]

After Tahiti the voyagers passed through Batavia, Sumatra, and the French colony of Mauritius on their return voyage. While Bougainville and the rest of the expedition continued on to France, Commerson and Jeanne Barret remained on Mauritius. By royal order they were to assist Pierre Poivre, a remarkable man, part scientific traveler and part philosophe, who had risen to the high rank of intendant (one of the administrators the French monarchy sent out as its direct representative to the different parts of the realm) on the island.[16] Poivre sent Commerson to Madagascar in August 1770, where he stayed until January 1771 and was dazzled by the botanical riches he could harvest. He also visited the neighboring island of Réunion before returning to Mauritius, where he remained until his death on March 13, 1773, assisted to the end by the faithful Jeanne Barret, torn between his desire to return to France and his immersion in his work. He would have been forty-six on November 18 of the same year.

The naturalist community in Paris devoured the work that Commerson had left behind. His papers, drawings, and cabinets of natural objects were all sent back to Paris. Commerson had been too busy collecting ever to publish the results of his investigations. None of his voyage companions or Paris colleagues put together a posthumous publication, as was later done for the world voyager Jean-François de Galaup de La Pérouse. Instead Buffon appropriated Commerson's works for the Royal Garden, where Antoine-Laurent de Jussieu used his botanical manuscripts and Georges Cuvier "removed all the drawings of fish."[17] What made its way into print under Commerson's own signature was not the results of his naturalist labors, but a vision of the original natural society that he thought he had seen in Tahiti.

Commerson was a radical social thinker. Among his papers he left an undated "sketch for the plan of the academic city," containing a detailed description of a circular village for the learned: an anticipation of either the utopian communities of the nineteenth century or Princeton's Institute for Advanced Study and its imitators in the twentieth. He expected three hundred houses to hold three to four thousand citizens. There would, of course, be a garden. There would also be a rotunda serving as temple, capitol, and observatory.

It would be dedicated "to all science, or eternal science." A self-contained retreat, it would include libraries, a press, and scientific collections. The whole would serve as a center of enlightenment dedicated to truth and beauty; in keeping with the practical spirit of the age he expected it to improve the useful arts, perfect navigation, and open up new branches of commerce. It would, of course, require a large sum to establish it, but he thought one shouldn't be scared by the necessary outlay. Some philanthropist—a new Alexander, Augustus, Frederick the Great, or French court minister like Sully or Colbert— ought to support it.[18]

This was not a thinker to be shy about sharing his impressions of an already existing utopia that he had actually visited. From Mauritius he sent a letter to several friends describing Tahiti. Lalande, one of the recipients, had it published in November 1769 in a prominent journal, the *Mercure de France*, where it could not fail to come to the attention of a wide public. So great was the sensation created by Commerson's letter that it has been called the starting point for the "myth of Tahiti," the transformation of a Pacific island with a complicated social structure, politics, and cosmology into a fantasy paradise.[19] It was a strange creation for someone who to the end of his life proclaimed his devotion to the memory of his departed wife, who never ceased to deny the intimacy of his relationship with Jeanne Barret, who pushed himself to the point of exhaustion to carry out his researches, and who proposed himself as a candidate for a history of the martyrs to biology.

Commerson was a serious man. In the will that he dictated just before his departure from Paris for the world voyage, he dedicated his cadaver to science (it was to be used for dissection and for making a demonstration skeleton "which can make permanently evident to the public my ardent desire for my entire life to be useful to it"). He dedicated a part of his fortune to establishing an annual prize for virtue (to be awarded annually to whoever "has done the best action to come to light in the moral and political order without any hint of ambition, vanity or hypocrisy").[20] He provided for his son. And he did not neglect Jeanne Barret, who was to get his household belongings. His essay about Tahiti was not intended as an exotic variation on erotic rococo. He wrote with a passion for social improvement.

His description of the island challenged first and last his readers' political prejudices. The normal assumption of educated eighteenth-century Europeans was that monarchy was the highest, indeed the most fully human political order; preference for any other form of government had a subversive edge to it. The exceptions were highly conservative social orders such as the Dutch Republic or the aristocratic Venetian Republic. When Rousseau wrote his Second Discourse, he introduced it with praise not for radical social experimentation but for the government of Geneva, another hierarchical republic whose elite ruled with Calvinist self-assurance and rigor. Europeans who ventured overseas were usually eager to find something corresponding to a monarchical form of government and viewed more democratic forms of political organization as a sign that they were dealing with inferiors.

Commerson's essay struck out from the first paragraph in a heretical direction. He gave the island the name of Utopia, which Thomas More, he reminded his readers, had given to his "ideal republic." If this was a republic, it was no Geneva. Bougainville called it "New Cythera," and the inhabitants themselves called it Tahiti, but Commerson stuck by his description of this new people as "good Utopians." And the government of this utopia? It was "ruled by family fathers rather than by kings." This structure was the setting for the religion of a people "who knew no other god than Love." The Tahitians—this we know today from the journal entries of the French, as well as from the testimony of the English on Cook's first voyage—expected these early visitors to make love in the full light of day, surrounded by spectators, a ritual that was beyond the imagination of most sailors and officers, who also took advantage of more furtive settings. Commerson certainly gave prominence to the attractiveness of the Tahitian women (calling them "the sisters of wholly naked Graces"). He set the encounter firmly, though, within the political order: it was the public celebration of "an act of religion." Society's self-reproduction brought forth the chants of the assembled people and finished with their applause. Commerson was proposing something similar to Émile Durkheim's later thesis that religion is a form of self-worship in which society affirms its collective unity.[21]

This political order was founded in nature. The public couplings of the Tahitians proceeded "from an instinct that is always sound because it has not yet degenerated into reason." Their language, which Commerson imagined was made up of four or five hundred words and without any syntax, entirely sufficed for their ideas and their needs, which it expressed with "noble simplicity." He contrasted Tahitian speech to the labyrinth of words that muddled the clarity of perception and spontaneity of judgment in European languages. "The Utopian, by contrast, names his object as soon as he sees it." It was a kind of paradise in which human beings lived in a state of sensuous immediacy, and reason was the abstract, planning faculty that pulled one apart from this harmony of word and object. His readers were not to think that Tahitians were simple or dumb just because they lacked this capacity for scheming. Their boats, baskets, cloth, orchards, and tools were all admirable. "Savage" men in his time and later were often associated with the mistreatment of women; but the Tahitian women "are not at all subjugated by them as they are by savages." He praised their horror toward the spilling of blood and their respect for their dead. They conducted themselves as dignified and appreciative guests at their meals with the French. The Tahitians were at one with themselves and were generous hosts.[22]

What was the origin of these Utopians? Writing with an enlightened indifference to the biblical narrative, Commerson viewed the world as peopled by distinct races and dismissed the notion that human beings shared a common origin. The Tahitians, he guessed, were an autochthonous people. "I therefore do not see why the good Tahitians should not be the sons of their own soil, that is, descended from ancestors who were always Tahitians, stretching back as far as the people proudest of its ancestry." Such a statement of polygenism, the notion of multiple human creations, could be used in the eighteenth century to justify a racial hierarchy favoring Europeans, implying that they were placed in just the right climate zone to develop hardy, energetic characters, but Commerson's letter suggested that the Tahitians were racially superior to Europeans, since their lineage was pure and undisturbed by migrations, and socially superior since they continued to live according to nature's original design. In conclusion he returned to a political topic. The Tahitians had no conception of property, an institution that did not belong to the state of nature but was an artificial convention. Their propensity to take things was only a redistribution of goods in a generous society where each gave and took what was needed. Europeans were self-condemning when they gave this behavior the name of theft. Commenting on an officer angered by a native who took his cane, he added, "Is such the soul of sailors, which Jean-Jacques Rousseau noted judiciously with a moment of doubt and a question mark?" Rousseau had included sailors in his list of doubtful travel witnesses, and now Commerson, having traveled with them, agreed. He corrected their insensitive reporting and offered a philosopher-traveler's countertestimony.[23]

With this remark Commerson completed the frame around his essay, situating it between two models of utopian writing. Thomas

More was an urbane and temperate public man but famously uncompromising about his principles; he offered his *Utopia* (1516) in
a spirit of jest, but it anticipated the modern era's will to political
experimentation. Rousseau for his part made his uncompromising
honesty part of his celebrity status and also, in the Second Discourse,
outlined a political order that was unrealizable (since the state of nature was irrevocably past) yet a spur to the utopianism of his own
time. Commerson drew from both sources as he wrote from the perspective of an intellectual and political radical. His friend and supporter Lalande was notorious for his atheism; Lalande and Commerson were both members of Freemason lodges, underground centers
of politically subversive ideas of fraternity, or "philadelphia," as he
called it in the essay. Commerson wrote at a late Enlightenment moment when radical thinkers were increasingly daring, increasingly
open about their disrespect for the established order, and increasingly emboldened to offer subversive alternatives. While More had
placed his utopia on an imaginary island in the Pacific and Rousseau
had placed his natural men in an irretrievable past, Commerson synthesized the two in his Pacific utopia, one that—unlike its predecessors—was a contemporary reality.

Commerson's account of the Tahitians had a disingenuous quality.
He was aware that the Tahitians were not as selfless as he portrayed
them, but were tough bargainers for the goods they received from the
French. Inconvenient incidents went unmentioned; there was no allusion to the sailors' killing of three Tahitians. The very way he began
his essay, with a comparison to More's utopia, suggested a certain wa-
vering between fact and fiction. To accentuate the unreality, he made
a point of mentioning that the island's longitude and latitude were a
government secret; while that may have been true at the moment he
wrote, mentioning it so prominently deepened the impression that
its "place" was somewhere in the imagination, at the fictive point

where climate and soil had met in just the right way to preserve human society in its natural condition.

What should we make of Commerson's account? He was not trying to titillate his readers; if anything he erred in the direction of earnestness. In a letter to Curé Beau (what did *he* think of the love-saturated utopia, one wonders) Commerson wrote: "Everyone sees and observes in his own way. I am by vocation a naturalist; I am supposed to speak the naturalist's language . . . I have seen new peoples, today still happily enjoying their primitive instincts. I have represented them with the mirror of truth. They do not wear flowing gauze, and am I supposed to dress them up like Eskimos or Lapps? Morality has been respected no less than physics so long as no one can tell me I have lied; I am deaf to every other reproach."[24] Commerson saw himself as a martyr to scientific truth; he was prepared to represent what he had seen with the "mirror of truth" regardless of the consequences. He defended his account as a faithful transcription of what he had witnessed. Other scientific travelers would proceed with a better feel for the dangers of hasty generalization, but with no less defiance toward the power-holders of their day, no less dedication to truthfulness.

George Forster

George Forster's father, Johann Reinhold Forster, was a polymath, adept at foreign languages and a self-declared Linnaean, who was living in London in 1772 when the Admiralty needed a replacement naturalist for Cook's second world voyage.[25] Casting about on short notice, they invited the brilliant, unemployed German.

Cook was to continue the search, already begun on his first voyage, for an enormous southern continent hidden somewhere in the South Pacific. This territory had to exist, speculated some geographers—

notably Charles de Brosses in his *Histoire des Navigations aux Terres Australes* (1756)—to balance the land masses of the north and keep the earth spinning smoothly. Cook's first voyage had already tested the theory for a large stretch of the Pacific; this time the Admiralty's Secret Instructions asked him to continue his investigations by traveling as close as possible to the South Pole. Not that this was the voyage's only purpose. As usual it was a catch-all expedition that would note longitudes and latitudes; survey shorelines; note soil, mines, minerals, valuable stones, birds, and beasts; and bring home "seeds of Trees, Shrubs, Plants, Fruits and Grains." And Cook and his companions were to be ethnographers: "You are likewise to observe the Genius, Temper, Disposition and Number of the Natives or Inhabitants, if there be any, & endeavour by all proper means to cultivate a Friendship and Alliance with them."[26]

Forster jumped to accept the opportunity with the condition that he be allowed to take along his sixteen-year-old eldest son George, a favor readily granted, especially since George already had his own reputation as a child prodigy. The trip was both glorious and difficult for George. The second voyage was a triumphant enhancement of the first, building on its achievements and complementing it with new discoveries. The voyagers visited islands and land masses across the South Pacific, many known to Cook from his previous expedition, including New Zealand, Australia, Tahiti, Easter Island, the Marquesas, the Tongan Islands, and Vanuatu, giving George Forster a rare historical opportunity to meet societies still intact and challenging his powers of theorization. His father's bad temper, however, made him ill-suited to a three-year voyage on a small ship; he quarreled with the officers, the sailors, and Cook, putting George in the unpleasant position of mediator who needed both to console his father and to conciliate the other members of the ship's company. Despite the trials of the voyage, the son wrote a narrative account that more than any other captures the freshness and brilliance of the early European encounters with the Pacific. Like Commerson, George Forster found support for his political ideals in a world of astonishing beauty, likable people, and profound challenges to Western moral and political conventions.

George took special care to justify the publication of his narrative. Cook was publishing a rival account, but the things that Cook would have observed and, more important, the seaman's perspective would be different from the facts and viewpoint guiding the younger man's report. George offered the public a second reason for publishing his version: his dedication to uncensored truthfulness. For the first Cook circumnavigation the Admiralty had hired a well-known man of letters, John Hawkesworth, to compile the participants' diaries into a cohesive narrative. Hawkesworth's account was a market success, but it was also condemned from many sides. Hawkesworth dressed up his story too much in neoclassical allusion and fancy for some and was too frank for others. Reading his words today one is struck by the mildness of the exaggerations, but Forster treated them as a disastrous precedent. Hawkesworth had not been on the voyage and had weighed his story down with "frivolous observations, the uninteresting digressions, and sophistical principle." "Few are able to determine," George added, "with what degree of justice the blame is thrown upon the compiler"—a comment implying that censorship may already have lurked behind the vulgarizations in this voyage account. George went on to accuse Bougainville of suppressing politically sensitive matter from his voyage account and to add that Cook would probably do the same in his narrative. So much for compromise with power-holders. George would give readers the unexpurgated story.[27]

Governments were thus one enemy of honest reporting. Another was "the philosophers of the present age": thinkers such as Rousseau (whom George ridiculed elsewhere for his speculations about whether orangutans were semihuman). He delivered a telling judgment against the tendentious tale-telling of Enlightenment thinkers: "Without being competent judges of the subject, they have assumed a few circumstances as facts; and wresting even those to suit their own systems, have built a superstructure which pleases at a distance, but upon nearer examination partakes of the illusive nature of a dream." Forster balanced this critique of the philosophes with a warning against pure empiricism: if speculative systems were bad, it was no better to give readers a "simple collection of facts," which Forster compared to "a confused heap of disjointed limbs, which no art could reunite into a whole." Going beyond either fabulation or facticity, the traveler "should have penetration sufficient to combine different facts, and to form general views from thence, which might in some measure guide him to new discoveries, and point out the proper objects of farther investigation." He did not mention another important dimension to his conception of social science in the preface, but held to it throughout the book: testing his preconceptions and altering them in response to the experiences of the voyage. This tugging back and forth between preconceptions and observation made good his claim to compose more than a philosophe's fable or a plodder's disjointed facts; the reader of his narrative witnesses the education of a young idealist whose notions of universal truth are again and again changed by what he witnesses in island societies.[28]

Forster's preface declared his intention "to connect the ideas arising from different occurrences, in order, if possible, to throw more light upon the nature of the human mind, and to lift the soul into that exalted station, from whence the extensive view must 'justify the ways of God to man.'" Twenty-first-century readers may look back with a certain skepticism on his faith that a beneficent providence helped the *Resolution* survive a hazardous exit from Plymouth harbor as it embarked on its world voyage. But Forster insisted: "We could not avoid reflecting on the tutelar guidance of *Divine Providence,* which had thus manifested itself in a critical moment, that might easily have put an effectual stop to our projects. We shall, in the course of this history, find frequent instances of impending destruction, where all human help would have been ineffectual, if our better fortune had not prevailed under the superior direction of *Him,* without whose knowledge not a single hair falls from our heads." Forster's was the conventional faith of the age; Hawkesworth had gotten into trouble with his readers for doubting this kind of providentialism. There was something of Candide about George Forster as he struggled to maintain his belief in divine intervention despite all the voyage's evidence to the contrary.[29]

Not that the voyage was without its satisfying moments. When an aged mother on Tahiti embraced Captain Cook as one who had known her deceased son and "wept aloud at the remembrance of her loss," Forster commented: "We paid the tribute of admiration due to such sensibility, which endears our fellow-creatures to us wherever it is met with, and affords an undeniable proof of the original excellence of the human heart." Observing a father's fondness for his little girl while the ship visited Vanuatu in August 1774, he added: "We observed an instance of affection among the natives of Tanna [Vanuatu] this evening, which strongly proves that the passions and innate qualities of human nature are much the same in every climate." When the travelers left Tahiti, he was touched to see tears in the eyes of their hosts despite the tensions of the visit. The philosophical traveler thrilled at every instance of a common humanity rising above the polarities of geography and culture.[30]

Nonetheless he had to account for the contrary behavior he often

witnessed during his three years around the world and was anything but a consistent sentimentalizer of the different peoples he
met. More than once he observed how women were abused in native
societies. On New Zealand in November 1773 his father and the *Reso-*
lution's first mate, Mr. Whitehouse, were bystanders to a family quarrel in which a boy threw a stone at his mother for denying him a
piece of cooked penguin; scarcely had the mother started to strike
him when her husband beat her and threw her to the ground. Other
members of the crew told Johann Reinhold that they had often witnessed similar scenes in which the husbands stood by to make sure
their children were not punished. "Among all savage nations," observed George, "the weaker sex is ill-treated, and the law of the stron-
gest is put in force." He tried, however, to grasp the deeper principle
underlying this kind of cruelty. Early man's oppression of women, he
thought, arose from natural law. The instinct of self-preservation did
not yet permit the growth of affection for a partner, which only came
in wealthier societies: "It is the practice of all uncivilized nations to
deny their women the common privileges of human beings, and to
treat them as creatures inferior to themselves. The ideas of finding
happiness and comfort in the bosom of a companion, only arise with
a higher degree of culture. Where the mind is continually occupied
with the means of self-preservation, there can be but little refined
sentiment in the commerce of the sexes, and nothing but brutal enjoyment is known." While human nature might have a universal capacity for goodness, realizing that capacity was the work of civilization. The process depended on material circumstances and a long
historical labor of self-improvement.[31]

George's education in the unpleasantness of his fellow human beings came from Europeans as well as islanders. On a day like Christmas 1773 the sailors' complete indifference to reason baffled him:

below sixty-seven degrees south, at the beginning of the sail northward after reaching their southern extremity, the sailors insisted on drinking themselves into a stupor instead of paying attention to the dangers surrounding them: "The sight of an immense number of icy masses, amongst which we drifted at the mercy of the current, every moment in danger of being dashed to pieces against them, could not deter the sailors from indulging in their favourite amusement. As long as they had brandy left, they would persist to keep Christmas 'like Christians,' though the elements had conspired together for their destruction." The sailors were especially instructive when it came to learning the limits of human kindness. Their cruelty to animals—Forster observed how they bought up fowls in Tonga to try to turn them, without much success, into cockfighters—disgusted him, as did their horrendous oaths. He also found their behavior toward him and his father infuriating. In September 1774, in New Caledonia, the Forsters were unable to pursue their botanizing after being poisoned by a fish they had eaten. A surgeon's mate came back from a hike with new shells and plants but refused to share them with the scientists. "It will not be improper to acquaint the reader," wrote Forster in an angry footnote, "that we were so situated on board the *Resolution,* as to meet with obstacles in all our researches, from those who might have been expected to give us all manner of assistance." The others on board the ship kept the most common knowledge from them, and their own discoveries aroused general envy, an atmosphere that made him exclaim how extraordinary it was that the "most enlightened nation in the world" should send out men of science to work in conditions "which would only become a set of barbarians." But despite the humiliations he and his father had suffered from the sailors, George did not lose his sympathy for them, reflecting instead that a life of hardship had numbed them to their own safety and made them incapable of feeling for others. He had a political point to make: not just the physical dangers but also the authoritarian regime of the navy had dehumanized them. "Subjected to a very strict command, they also exercise a tyrannical sway over those whom fortune places in their power." And so they were eager for the slightest provocation to fire on the native peoples they met. Altogether he sized them up as barbarians with all the virtues and vices of their kind. "Though they are members of a civilized society," he wrote, "they may in some measure be looked upon as a body of uncivilized men, rough, passionate, revengeful, but likewise brave, sincere, and true to each other." It was a sorrowful reckoning with his own three years of suffering as a boy thrown in with these men and with the demoralizing effects of service in the British navy.[32]

Recognition of human selfishness and cruelty was not alien to the Enlightenment, whose central representative and popularizer, Voltaire, taught his readers not to expect much from the world as they quested for happiness. A more unsettling question was whether a scientific voyage helped the people it looked in on. Sometimes Forster took pride in European technical prowess, as in the scene on Goose Cove on April 26, 1773. The voyagers named this area on the northwest part of Dusky Bay, New Zealand, after the animals they released there to multiply "for the benefit of future generations of navigators and New Zeelanders." After the Europeans cleared a little settlement for themselves, Forster admired the transformation:

The superiority of a state of civilization over that of barbarism could not be more clearly stated, than by the alterations and improvements we had made in this place. In the course of a few days, a small part of us had cleared away the woods from a surface of more than an acre, which fifty New Zeelanders, with their tools of stone, could not have performed in three months. This spot, where immense numbers of plants left to themselves lived and decayed by turns, in one confused inanimated heap; this spot, we had converted into an active scene, where a hundred and twenty men pursued various branches of employment with unremitted ardour.

Forster then ascended through the representatives of civilization at work: the craftsmen who felled trees, turned them into planks, cooked, caulked, and rigged; the visual artist who imitated nature in his images; the scientist who built an observatory; and the philosophers of plants and animal creation. "In a word, all around us we perceived the rise of arts, and the dawn of science, in a country which had hitherto lain plunged in one long night of ignorance and barbarism!" This bustle foreshadowed the clearing and building to come, for Forster was already thinking ahead to European colonization of the Pacific. His entry for November 25, 1773, reflected that "perhaps in future ages, when the maritime powers of Europe lose their American colonies, they may think of making new establishments in more distant regions; and if it were ever possible for Europeans to have humanity enough to acknowledge the indigenous tribes of the South Sea as their brethren, we might have settlements which would not be defiled with the blood of innocent nations." It was a cautionary look forward, but not without hope that Europeans could make the Pacific a place of peaceful conquest.[33]

At the same time he confronted evils that made him wonder whether the great adventure of opening up the Pacific was justifiable at all. On Wednesday, June 23, 1773, on the passage from New Zealand to Tahiti, it became apparent that one or two men on the *Adventure* had contracted a venereal disease, apparently from native women in New Zealand. The travelers went through the list of European voyages to the region and could not imagine when there would have been a prior opportunity for contact. They satisfied themselves—erroneously—that the disease must have been indigenous, but Forster did not suppress reflection about possible European guilt:

> But if, in spite of appearances, our conclusions should prove errone-ous, it is another crime added to the score of civilized nations, which must make their memory execrated by the unhappy people, whom they have poisoned. Nothing can in the least atone for the injury they have done to society, since the price at which their libidinous enjoy-ments were purchased, instils another poison into the mind, and de-stroys the moral principles, while the disease corrupts and enervates the body. A race of men, who amidst all their savage roughness, their fiery temper, and cruel customs, are brave, generous, hospitable, and incapable of deceiving, are justly to be pitied, that love, the source of their sweetest and happiest feelings, is converted into the origin of the most dreadful scourge of life.

His reflection fed into wider doubts about the travelers' civilizing mission. Tahiti had an erotic life with its own rules, which Forster, like other sympathetic travelers, tried to get his readers to recognize by arguing that married and upper-class women kept aloof from the sexual traffic with Europeans; one would hardly make judgments about the virtues of the natives of England, he added, from the be-havior of women in the Strand. He observed, too, the breakdown of cultural mores and transformation of Tahitian sexual behavior into prostitution when the voyagers returned in May–June 1774 with red feathers, an item of the highest social and political value. The feath-ers caused such a frenzy of bidding that, much to Forster's disgust, a chief's wife offered herself to Cook in exchange for a supply. Prosti-tution accompanied the overall progress of European commerce; the venereal canker was its consequence.[34]

At times an enthusiast for European civilization and at times its critic, Forster in some passages left his shifting moods side by side, unreconciled. He yearned for universal human brotherhood, and on occasion thought he could glimpse such a thing and help bring it about; but then he confronted the misunderstandings and follies that undermined it. In Vanuatu on August 19, 1774, he went off alone into the woods, where he strolled for miles and saw natives working in plantations. The "gentle elevations, and spacious vallies" gave him a broad view of the surrounding country. "Those who are capable of being delighted with the beauties of nature, which deck the globe for the gratification of man, may conceive the pleasure which is derived from every little object, trifling in itself, but important in the moment when the heart is expanded, and when a kind of blissful trance opens a higher and purer sphere of enjoyment." After describing this landscape and the "golden clusters of fruit" in the plantations, "the emblems of peace and affluence," he carried his meditation to its lofty conclusion, describing how the travelers gradually overcame their hosts' mistrust:

> The mind at rest, and lulled by this train of pleasing ideas, indulged a few fallacious reflections, which increased its happiness at that instant by representing mankind in a favourable light. We had now passed a fortnight amidst a people who received us with the strongest symptoms of distrust, and who prepared to repel every hostile act with vigour. Our cool deliberate conduct, our moderation, and the constant uniformity in all our proceedings, had conquered their jealous fears. They, who in all probability had never dealt with such a set of inoffensive, peaceable, and yet not despicable men; they who had been used to see in every stranger a base and treacherous enemy, now learnt from us to think more nobly of their fellow-creatures. This retrospect was honourable to human nature, as it made us the benefactors of a numerous race. I fell from hence into a reverie on the pre-eminence of our civilized society, from which I was roused by the sound of approaching steps. I turned about and saw Dr. Sparrman, to whom I pointed out the prospect and communicated my ideas.

They walked back and were surprised to see natives running away from them in fear. "At last, when we stepped out of the wood, we beheld two natives seated on the grass, holding one of their brethren dead in their arms. They pointed to a wound in his side, which had been made by a musket-ball, and with a most affecting look they told us 'he is killed.'" A sentinel had been stationed on the beach to separate natives from Europeans; one native had gotten into a fight with the sentinel and been shot and killed. At that moment Cook landed, had the sentinel arrested, and then worked to restore peace. Meanwhile George waited for his father, who had gone off alone. He soon appeared unharmed.

He had met with the same good treatment from the natives as ourselves; they had learned to know our disposition, and seemed to be too good tempered to confound the innocent with the guilty. Thus one dark and detestable action effaced all the hopes with which I had flattered myself. The natives instead of looking upon us in a more favourable light than upon other strangers, had reason to detest us much more, as we came to destroy under the specious mask of friendship; and some amongst us lamented that instead of making amends at this place for the many rash acts which we had perpetrated at almost every island in our course, we had wantonly made it the scene of the greatest cruelty.

Captain Cook resolved to punish the perpetrator. But it turned out that the sailor's superior had given orders to kill. The sentinel was declared innocent, and the officer remained in his command. Forster did not spare himself and his fellow scientists when he reflected on how their pretensions to peaceable relations were inextricable from the sentry's deadly show of force. His recounting of this incident was a self-contained meditation that worked his experience into the literary form of the elegy: first came the removal from earthly affairs, both physical and spiritual, as he ascended a mountain; then the return to consciousness of human afflictions that deepened with his descent. The genre embraces humanity's alternation between solitary hopes and social cares and permits the practitioner to synthesize them in his vision of the human condition; Forster's elegy contained his own deepening wisdom as the moment of friendship between strangers gave way to violence.[35]

On a voyage through Oceania a social scientist could observe more than just technological differences and moral dilemmas; it was also a laboratory for different kinds of political organization. It was one thing for European philosophers to speculate on natural man; the Pacific presented an extraordinary diversity of political societies within the clearly defined boundaries of isolated island societies. Forster was one of the first observers to reflect on the cultural similarity of Polynesians across their vast range of island settlements. Why should their political organizations differ widely from place to place? What were the effects of their different regimes on human virtue and happiness? These questions preoccupied him as he pondered all that he had seen during the voyage.

The place that especially captivated his imagination, as it did visitors before and after him, was Tahiti. Soon after the voyagers first saw it on August 16, 1773, peacemaking and trade mixed with its appeal to the senses. "It was one of those beautiful mornings which the poets of all nations have attempted to describe, when we saw the isle of O-Taheitee, within two miles before us." A perfumed breeze, mountains that "rose majestic in various spiry forms," the plains with their breadfruit trees and, rising over them, the palm trees; and before long, a canoe to greet them, and two men sitting in it who "waved a large green leaf, and accosted us with the repeated exclamation of *tayo*." Symbol of peace, call of "friend": what better way to captivate George Forster, ever hopeful of enlarging the circle of human friendship? Soon the trading began: "We let down a present of beads, nails, and medals to the men. In return, they handed up to us a green stem of a plantane, which was their symbol of peace." Within an hour a hundred canoes surrounded the ship, with the sound of *tayo* echoing on all sides. The trading continued: "Coco-nuts, and plantanes in great quantity, bread-fruit and several other vegetables, besides some fresh fish were offered to us, and eagerly exchanged for transparent beads, and small nails." Forster does not mention—perhaps he did not yet know—that this was an armaments deal, for in a society without metals, iron nails brought an enormous leap in the deadliness of weapons that could be put to effective use against other districts of Tahiti and the neighboring islands. He does not tell us what he traded for his own interests, but within a half hour he "had got together two or three species of unknown birds, and a great number of new fishes, whose colours while alive were exquisitely beautiful." For the rest of the morning he set to work "sketching their outlines and laying on the vivid hues, before they disappeared in the dying objects."[36]

He was hardly less proficient in remembering for his readers his initial impressions of the islanders as he observed them through his ship cabin windows. He particularly admired how the women draped themselves in strips of tapa, the supple cloth that Polynesians manufactured from tree barks: if not quite as perfect as the clothing on Greek statues, still "much more advantageous to the human figure, than any modern fashion we had hitherto seen." The canoers were pleased to find their visitors to be attentive students of their language, which Forster found easy to learn, quickly tuning his ear to the fine inflections of the vowels and noting that the initial *O* or *E* (as in "O-Taheiti") was the article ("the"), not part of the word. Later a man whom Forster judged to be "a person of some consequence in this part of the island," O-Taï, came aboard with his wife and two sis-

ters. Maroraï, one of the sisters, "a graceful figure, with the most deli-
cate and beautiful contours, in the hands and all above the zone,"
took a fancy to a pair of sheets in an officer's cabin. She "made a
number of fruitless attempts to obtain them from her conductor.
He proposed a special favour as the condition; she hesitated some
time, and at last with seeming reluctance consented; but when the
victim was just led to the altar of Hymen, the ship struck violently on
the reef, and interrupted the solemnity." In one day, the trade in
weapons and in sex joined the banner of peace, the language lesson,
and the disinterested pursuit of science. Whatever disconcerting un-
dercurrents there were, Tahiti and the Tahitians enchanted George
Forster.[37]

Forster's approach to politics was indirect. He did not pay much
attention to local power struggles or the deliberations that were
shaping up between Cook and local power-holders, although these
were crystallizing into a regular alliance between the British and one
family, later called the Pomares, who over time rose to predominance
as the "monarchs" of Tahiti. George was too busy with his field research and too young to be included in the ongoing diplomatic negotiations. Instead it was the moral condition of the Tahitians that he
felt in a position to observe and that he used as the starting point for
his observations about different societies and their political regimes.
His mood about the significance of the Tahitians for a general view
of human nature oscillated over the course of their sixteen-day first
stay. Walking through a plantation district two days after their arrival, he admired the "neat simplicity" of Tahitian cottages and the
"artless beauty" of the surrounding groves of fruit trees. A friendly
crowd followed George and his companions, while others, chatting
or resting, "only pronounced a kind *tayo* as we passed." On his walk
the next morning a man treated him to breadfruit baked in an underground oven, which, he noted, came out much better than the

The naturalists at work: George and J. R. Forster. Untitled painting by John Francis Rigaud (1780).

boiled vegetables he knew from home. He and his companions did not find many collectible plants on their walks, but enjoyed the native industry and hospitality.[38]

At the end of a hospitable walk on their fourth day, August 20, he and some of the others encountered

> a neat house, where a very fat man, who seemed to be a chief of the district, was lolling on his wooden pillow. Before him two servants were preparing his desert, by beating up with water some bread-fruit and bananas . . . A woman who sat down near him, crammed down his throat by handfuls the remains of a large baked fish, and several bread-fruits, which he swallowed with a voracious appetite. His countenance was the picture of phlegmatic insensibility, and seemed to witness that all his thoughts centred in the care of his paunch. He scarce deigned to look at us, and a few monosyllables which he uttered, were only directed to remind his feeders of their duty, when we attracted their attention.

A dispiriting sight for philosophical botanizers: until then he and his companions thought they had found one spot in the world where people lived in a state of orderly equality and balanced work and rest. "Our disappointment was very great," continued Forster, "when we saw a luxurious individual spending his life in the most sluggish inactivity, and without one benefit to society, like the privileged parasites of more civilized climates, fattening on the superfluous produce of the soil, of which he robbed the labouring multitude." Despite this revelation, as the voyagers prepared to sail up the coast on the twenty-fourth he still believed "that this island is indeed one of the happiest spots on the globe." When they landed at Matavai Bay and chatted with the inhabitants there about common acquaintances from the last voyage he was more convinced than ever of their good and gentle character. "It must surely be a comfortable reflection to every sensible mind," he added, "that philanthropy seems to be natural to mankind, and that the savage ideas of distrust, malevolence, and revenge, are only the consequences of a gradual depravation of manners."[39]

Like Rousseau, Forster believed there was a state of equilibrium for human societies; he thought he had seen it in Tahiti. Two days later he saw the equilibrium disturbed when women stayed on board overnight. Amid the dancing, the lovemaking, and the exchange of "every bead, nail, hatchet, or shirt which their lovers could muster," he again singled out native gluttony as the symbol of riotous sensuality. Below deck the women ate with their lovers, a capital breach of tabu ("taboo") regulations, and if their lovers could afford pork the women ate it with a greediness that George found shocking, even though he reflected that they must rarely if ever have eaten it in their own homes. His earlier impression of Tahitians' simple and satisfied way of life gave way to a troubled awareness of how easily human beings could lose their self-restraint. Nonetheless, at the end of the visit, on September 1, he was sorry to leave Tahiti and judged its inhabitants to be among the happiest in the world.[40]

Forster took in stride the division of the Tahitians into three social ranks, for, he noted, the material simplicity of their way of life did not make the gap between the highest and the lowest so great. The Tahitians seemed to feel genuine affection for their rulers, and "the lowest man in the nation speaks as freely with his king as with his equal." When native behavior offended his moral categories he tried as far as possible to offer explanation rather than judgment. What aroused his consternation was the overturning of the existing cultural system. Over time, he thought, the well-fed, indolent chiefs would grow disproportionately in number and oppress the laborers ever more heavily. "This addition of labour will have a bad effect on their bodies, they will grow ill-shaped, and their bones become marrowless: their greater exposure to the action of a vertical sun, will blacken their skins, and they will dwindle away to dwarfs, by the more frequent prostitution of their infant daughters, to the voluptuous pleasures of the great." Meanwhile "that pampered race" would get bigger, more beautiful, lighter, more gluttonous, and idler. He predicted a revolutionary finale: "the common people" would rise up and "a proper sense of the general rights of mankind awaking in them, will bring on a revolution." "This," he added, "is the natural circle of human affairs."[41]

Forster's observations contributed to a long-standing discussion of the fate of republics: looking back to classical writers and the history of Greece and Rome, Europeans asked whether it was inevitable for republican virtue to give way to a concentration of power and moral decay. Rousseau outlined such a cyclical movement from equality to hierarchical decadence and destruction in his *Discourse on Inequality*.[42] Forster's predictions were certainly an indirect critique of aristocratic decadence in Europe. They were not, however, a call to insurrection, but an expression both of a cyclical philosophy of history and of fear for the decline of the happiness he had observed among the Tahitians.

He sounded a more urgent note of concern in his critique of incipient European colonialism. "At present," he continued, "there is fortunately no room to suppose, that such a change will take place for a long series of years to come; but how much the introduction of foreign luxuries may hasten that fatal period, cannot be too frequently repeated to Europeans. If the knowledge of a few individuals can only be acquired at such a price as the happiness of nations, it were better for the discoverers, and the discovered, that the South Sea had still remained unknown to Europe and its restless inhabitants." Even though Forster had caught only a brief glimpse of Tahiti and was self-conscious about how little time his natural history duties had left him for social observation, he was a keen reader of the local culture and the dangers of exposure to luxuries. His worries for Tahiti were realized in Hawaii, where the chiefs' culture of manifesting power through brilliant display led to gross conspicuous consumption and exploitation of laborers after the death in 1819 of Kamehameha I. Tahiti was by then off the main highway of international trade. Whatever the future would bring, Forster in this passage recognized that the enlightened expedition of a Cook was inseparable from the introduction of a new and, for the islanders, destructive economy.[43]

His comments on other islands took up the same theme of luxury and equality in comparative perspective. On October 2, 1773, the *Resolution*'s first day on 'Eua, as they were enjoying their warm reception and the general signs of neatness and industry, Forster compared this Tongan island to Tahiti. Less generously endowed by nature, it had more egalitarian and industrious inhabitants. This contrast stirred more general reflections on equality:

> Their attention to separate their property seemed to argue a higher degree of civilization than we had expected. Their arts, manufactures, and music were all more cultivated, complicated, and elegant than at the Society Islands. But, in return, the opulence, or rather luxury, of the Taheitians seemed to be much greater. We saw but few hogs and fowls here, and that great support of life, the bread-tree, appeared to be very scarce. Yams, therefore, and other roots, together with bananas, are their principal articles of diet. Their cloathing too, compared to that of Taheitee, was less plentiful, or at least not converted into such an article of luxury as at that island. Lastly, their houses, though neatly constructed, and always placed in a fragrant shrubbery, were less roomy and convenient. We made these reflections as we advanced towards the landing place, where several hundred natives were assembled; and their appearance immediately struck us with the idea, that if they did not enjoy so great a profusion of the gifts of nature as the Taheitians, those gifts were perhaps distributed to all with greater equality.[44]

The Marquesan islanders inspire similar reflections. Since the ethnic origin of the islanders was the same as the Tahitians', he turned to environment to account for differences in social organization. The Marquesans had only enough land for subsistence and none left over for mulberry plantations of the kind he had observed on the plains of Tahiti; the result was a greater equality and a greater sum of social happiness:

> They are all equal among themselves; they are active, very healthy, and beautifully made; there is nothing which can make them unhappy, by debarring them the means of obeying nature's voice. The Taheitians have more comforts and conveniencies; they have perhaps superior skill in the arts, and these things give them a greater relish for the enjoyment of life; but to balance these advantages, they are no longer upon a level; one part lives by the labours of the other, and diseases already wait upon their excesses.[45]

The contrast between Tahiti and its Polynesian cousins introduced a note of uncertainty into Forster's theorizing. Elsewhere he discussed material and technological civilization as a positive good; yet when he came to consider political regimes and their relationship to social well-being, he argued almost the reverse. The *juste milieu* of human society fell to a sparse level of enough goods for the subsistence of all. The Tahitians' greater wealth and refinement, the Tongan and Marquesan examples revealed, came at a high moral and political cost.

The tension between Forster's belief in a European civilizing mission and his criticism of civilized decadence came together in his description of Mai (Omai), the Tahitian whom Cook had picked up on his first circumnavigation. Mai had been feted by London high society, to the disgust of observers who disliked both his shallow behavior and the frivolity of his admirers. George Forster rued that Mai had been exposed to the superficial life of the court and had imitated it instead of being educated in the true benefits of civilization: "The continued round of enjoyments left him no time to think of his future life . . . It can hardly be supposed that he never formed a wish to obtain some knowledge of our agriculture, arts, and manufactures; but no friendly Mentor ever attempted to cherish and to gratify this wish, much less to improve his moral character, to teach him our exalted ideas of virtue, and the sublime principles of revealed religion." Attacked later by one of his critics for lamenting the treatment of Mai, Forster stuck by his condemnation and regretted that Mai was not taught agricultural skills to take back to the Tahitians. His example did not, however, lead Forster to despair over the possibility of international aid. Instead he hoped that there would be wiser attempts and noted that ships were going out with domestic animals that could be of real use to the Tahitians. Here was the point where he could revert from his own doubts to a justification for voyages of exploration.[46]

Searching and reflective—remarkably so, given his youth and the forced pace of his writing—Forster confided in his readers, asking them to consider all the effects of European contact, from the physical and moral evils to the benefits. In the end he came down in favor of a paternalistic European regime of settlement and economic exchange that would rid Pacific islanders of their "barbarism." In an unusually effective ending—most voyage accounts go into a narrative decline once the travelers have done their business and are returning home—Forster realigned the expedition's lonely wanderings with the progress of civilization, which had not halted in their absence. The voyagers were able to read journals and newspapers when they arrived at the Cape of Good Hope in March of 1775. They found so much good news of peace in Europe and the doings of enlightened monarchs like Catherine the Great in Russia and Frederick the Great in Prussia that their return seemed to coincide with "prospects, which all at once opened to our eyes, which promised general happiness to the human race, and seemed to announce a period of time, when mankind will appear in a more exalted light than ever!"[47]

Back home in London, surrounded by creditors, fearing for the well-being of his mother and siblings and ruining his health with overwork, George Forster shared with his readers his pride in living at a moment of the forward movement of history. Near his conclusion he paused to list the extremes of the human condition the *Resolution* voyagers had known from the "dull, hungry, deformed savages of Tierra del Fuego" to the "happier tribes of the Society Islands." Summing up all he and his fellow voyagers had seen and done, he continued:

> From the contemplation of these different characters, the advantages, the blessings which civilization and revealed religion have diffused over our part of the globe, will become more and more obvious to the impartial enquirer. He will acknowledge, with a thankful heart, that incomprehensible goodness which has given him a distinguished superiority over so many of his fellow-creatures, who follow the impulse of their senses, without knowing the nature or name of virtue; without being able to form that great idea of general order, which could alone convey to them a just conception of the Creator.[48]

He and his father had risked their lives and endured insults and deceptions, but it had all been for a higher end. He wished the native peoples of the world well; he thought the scientific voyagers were the instruments of enlightenment and the princes of Europe its patrons.

Forster's faith in a paternalistic Enlightenment deepened in his later writings on Cook and the Pacific. The most important of these was the essay "Cook the Discoverer." Commenced as an independent essay, it turned into the introduction to his translation into German of the official narrative of Cook's third voyage. He approached the essay as an important work, one that he composed with special care between December 21, 1786, and March 31, 1787; in the edition of his writings that came out in 1789 he placed it at the beginning. Forster's friends admired the essay and the translation as a whole, as did the many reviewers.[49]

The essay is a monument to a slain hero, placing Cook, who had been killed by Hawaiians at Kealakekua Bay, Hawaii, in 1779, among the benefactors of humanity. Near the beginning of the piece, Forster confronted the ethical dilemmas of scientific discovery. "Who," he asked, "could seriously deny the devastation that is inseparable from the development of various abilities in human beings?" But to stop with a recognition of the evils of scientific knowledge and the resulting expansion of Europeans beyond their homes would have been to deny the actual course of human history without showing the possibility that it could have developed differently, "and until this has been proven it will be pointless to call us back into the forests." Cook represented the European spirit of advancement. Forster reminded his readers that Cook's predecessors had hewed to a narrow route around the globe, whereas the great discoverer had broadened out to bring ever wider realms into the domain of science. The voyages had also proved that there was one, undivided humankind: "that human nature is different everywhere in keeping with climate, but overall and with regard to its organization as well as its instincts and the course of its development is specifically the same." Every people of the earth had the capacity for speech, and along with speech, the capacity for reason. Nonetheless he cautioned against an exaggerated egalitarianism, concluding "that just as a complete and absolute equality among men does not exist physically, so it is also morally impossible." While Europeans could educate their brothers in other parts of the world, it was by no means clear that they could ever elevate them to the status of equals.[50]

In conclusion Forster associated Cook with two kinds of causes. One was the party of work versus the party of indolence. Everywhere Cook went, wrote Forster, from the poles to the equator, he and his companions found human happiness to be in proportion to the degree of physical and mental activity. "In Tahiti as in Europe the gluttonous idler is just a congenital defect of the political system who exists at the cost of a working and useful class of human beings. Shouldn't his condition fill us with revulsion rather than longing?" The other was the advance of Europe at the expense of static Asia: Forster was astonished that the ancient peoples of Asia "in Bengal, Java, the Moluccas and Philippines" had seemingly stagnated in their level of culture. By contrast he thought that countries with small numbers of indigenous people could be the seats of new colonies to which Europeans could transplant their spirit of dynamic enterprise; Australia especially appealed to him as a new hub linking India and America.[51]

"Cook the Discoverer" has a more consistently triumphal tone than the voyage account, which incident by incident revalues European values. Was this European self-assurance an abandonment of the peoples who, he repeatedly emphasized, befriended the voyagers on their journey? Such a rejection was certainly not his intent. One might speak more accurately of a growing awareness of the dynamic forward movement of history in the last years of George Forster's life. The question he faced in his essay on Cook was one Rousseau had already confronted: if there had been an earlier period of equilibrium in human history, of rough equality and simple material culture, and if the peoples of Oceania were living representatives of that period, what was one to make of Europe's relationship to them now? Rousseau himself was pessimistic; he saw no possibility of a return to an earlier moment in the history of the human species. In his travel account Forster balanced his awareness of the strengths, and in some ways the superiority, of native cultures against his loyalty to the Enlightenment and belief in the working out of a providential design in human history. By the time he wrote "Cook the Discoverer," he subscribed more uniformly to a faith in the spread of reason, with Cook as its agent and its martyr.

Forster himself was to be reason's martyr as well. After his return to Germany he found employment first as a professor in Kassel, then at the University of Vilna, and finally as the chief librarian of the local prince's collection in the Rhineland city of Mainz. There he was when the armies of the French Revolution burst across the river and, to the surprise of contemporaries, repulsed the army of aristocratic enemies. Entering Mainz, the conquerors established a revolutionary republic. Forster did not run away, but stayed and represented the people of the city to the occupiers. Soon Forster himself turned into an advocate of the revolutionary regime, and the people of the city elected him to be one of three German delegates to the revolutionary government in Paris. The Holy Roman Empire banished him as a traitor, his wife abandoned him, and in Paris he lived in poverty, a disillusioned witness to the Jacobin regime. He died there on January 10, 1794, probably of pneumonia, bereft of friends, his body tossed into an anonymous grave. At a time when others were too worldly, too beholden to the past, or too calculating, Forster threw in his lot with reason in history. Like the delegates who had been called to the Estates General in Paris in 1789, he did not start out a revolutionary, but got caught up in the accelerating whirl of words, ideas, and events.[52] A more compromising personality would have made for a cannier careerist, but a lesser participant in a revolutionary age.

Adelbert von Chamisso

A curious crossing of destinies took place in 1792. On the right side of the Rhine, the French invasion threw George Forster's former life as an established German man of letters into disarray and turned him into a revolutionary. In France, one of the noblemen who decided to flee the growing menace of terror was Count Louis Marie de Chamisso, who with his wife and seven children left the family estate in Champagne and joined an émigré army in the Netherlands, a monarchist misadventure that led to years of wandering through Lüttich, The Hague, Würzburg, and Bayreuth. Finally in 1795 the family found a haven in Berlin.[53] While the Revolution drove Forster into France, the Chamisso family fled to Germany.

This experience was the early "education" of Adelbert von Chamisso, born in 1781 as the sixth child in this refugee family. Along with two of his brothers, Adelbert (born Louis Charles Adélaide) helped support the family during their homeless years by painting portrait miniatures and selling the paper flowers his mother made; when he arrived in Berlin in May of 1796, he was sent to paint in the royal porcelain factory. In the same year came his deliverance. The Prussian queen, Frederike Luise, charming, domestic, and beloved by the Romantics, rescued him by making him one of her pages; under her protection he was also able for the next two years to visit the French Gymnasium in Berlin. After this incomplete schooling, in 1798 he entered a Prussian army regiment and was stationed in the city garrison of Berlin. Three years later his parents returned to France, just after he was promoted to lieutenant.[54]

Like George Forster, Chamisso moved at an early age between countries and languages. But under what different circumstances! Forster inhabited a unified Enlightenment Europe with common challenges and ideals to ease his passage as he moved from Ger-

many to England and back to Germany. During the years of his up-
bringing he experienced a world of fierce intellectual debate but
intra-European peace. Chamisso struggled to stay afloat in a Europe
flooded with armies and ideologies; he acquired a double French
and German cultural identity as his family searched for a haven.
Berlin turned out to be a place where he continued to absorb French
culture even as he assimilated into his adopted homeland, for the
Prussian capital had its own strong traditions of openness to French
literary and philosophical influence. The Prussian monarchs had
welcomed in prosperous and industrious French Huguenots after
their expulsion from France a century before by Louis XIV. Frederick
the Great preferred the French language and literature to the German, and he imported French intellectuals to his court, most famous
among them Voltaire. During and after his rule, Berlin was a provincial outpost of the French Enlightenment, with intellectual leaders
who promoted a particularly doctrinaire version of the ideas they
imported from Paris. The Huguenots, who remained a distinct sub-
community, ran the Gymnasium Chamisso attended for his few years
of formal schooling, getting an education in the classics of his home
country.

By 1800 Berlin had turned into the setting for one of the first
groups of Romantics to appear in Germany, who assaulted the literary conventions of their enlightened elders and offered their own
brilliant counterexamples of criticism and imaginative writing. In his
literary theory and history Friedrich Schlegel announced new principles of sympathy with one's subject and analysis of its specific structure, while the poet Novalis (Friedrich von Hardenberg) demonstrated how to bring alien historical epochs such as the Middle Ages
to life for modern readers. These writers showed an astonishing energy in expanding the literary canon to argue for the centrality of
Dante and Shakespeare to modern literature and for the importance

of Rabelais. They urged on their readers an attitude of self-criticism to be furthered through wit and irony. Their urbanity, their playfulness, their exploration of imaginative highs and everyday lows, appealed deeply to Chamisso, torn as he was between his literary ambitions and the discipline of the Prussian army. Irksome though his military duties were, they left him with plenty of free time, and with the latecomer's thirst for knowledge he threw himself into the Berlin literary scene as a junior follower of the Romantic School, as they came to be called; his first German poems appeared in 1803.[55]

Later he joined the Parisian circle around Germaine de Staël, daughter of the Genevan banker Jacques Necker, who had served as minister of finance to Louis XVI; she attracted cultivated admirers such as Benjamin Constant, the political philosopher and novelist who took seriously the French Revolution's principle of liberty and repudiated its manifestations of democratic despotism, whether in the Terror of the early 1790s or in the authoritarian regime of Napoleon. Another member of her circle was August Wilhelm Schlegel, who like his younger brother Friedrich spoke for a new conception of world literature that would appreciate the diverse productions of different times and places (later he became a professor of Sanskrit). Mme de Staël herself wrote in the same spirit of appreciation of diversity when she published *De l'Allemagne*, which advertised the achievements of German literature and philosophy to her French contemporaries. It was implicitly a critique of the policies of Napoleon, who wanted French culture to beam out from Paris across Europe. When de Staël fled from the wrath of the emperor, who was not slow to notice that she had challenged his program for French hegemony by praising the land of poets and thinkers, Chamisso accompanied her into Swiss exile at Coppet, her estate near Geneva. "I spent unforgettable days," he wrote, "with this absolutely wonderful woman, met many of the most important men of the day, and experienced a portion of the history of Napoleon, his enmity toward a power which would not be subservient to him; for nothing independent was allowed to exist around or below him."[56] Chamisso was an offbeat, bohemian figure there, arousing the jealousy of her lover, the humorless August Wilhelm Schlegel, and annoying everyone with his perpetual pipe smoking.

Chamisso was a displaced man, buffeted between French and German hostilities. At one point he was in danger of being captured by French troops and executed as a traitor to his country of birth. (This would have been in terrible symmetry with the fate of George Forster, who was condemned as a traitor to the Holy Roman Empire.) Later he left Berlin in fear of anti-French rioting. His occupation was no more fixed than his nationality: in 1808 he resigned his lieutenant's commission before going off to join Mme de Staël, disgusted with army life and desperate to make a full-time go of literature though unable to find a stable position to permit him to do so. Then he stumbled on something that promised a kind of stability amid the disturbances of the Napoleonic era. In 1811, while at Coppet, he went on botanical walks with Mme de Staël's son, Auguste-Louis, and began to discover his calling as a naturalist. The following year he was able to study natural science at the recently founded University of Berlin. Without a career, without a family, and menaced by anti-French xenophobia, Chamisso conceived the ambition of hiring himself out for plant collecting in some distant part of the world. He offered his services to Prince Maximilian von Wied-Neuwied, who was preparing to go to Brazil, but Maximilian (like Chamisso a demobilized Prussian officer who had had only a brief opportunity for university study) was financing his own trip and had no means to support a travel companion. It was a crazy idea anyway: in his thirties, with a hard life behind him, Chamisso was too old for a journey that would test the endurance of a man ten years younger.

Besides, he had done none of the networking that landed self-pro-
moters like Commerson and the elder Forster their assignments.
Then, in a chance turn of events, an invitation came his way. It
was like something out of a Romantic tale by his friend E. T. A.
Hoffmann.[57] Count Nikolai Rumiantsev, until recently first minister
of state in Russia, was sponsoring a voyage around the world. The
naturalist designated for the voyage, the professor of botany Carl
Friedrich Ledebour, at the University of Dorpat (today Tartu, Estonia), was too sick to go.[58] Would Chamisso like to take his place? His
friend Julius Eduard Hitzig, a government attorney and also a book
dealer and friend of the Romantics, knew the playwright August von
Kotzebue, who was the father of the voyage commander, Otto von
Kotzebue. When Chamisso declared that he was game, Hitzig made
his wishes known to the voyage organizers. Before long Chamisso
was accepting an invitation from Adam von Krusenstern, a captain
of the Russian navy, to join the expedition.

In the fall of 1814, shortly before receiving the invitation, Chamisso
wrote a novella, *The Amazing Story of Peter Schlemihl*, that oddly anticipated the voyage. It was a variation of the Faust story of selling one's soul to the devil that fascinated the era; Goethe had published Part I of his *Faust* drama in 1806. Chamisso's protagonist
was not a learned doctor, a man of dignity and honor, but a marginal
figure. His last name indicated that he was a Jew, or rather a Jewish
folk figure, the schlemiel, a bumbler always getting into trouble: as
Chamisso wrote to his brother Hippolyte, he not only sleeps with the
rabbi's wife but gets caught, unlike the rest of the world.[59] Peter
Schlemihl, a low-life comic Faust, exchanges his shadow for a magic
leather pouch that produces gold. Right away he discovers that without a shadow he cannot live among men; old ladies tell him he has
lost it, schoolboys taunt him, and he is forced to flee. Disguised as
an anonymous wealthy man and provided with servants, he settles

among villagers who first mistake him for the king of Prussia and then settle on calling him the Count. His misfortunes only grow. He falls in love with a village girl only to lose her to one of his servants, who betrays him as a man without a shadow. The man in a gray coat who bought his shadow for the magic pouch pursues him, offering to give him back his shadow and the girl in exchange for his soul. This time Schlemihl is wiser. He resists temptation and throws away the sack. As he finds himself, fortune begins to turn his way. He buys an old pair of boots that turn out to be the Seven League kind and carry him in a few steps across the face of the earth. No longer acceptable to human society, he finds redemption in nature. His watch will do as a chronometer. He outfits himself with a sextant and books. Back and forth across the earth he wanders, "now measuring its heights, now the temperature of its waters and those of the air, now observing animals, now investigating plants; I hurried from the equator to the pole, from one world to another, comparing experience with experience."[60] He becomes a botanist and plans to will his papers to the University of Berlin. This is a Faust story, but with a few special twists. What he loses is not his soul but his social existence. What he gains at the end is what Goethe's Faust initially rejects, the solitary pursuit of knowledge. Schlemihl's science, however, is not the abstract bookish studies that drove Faust out of his study, but the collector's tramping that leaves mud on one's boots. After exile from the company of his fellow human beings, he discovers the consolations of Linnaean botany.

Chamisso had no Seven-League Boots. He boarded a brig, the *Rurik*, for his journey around the world. His companions were an unusually gifted group of observers, making this one of the most important ethnographic expeditions of the era of scientific exploration. The captain, Otto von Kotzebue, was not only the son of August von Kotzebue, who enjoyed international popularity as the creator of light social dramas; Otto was a literary talent in his own right, whose account of the *Rurik* voyage kept technical details to a minimum, did not dwell on natural phenomena, and fluently narrated the voyagers' encounters with different societies around the world. He and Chamisso tested each other's patience; yet Otto was an excellent captain in the mold of Cook, autocratic but solicitous of his men's welfare and—despite Chamisso's complaints—not insensitive to the voyage's scientific mission. A Danish lieutenant named Morton Wormskiold joined the expedition as a volunteer naturalist. At first welcomed by Chamisso, he turned into a jealous rival, persuaded that others were cutting him out of the best plant collecting, and finally left the expedition in Kamchatka, the Siberian peninsula facing the Aleutian Islands.[61]

If Kotzebue was difficult and Wormskiold was impossible for Chamisso, his relationship to the other two members of the scientific staff could not have been better. The physician Friedrich Eschscholtz, like Commerson and many others, had a medical education that carried over into a professional expertise in natural history; he became Chamisso's inseparable companion in all his scientific activities. (Later he was appointed professor of botany at the University of Dorpat.)[62] No less affable was Chamisso's relationship with the artist on board, Louis Choris. From a Ukranian German family and fourteen years Chamisso's junior, he was warm-hearted, ambitious, and eager for scientific training. Chamisso's broad human sympathies stopped short of the sailors. Despite his years of military service, this linguistic virtuoso found their behavior so disgusting that he made a point of not learning their language. His antipathy toward Russians on the ship blended with his more general dislike of the tsarist autocracy.

The *Rurik* voyage had the status of a Russian warship. Its primary scientific mission was an *idée fixe* of the post-1815 period: to continue

The Romantic artist: Louis
Choris. Artist unknown, lithographed by Langlumé.

the search for a northern waterway that would lead via the Bering
Straits from the Pacific to the Atlantic. Explorers had tried unsuccessfully for centuries to find a northern passage across the American
land mass, with all the obvious advantages for commerce it would
bring, and the period after 1815 was one of high confidence and ambition, when Britain and Russia competed for the glory as well as the
material gain of such a new discovery. The *Rurik* was also to look in
on Russian fur-trading posts and to scout out new locations for trading and colonizing in the North Pacific. Even though the expedition
was a scientific one, Kotzebue had to think of imperial interests on
almost every station of the journey; the tensions between him and
Chamisso had much to do with the conflicting roles of diplomat and
scientist.

Chamisso joined the ship for its departure on August 17, 1815, from

Copenhagen. After rounding Cape Horn on January 22, 1816, and visiting Concepción, Chile, it crossed the Pacific via Easter Island and the Tuamotu Islands on its way to Kamchatka, Kotzebue Sound, and the Aleutian island of Unalaska; then it headed south again, visiting San Francisco from October 2 to November 1 and Hawaii from November 22 to December 14. Next came a smaller Pacific triangle within the larger triangle of the first year: atoll-hopping through Micronesia during the remaining winter and spring of 1817, a northern tour during the summer months, Hawaii from September 28 to October 14, and a return to Micronesia. The long route home passed through Capetown, St. Helena, and Portsmouth on the way to St. Petersburg, the voyagers' final destination, in late September 1818. The *Rurik* traveled after the shift northward of European great-power rivalries in the Pacific. Chamisso did not stay in Tahiti, as Commerson and the Forsters had done; instead he got to know Hawaii and to explore the still little-known Marshall and Caroline Islands.

When it came to his work as naturalist, Chamisso's forte was the botanical collecting that had captivated him since his days with Auguste de Staël. He came back from the voyage with a "herbarium"—a collection of dried plants—of 2,500 species. It was a precious capital, the starting point for a modest but sufficient career as botanist. In August 1819 he received a position as supervisor of the Prussian monarchy's Royal Botanical Garden, where the curator, Diederich Franz Leonhard von Schlechtendal, was a friend from his student days. Chamisso's ongoing botanical research, much of it carried out in cooperation with this friend, appeared after 1826 in the professional journal edited by Schlechtendal, *Linnaea*. By the end of Chamisso's career his name, by itself or with Schlechtendal's, was associated with more than 1,280 genus and species names. After Chamisso's death, his herbarium of 10,000–12,000 species was bought by the Russian Academy of Sciences in St. Petersburg, whose botanical garden still houses it today.[63]

The politics of a new era defined the voyage. In March 1815, Napoleon returned from Elbe, beginning the adventure of the Hundred Days and a renewed victory for conservative rulers across Europe. In September of the same year, a few weeks after the departure of the *Rurik*, Chamisso's two masters—the Russian and Prussian monarchs—and their Austrian counterpart announced the formation of the Holy Alliance in order to combat revolution and promote Christianity in Europe. In Concepción, Chile, Chamisso could observe the decay of the Spanish old regime and the stirring of nationalist and revolutionary movements. On their return trip the voyagers representing the most reactionary European power could contemplate St. Helena, the island home of Napoleon after his final defeat. After the travelers' return politics again impinged on their consciousness, this time violently: during a theater performance in Mannheim, an enraged student, Karl Sand, shot and killed August von Kotzebue for serving as an intelligence gatherer and propagandist for the tsar. The assassination triggered the Karlsbad Decrees, repressive measures to limit freedom of expression throughout the newly formed German Confederation. To be part of a Russian imperial expedition created an uncomfortable situation for Chamisso, who did not fit in easily on either side of the age's conflict between Napoleonic and anti-Napoleonic regimes. As a friend of Mme de Staël he was allied with the opponents of Napoleon, the leveler of national liberties and freedom of expression in Europe; but he was no less opposed to the repressive policies of the restoration monarchies.

Chamisso wrote two descriptions of the voyage. The first was his contribution to the official account, which was first published in German as part of Otto von Kotzebue's voyage account. He wrote it in less than a year after his return—he arrived in Berlin on the last day of October 1818, and his preface is dated December 1819—for inclusion in the third of three volumes of the Kotzebue work, which appeared in 1821. Far from experiencing the restrictions on his freedom of expression that one might have expected from a book published at the most reactionary moment in the nineteenth century under the sponsorship of its most reactionary regime, Chamisso was able to make his work a commentary on personal and national freedom around the world. In his observations on Chile he worried about a society with a languishing economy that was edging toward revolution. History, he wrote, had judged that the United States owed its prosperity to throwing off its colonial master; "all the peoples of Europe openly wish the Spanish possessions good luck in their struggles for an end to their dependence." He doubted, however, that the Chileans could look forward to a similarly prosperous future. "Separation from the mother country is already foreseeable," he wrote, "but it is doubtful when wise calm development will seal the transition from repression to free independence." He felt a special sympathy for the Indians who worked as day laborers, the shattered remnants of the Araucanians, who, he wrote, did not give a true impression of "that warlike, eloquent, strong and pure nation whose devotion to freedom and military skill were an insuperable armed bulwark first against the Incas and then against the leveling conqueror of the New World."[64]

At the northern end of Spain's American empire, Chamisso was angered by Spanish restrictions on trade in San Francisco. The provincial governor prohibited all trade along the California coast when "a little freedom would soon make California into the granary and market of the northern coasts of these seas and the ships sailing them." The Franciscan mission in San Francisco horrified him. The monks had no training in the crafts they were supposed to teach and no knowledge of Indian languages; the Indians were dying of European epidemic diseases without receiving medical attention. Chamisso thought the Indians were on a lower cultural level than those of the interior or the Northwest, but he regretted the missionaries' contempt toward them, their dismissal of anything originating with the "savages," and their refusal to learn anything about them. Nor was the Spanish Empire the only place where Chamisso made observations like these. He protested, as did many Russian naval observers, the Russian enslavement of the Aleuts, whose men they used as fur hunters; Chamisso contrasted their poverty and misery with the wealth and strength of the nearby free Chuchkis. In the Philippines he wanted to know more about the "free tribes" of the interior than he could learn on a short visit, also commenting that greater economic freedom could permit Manila to surpass its rival, Canton. The yearning for freedom—indigenous, economic, and constitutional—resounded through his text.[65]

Chamisso inhabited a political world remade by decades of revolution. Commerson and George Forster had lived in a Europe defined by privilege; on their voyages around the world they sought to learn whether human beings could function in a different kind of political system, one defined by human equality, and whether a democratic order would increase human dignity and happiness. Neither one could resist the pull toward a democratic utopia: Commerson imagined he had found his in Tahiti, Forster in the Jacobin republic. Chamisso lived at the other end of the revolutionary and Napoleonic era and reflected on its transformations, triumphs, and excesses. Within the revolutionary triad of liberty, equality, and fraternity, his writings mark a shift from a radical Enlightenment preoccupation with equality to an early-nineteenth-century preoccupation with liberty, which he upheld against repression in all its varieties, French, Russian, and colonial. The background of his observations in 1819 was the victory of the Allies over Napoleon, the conservative peace settlement at the Congress of Vienna, and the reactionary Holy Alliance. It was also, however, an awareness that the revolutionary spirit of freedom had by no means been permanently suppressed. If 1819, when he completed his work, was a low point, there were nonetheless liberal uprisings in Spain and Naples, and the onset of the Greek independence movement, by the time his words were printed in 1821. Just as Commerson and Forster sought to test the possibilities for equality, so Chamisso sought to take measure of the gains and losses for freedom around the world.[66]

Nowhere was this more visible than in his description of the Hawaiian Islands (or Sandwich Islands, as the British named them). It was, he knew, a hierarchical society: there were no illusions in his report about an elite and a landholding system that he compared to European feudalism. The *Rurik* visited the islands just before the disintegration of ancient Hawaii. Since the late 1790s a skilled, energetic ruler had arisen, Kamehameha, who forged a protective relationship with the British, outvied political rivals, styled himself a monarch, and carefully controlled incoming trade to increase his wealth without corroding the social system. Chamisso was disgusted by the widespread prostitution and ruthless pursuit of profit that Europeans had introduced into Hawaii. He was fascinated too, though, by these people who he thought could never be conquered. Even if the kingdom fell apart after Kamehameha's death as the *ali'i* (the social and religious elite) reasserted their political power, Chamisso thought that "the Sandwich Islands will remain what they are: the free harbor and stockpiling place for all those mariners who sail these seas." Looking over the fortifications and the weaponry of Honolulu, the former Prussian lieutenant thought an invader might be able to take the place by force, but could never keep it. "This people will not subject itself to foreigners, and they are too strong, too nu-

merous, and too fond of warfare to be quickly extirpated, like the natives of the Marianas." The Hawaiians' aggressive character made
them less pleasant than the gentle Micronesians, but equipped them
to resist the Europeans swarming into their ports. His prophecy was
correct that no armed force would ever take Hawaii; it was instead
religious and economic invasion, as well as epidemic disease, that
undermined the islands' independence.[67]

Chamisso's contribution to the official voyage account was not his
last word on his voyage around the world. In the mid-1830s, when he
was an honored representative of Berlin arts and letters, he brought
out a four-volume edition of his collected works. It included an entirely new voyage account, which he titled his *Tagebuch* or journal.
This name was curious, since the work was not a journal as the term
was then used to name the day-by-day record that officers, scientists,
and other voyagers commonly kept, but a remembrance of events
from almost two decades before. Perhaps Chamisso meant in this
way to indicate that it was a narrative history in contrast to his ana-
lytically organized contribution to the Kotzebue compendium. It
also had the greater personal intimacy of a private journal: in contrast to the laconic scientist's report of 1819, the *Tagebuch* included
his personal response to his experiences. Since his return, he explained, he had advised young would-be travelers to suppress their
scholarly impulse and write a narrative that would "seek only to
present the strange land and the strange people, or rather present
myself in the strange surroundings to the participating readers, and
if the success were in proportion to the intent, then everyone would
have to dream along with me wherever the voyage took us."[68] He
packed plenty of empirical observation into this account, too, in a
style no less disciplined than before. Compare his statement, though,
to George Forster's declaration of *his* intentions: for Forster the voyage narrative was to "justify the ways of God to man," to place the

voyage within a rational universe and the forward movement of history, with Cook and his passengers doing their part to spread enlightenment across the face of the earth. Chamisso promised no such providential rationality. Instead he led his readers into the psychological drama of European–islander encounters.

The European political setting had changed by the time Chamisso wrote his second account. In 1818 the dynastic successor from the Bourbon family, Louis XVIII, older brother of the unfortunate Louis XVI, had returned from exile to be propped up on the royal throne by the Allies, who hoped that he would bring historical continuity and stability to France. He ruled for seven cautious years, too singed by misfortune to object to the constitution that the Allies imposed along with the opportunity to return to power. His successor, Charles X, quickly created unease with measures that looked like the beginnings of a right-wing coup d'état. A brief, almost bloodless revolutionary convulsion toppled him in 1830. His replacement was Louis Philippe, from the closely related Orléans dynasty. He was a man of a different temper who had spent part of his years of exile in North America, took an interest in commerce and industry, established a liberal history professor, François Guizot, as his prime minister, and sent his sons to Oxford.

The Revolution of 1830 signaled to contemporary observers that the political changes initiated in 1789 had only paused, but not stopped, with the defeat of Napoleon. Chamisso was among those who welcomed the change, which brought an end to legislation such as antiblasphemy laws in France (with severe penalties for those who wrote disrespectfully about the Catholic Church) and promised an era of greater civil liberty for all of Europe. He also, however, recognized the ambiguities of progress, which was as much a name for cultural destruction as it was for the spread of political freedoms. The multiple perspectives of past and present, of regret for vanishing aristocracies and affirmation of the new era of democratic freedom, gave special depth to his psychological insights as he recalled his visits to Hawaii.

Chamisso emphasized the aristocratic warrior qualities of the Hawaiian *ali'i*. He noticed them as soon as he and Eschscholtz left the new arrivals' initial audience with Kamehameha—which dispelled tensions surrounding the Russian warship's arrival—and began to look for plants:

> A chief, unmistakable from his demeanor and his almost gigantic stature, laughingly brandished his javelin at me as he came along the path toward us, then shook my hand, calling out the greeting of peace, "Arocha!" What he then said might have meant, "Have you spoiled our fun again? We thought we were going to have a good fight, and now you are our good friends!"

It was an unusual portrayal of a native–European encounter: the Hawaiians as military equals, fearless and relaxed; Chamisso not resentful of this patronizing behavior, but impressed by the man who greeted him with the weapon of war and the greeting of peace. Another incident carried a similar message: at a dance arranged for the visitors, Chamisso pushed aside a boy who kept stepping on his feet. Seeing that he had hurt the boy's feelings, he made a face and pretended to hurl a javelin at him, in this way bringing a smile to the boy's face. "As long as I considered him capable of bearing arms and my equal everything was all right," wrote Chamisso, "but he would not let himself be shoved or kicked." It was a small anecdote, but revealing, he thought, for the national character. The European aristocrat discovered corresponding aristocratic values in Hawaii. "People have been surprised to hear me speak of nobility among the Polynesians. To be sure, I find nobility there the way I imagine it used to exist among us, where, already discarded, it lives on only in faint memories." He caught a late glimpse of what had already vanished in Europe, the inner ethos of nobility, not the titles that a Napoleon could dispense.[69]

Despite his yearning for nobility, Chamisso, who had seen the world from the bottom up and was always ready to mock the social pretensions of high society, wrote with a populist edge. He was an avid reader of folk literature and of Rabelais and had first made a name for himself with the story of down-and-out Peter Schlemihl. Recounting his weeks on Hawaii he was an unusually sympathetic observer of ordinary people, and even though his encounters with them were not close, he took a certain glee in pointing out how they viewed him and his non-native clumsiness. On one of his botanical excursions he tried to show off by swimming for the first time and made some forward motion across a shallow stream. He was pleased with his progress until he heard onlooking Hawaiians' "incessant peals of laughter" at his clumsy movements. "But laughter here does not contain anything hostile in it. Laughter is a person's right; everyone laughs at everybody else, king or commoner, without detriment to their other relationships."[70] It was "equality" of a sort: not the abstract equality preached by Rousseau and sought by Commerson and Forster, but the kind that came from a moment of carnival, dissolving the pretensions and anxieties of high and low alike. This was a mood that crossed hemispheres. The Hawaiian counterpart to carnival was the Makahiki festival. During this celebration of fertility, difference was dissolved by public dancing, satire, laughter, copulating, and mingling between *ali'i* and lower-rank people in a generalized community.[71] From their different ends of the earth, Chamisso and his audience had their ritualized forms of comic affirmation of fellowship.

If flashes of communication were one possibility of a trip to a foreign country, so were misunderstandings. Chamisso brought his reader up against the limits of the traveler's insight. His impulse nearly got him in trouble when he, the trained botanist, started pulling out an unfamiliar kind of grass, only to have a Hawaiian berate him; later he learned, to his embarrassment, that the strange grass was rice, which a European plantation owner was cultivating. Later the same day, Kotzebue had one of his men put up flags to take measurements for mapping Honolulu harbor. An adventurer had recently hoisted a flag as a sign of possession of Oahu, "and now everyone seized his weapons, all promising themselves the festival of a battle." John Young, an American-born advisor to Kamehameha, spotted the confusion and warned the captain to bring down the flags before anyone got hurt.[72] Again Chamisso's literary background made him an acute observer: his variety of early Romanticism savored the false projections, misreadings, and misunderstandings that clung to attempts at mutual understanding. He made a special point of noting how often Kotzebue misjudged the intentions and customs of others, as when he took offense at Spanish women's custom of throwing coins at the window of their guests in Concepción, or threw away some of a precious gift of food in the Marshall Islands. There was also much confusion over who Dr. Chamisso was—this "Russian," as he was often assumed to be, who in a distant valley of Hawaii was introduced to a supposed fellow countryman and could not speak a word to him.

Incomprehension also awaited the traveler after his return. On December 4 and 6, 1816, Kalanimoku, governor of Oahu, arranged for his Russian visitors to see Hawaiian dancing. Chamisso hardly had words to compare the "magnificence of that spectacle" to the "repulsive gyrations" of European ballet. "We barbarians! These peoples so endowed with a sense of beauty we call 'savages.'" As he wrote in the 1830s, he knew that he was looking back on a vanished art, suppressed by the missionaries of Tahiti and Hawaii. "I must give some evidence that I am speaking the truth," he wrote—but what could that evidence be? He could only comment that the male dancers were better artists than the females, although the women were attractive and the men were plain. Choris's pictures of the hula were "poor sheets." He wished a real artist, not just a draftsmen, had visited the islands, but in the end, "dancing cannot be painted."[73] Words failed him: an old problem in the history of travel, but one presented with a new insistence in his writing, shaped as it was by a Romantic sensitivity to the inadequacy of language to human communication.

The difficulties of conveying one's experiences sometimes had to do with the social setting of the expeditions. Official voyage naturalists wrote with their first and most important readers at home in mind, the monarchs and ministers who were their sponsors. Their future depended on their ability to win these power-holders' favor. With their approval came publications, honors, employment; without it all the travelers' work could come to nothing. Their sponsors might be intelligent and discerning critics, with a sincere appreciation of scientists' work, and travelers might be devoted with equally sincere interest to European projects of commerce and colonization; but whether or not the match was a good one, travelers had to write for the guardians of privilege who gave them their instructions before they left and their rewards after they returned. Their writings were inseparable from the emotionally felt, personal relations with the men who were their patrons.

CHAPTER 2

Patrons

Scientific travel depended on patronage. Most travelers on world voyages were young, poor, and painfully dependent on the goodwill of masters who paid their way and provided other vital services to ease their passage to distant parts. From the world of the travelers we best remember Charles Darwin, who did not fit these generalizations and went on the *Beagle* voyage as a well-to-do young man—but even Darwin depended on his father's goodwill for permitting him to go on the trip and then for footing the bill for his years of travel. Rarer still was the situation of the young Alexander von Humboldt; the early death of his parents brought him into a huge inheritance that freed him to pursue his studies, his long years of preparation, and finally his journey through the Americas. Most travelers had to get by without rich parents: they clung to the lower end of gentlemanly status and hoped for a patron who would pull them up into full-time respectability. In order to understand the world of the travelers we must consider how their relationship to their power-holders shaped their routes and their writings.

Patronage as Max Weber analyzed it in "Politics as a Vocation" intertwines emotional loyalty and material interests to bind together unequal social partners. Until the end of the old order in Europe, it was normal and legitimate for political and economic life to be built around patronage. A high-ranking patron in the eighteenth century could deliver large favors: an officer's commission, for example, or a writer's sinecure. This kind of largesse could cement an alliance between two families at a time when individuals lived far more than today with a clanlike devotion to family interest and honor. Writ large across society, up and down the social ladder and across the ranks of social peers, the distribution of patronage created clusters of people held together by mutual interest. This kind of mutual interest went further than our modern relationships usually do, for they worked on more than just rational calculation. Feelings of gratitude, personal devotion, and honor sank a patron's gift deep into the protégé's emotional life.

Patronage relationships involve a gift exchange. In the famous analysis of the anthropologist Marcel Mauss, the gift is a widespread and enduring human institution, one that could be found in precapitalist societies around the world. A people like the Kwakiutl Indians of the American northwest coast also distributed favors, and they did so on a scale that demonstrated their personal grandeur while forcibly binding their society into a whole held together by mutual obligations. For Europeans as for Kwakiutls, the patron's gift had an aristocratic nimbus. It was a visible manifestation of power and glory designed to impress the receiver and the larger society. You didn't have to be an aristocrat to give a gift, of course, or to be a patron. But in this as in many other practices of the old regime, aristocrats set the tone and gave the example for lesser human beings to imitate. They had the means and the confidence to win the loyalty of their social inferiors with these visible manifestations of greatness. When they made their gifts they also reinforced the social hierarchy, announcing their own high rank while gaining the gratitude of social inferiors.

Throughout Polynesia gift giving and power relations went together too. The more traditional Europeans were, the better they were able to build a web of mutual obligations with Pacific peoples; the more utilitarian, capitalist, and legalistic they were, the more likely the voyagers were to arrive with false expectations and promote mutual recriminations.[1]

Patronage goes on today, of course. Yet moderns feel less comfortable with it than did Europeans of an earlier age. With good reason: contemporary Western society is based largely on the principle of merit, and merit depends on objective achievement, judged without regard to personal or family connections. Westerners do not mind gifts in the private sphere, between parent and child, guest and newlyweds, or donor and charity. (Even here, though, gifts carry informal expectations of gratitude that are not always recognized and that may cause trouble—whether the parent's expectation of a phone call from summer camp or the donor's expectation of a dinner in his or her honor.) In the public sphere, however, gifts overlap with the Western definition of corruption. The rules have changed: the gifts back and forth that were once the substance and acknowledgment of existing hierarchies can now look like an undertow that distorts professional detachment. It is in the logic of a meritocratic society to dispense as far as possible with the gift.

The late eighteenth and early nineteenth centuries were a moment when patronage and impersonal evaluation of merit jostled. In Britain the Admiralty decided on who would command royal vessels, and it often rewarded these juicy social plums to the highborn. The commanders chosen to lead important world voyages included aristocrats like George Anson (who led a prominent voyage before Cook) and Robert FitzRoy (Charles Darwin's captain on the *Beagle*). Yet the naval leaders could also put aside considerations of privilege: after the Royal Society recommended Britain's first scientific circum-

navigation, a voyage with an obvious promise of celebrity and reward, the Admiralty turned to a humble unknown, James Cook.
Monarchs and other patrons had good reason to be deft at combining considerations of rank and Enlightenment conceptions of efficiency; they could not safely ignore the interests of the most powerful classes in their own society, but they had to muster enough
intelligence and skill in those chosen to compete successfully with
other European rulers. For their part, aspiring artists and scientists
might begin outside the circle of the wellborn, but aggressively charge
their way upward. In practice, patronage and merit were deeply com-
mingled.[2]

Patronage posed a special dilemma for scientific travelers. For those
who sought to be members of official expeditions there was no getting around the assistance of powerful patrons. One could not join
an expedition without the approval of its sponsor, who provided
equipment, defined rights and tasks, granted permission to publish, and made the recommendation for a professorship upon one's
return. If travelers were men of modest means, their patrons were
most likely just the opposite: high-ranking naval officials, ministers
of state, or monarchs. These masters had their own conception of
truth, and it was rigorous and exacting. They expected their scientists
to make exhaustive efforts to gather botanical specimens, shoot and
preserve animals, make sketches, observe peoples, and comment on
anything else of interest.

The scientific travelers were paid to be reporters. But reporters,
then as now, see unpleasant things, sometimes more than their audience would like to learn about. Did Russian patrons want to know
about the abuses of their country's fur empire? Did British masters
wish to hear about the evils of plantation slavery in their Caribbean
colonies? Did French bureaucrats relish tales of corruption in Guiana
and Mauritius? Alejandro Malaspina gave a horrifying example to

his contemporaries of the risks of frankness. After brilliantly leading his Spanish expedition around the world, he returned to Cádiz in 1794 brimming with plans for turning the Spanish Empire into a commonwealth with far-reaching autonomy for its colonies. Naively self-confident, he broadcast his radical Enlightenment views and intrigued against the government until its chief minister, Manuel Godoy, had him arrested and sentenced to life imprisonment in November of the following year. He was not released until Napoleon intervened on his behalf in 1803. An official voyage account, which would almost certainly have brought fame to Malaspina and his sponsors, and would have been rich in ethnographic and political insights, was never published. Malaspina's misfortune was an extreme example of the dangers of political naiveté. Nowhere more than in travel writing was truth telling considered part of the special mission of the age, but travelers sometimes ran up against a version of veracity hostile to their own.[3]

France

Early in the eighteenth century France undertook the systematic, large-scale support of scientific travel. Anglo-American histories of exploration gravitate to the grand epic of the Cook voyages and tend to underestimate ventures from the other side of the Channel.[4] Yet many decades before the British, the French state took a direct role in organizing expeditions with scientific ends, method, expertise, and organization. The French monarchy generally had a much more aggressive policy of intervention, whether in the economy, the arts, or the sciences, and its activism extended to expanding scientific knowledge through global research. The scientists in its state-sponsored academies worked closely with navy officials and chief ministers of state to gather useful information from abroad. In other countries great founding figures, often notable scientific travelers in their own right, took the lead in sponsoring scientific travel, but in France it was the bureaucracies that played the entrepreneurial role, even though a series of impressive personalities worked within them to organize and fund scientific missions to distant points.[5]

One of the most important sponsors was the Paris Academy of Sciences. Its own members sometimes traveled, and other travelers were sometimes awarded membership for notable achievement abroad. Equally important, though, its members could stay at home and enjoy the comfort of living and working in the metropolis while processing reports from the rest of the world. The academy awarded the status of corresponding member to its distant foot soldiers, who could come from almost any kind of background so long as they furnished information; they included colonial doctors and locals with a scientific bent as well as travelers commissioned to journey from Paris to the peripheries. The academy had an elaborate structure, with these corresponding members somewhere near the bottom. As Charles Gillispie has written, its structure was a microcosm of the character of the old regime, "monarchical, hierarchical, prescriptive, and privileged." At the top were twelve honorary members, usually drawn from the upper nobility or magistracy; they were "patrons and ornaments." Below them came the senior rank of men of science, eighteen in all, who qualified for a stipend, and below them came two lower ranks of scientists. The academy was organized into six sections: geometry, astronomy, mechanics, anatomy, chemistry, and botany. One could try to advance upward through the ranks; the whole organization functioned as a typical old regime mixture of birth, money, and merit.[6]

The academy was a brilliant body, but skill at winning the favor of the powerful was an indispensable ingredient of advancement. Take the case of Buffon, who became one of the great scientific patrons of his day in his role as intendant of the Royal Garden from 1739 until his death in 1788. He started out with only a modest amount of social capital but used it shrewdly as a young man to make his way into the academy. When Maurepas, the chief minister of state, was looking around for someone to run tests to improve the quality of wood used for ships, Buffon started experiments with the wood from his estate in his native Burgundy, an act of generosity soon followed by his election, at Maurepas's request, to the academy. The wood story may also have earned him the goodwill of Louis XV, who is supposed to have invited him to Fontainebleau for a discussion of his experiments. The king granted him a pension of two thousand livres to compensate him for his efforts and to encourage him to continue.[7] Here we see one of those "voluntary" gifts that were in fact part of the economy of patronage; Buffon knew how to recommend himself through an act of selfless service to the state. He was a gifted scientist, but he would never have risen to the heights of administrative power without a firm grasp of the law of *do ut des* (literally, "I give so that you may give"), giving so that those above could return the favor.

From the standpoint of patronage relationships, Philibert Commerson was well placed to win a choice post as official voyage naturalist. His father provided him with a fine education and indulged his decision to turn away from the law and study medicine instead. Commerson enjoyed the early acclaim of the republic of letters: passionate and dedicated to his studies, he impressed those who met him in Montpellier, and his reputation spread. Linnaeus asked him to prepare a work on the rare fish of the Mediterranean; the prominent Bernese scientist Albrecht von Haller invited him to further his botanical collecting by visiting Switzerland. But it was above all his childhood friend Joseph de Lalande who retrieved him from the provinces and brought him to the center of French intellectual life. Lalande invited him to leave behind the botanical garden he had already assembled at his home in Châtillon-les-Dombes and come to Paris, which he did in August 1764. There he lived adjacent to the Botanical Garden and struck up a friendship with the botanist Bernard de Jussieu. It was hardly surprising that when the government sought a naturalist for a scientific world voyage, it turned to Commerson. On board his luck continued; Bougainville was a scientist himself as well as an able commander and—no less important—a man with a generous disposition toward a fellow scientist, unafraid of having his glory stolen, unperturbed by the unmasking of Jeanne Barret, unprovoked by Commerson's peevish personality. And yet another lucky coincidence: on the return trip to France, the Bougainville expedition stopped off at Mauritius. Pierre Poivre, whom Commerson was asked to assist, was a noted traveler, administrator, and scientist in his own right, with a special expertise in the study of agriculture. Delighted with his new companion, he installed Commerson and the ever-faithful Jeanne Barret in a large house next to his own. He then gave the naturalist a rich new field for his activity by sending him to neighboring Madagascar, where Commerson found thousands of species awaiting names and classifications. Only after Poivre was called back to Paris did his fortune take a sudden turn for the worse; Commerson stayed behind, and the new governor, a man with scientific pretensions of his own, took a dislike to him and booted him out of his house. Commerson was still struggling with his new boss when he died on Mauritius in 1773.[8]

Commerson wrote a work entitled "Martyrology of Botany," a history of all those botanists who had suffered and died in the service of their calling. If Commerson was a martyr, then much of the suffering was either accidental or self-imposed. He was a man of privilege and early success who enjoyed the friendship and protection of well-placed scientists and administrators for most of his life. His misfortunes were mostly familial: the death of his wife in childbirth, the pain of separation from his son (who later became a distinguished jurist), the months of agonized waiting after a soldier related to him that one of his parents had died—but could not remember which one. And then there was, of course, the self-imposed embarrassment of the disguise of Jeanne Barret and (if really unintended) the publication of the letter on Tahiti. Yet beyond this, we can see how even such a success story was marked by hardship, and how even influential friends could not stave off unpleasant service when the monarchy called. Even a scientist with a European reputation could get stranded in the colonies and end up dealing with a hostile superior. With his many well-placed friends, Commerson would probably not have remained on Mauritius indefinitely, but his early death created an aura of tragic incompleteness around a life of service to the state.

Commerson's commander deserves our special attention as an agile manipulator of patronage as well as a brilliant ethnographer, mathematician, and navigator. Louis-Antoine de Bougainville, the first and most famous French circumnavigator, combined, like Buffon before him, genuine scientific achievement with virtuoso social climbing skills. By family circumstances, too, he was poised for success. His father received his patent of nobility in 1741. His elder brother, Jean-Pierre, was a man of learning who turned his attention early to geographic questions and introduced him into scholarly circles. His wealthy uncle, Jean-Potentien d'Arboulin, had good relations with Madame de Pompadour, the mistress of Louis XV, and eased his way into court circles. A friend of the family, Catherine Hérault, widow of René Hérault, lieutenant general of the police of Paris, took over a maternal role for the Bougainville children—he addressed her as "chère maman"—after their mother died when Louis-Antoine was young. Through her influence, Bougainville was assigned as aide-de-camp to the French general Louis-Josephe de Montcalm and went with him in 1756 to North America, where he had firsthand experience with the Indian allies of the French as their army was defeated in the French and Indian War.[9] (His role as assistant to Montcalm also qualified him for a bit part in James Fenimore Cooper's *The Last of the Mohicans,* in which he is lampooned as a decadent French nobleman.) After his return to France, he assiduously courted the favor of his uncle and cultivated good relations in the salons of Paris.

Bougainville was a strategic thinker who realized right away that with the loss of its North American empire, France would want to compete for trade and colonies elsewhere in the world—and would vie with Britain for control of trade routes in the southern hemisphere.[10] During the negotiations leading up to the French admission of defeat in the Treaty of Paris, between November 1762 and February 1763, he approached the Duc de Choiseul, Louis XV's foreign minister, with a plan for colonizing the Falkland Islands, a place en route to Cape Horn that could support a self-sufficient colony and serve as a stopover for ships on their way to the Pacific. He was catching Choiseul at just the right moment, when, in his despair over France's crushing defeat, the policymaker was on the lookout for new colonial designs. Choiseul introduced Bougainville to a senior colonial administrator named Accaron, who had slowly made his way up the bureaucratic hierarchy; the minister asked the junior officer to give Accaron an outline of his project for criticism and revision. Accaron received Bougainville generously—not least because he was looking to marry off his three daughters; he invited Bougainville into his home, and after the daughters were charmed by this witty, affable young man, he had no hesitation about taking up his visitor's project, which Choiseul approved as well.[11] Bougainville carried out his mission to found a colony on the Falklands in two voyages from 1763 to 1765.

When he returned to Paris from the second voyage in August 1765 and reported that he had left the colony in good shape, Choiseul abruptly told him that he had reached an agreement to hand the colony over to Spain. Instructions had already gone to the governor of Buenos Aires, and Bougainville himself would be asked to go to Madrid for a debriefing with the Spanish foreign minister. The project had been ill-conceived from the start; Choiseul, burning to put himself back in the race for colonies, had not reckoned with Spain's anxiety and Britain's quickly rising opposition. The news came as a shock to Bougainville, but after pleading his case unsuccessfully he carried out the Spanish mission. Faithful servant that he was, Bougainville remained a favorite of Choiseul and also pleased his cousin, the Duc de Praslin, whom Choiseul installed as naval minister in April 1766. They thought next of appointing Bougainville to be governor of Mauritius and Réunion, an offer Bougainville accepted. A month later, while plans for this appointment were still under way, the British commander John Byron returned from his circumnavigation. His enterprise further jolted French thinking in the direction of the Pacific as a field for colonies and strategic outposts. In response to a proposal from the Academy of Sciences for a round-the-world scientific expedition, the policymakers turned to Bougainville to lead the voyage. It was a choice that passed over the many talented officers bred to naval service and awarded the expedition to an outsider. He was a master courtier, however, who had doggedly persisted through all the ups and downs of serving a fickle master and was finally receiving his reward.[12]

Bougainville was to have many successors. After the three Cook circumnavigations, the French state mobilized its resources in 1785 to send out a large-scale scientific voyage to the Pacific led by an experienced world traveler, Jean-François de La Pérouse. As was usually the case, the voyage had practical as well as scientific motives. Cook's third voyage had returned with a commercial discovery: a few furs that his men had taken from the northwest coast of North America had fetched a large price in China, where they sold them in Canton. Statesmen and merchants dreamed of the fortunes to be made in the fur trade and scrambled to send ships to scout out sites for trading posts and carry the valuable commodity across the Pacific. In the mid-1780s French administrators began planning a French enterprise to compete with British, Russian, and American contenders for control of this trade. Louis XVI took a direct part in planning the voyage and wrote one set of instructions for it, even though the day-to-day responsibilities were in the hands of the navy's director of ports and arsenals, Claret de Fleurieu. The organizers outfitted the ships with a stove that could cook French bread, a distilling machine, and a windmill to provide flour. They also stuffed them with tons of food, water, wine, poultry, pigs, and woolens. After planning the itinerary for a voyage of two ships that would explore the American northwest coast and then cross over to China, Fleurieu approached leading scientists, including the mathematician and philosopher Nicholas de Condorcet (who was permanent secretary of the Academy of Sciences), Buffon, the chemist Antoine-Laurent Lavoisier, and experts in mathematics and astronomy. The ships carried twelve scientists and artists—most of them accomplished professionals—and four surgeons. The voyage, which began in August 1785, turned into a mysterious disaster after the ships disappeared in June 1788. To the end of his life, Louis XVI asked whether there was any news of La Pérouse. There was not; only four decades later did Europeans begin to find bits of the vessels, which had crashed off the South Pacific island of Vanikoro. One expedition member had been dropped off in the Kamchatkan outpost Petropavlovsk in September 1787 and carried La Pérouse's journal with him across Siberia and back to France. The French government published it in a handsome, illustrated edition in 1790 and rescued national glory from the tragedy. While Malaspina returned safely but died in ignominy, La Pérouse

Europe enlightens the world in this title page for Jean-François de La Pérouse's *Voyage de La Pérouse autour du monde, Atlas* (1797).

had champions even after his disappearance and became a national hero.[13]

The French Revolution swept away the old regime in learning as in politics. The Academy of Sciences, which had twice rejected applications from Marat before 1789, was abolished. The threats to the Revolution from reactionary powers abroad and Napoleon's mobilization of national resources for imperial expansion quickly led, however, to a rebuilding of the connections between science and the state. Scientific institutions changed, but they continued to rely on patronage for the awarding of prize positions and assignments. The status of patronage itself, however, was different after 1815: France was a society of legal equals, and aristocrats had neither the privileges nor the ability to dispense favors as before. Yet a mixture of old habits and a new emphasis on merit characterized post-Napoleonic France. It was an age of merging elites in which old and newly empowered families together dominated government institutions, and old patterns of social network-building integrated rising talent. Nowhere was this truer than in the case of scientific expeditions, closely tied as they were to state financing and French foreign policy.[14]

In the early nineteenth century bureaucratic pressures from many different sides continued to shape scientific enterprises. Ambitious officers did their best to get a hearing for their projects and could submit them to the Ministry of the Navy. If a voyage was approved, the organizer received instructions from the ministry sketching its aims and itinerary. A separate memorandum specified technical details of the trip and listed technical tasks of observing seasons, winds, currents, and hydrography. Outside the ministry, the Academy of Sciences weighed in with a commission named by the ministry, which prepared scientific instructions.[15] The instructions for a successful voyage proposal mobilized expertise from many sides and a mixture of political and scientific goals.

It was not enough to be a virtuoso captain on the high seas; for success a commander had to be equally adept at managing turbulent political waters at home. The naval ministry provided the scientist-captain Jules Dumont d'Urville with pointed political goals in its instructions of April 8, 1826; he was to look for suitable sites for anchoring large warships and find a spot for a penal colony. His commission included leaders of France's scientific establishment—Pierre de Laplace, Georges Cuvier, Alexander von Humboldt, and François Arago—who made detailed requests that ranged across botany, zoology, the study of magnetism, meteorology, physical anthropology, and linguistics. Dumont d'Urville led a triumphant voyage, afterward memorialized in volume after volume of scientific reports, but his navigation through the shoals of bureaucracy was less sure. A superb sailor, scholar, and scientist, he lacked the courtier skills of a Bougainville. D'Urville was arrogant and impatient; he was also a republican in his politics, and his views did not endear him to supporters of the deposed Bourbon monarchy in the navy administration.[16]

Old patterns of bureaucratic control of scientific travelers continued in the postrevolutionary era, but one can also observe the emergence of a new professionalism that combined the elite-dominated character of eighteenth-century science with a movement in the direction of disciplinary expertise. One novel French experiment of the postrevolutionary era was an attempt to create a school for naturalists.[17] No professional education for scientific observers had ever existed before. Eighteenth-century travelers qualified with a medical or other university education, with gardening or artistic skills, or with gentlemanly status and money. French administrators gathered a considerable body of experience in assessing their colonial and commercial needs and in drawing up instructions. But a formalized program of study had not existed in France or in any other country.

The Museum of Natural History, successor to the prerevolutionary

Royal Garden, was a natural home for such a school. André Thouin, the head gardener from 1764 until his death in 1793, had nearly 1,800 botanical correspondents from France, Europe, and around the world. Thouin was a product of the patronage system; his father, Jean-André Thouin, was head gardener before him and came from Buffon's hometown of Montbard in Burgundy. An expert, efficient manager, who came from a humble social background by the standards of his society but gained the respect of administrators and scientists, Thouin took care in the 1780s to train travelers in properly caring for and preserving their plant specimens. But this was one man's advice, not an institutional program.[18]

A collective enterprise began in December 1817, when the minister of the marine, Comte de Molé, invited the scientists of the Museum of Natural History to prepare instructions for potential collectors. The museum's zoologists, botanists, and mineralogists responded with alacrity; they wrote up a forty-seven-page set of instructions on how to collect specimens, what they were looking for, and where to find them. By January 1819 a new minister of the interior, Élie Decazes, was proposing a school to send naturalists on voyages to different parts of the world. It was to be funded with twenty thousand francs per year, a big sum, perhaps 7 or 8 percent of the museum's budget. In April of the same year, the museum professors chose six men for admission to the school and three additional naturalists for immediate voyage commissions. The voyages were disappointing for the museum and dangerous for the travelers, however. Only one, Alcide d'Orbigny, fulfilled the traveler's dream of becoming a museum professor.[19]

The Geographic Society of Paris, founded in 1821, was a new kind of lobby for travel-related research. Its leaders prided themselves on founding a venture of tremendous importance, they thought, for their time. There was some truth to their claims; while theirs was not the first geographic society ever founded—there were a few attempts in the eighteenth century, and geography as a branch of learning had a venerable history—they created the model for the kind of geographic association that has had a continuous history ever since. The founders combined high scientific competence with a clubby atmosphere and a boyish enthusiasm for exploration and discovery. The society had only a few hundred members, and until the mid-1880s it remained a small, elite organization. Many of the founders were professional geographers such as Barbié du Bocage, geographer of the Ministry of Foreign Affairs; Edme-François Jomard, creator of the division of maps at the Bibliothèque Nationale; and Conrad Malte-Brun and Jean-Baptiste-Benoît Eyriès, coeditors of a journal of exploration and discovery, *Nouvelles Annales des Voyages.* Civil servants, officers, and politicians joined too. Every one of the six central officers named at the founding meeting of December 15 had a title, including René de Chateaubriand, the famous writer, traveler, and diplomat. Prominent scientists led some of the real work of the organization: Cuvier agreed to take charge of publications, and Humboldt took over the correspondence section.[20]

Initially the society had hopes of sponsoring journeys of exploration and set its sights on a polar expedition. It hoped that an aristocracy of birth and wealth would provide it with an endowment substantial enough to support bold expeditions. None of this happened. Only in 1866 did the president of the society organize a trip to the Mekong Delta of Vietnam. As an organizer of geographic knowledge, however, the society was a success from the start. Its *Bulletin* was a clearinghouse for all sorts of geographic information, much of it travel reports from around the world. It had a certain cosmopolitan flavor, with members like Humboldt and the Danish Malte-Brun prominent in its leadership, and it engaged in polite correspondence with learned societies and individuals from other countries. In part this cosmopolitanism was a continuation of the "republic of letters" habits of the previous century. Society members were glad to think of their scientific elite as having no political boundaries. But the society was also an organization of specialists, and it pointed the way toward the scientific division of labor that would deepen by the late nineteenth century into the kind of academic disciplines that we know today. Even though the society did not yet have a rigorous conception of geography, it was part of a thickening network of geographic knowledge, much of which took the form of travel reports.[21]

Many of the strands of the French scientific travel network came together in the career of Louis Choris, Chamisso's young traveling companion and friend on the *Rurik* voyage. After his return to St. Petersburg he was itching to continue his artistic education. By early June of 1819 he was ready to depart for Paris, where he arrived in August. From Paris he sent his first letter to Chamisso on April 3, 1820. By then he could boast that scientific stars of the capital were showing a friendly interest in his work, including Georges Cuvier, the great comparative anatomist, who was head of the Museum of Natural History, and Franz Gall, Vienna-trained physician and founder of phrenology (the disputed science of reading character from skull shape). Gifts from the world voyage helped win their favor. These were the currency of patronage, helping Choris prove his usefulness and eagerness to please the powerful. He had given Gall a skull from the Bering Straits, "which gave him great pleasure," and he gave Cuvier his birds, three of them new species, for the museum. He could even report that Alexander von Humboldt had honored him with a visit. Choris was not exaggerating when he spoke of winning their favor. Two years later he published his world tour in pictures, *Voyage pittoresque autour du monde*. As the title page announced, Cuvier provided some of the descriptions of natural objects, and Gall analyzed a skull. There were important cross-connections, too, to the entrepreneurial geographers of the *Annales des voyages*. Eyriès did him the very substantial favor of turning his written commentary into fluent French prose. For the prominent *Journal des Débats*

Malte-Brun wrote a lengthy, extravagant review. The young provincial had turned in his small way into a protégé of the capital's scientific elite.[22]

By October 1822 Choris was impatient. Plans for a trip to London had fallen through. He was waiting for movement, asking Chamisso whether he thought the Prussian government would have work for a botanical illustrator in Berlin. At the same time, he was beginning to show up at the meetings of the Geographic Society. He had presented his *Voyage pittoresque* to the society's central commission on September 6 (this was not a great honor in itself—five other works were presented on the same day). A week after his job query to Chamisso, he showed up at another of the society's sessions and commented on the striking resemblance between tattoos on a figurine from Ohio (portrayed in a journal illustration) and the tattoos he remembered from the natives of the American northwest coast. By then he was a member of the society, which in contrast to just showing off his book was a mark of social distinction.[23]

For the next five years he left no traces in the geographers' minutes. Then, on February 16, 1827, he wrote to the president of the society with a proposal for a scientific voyage. His ambition was to make a trip from New York to Patagonia, with stops in Mexico, Guatemala, Quito, and Chile. The trip would last five or six years, he thought. From the society he wanted whatever aid it could provide in the way of recommendations, instructions, and advice. Jomard, an expert on Egypt, was interested. Replying in August of the same year, he thought that a good match for Choris's talent would be a close examination of the ancient monuments of Guatemala. He asked Choris to look at some earthen Guatemalan vases that he could view in Paris; to make sketches of the sculptures he could see in Guatemala; to make geometric plans of the monuments; and to study their stones and the means of transporting them to the sites. Choris was also to attend to indigenous traditions, the situation of the mountains, and the course of the rivers. Probably thinking of Choris's earlier work in the *Voyage pittoresque* he emphasized to the young artist his hope of receiving a gallery of portraits of native physiognomies, with due attention to skull structure, facial angle, hair, lips, jaws, and eyes. It would be good, too, if he could bring back some skulls of the ancient inhabitants. All in all, he hoped Choris's attention to customs, commerce, religion, population, language, laws, communications, and monuments would add up to a complete overview of the different societies he visited.[24]

Choris needed more than just instructions, however; he needed money, he needed transportation, he needed a title, and he needed protection. Some of this the Geographic Society could help to arrange. At the behest of the society, the minister of the navy wrote to the society that he was pleased to recommend that Choris (and three other travelers) receive the protection and goodwill of the navy and the French consulates. On the society's recommendation, Choris and others were elected members of the Medico-Botanical Society of London, which would forward diplomas to them. For funding, though, it was the Museum of Natural History which came to his aid. The minister of the interior wrote to announce Choris's project of a voyage to Central America and his offer to gather materials for the museum. Could it reward him from its fund for travelers? It could, replied the professors on May 1, 1827, though they made it clear then and later that they were paying him a wage, not a salary, for the objects he sent: six hundred francs per year beginning January 1, 1828, and more if his specimens merited it. They also outfitted him with a letter certifying his status as Naturalist Traveler and with a diploma certifying him as a Correspondent of the Museum. On October 6, 1827, he left aboard a royal frigate, the *Jeanne d'Arc*. After thirty-six rough days of sailing into contrary winds, the ship arrived ahead of the rest of its convoy at Fort-Royal, Martinique, in the West Indies (today Fort-de-France).[25]

From Fort-Royal Choris wrote to Cuvier. The ship had made a number of excursions around the West Indies without enough time for Choris to do any collecting, but he had been able to gather some things at Fort-Royal. He was sending a barrel marked on the outside with his initials, containing specimens that he described in over five pages, including a giant tarantula, a lizard, a new kind of poisonous snake, crabs, spiders, and insects. He was sending sketches too; the colors were exact, he emphasized, but he had taken less care to render the form, since Cuvier would see the specimens. His next shipment of a box and a barrel full of specimens came from Havana. The story comes to an abrupt end: the museum professors' meeting minutes of June 18, 1828, record that Choris was murdered in Mexico on the road to Jalapa. Choris had arrived in Vera Cruz on *L'Éclipse* from New Orleans. On March 21, two days later, he lost his life when he and his traveling companion were attacked by four bandits. Meanwhile, the professors were still receiving letters and specimens. More packages and boxes from Martinique and Havana had arrived, according to their meeting records for August 27. The minutes recording receipt of the collection rolled on, regardless of the fate of the collector, registering his gains for the empire of science.[26]

Choris was only one of many casualties among those who departed overseas in service to science. A filament had burnt out; other travelers would continue collecting for the scientists of the metropolis.

Great Britain

In Great Britain as in France, the pursuit of knowledge through large-scale scientific expeditions was inseparable from the need to find money and means to support them. The pattern of support, however, differed; private advice and voluntary associations played a far larger role.[27]

One can almost write the history of voyage patronage in late-eighteenth- and early-nineteenth-century England through the career of one individual, Sir Joseph Banks. Banks came from a wealthy Lincolnshire family, and at eighteen, after his father's death, he moved to London, bought a house, and made a name for himself as a naturalist-collector and as an affable companion, winning friends in both scientific and political circles. While plans were taking shape in 1768 for what became the first Cook voyage to the Pacific, he worked hard to have his own name put forward for the position of naturalist. The secretary of the Royal Society made the following comment on his application before sending it on to the Admiralty: "Joseph Banks Esqr Fellow of this Society, a Gentleman of large fortune, who is well versed in natural history, being Desirous of undertaking the same voyage the Council very earnestly request their Lordships, that in regard to Mr Banks's great personal merit, and for the Advancement of useful knowledge, He also, together with his Suite, being seven persons more, that is, eight persons in all, together with their baggage, be received on board of the Ship, under the Command of Captain Cook." Banks's knowledge made him a fit candidate, but so did his personal fortune and status as a member of the Royal Society, which was as much a meeting place for gentleman-amateurs as it was for thoroughgoing scientists.[28]

There were limits, too, to the persuasive powers of even a wealthy, successful, and polished gentleman, as Banks himself soon discovered. In 1771 he returned from the first circumnavigation a hero, far more celebrated in London society than was Cook.[29] When designs began for a second voyage in November 1771, Banks thought of himself as the logical choice for naturalist and began planning for the voyage, as did the Admiralty on his behalf. Banks was so bold and unyielding in his demands for space and entourage, however, that he found himself at odds with Cook. In May 1772 Banks announced that he would not go on the voyage and began making personal attacks on John Montagu, Earl of Sandwich and First Lord of the Admiralty. Sandwich had been a friend to Banks in the past and would be again in the future; but at this moment Banks, with his obstreperous behavior, overreached himself. The response to his political campaign was that the invitation to serve as naturalist instead went out in June to Johann Reinhold Forster, who then brought along his son George.[30]

The senior Forster was for his part a hungry patronage hunter. Born near Danzig and educated in Berlin and at the University of Halle, he escaped his life as small-town pastor by accepting Catherine the Great's invitation to investigate the condition of the so-called Volga Germans, peasants who had taken up the Russian government on its promise of land near the garrison town of Saratov. Forster handed in a frank report on how poorly the peasants were faring and submitted a constitution for the Volga Germans in May 1766. He was never paid more than a small sum for his work, and he next left for England, seeking to improve his fortunes there. He received a teaching post at Warrington Academy, a secondary school for children of dissenters from the established church and a "beacon of liberalism," where among others he met the scientist Joseph Priestley. But Forster was fired for his intemperate behavior toward the boys and moved with his large family to London. Admirers helped ease his way into the intellectual life of the capital; already an accomplished naturalist, he was elected a fellow of the Royal Society in February 1772. When he received the invitation to join the Cook voyage, Forster agreed with alacrity—even though he had been cultivating Banks's favor until then, and even though Banks was still hoping that Cook and Sandwich would accede to his demands. On the voyagers' return to England, Forster expected to write the great narrative of the expedition. When Sandwich, dissatisfied with Forster's Germanic style, tried to appoint a man of letters to serve as a stylistic editor, Forster smelled a conspiracy to censor his writing and refused to permit any alteration of his work. Sandwich was initially eager to reward Forster generously, but expected him to behave civilly and submit to a reasonable request. In the end Forster received almost nothing for his labors.[31]

As for George Forster, he grew up in the unhappy atmosphere of his father's quarrels with Cook and Sandwich. It was George who had to bear the burden of his father's quarrel. J. R. Forster was not allowed to write a narrative of the voyage, but the prohibition did not apply to George, who upon their return sat down to nine months of churning out the pages of his epic work. It was then George, too, who dispatched letters pleading for help to rescue his father from the threat of debtors' prison; and George who wrote a public letter to Sandwich upholding the claim that his father had refused to compromise his intellectual independence by accepting an editor for his work. J. R. Forster had first ostentatiously courted Joseph Banks's favor, then snatched the naturalist post without a moment's hesitation or consultation; George subsequently had to write humble letters to Banks asking him to wait for repayment of a debt that his father owed him. It was still unpaid at the time of J. R. Forster's death and threatened to ruin his widow's finances, but Banks finally agreed at that point to forgo the sum.[32]

By the time the voyagers returned, Banks was already fashioning a new vocation for himself as organizer of scientific voyages. Linnaeus in Sweden was an obvious model for this kind of entrepreneurship. His student Daniel Solander had been Banks's companion and fellow collector on the first Cook circumnavigation; another, Anders Sparrman, went on the second.[33] Whereas Linnaeus organized expeditions to stem Swedish national decline, however, Banks worked when Britain was climbing to its role as the dominant imperial power.

By corresponding with naturalists around the world, he could make his global network of knowledge fateful for entire peoples and places.

Banks was elected president of the Royal Society in 1778, and under his leadership it played a large role in initiating Cook's third circumnavigation. He also drew on his experience from the first voyage to help plan the Australian penal colony; initiated the voyage of the *Bounty,* which under the command of William Bligh was supposed to transport breadfruit from Tahiti to England's Caribbean colonies to serve as a foodstuff for plantation slaves; recommended Matthew Flinders for the command of the *Investigator,* instructed to make a systematic survey of the coasts of Australia; and recommended Archibald Menzies to serve as naturalist on George Vancouver's circumnavigation. Banks gave a boost to other, less well remembered ventures, too, including one scheme to open up Japan to British traders and another to compete with the Russians in the North Pacific sea otter trade. When bright young men had ideas for expeditions, they turned to Sir Joseph, rightly believing that his support could carry them far toward realizing their hopes for funding.[34]

A notable feature of Banks's influence is just how far it depended on informal channels of influence. He was not only a government employee but also a private gentleman, and his wishes went only as far as his ability to persuade the decision makers. He cultivated a succession of politicians who in fact turned to him for advice. The first of these was the Earl of Sandwich. Despite their disagreement over the second Cook voyage, Sandwich continued to work with Banks and gave him crucial support for his election to the presidency of the Royal Society. Banks was also on good terms with George III and helped persuade his monarch to appoint William Herschel to be astronomer at the private royal observatory at Kent in 1783. Sir Evan Nepean, undersecretary of the Home Office, worked closely with Banks on some of his most important projects, such as the first con-

The gouty patron: Sir Joseph Banks. Painting by Thomas Phillips (1810).

voy of convicts to the Australian penal colony and the voyages commanded by Flinders and Vancouver. Banks's dependence on these personal relationships became evident in the planning of the Vancouver voyage: he could plead for good working conditions for his protégé Menzies, but only so long as Nepean was available; when Nepean left on a trip to the Caribbean in November 1791, Banks could do little.[35]

A second striking point about Banks's career is its close linkage of utility and knowledge. Banks was a naturalist and explorer himself, a man of science who cultivated friendships with other scientists throughout Europe; but he was also a visionary of empire, with project after project designed to nurture industry at home, plant new colonies, link the different pieces of empire together, and ensure Britain's commercial and military superiority. From 1773 Banks controlled the Royal Botanic Gardens at Kew and turned it, in the words of one biographer, into "virtually an institute for economic botany." Expedition after expedition brought back specimens to Kew, and Banks was keenly practical in his aims for them. If necessary, he was prepared to send out a botanist as an industrial spy. In 1787 he persuaded the government to send a Polish naturalist, Anton Hove, to Bombay in search of finer strains of cotton than were currently available for British manufacturers. Indian manufacturers controlled the production of cotton there, and Hove would have to work secretly and gather his samples without arousing their suspicion. Outfitted with public instructions ordering him to look for specimens wherever he traveled and private instructions directing him to the Bombay vicinity, Hove carried out his mission in the first half of 1788, surviving bandits, borrowing exorbitant sums to hire armed guards, and returning to London with twenty-three varieties of cotton seeds. Patron and naturalist did their work as part of a larger web of burgeoning industry and empire.[36]

Banks's correspondence documents a global network of knowledge. Over twenty thousand letters survive, and of those some six thousand were written by Banks himself between 1766 and 1820. Statesmen, captains, and other men and women of high rank wrote back and forth to Banks, but so too did scientific travelers, from the wealthy and well-placed to the modest and indigent. To leaf through the letters is to encounter the great variety of human beings who were employed—or sought, with Banks's help, employment—in gathering objects for the collections of the learned in England. Transported at a preindustrial pace, the messages record the need for employment, the instructions for travelers, the hardships of executing them, and the dangers of travel.[37]

To make this network function, Banks had to be a patron on a large scale. He knew the role well from his status as a landowner in Lincolnshire and years of dealing with everything from wool-breeding to quelling riots against the militia draft. As a scientific patron he attracted a Hogarthian riot of characters, including a good number of kooks and confidence men, like George Augustus Pollen: in an irregular script with scratches and blotches he presented a plan in 1804 for an expedition overland from Berlin to Lhasa to investigate manuscripts in the library of the Dalai Lama. When Banks refused him support, Pollen wrote back calling him "hasty and impolite." Banks noted by hand that the plan of the journey was not Pollen's but someone else's. Serious travelers, too, turned to Banks for aid. Sigismund Bacstrom, who had served as a secretary to Banks in the 1770s, began his supplication by thanking Banks for all his past help before going on to recount his subsequent adventures in misery: six voyages from London in the ensuing seven years on merchant ships to Greenland, Guinea, and Jamaica; temporary blindness in Jamaica when he caught an "epidemical distemper, which was among our slaves," and a five-month stay there at his own expense; near-shipwreck on one of the trips to Greenland; and now, a return to London poor and friendless. He begged Banks to help him find employment as a tutor, traveling companion, or nurse to a gentleman, or as an assistant to a gentleman chemist. Banks treated him kindly and later offered to pay him for botanical specimens he might gather on a voyage that was to take him around Cape Horn to the South Seas, Nootka Sound, the East Indies, and the Cape of Good Hope. Banks stood by his protégés: after Flinders, suspected of being a spy, was imprisoned at the end of 1803 by the French governor of Mauritius, Banks negotiated on his behalf and consoled him and his wife during the long years until his release in 1810.[38]

Competition with other great powers thickened the network. Banks was acutely aware of their collecting activities and was determined to keep Kew the greatest botanical collection in the world. During the revolutionary and Napoleonic eras, war between France and Britain made it dangerous to send out scientific expeditions and greatly slowed the pace of collecting. As he wrote to William Townsend Aiton, the superintendent of gardening at Kew, it had become almost impossible to send home collections of live plants, since ships were liable to wait until military convoys could accompany them. Within days after the first Treaty of Paris was signed on May 30, 1814, Banks jumped into action. The arrival of peace with France and the certainty that collections could sail as they used to without delays, he continued, "makes me anxious to see the establishment of Foreign Collections resumed." He worried about the emperor of Austria, "who has formerly freighted Ships at an immense expence, & sent well educated Botanists to collect for his Garden at Schönbrun[n], the only rival to Kew that I am acquainted with" and who would, Banks thought, "resume the business of improving it."[39]

He went on to propose sending out two collectors, James Bowie and Allan Cunningham, and followed up with a report to George Harrison, assistant secretary to the Treasury. His plan was accepted, and they departed on October 3, 1814, on the *Duncan* for Rio de Janeiro, the Cape of Good Hope, and New South Wales. Once they were on their way Banks kept in touch with them as much as the mails permitted. It was not enough just to send the men out; he had to make sure that they survived and had the freedom to carry out their work. From Rio they wrote in March 1815 to Aiton that the Portuguese refused to find them a soldier to act as their guard, even though they offered to pay, so they ended up buying pistols at great expense, paying for them out of their own pockets since they feared Banks might not approve of their putting them down as public expenditure. Banks was indeed concerned about how much his charges spent, and appreciated their careful handling of accounts as well as the quality of the species they sent back from Brazil. When they had finished their business in Brazil he urged Cunningham on to Australia, sharing his impatience to keep Kew ahead of the botanical garden in Paris. Once Cunningham got there (the two travelers separated, with Bowie heading for South Africa, where Banks admonished him for buying two wagons without explaining his need for "so heavy an expence") he ran into new difficulties: this time not with disorderly locals but with Alan Macquarie, the governor of New South Wales. Macquarie thought that Cunningham was complaining to Banks about the way he was being treated and called him in for an upbraiding about his "false and ungrateful Conduct"; Banks wrote a soothing reply to Macquarie stating that "nothing in Cunningham's letter had the appearance of a complaint." Beating out the Austrian and French competition for glorious gardening took more than just finding good men and paying them; they needed advice and diplomacy.[40]

Competition speeded up the pace of global network building, but so did cooperation. Throughout the long years of war with France, Banks took great pains to keep alive good relations with French scientists. The collections of a republican French botanist, Jacques de la Billardière, were first seized by a royalist French commander and ended up in the hands of the British, who gave them to Queen Charlotte. After his return to France, Billardière and the French government at the time, the moderate Directory, argued for their return. Banks agreed and was able to help bring about their transfer to their owner. "Surely nothing is so likely to Abate the unjustifiable Rancour that Politicians frequently entertain against Each other as to See Harmony and good will Prevail Among their Brethren who Cultivate Science," wrote Banks when he was assuring Billardière of his efforts on his behalf. In the same spirit, Banks worked to keep open communications between the Royal Society and the Institut National (the comprehensive scientific and artistic organization founded in 1795). He also helped lead the campaign for the release of the French geologist Déodat de Dolomieu (who was imprisoned in solitary confinement by the Neapolitans for twenty-one months on his return from Egypt), and provided financial aid to his friend Pierre Broussonet, who fled the Revolution and got stranded in Spain. Banks had unfortunates of his own to plead for, such as Flinders, stranded on Mauritius. Yet Banks did not restrict his efforts to France: in the midst of the revolutionary decade, despite all the cares of wartime, he arranged for a gift of plants to Russia. His acts of friendship, generosity, and exchange had practical motives, but Banks was also serving the Enlightenment ideal of a republic of letters. In the early nineteenth century this sentiment took on new importance as part of the solidarity of upper classes across Europe, determined to prove to one another and their contemporaries that more than just selfish interests bound them together.[41]

One of Banks's most skilled collectors and ethnographers, Archibald Menzies, needed all his patron's pull after he ran into trouble on board the *Discovery,* commanded by George Vancouver on its voyage around the world from 1791 to 1795. Vancouver had served as a junior officer under Cook. Like William Bligh, another junior officer on the third circumnavigation, he seems to have caught something of the irascible temper that bedeviled Cook and contributed to his disastrous end. Vancouver went out with clear strategic goals. He was to search for the Northwest Passage that had eluded Cook, to advance British interests in the fur and whaling trades, and to further British claims throughout the Pacific to strategic outposts for refreshment and refurbishing. To read his voyage account is to observe the masterful execution of a new imperial design. Unfamiliar native behavior, however, was enough to set off a paroxysm of paranoid suspicion, and the faintest pretext provoked violent rage toward his own men. He whipped them far more often than did Bligh.[42]

Menzies was a gardener and botanist at Kew. He was more learned than his status as gardener might suggest, for he had studied at the University of Edinburgh and qualified as a surgeon. He had steadily proved his worth to Banks, in 1784 sending to his patron seeds gathered in New York, the Caribbean, and Nova Scotia on an American tour, and faithfully gathering more specimens while serving as surgeon on a commercial circumnavigation from 1786 to 1789. For the Vancouver voyage Banks provided him with detailed instructions that went beyond just collecting; he was to report on the suitability of different places for colonization and to write down whatever he could learn about native societies and cultures. While the voyage started out routinely enough, he and Vancouver quarreled over whether his plants were being mistreated. Captains often resented naturalists and their demands on space and time, but Vancouver took the unusual steps of arresting him and taking away his servant, with the result, Menzies wrote to Banks, that his plants for Kew were ruined.[43]

Menzies also provoked Vancouver's rage by refusing to hand over his journal, which he claimed he owed to Banks and to Lord Nepean of the Treasury, the voyage's government sponsor. No wonder: he and Vancouver tell two very different stories. To compare them is a lesson in the contrasting perspectives of captain and naturalist. Vancouver opens his travel account with praise for "the rapid progress of improvement in the sciences, and the general diffusion of knowledge since the commencement of the eighteenth century" that had inaugurated a new age of discovery. His account is an act of state and upholds the dignity of his role as emissary of the king of England on a historic mission of founding new relationships with the peoples and places of the Pacific. It breathes the eighteenth century's language of humanitarianism, goodwill toward strange new peoples, and a European civilizing mission. Even this version of the voyage, however, gives away glimpses of uncontrolled fury. After thefts culminating in the disappearance of a hat, the captain had the two guilty Tahitians set on shore and whipped somewhere between one and three dozen lashes: Vancouver termed this punishment "a slight manual correction." Someone stole a bag of shirts and some axes, too. Vancouver, wrote Menzies, declared on January 20, 1792, that if he didn't get the things back soon "he would desolate the whole district & destroy all their Canoes." On March 11, while encamped on the island of Kauai, the voyagers saw a fire in the distance. Vancouver was alarmed, for he "supposed that it might be a signal for commencing hostilities on the part of the islanders" and started threatening the surrounding Hawaiians. Some of them explained that the fire was used to burn down old brush, and Menzies remembered seeing the same fields burned down on a previous visit. The same day a native canoe carrying Vancouver tipped over. He "ordered two launches manned and armed" to be ready for an attack that night; meanwhile Menzies, to reassure the chiefs, went and slept peacefully in a village house. As Menzies recounted the story, the captain's cruelty disrupted the rites of hospitality and friendship.[44]

It would be mistaken to dismiss Vancouver's account as simply captive to imperial ideology. It is detailed, precise, and acute. There was no better judge of political relations—it was he who picked out the young Kamehameha as the coming man in Hawaiian politics—and he carried his fine political judgment into his narrative. Something more complicated was going on in the conflict between Vancouver and Menzies: captains such as Vancouver, Bougainville, and Cook all had the privileged vantage point of power-holders, and they had insights not available to a Menzies, a Commerson, or a Forster; at the same time the captains felt the constraining, sometimes distorting tugs of patriotism, empire building, and career interests. Menzies's journal notes open up a different perspective, useful to us, embarrassing to his captain. They were not published in

Menzies's lifetime; and without the counterforce of Banks as Menzies's patron, they might have disappeared into Vancouver's hands.

The uses of patronage outlived Banks and continued in the first half of the nineteenth century. It was Banks's protégés who formalized and institutionalized his creation of a network of knowledge, turning it from a gentleman's personal achievement into a state-controlled enterprise. A few key entrepreneurs dominated the organizing of scientific expeditions. A Banks protégé who developed into a master entrepreneur of scientific travel was William Jackson Hooker, who in 1841 was appointed the director of the Botanic Gardens at Kew. Before then Hooker had enjoyed decades of success as a scientific collector in his own right, thanks in no small measure to Banks's steady support for his work. Born in 1785, Hooker, the son of a wool merchant, inherited landed property when he was four as a result of the untimely death of a cousin who was also his godfather. He had an early fascination with birds, entomology, and botany, and sent some samples of his botanical collecting to Dawson Turner, a banker and fellow of the Royal Society who invited him to visit and subsequently eased his way into the learned world. In 1806 Hooker was elected a fellow of the Linnaean Society. In the same year he visited London and met many of the leading naturalists there, including Banks, who opened his house and his personal library to him. Hooker was eager to visit a tropical country, but plans for travel to one fell through, and instead, on three days' notice, he took up an offer arranged by Banks for him to accompany a merchant ship to Iceland. In 1814 he visited Paris and met the leading botanists at the Institut; in 1815, on a return trip, he met Alexander von Humboldt; in the same year he married his patron Turner's eldest daughter. Five years later he wrote to Banks asking whether a position was open that could help him support his growing family, and Banks facilitated his appointment to the chair of botany at the University of Glasgow. Before and after his appointment Hooker developed an enormous, worldwide correspondence. According to his son, J. D. Hooker, he received about 29,000 letters from 4,420 individuals, most of them from the period after 1820; they included letters from eminent botanists and travelers as well as government officials, merchants, owners of horticultural establishments, and nurserymen. Hooker continued Banks's project of turning Kew Gardens from a pleasure garden into a scientific laboratory for the collection, study, and breeding of plants useful for Britain's global economy.[45]

A second Banks protégé who developed into one of the era's great proponents of exploration and discovery was John Barrow. Barrow's appointment as Second Secretary to the Admiralty began in 1804, and he stayed there almost continuously for the next forty-one years. Unlike Banks, Barrow came from a modest background—his father was a farmer in north Lancashire—but a lucky break provided patronage. He tutored a boy whose father was a baronet and connected to Lord Macartney; Barrow followed Macartney to the Cape Colony (in the southern part of today's South Africa) when he was appointed governor there; during his stay his excellent administrative talents also came to the attention of General Francis Dundas, who took over the governorship in 1798; Dundas's uncle was Lord Melville, appointed First Lord of the Admiralty in May 1803; the day after Melville's appointment, Barrow was made Second Secretary of the Admiralty. Melville was impeached two years later for crimes of corruption, but Barrow stayed on through administration after administration. He knew how to play the role of unassuming civil servant, avoiding politics and putting the decisions of others into practice. His passion, however, was the sponsoring of voyages. He became an expert on geography and wrote reviews for the Tory journal the *Quarterly Review*. He also cultivated the goodwill of the journal's publisher, John Murray, seeing to it that Murray became the official publisher for the Admiralty. In 1806 Barrow was elected a Fellow of the Royal Society, and he cultivated a friendship with Banks. After 1815, Barrow was the initiator of a steady succession of voyages, especially Arctic expeditions; he was also concerned with keeping Australia a purely British continent and in the 1820s took up the problem of founding a settlement on the north coast to keep away the French and the Dutch. While highly placed, Barrow had no direct power, and indeed no obligation or authority, to initiate voyages; they were his extracurricular hobby and his passion, and he was effectively able to mobilize support for them.[46]

Barrow took the lead in creating the Royal Geographical Society as a center for exploration and discovery outside the country. The society had several forerunners. The Royal Society had played a sponsoring role for the Cook and other voyages, and Banks, during his long tenure as its president, made sure that it maintained an interest in the accumulation of geographic knowledge. Banks was also one of the founders of the African Association, formed in 1788 to further exploration of northern Africa and the sub-Saharan continent, and which sent out one ambitious young adventurer after another. Finally, there was the immediate example of the French; their geographic society provided a rival model for British patrons of exploration to emulate.[47]

The Royal Geographical Society developed out of the Raleigh Club, a private gentlemen's establishment. At its meeting of May 24, 1830, Barrow proposed the formation of a geographic society. The members assented, and a committee of six was able to bring the society into existence by the end of the same year. By 1832 the first volume of the society's *Journal* listed over five hundred members. The many titles and honorifics next to their names announce a decidedly privileged organization, with a mixture of social ornaments, statesmen, officers, and members of the Royal Society gathered together under the patronage of William IV. There was nothing dilettantish about the society's statement of aims, however, which marked it out as the eminently practical instrument of empire builders. The science of geography was announced to be "paramount to the welfare of a maritime nation like Great Britain, with its numerous and extensive foreign possessions." The aims it then went on to list were utilitarian and undramatic: to collect and disseminate "new, interesting, and useful facts and discoveries"; to accumulate a geography library and map collection for the use of travelers; to collect samples of scientific instruments that travelers could examine; to prepare travelers' instructions; to correspond with other societies, foreigners, and British residents abroad; and to open communication with scientific societies in related branches of learning. An omission is as significant as the items on the list: there was no single point promising the support of expeditions, only an incidental hope, added to the item about preparing instructions, that the society might eventually offer travelers aid to achieve "some particular object of research." In contrast to its French rival, however, the society soon turned into a generous voyage sponsor: it sent out six expeditions by the end of 1840, including trips to the Arctic, the Antarctic, Guiana, South Africa, Australia, and Kurdistan.[48]

Yet such efforts were not the organizers' main goal. What Barrow and his fellow founders sought was a center for the systematic organization and dissemination of practical knowledge. His imagination fixed on down-to-earth and down-to-water things, foremost among them advances in hydrographic knowledge. The most important object of the society's attention, he stated in his remarks to the inaugural meeting, would be improved maps ("especially those relating to orology, hydrology, and geology"); new analyses of the earth's surface, especially those "founded on physical and geological characters, on climate, and on distinctions of the human race, or of language"; a more systematic and complete list of place-names; and—at a time when travel guides did not yet exist—"the preparation and improvement of road-books for different countries, of gazetteers, of geographical and statistical tables, and all such matters as are of general utility." While membership in the society was a lofty affair, Barrow hoped for contributions from humble outsiders; for everything from travel routes, to meteorological and magnetic observations, to the features of the soil, to latitudes and longitudes, the society would rely on Britons traveling and living around the world. Before concluding his remarks to the organizing meeting, Barrow felt it necessary to mention that he and the other organizers were not "hostile to theory."[49] Overall, though, the stated aims made it clear that the society members were busy men with an empire to build.

The early issues of the society's *Journal* may in retrospect have a random look, for under the rubric of geography it collected information that by the end of the nineteenth century was divided and disciplined across the whole range of social sciences. But in its time the society stood for a real concentration of knowledge that served the open-air ends of world travelers and administrators. That it quickly spilled beyond its original aims and became a sponsor of expeditions was a sign of its success. It was, after all, the applied scientific servant of an empire that already dominated the waterways of the earth and was soaring past France to a midcentury zenith of global power. The Geographical Society was the gathering place for a wealthy, knowledgeable, and confident social elite, firmly grounded in civil society, naturally extending to the state, and brimming with energy to promote commerce, colonies, and science.

Russia

When we look back at the movement of European ships and peoples into the Pacific, it is easy to focus on France and Britain to the exclusion of any other country. Their competition for mastery of North America and the Pacific occupies the center stage of late-eighteenth-century imperial history, with the French expulsion from North America, ratified by the Treaty of Paris in 1763, a first dramatic climax, followed by rival voyages like Bougainville's and Cook's. Yet to limit the story to the Anglo-French rivalry would be to miss another dramatic development of the decades after 1800, the arrival of Russian expeditions in the Pacific. Russian ambitions got a powerful boost from Cook's third circumnavigation and the subsequent race (especially after publication of the official voyage account in 1784) to dominate the fur trade. Traders from different parts of the world—the North West Company based in Montreal, the Hudson's Bay Company, a Russian merchant corporation, and John Jacob Astor's interests—vied to control the commerce in sea otter skins.[50] Statesmen turned their attention to the North Pacific too, intensifying their search for a water passage across the American continent, experimenting with ventures to occupy and colonize the northwest American coast, and trying to establish forts and colonies at strategic points throughout the Pacific—a mixture of scientific and colonial designs on the region, furthered by ships that had both military and scientific missions. Russian patronage of overseas voyages diminished in the late 1820s, but only after an impressive series of voyages that produced rich reports on the peoples of the Pacific.

Since the early eighteenth century the Russian state had been organizing expeditions to explore its Siberian territories and the Pacific regions that lay beyond them. The first systematic Russian attempt to colonize the northern Pacific came from a group of merchants who in 1785 formed a monopoly corporation, the Russian-American Company. It set up a station on Kodiak Island and smaller forts on almost all the Aleutian Islands. To collect its furs the company kidnapped Aleutian men and used them as hunters. Despite widespread public criticism of the hellish exploitation of the Aleuts, the company had its privileges confirmed by the monarchy in 1799. In opposition to these destructive practices, naval officers dreamed of a systematic occupation and domination of Pacific territories. Taking British technical know-how and Cook's treatment of sailors and native peoples as their example, they launched a series of circumnavigations with the Pacific as their strategic focus.[51]

The first person to conceive a global strategy for Russia was Adam von Krusenstern. From the German nobility of Estonia, which had a tradition of naval service to the Russian monarchy, he attended the naval academy in Reval and entered the naval service. From 1793 to 1799, during the wars of the French Revolution, he served on British ships and, eager to see British trade in Asia firsthand, managed to spend a year in India beginning in early 1797 and to stay in Canton during 1798–99. He returned to Russia with a memorandum arguing that the monarchy should train an elite cadre of non-nobles for merchant service, send out well-equipped ships, and create one or more colonies that could build their own ships and link the Aleutian Islands, the northwest coast of America, eastern Siberia, and the Chinese and Indian merchant ports. At the time he wrote, the Russian-American Company sent supplies to their Pacific stations by land route via Yakutsk (north of Mongolia) to Okhotsk. Everything from wheat to anchors had to follow this path across Siberia. It was not an efficient way to do business; many of the goods were plundered along the way, anchors and anchor chains had to be hacked into parts and then reassembled in Okhotsk, and the poorly built ships that set out from Okhotsk did not always survive the cold and stormy route to the fur-trading stations. Krusenstern instead proposed sending ships on voyages that would go out laden with supplies, carry furs to Canton and other ports, and return with Chinese goods for the north German market. Krusenstern had a keen appreciation of the kind of applied science that facilitated the voyages of Cook and Bougainville,

The patron as international benefactor:
Count Nikolai P. Rumiantsev.

but his attention was firmly fixed on building up a Russian commercial empire that could surpass its European rivals.[52]

For two years after his return to Russia, Krusenstern could find no advocate in official circles for his proposal. Finally in early 1802 his ideas came to the attention of Count Nikolai Rumiantsev, who had recently been appointed minister of commerce. Rumiantsev, at the beginning of a career carrying him to the heights of power, was Krusenstern's equal for worldliness, devotion to Russian commerce, and appreciation of scientific travel. From one of the most privileged families of the Russian Empire, Rumiantsev completed his education with a grand tour of western Europe from 1774 to 1776. He was a Russian consul in Frankfurt am Main from 1782 to 1795 and held prominent financial and banking posts before entering the commerce ministry.[53]

With Rumiantsev's leadership, the naval minister's cooperation, and Alexander I's assent, the Krusenstern voyage was outfitted to emulate the standards set by Cook. The expedition's ships, the *Nadeshda* and the *Neda,* were purchased in England. German scientists were hired for the voyage, including Wilhelm Gottfried Telsius von Tilenau as naturalist, Johann Caspar Hoerner as astronomer, and Georg Wilhelm Langsdorff as physician. The St. Petersburg Academy of Sciences provided maps and books. Tsar Alexander himself visited Kronstadt to inspect the preparations for the voyage, and he declared that the revenues of an estate would be paid to Krusenstern's wife for twelve years. The voyagers departed from Kronstadt in the two ships in August 1803, rounding Cape Horn and visiting the Marquesas, Hawaii, Kamchatka, Nagasaki, Sakhalin, Macao, and the Indian Ocean before their return in August 1806. They could not open up commercial relations with the Japanese, who were highly suspicious of them when they tried to land in Nagasaki. On the scientific and navigational side, however, the voyage was a success, with important ethnographic observations in the Marquesas and a survey of Sakhalin among its achievements.[54]

When the *Neva* arrived at Kronstadt in 1806, Alexander and his mother went to congratulate the arrivals, with his mother leaving jewelry and gold pieces as homecoming presents. Thanks to Rumiantsev's recommendation, all the officers on board both ships were raised one grade in the Russian hierarchy of social ranks, and all the voyagers, from the officers to the sailors, received lifelong pensions. Krusenstern himself felt that from the time of his return he was only modestly rewarded for his achievements. He was made captain second class and only slowly rose through the naval ranks to be promoted to the rank of counter-admiral in 1826. An Anglophile, and a protégé of the Francophile Rumiantsev, he was never taken into the admiralty's strategic corps, but instead functioned as a scientific and academic advisor, first spending three years writing up his account of his own voyage and then turning his attention to the preparation and planning of new scientific expeditions. His last great achievement in the 1820s was the preparation of a scientific atlas of the South Pacific.[55]

Like the Cook voyages, Krusenstern's circumnavigation was the school for a generation of ambitious young naval officers who either accompanied him on the journey or were motivated by his example. They championed competition with the other great European powers for commerce and colonies in the Pacific, fought the Russian-American Company as their internal rivals, and planned scientific expeditions to match their French and British counterparts. For the Russians, as for the British and French, the end of the Napoleonic wars led to a burst of ambitious voyaging. Navigators such as V. M. Golovnin and F. G. Bellingshausen crossed the vast spaces of Oceania during the early years of the Restoration with virtuoso ease—Golovnin's voyage lasted from 1817 to 1819, Bellingshausen's from 1819 to 1821—demonstrating Russian skill in all the arts and sciences required for a circumnavigation and asserting Russia's place as a rising global power alongside France and Britain.[56] The most important ethnographic expedition of the era, however, was the 1815–1818 voyage of the *Rurik*.

The choice of Otto von Kotzebue as voyage captain was a triumph of patronage. The Kotzebue and Krusenstern families were closely intertwined. Otto's father was married three times to members of the Krusenstern family. August von Kotzebue and Adam von Krusenstern were close friends who wrote frequently to each other, and Adam took Otto and his brother Moritz as cadets aboard the *Nadeshda*. Their father, August von Kotzebue, whose light social dramas were favorite fare throughout Europe, read through the captain's world voyage account and gave him publication advice. When Otto received his own commission as commander of the *Rurik* nine years later, it was on a voyage that was the personal project of the two

Pacific enthusiasts, Krusenstern and Rumiantsev. The two friends began planning the voyage in 1812, spending hours together discussing a new search for a Northwest Passage that ships could traverse from the Pacific to the Atlantic. By 1814 Rumiantsev had retired from state service and turned his full attention to philanthropy. He financed the entire *Rurik* expedition from his personal fortune, an amazing act of munificence. The *Rurik* had the status of a Russian warship, but Otto enjoyed the prestige of commanding a voyage that was above all a mission for the advancement of science. Krusenstern took over the planning and preparations for the voyage, deciding that the vessel should be a brig—a small, stable two-master—ordering the building of a new ship in Finland, and traveling to England in the spring of 1814 to supervise the purchase of the astronomical instruments, the chronometer, the surgeon's tools, medicines, herbs, and clothing; he was also delighted to make the discovery of newly invented canned foods and brought back large quantities for the voyage. After the *Rurik*'s return, Krusenstern touted its achievements in learned journals.[57]

If Kotzebue was the ultimate insider, the special favorite of a patron who had watched over him since boyhood, Adelbert von Chamisso began and stayed an outsider to the planners' circle. He got the assignment to serve as naturalist by chance when the German scientist originally picked for the post backed out at the last minute. He knew neither Rumiantsev, nor Krusenstern, nor Kotzebue, had had no naval apprenticeship, and had no experience with Russians. His relationship to the insiders started out promisingly enough. In his letter of invitation, Krusenstern underlined the unusually idealistic and scientific nature of the voyage. It was being financed not by the tsar, he pointed out, but by an individual (Rumiantsev), and the participants could not expect a large salary or a pension; "the prospect before you is only the glory of taking part in an enterprise which is unique for its kind and highly promising." But he emphasized his confidence in Chamisso: "I see with intense pleasure from Professor Lichtenstein's letter," he added, "that your motives for traveling are no less noble."[58] Whether Krusenstern knew it or not, his assessment of his naturalist's character was more than a rhetorical flourish. Perhaps most other travelers would have looked forward to pensions and gold of the kind granted to the members of his own expedition after their return, but not Chamisso. The appeal to nobler motives perfectly matched the temperament of a naturalist who was contemptuous of calculation and eager for a chance to fulfill his new scientific calling.

At first Chamisso's liking for Kotzebue bordered on adulation, but his bohemianism and Kotzebue's careerism did not wear well together over a three-year voyage. Even though Chamisso, at thirty-four, was the oldest person on board the ship, Kotzebue mocked his enthusiasm for the wonders of the Pacific. While they were staying in Hawaii in December 1816, Chamisso asked if he could stay for a year, to be picked up when the *Rurik* made its scheduled return stop on the islands; Kotzebue answered that if Chamisso decided to stay, he was on his own and could not expect the *Rurik* to return him home. Chamisso sensed the rapid changes taking place in Hawaiian society, and we can admire his demand for the opportunity of a year's fieldwork, which in retrospect seems like a marvelous opportunity lost; but from a captain's point of view, a leave of this kind would have been abandonment of one's post. At the end of the voyage, the two men patched up their differences; but Chamisso returned home outraged over the way he had been treated.[59]

Disagreement broke out again after they returned to Europe. Chamisso went to work on putting together his naturalist's account of the voyage. On September 3, 1819, he reported to Rumiantsev that he hadn't expected the work to take more than a winter; in fact he had dedicated a year to it. At the beginning of the summer he had sent off the first part of his work and was now about to send off more. Chamisso was eager to publish his voyage observations as a separate volume; Kotzebue, backed by Rumiantsev and Krusenstern, firmly refused him permission. Rumiantsev made it clear in a letter of November 12, 1819, that Chamisso could not publish his general observations of the voyages, in particular remarks touching on new discoveries, but granted him permission to publish a separate work limited to natural history. At the end of January 1820, he sent Chamisso a rather kind letter indicating his pleasure that the naturalist's portion would appear within the work under Chamisso's own name, with nothing changed or added. While refusing Chamisso's request for a separate publication, he added his polite enough understanding of authorial impatience: "I find it very natural that you wish to relate your surely most interesting observations to the world without delay; however I am also convinced of the decency of your sentiments that for the time being you will gladly wait when you learn that an earlier edition of your book corresponds neither to the chancellor's wish nor to that of your former captain." Compared with other voyages the publication went quickly and smoothly, and Chamisso received his fair share of recognition; but he felt he had been badly used and came away with lasting resentments. Kotzebue for his part garnered glory and advancement. He went on to command a second circumnavigation, with visits to Tahiti and Hawaii on its route, from 1826 to 1830. His was the name known to readers of travel accounts around the world. Chamisso was the superior intellect and a penetrating observer of local life wherever he went; his difficulties are a vivid demonstration of how deeply social knowledge was intertwined with social status and power, how it flowed or was checked by the authority of metropolitan power-holders.[60]

Germany

Late-eighteenth-century Germany was home to a fascination with travel writing. Reports on foreign peoples and places flooded journals and bookstores. Authors commented on the overwhelming assortment of information; they justified new literary ventures by calling for order and system. Friedrich Gottlieb Canzler, private tutor of historical, geographic, and statistical sciences in Göttingen, was not modest about the importance of the service he was offering his readers. He wrote in the introduction to his magazine for modern history, geography, and ethnography that he was offering them "an extremely pleasant gift," to judge from the high esteem of experts for his work. His ambition, he announced, was to gather together all the scattered material he could find about little-known parts of the globe and from time to time to synthesize it into a system.[61] Other journal editors, too, began with a proclamation that their readers needed help in gaining news about the nature of the wider world rescued from manuscripts, obscure places of publication, or larger works and digested into an easy-to-use form. This public was a broad one and comprehended several different audiences. At the level of highest expertise a university expert like F. C. G. Hirsching edited a geographic and anthropological journal suited to administrators and fellow academics. Writing in 1791 from the University of Erlangen, he welcomed many different kinds of reports for his journal, but his special interest was "knowledge of nutritional conditions"; the main path to this knowledge was statistics, including a place's figures for the number of households, businesses, and craftsmen.[62]

Early nineteenth-century writers took the new geographic knowledge beyond the educated public to popular audiences. One book imaginatively named *The Bee* went on in its subtitle to promise "curiosities from foreign countries and folklore. A very entertaining and instructive reader for all classes of readers, who will pass the time most pleasantly with its varied and titillating contents; provides materials to cheer up conversations, especially for travelers, lonely walkers, the mildly sick, etc." The contents were a kind of Believe It or Not with nonsensical tidbits from everywhere, including India, Siberia, ancient Egypt, Turkey, the East Indies, and indigenous North America. Piquant anecdotes filled the pages: "The inhabitants of Nootka Sound in Northwest America have no spices for their food, not even salt; instead they use their tears for their food. Enjoy your meal!"[63] This was anthropology as folk anthology, a source of entertainment and homely morals. These popular writings were more than just a means to kill time, however; no less than the reports for professors and bureaucrats they gave voice to a hunger for experience of a wider world beyond the boundaries of Germany's petty principalities.

Germans read about voyages, but they had no state tradition of sponsoring them. "Germany" was not a political entity in the late 1700s and early 1800s. It denoted not a centralized monarchy comparable to France or Britain or Russia, but a cultural region crisscrossed by political, religious, ethnic, and linguistic differences. "Germans" were Catholics, Protestants, and Jews; lived in regions as culturally distinct as Bavaria and the Baltic; and knew the liberties of free cities and the drill of monarchies. Austria and Prussia, its two major states, asserted their great-power status by marching their armies; they had no overseas colonies and no more than a smattering of overseas commercial interests. Their statesmen, with their attention turned almost entirely toward European affairs, had little reason to sponsor extra-European scientific voyages.[64]

Individual Germans managed to go abroad, however. One of the outstanding early German travelers, Carsten Niebuhr, made his journey with Danish patronage. From a North German home, Niebuhr emigrated when he was twenty-seven to Denmark and became an engineering lieutenant in Copenhagen. A year later he became one of six scientists on a journey to the Middle East sponsored by the Danish king, Frederik V. The planners of the trip were the Göttingen biblical scholar Johann David Michaelis and the Danish foreign minister, J. H. von Bernstorff. Pioneers of a modern kind of scholarship, they wished to provide an empirical context for biblical studies by returning to the holy sites of the eastern Mediterranean and bringing back information that could deepen the learned world's understanding of peoples, places, and objects that were still known in northern Europe only as literary artifacts in the sacred text. It was a perilous undertaking. Out of the six scientists, Niebuhr was the only survivor; he returned to Europe and went on to publish two memoirs of his travels in 1772 and 1774–1778. Niebuhr's voyage was a European sensation. His travel accounts were translated into multiple foreign languages, and Michaelis's planning of a scientific voyage—one that predated Cook and Bougainville—was an example not lost on his contemporaries. Tiny, landlocked Göttingen demonstrated its importance within the voyage culture of the eighteenth century; at the same time Carsten's travels illustrate how Germans went into foreign service in order to fulfill their ambitions.[65]

A partial exception to the German states' lack of patronage for scientific expeditions was Austria, which developed a significant tradition of sponsoring naturalist collections. This patronage was due not to the stimulus of empire building but to the connoisseurship of a highly cultivated royal family and aristocracy that took a personal interest in collecting. Emperor Francis I sent a Dutch naturalist, Nicolaus Joseph von Jacquin, on a collecting expedition to the Caribbean, and from 1755 to 1757 ships filled with "plants, fossils, corals, tools and idols of the islanders, with living animals, minerals" and other items returned to Europe and enriched the imperial collections in Vienna. Jacquin enjoyed a successful career as professor of botany and chemistry at the University of Vienna and as director of the Schönbrunn palace botanical garden. Like Banks in England and Krusenstern in Russia he became a founding figure, his success and his advice serving as a starting point for further ventures. His son, Joseph Franz von Jacquin, succeeded him as professor at the university and later took over the gardens of another Habsburg palace in Vienna, the Belvedere. When Emperor Joseph II decided to organize an expedition—there was talk of a circumnavigation along the lines of the Cook voyages—Nicolaus Joseph de Jacquin was one of the experts he turned to for advice. The naturalist Franz Josef Märter ended up leading an expedition along the American coast from Philadelphia to the Bahamas from 1784 to 1788 and sending sixty-five boxes stuffed with specimens back to Vienna. Joseph II sent another successful expedition to southern Africa in 1785 (the last member of the party, Georg Scholl, did not return to Vienna until fourteen years later).[66]

Despite all the disruptions and financial worries caused by war with France, Austrian monarchs, nobles, and scientists remained passionate collectors. Chancellor Klemens von Metternich, after completing his duties as host of the Congress of Vienna and organizer of post-Napoleonic Europe, played a role in sponsoring a scientific voyage. On the occasion of the marriage of a Habsburg archduchess, Leopoldine, with Pedro, the heir to the Portuguese throne, he arranged for a large contingent of Austrian scientists (and, at the request of the Bavarian king, two Munich colleagues) to accompany the newlyweds to Brazil and explore the country's interior. Metternich sought—and gained—a scientific achievement that would bring Austria international prestige. Never was scientific travel more attractive to highly placed sponsors than in the early Restoration years, when this Austrian expedition vied with Russian, French, and British voyages for scientific glory.[67]

No other German-speaking state developed a comparable appetite for state-sponsored natural history collections. Bavaria, Saxony, the Rhineland, and the Southwest German states had their own traditions of scientific and artistic patronage, but were simply too small and too landlocked to begin the extravagant game of sending scientist-laden ships abroad. Prussia too had only modest ambitions for overseas exploration.

North Germany did, however, have an excess of one valuable resource for scientific travel: its university graduates. Central Europe was rich in mathematicians, life scientists, and applied scientists in fields like mining and engineering as well as experts in non-European languages and cultures. Elsewhere, learned academies provided the most important meeting places for the erudite, but Germany had a network of universities stretching north, east, south, and west across the central part of Europe. While most European universities (including the German ones) were sleepy places in the eighteenth century, two German creations of that period, the universities of Halle and of Göttingen, were exceptions. They set examples of higher learning for the founding of the University of Berlin in the early nineteenth century, the great model of the modern university as an institution combining teaching and research. With Berlin at the forefront, the university triumphed over the academies of the eighteenth century and the Napoleonic model of specialized knowledge to become the dominant modern institution for the production of scientific knowledge. In the late eighteenth century the German universities already produced a surplus of graduates who could not find employment in the bureaucracies of their principalities and needed to search for other kinds of employment. They became a reservoir of educated knowledge, ready for hire by foreign empires.

Göttingen was the setting for North Germany's patron-entrepreneur of scientific travel, Johann Friedrich Blumenbach. Like many naturalists of the late eighteenth and early nineteenth centuries, Blu-

menbach was trained in medicine. From an early age he was fascinated by the travel literature of the period, and he read systematically
through the large collection of travel accounts available to him in
Göttingen. Blumenbach was one of the major voices in his era's discussions of race; he argued emphatically for the unity of the human
species, but believed that Europeans represented a physical norm
that in other races was modified by environmental factors. To gather
evidence for his views Blumenbach collected body parts; his skull
collection was famous throughout Europe. Through his good relations with the powerful he was able to help plan trips and to place
his students on them. He and like-minded fellow professors created a
milieu for scientific travel, turning Göttingen into a center that attracted gifted intellectuals and put them in touch with the holders of
money and power who could send them abroad.

Blumenbach came from a respectable but modest background. His
paternal grandfather was a tailor in Leipzig; his father was a professor
at the Gymnasium in Gotha. A politically opportune marriage eased
his rapid rise in the German academic world. In 1772 he arrived as a
medical student in Göttingen, and there he married the daughter of a
highly placed state administrator. His brother-in-law was now Christian Gottlob Heyne, a classical philologist and one of the university's
luminaries. On October 11, 1778, Heyne wrote to the Geheimes Rats-
Kollegium (the governing board in Hannover responsible, among
other things, for university governance) and petitioned for a professorship in medicine for Blumenbach, pointing out that he had done
an excellent job of organizing a local collection of natural history
and coins and that his lectures—he had begun teaching in the summer semester of 1776—were very popular. The privy council must
have assented and forwarded the request for royal approval with remarkable speed, for a month later George III wrote to the council
and granted Blumenbach his professorship.[68] Whatever his real merits, it was his brother-in-law who made sure that they did not go un-

noticed and who secured him the post at the leading university in North Germany and one of the most notable centers of university learning in all of Europe. Once installed in it, he cultivated good relations with the political power-holders of his time and counted aristocrats and princes among his students.

Blumenbach made astute use of personal relationships to enhance his reputation and his passion for skull collecting. During the 1780s and early 1790s Joseph Banks tried to provide him with new samples. In July 1789 Banks wrote that he had the skull of a Carib chief from the Caribbean island of St. Vincent's, but mentioned the difficulty of getting a skull of a "yellow" Carib as most of the members of this group had been extirpated by the "black" Caribs. Four years later, the outbreak of the French Revolution and the rule of the Jacobins did not keep Banks from scouting for skulls to round out his friend's collection. He had heard a rumor, he wrote on February 6, 1794, that "the King displeased at the great use which was made of his quarterly messengers has abridged very much the space allotted to their packages." He did not know, he continued, if Blumenbach had yet received a "perfect Otaheite" (Tahitian) skull.[69]

By then Blumenbach had firmed up the friendship with a visit to London, where he stayed for two months in 1791–92. He seems to have enjoyed himself hugely and looked back on the visit with the feeling that all his expectations had been fulfilled. "Nowhere have I found such civility," he wrote to a friend in Vienna, adding that he looked forward to helping any English travelers who visited him at home. Blumenbach's most direct service to Banks, however, was to recommend talented explorers for the African Association. Blumenbach sent four students to Banks—Friedrich Hornemann, Ulrich Seetzen, Heinrich Roentgen, and Johann Ludwig Burckhardt—all of whom died in Africa, as did most of the association's other travelers.[70]

After the founding of the University of Berlin in 1812 and the return of peace to Europe three years later, the Prussian capital took on a greater significance as a center for naturalist studies. It was still a far remove, though, from the ambitious imperial capital of the late nineteenth century.[71] Prussia sent its first naturalist around the world as part of a cautious state attempt to place manufactured goods in world markets. In 1820 Friedrich Wilhelm III appointed a financial administrator, Christian von Rother, to be president of a mercantile venture, the Royal Prussian Sea Company (Königliche Preussische Seehandlung). With a small fleet of ships, the company tried to export linen, wool, and other goods to China, South America, Mexico, and the West Indies. The company was never able to compete with the quality or quantity of British goods flooding the world markets; its very existence was a sign of the backwardness of Prussian industry, which needed to turn to the state for the capital and initiative to undertake such a venture.[72]

At the recommendation of Alexander von Humboldt, a young botanist named F. J. F. Meyen was allowed to hitchhike on one of the company's ships, the *Prinzess Luise,* which traveled to South America and the Pacific in 1830–1832. Unlike the great French, British, Russian, and Austrian voyages, with their teams of scientists on voyages specially commissioned for scientific research, Meyen went alone on a trip that was supposed to pay for itself. Under the circumstances he did admirably, bringing back large collections for the zoo, the anatomical museum, the botanical garden, the mineralogical museum, and the royal library. The royal collections now contained hundreds of new creatures packed in wine, thousands of insects, a mummy from the high plains of Peru, some 2,560 plant species, a catechism and a declaration of Christian doctrine in Quechua, and a copy of the Chilean constitution.[73] Karl von Stein zum Altenstein, the responsible Prussian minister, declared himself very satisfied with Meyen's industry in his report to Friedrich Wilhelm III and arranged for a modest two-year stipend so that Meyen could write up his travel account, which duly appeared in two volumes.[74] Despite this promising start there was no follow-up: the company did not sponsor further naturalists.

A geographic society was formed in Berlin in 1828. Its initial aims were modest. From his earliest planning stages in 1822 in correspondence with the government, the geographer Carl Ritter imagined a local organization for the exchange of scholarly knowledge and technical skills.[75] At the 1832 meeting of the Berlin Geographic Society (its first with printed protocols) Ritter pronounced the noblest aims for the organization, a humane and universal science for the uplift of humanity, now to be practiced with a new comprehensiveness: "The tremendous breadth of general geography has only been conceived in its fullest, most philanthropic reach by Herder, although known to the soul of all cultured peoples and through all branches of science, nature and scholarship; so broad is the field now opened up that all too often the relevant facts are treated in isolation and not as part of a scientific totality." The topics discussed at the meetings were as varied as the ones in Paris and London, including astronomical observations, magnetism, the temperature of the sea, progress in measuring techniques, and discoveries of pre-Columbian artifacts.[76] Little had changed by the late 1830s, when Ritter's successor could still declare that the work of his organization, in contrast to the London and Paris geographic societies, consisted "in the generalization, purification, and summary of the geographic results that we and others have achieved."[77] The aims were not quite as impractical as its leaders made them out to be; army officers, who had sound practical motives for improving their knowledge of geography, made up 39 out of the 110 participants at the 1832 meeting.[78] Nonetheless, the composition and tone of the organization were strikingly different from the worldly, ambitious organizations in the imperial capitals. While the

Prussian geographers might have some uses for the army, in these early years they had no role in supporting ventures to map and master the extra-European world.

Germany north of Austria thus had significant centers of interest in scientific travel, including Göttingen in the late eighteenth century and Berlin after 1815; but a country that actually sponsored independent voyages overseas did not exist. A sole venture for Meyen on a merchant ship was the best Prussia could offer. Wellborn naturalists in Germany who wished to emulate French and British collectors had to emigrate or use their own means. Duke Paul Wilhelm of Württemberg, for example, was a nephew of the king of this wealthy, cultivated principality. He used his private wealth to take overland trips in North America and other parts of the world from 1822 until his death in 1860. Maximilian von Wied came from the ruling dynasty of a progressive, independent Rheinland territory. He entered Prussian military service but also had strong naturalist interests, studying with Blumenbach at the University of Göttingen during winter semester 1811–12. From 1815 to 1817 he made a scientific expedition to Brazil and from 1832 to 1834 he visited North America, carrying out both journeys at his own expense.[79] Like Bougainville and Dumont d'Urville these German naturalists combined military with scientific training, but unlike their French counterparts they had to leave state service in order to fulfill their scientific ambitions.

Another German who could afford to travel by paying his own way—and also left state service in order to do so—was Alexander von Humboldt. Alexander trained and briefly served the Prussian monarchy as a mining engineer while making preparations of a half-dozen years for a scientific journey that lasted from 1799 to 1804, as he and his companion Aimé Bonpland traveled through the Americas. In 1808 he went to Paris—initially as a companion to a Prussian prince—and stayed on to enjoy the stimulation of French scientific colleagues and to assemble a team of coworkers to help him publish the scientific results of the voyage. Humboldt became one of the era's scientific patron-entrepreneurs, arranging for stipends, recommending job candidates, and furthering publications, a role he played both in Berlin and in Paris. In Paris his efforts were aided by his warm friendship with François Guizot, the liberal historian who in 1830 became prime minister.

The expenses of leading this brilliant life in Paris and of publishing his travel account in twenty-nine volumes accompanied by hundreds of copper engravings for maps and prints (at a time when the new technology of lithography offered a cheaper alternative for illustrations) exhausted even Humboldt's wealth. Reluctant to reenter Prussian government service, he had to turn for support to a patron. He was a personal favorite of Friedrich Wilhelm III, who supported his eighteen-year stay in Paris for the sake of the travel account. Humboldt began to receive advances for the multivolume work in 1815, which were to be "paid" back in the form of four luxury editions for the Prussian universities of Berlin, Breslau, Halle, and Bonn. This financial support and other gifts came at a certain cost. After Friedrich Wilhelm III arrived in Paris on March 31, 1814, at the head of his troops, he sent the next day for Humboldt, useful because of his exact knowledge of the city, but also valued as a conversationalist; two years later, by a cabinet order of May 1816, Humboldt was given 1,500 thalers for his services during this visit. In June 1816, Friedrich Wilhelm went on a visit to London; he took along Alexander and Wilhelm von Humboldt. In 1827 the king ordered Alexander to return to Berlin; Friedrich Wilhelm, though generally reserved and careful with his spending, gave Humboldt a pension and asked his courtier for nothing more in exchange than conversation and advice on scientific and artistic matters. Later he permitted Humboldt to return to Paris for four months per year and to go on an expedition to

Siberia in 1829–30. It was a generous but uncomfortable arrangement for the sarcastic, impatient Humboldt, used to the impertinent tone of Paris salons and now set down among the dowdy bureaucrats and burghers of Berlin.[80]

North German rulers may not have sponsored their own voyages, but they knew how to nurture and reward them. The Forsters, Chamisso, and Humboldt had to go abroad in order to satisfy their ambition to see new worlds, but were eventually able to return to sinecures and honor. It was not a bad situation for these independent-minded intellectuals: they had some distance from their former employers, and could therefore afford to write more critically about their voyages than travelers who remained within their home state; at the same time they were surrounded by a literate, curious, educated audience with a real interest in their news from afar. There was a rising note of national pride in this conversation between travelers and stay-at-homes, an appreciation of the contribution that they as Germans had made to the second age of discovery and a sympathy for the potential indignities they had to suffer as outsiders. From monarchs and from their educated compatriots, the travelers could anticipate a warm welcome, and along with it, a considerable degree of intellectual freedom.

J. R. Forster is a good example of this domestic tolerance for a traveler who had not fared well with foreign patrons. After the Forsters' dispute with Sandwich and their return to the Continent, George was a celebrity in his own right, made famous by his publication of the voyage account. He now had his own dealings with monarchs who might provide him with employment. As his and his father's fortunes shifted, they became better at managing their relationships with princely patrons—became, indeed, highly successful entrepreneurs who milked a succession of enlightened rulers for favors. Ferdinand, Duke of Braunschweig-Wolfenbüttel, paid off J. R.

Forster's large debts to almost all his English creditors, permitting him to leave London and return to Germany. Soon Frederick the Great of Prussia was one of the elder Forster's admirers and a generous and steady supporter of him at the University of Halle.[81]

George Forster never received a professorship from the Austrian ruler Joseph II, but on his way to taking up a professorship in the Polish city of Vilna, he did visit Vienna and had an interview with the enlightened emperor and radical reformer. After keeping Forster waiting for two hours, as he recorded in his diary, Joseph looked at him sharply and asked him what his business was in Poland. He explained that he didn't know the place at all, but sought to live where he could practice his science; hence he had left his previous job in Kassel. "So," replied Joseph, "the Count [of Hesse-Kassel, his former employer] doesn't have the will, and the king of Poland won't have the means." "It is sad, Your Majesty, that these two things so seldom come together," responded his guest. The emperor went on, "I know the Poles, they will be long on talk, but there's no chance that they'll keep their word. You certainly won't stay there long; if you want to work, you won't be able to do so there, you can believe me." Joseph then questioned him about Cook, Banks, and Linnaeus's student Solander—and then at the end came back to Forster's fate in Poland: "I think I'll see you again before long. I don't believe that you are the man who would change and do nothing just to have a bigger wage; I don't think you are the man." "No, Your Majesty, my only wish is to be happy in order to be able to work." "Now, you will not stay in Poland."[82]

From Vilna, Forster wrote to Joseph that he had written an appreciation of Cook which would appear in a German translation of the narrative account of Cook's third voyage. Might he dedicate the essay to the emperor? "Since Cook's voyages have resulted in so many new conceptions and corrected so many incorrect ones, they are true contributions to the Enlightenment, and as such I should like to present them to the German people under the sanction of its greatest authority. I therefore venture to ask Your Imperial Majesty for permission to dedicate this work to you." Joseph replied three weeks later that as a rule he did not accept dedications, but in this case, the thought of planting the famous work in German soil led him to make an exception. He also sent along a fine ring.[83]

While Joseph contented himself with praise, another enlightened monarch, Catherine the Great, tried to hire Forster. She had plans for a voyage around the world and engaged him to join the voyage as its historian; he had already sent her an acceptance letter with a long list of conditions, including a pension for his widow (in the event of his death), before the project fell through.[84] Catherine then offered him a professorship in St. Petersburg, but Forster had to consider the wishes of another patron, his father-in-law, Heyne (the influential philologist at the University of Göttingen who had secured Blumenbach's professorship). Heyne shuddered at the thought of his daughter and son-in-law going to Russia—a land of "barbarians," he called it—and at his urging Forster declined the offer, not without considerable discomfit.[85] Heyne instead arranged for a more suitable position for his son-in-law as director of the university library in Mainz. Heyne thought the Elector of Mainz had a real feel for "useful Enlightenment" and would understand the value of a man like his son-in-law.[86] By mid-August 1788 the former world traveler had been hired for the position and was learning how to catalogue, noting library rules for lending books, and looking for titles to acquire.[87] Mainz was a comfortable spot, in the middle of the Rhine, an intersection for commerce and ideas from across Europe. Not yet thirty-four, Forster already enjoyed fame and a secure home in Germany.

Like the Forsters, Chamisso returned to honor. When he left Berlin in 1815 he was still at loose ends, a writer with a growing reputation but no secure employment. On his return he received a position as custodian in the royal garden in Schöneberg. This was a modest status, at a far remove from the exalted title of professor, but one well suited to his personality; it did not confine the bohemian traveler to the rituals of court and civil service, and it left him free for his literary pursuits and his beloved field trips for plant collecting. The civil servants were proud of him. One of them wrote on December 30, 1822, to the king to make him aware of Chamisso's gifts to the royal collections: books to the library, objects for the museums, and specimens for the herbarium, for which Chamisso initially refused any recompense ("With noble selflessness he has refused any payment for these objects . . .").[88] Chamisso could be a social klutz, but he understood the rules of gift giving. He became an honored figure in his adopted country, his eccentricities and his liberal political opinions tolerated, his status confirmed as one of Germany's leading men of letters. Acknowledging a copy of Chamisso's newly published travel journal, Alexander von Humboldt wrote: "How could my thanks be heartfelt and enthusiastic enough, most honored friend and colleague, for your handsome and fitting present! First I have to tell you how happy I am that your autobiography, your so winning and noble and solid portrait, has made such a deep sympathetic impression on our dear crown prince. We have begun to read from your first volume with the king in Potsdam. It is rare that a poet like you, so harmonious and enthusiastic in verse, can write such spontaneous, simple and free prose. You have *both* gifts. This voyage around the world may be old by now, but your personal stamp has given it the charm of a new world drama."[89] The crown prince himself—the future Friedrich Wilhelm IV, a man of highly cultivated tastes—wrote directly to Chamisso on May 16, 1836, to tell him how much he had enjoyed the work and that it now was entertaining the court between dinner and bedtime. "I wish I could thank you again and again in

person. I haven't seen and spoken to you for so long. Now A. von
Humboldt tells me you've been sick for the whole winter. That dam-
ages my hopes, I'm very sorry to say, for seeing you at my table. If you
can risk it, then please let me know."[90] Alexander von Humboldt saw
to it that Chamisso got scientific recognition too, nominating him,
after the death of his brother Wilhelm vacated a space, to membership in the Prussian Academy of Sciences.

German travelers had greater intellectual autonomy than their
counterparts in other European countries. It was their personal misfortune that they came from a region with little interest in sponsoring voyages and had to hire themselves out to foreign patrons, a situation that could lead to unhappy histories like the Forsters' and
Chamisso's. But precisely their outsider status allowed them a position of greater detachment from metropolitan prejudices. They surveyed a widened social space as they moved back and forth between
different European masters, an expansion of horizons that made
them unusually cosmopolitan observers of non-European peoples.

CHAPTER 3

Collaborators

Coming from thousands of miles away, with little more than a few accounts by predecessors to guide them, travelers depended on indigenous peoples for guidance through a strange countryside, for insight into society and culture. What filtered through? How did it shape naturalists' notions of the peoples they encountered? We cannot separate the hosts from the reports of the Europeans who visited them. But we can observe how collaborations worked between travelers and the people they visited.

The word has a double meaning here: collaborations took place in the simple sense that travelers worked together with the people they met, relationships that they often described as founded in friendship or hospitality. Yet there were many other motives on both sides. Travelers on voyages of discovery had powerful military means at their disposal; islanders and settlers were aware of their visitors' potential for violence as they cooperated with them. This alone, however, would never account for the often spontaneous, outgoing conversation and guidance that permitted travelers to learn as much as they did about Polynesian languages and cultures. Collaborations resulted from the mutual interests that were as strong on the locals' side as on the travelers'. For the travelers, collecting ethnographic knowledge was a means of fulfilling their obligations to their patrons, furthering their careers, and satisfying their scientific curiosity. For their part, locals had equally powerful ambitions and sought protection from enemies, social prestige, and an opportunity to satisfy their own curiosity about the larger world. The mutual interests of elites, too, were a ground for lasting collaborations: powerholders in Europe (represented by their emissaries, the captains) and local power-holders quickly found one another and developed strategies of cooperation that lasted over decades. These collaborations from above created the peaceful conditions that permitted travelers to carry out their ethnographic work. Overall, collaboration, like patronage, was a relationship that combined power and emotional bonds; this mixture of interest and feeling deeply informed travelers' ethnographies.

Because native societies were nonliterate, our knowledge of them is mediated by Europeans, nativized Europeans, or europeanized natives. Confronted with this lack of direct native testimony in the written record, one could argue that any attempt to speak about Oceanic peoples in the early days of contact is radically flawed as one more attempt to arrogate native voices and speak for them. But this kind of radical agnosticism—the belief that we cannot know anything about Hawaiians or Tahitians or other islanders—has its own dangers, for it leaves us completely at the mercy of European opinion. There is then a very real possibility of leaving long-standing stereotypes unchecked and unchallenged. Agnosticism would also ignore the painstaking research that *has* taken place: the efforts of archaeologists working around the Pacific, the careful comparison of sources for insights into native societies, the theories that challenge us to imagine ways of thinking alien to our own. We see through a glass darkly, but that is not to say that we cannot see at all. On the contrary, historical anthropologists have combined different kinds of evidence—from archaeology, language, and oral testimony—to arrive at a picture of Polynesian societies before and after Cook. While we should not lose our sense of how little we know, we gain from many-sided reconstruction. A skeptical but not dismissive approach repeats the learning experience of the generations of travelers who visited the Pacific from the 1770s to the 1830s: that cultural insight grows from repeated exposure over time.[1]

To imagine just two opposed categories, natives and non-natives, would be to simplify the nature of cultural encounters in general and specifically in the islands of the Pacific. In fact people on both sides moved beyond this polarity to take advantage of a multiplicity of roles between native and European societies. Europeans quickly began to play a visible role in Oceanic societies, sometimes preying on them, sometimes caught up beyond their own control in internecine violence, sometimes allying with native leaders or serving as their advisors. In Hawaii a chief tried to persuade Cook in January 1779 to leave behind Lieutenant James King, and from then on Hawaiian leaders steadily made attempts to bring Europeans to their side. In 1789 Kamehameha persuaded a European captain to supply him with arms; in 1794 Vancouver helped him to build a ship, the first to be assembled on the islands. In 1790 Kamehameha detained two sailors who had ended up in Hawaii, Isaac Davis and John Young, and refused to let them leave. "They were given wives, lands, and servants," writes the historian of Hawaii, Ralph S. Kuykendall, "and became in effect Hawaiian chiefs." After Kamehameha's death foreigners overwhelmed the Hawaiian kingdom, but during his lifetime he was skilled at turning them to his advantage, relying above all on Davis and Young for advice. Collaboration between islanders and Europeans was a two-sided process of accommodation in which both parties sought to profit and sometimes one, sometimes the other, operated from a position of strength.[2]

Ahutoru

The Bougainville voyagers had no European mediators to guide them into native cultures: absent were the missionaries, colonial hands, or métis to guide and translate. Instead they needed to begin to spin their own web of intermediaries. One of the ways they did so was by taking a native on board. This was an old practice: in 1534 Jacques Cartier took two Indian boys to France and left behind two French boys to learn the local language; in 1562 Michel de Montaigne traveled to Rouen in order to have a chance to see and talk to some visiting Amerindians, an incident he relates in his essay "On Cannibals," his protest against European derision toward indigenous peoples.[3] Authentic natives proved as nothing else could that a European voyager had actually been to someplace new, and they provided entertainment for kings and courtiers.

From the beginning there was a double function to bringing back natives: they were partly scientific sample, partly circus display. They continued to have this double function during the late nineteenth and early twentieth centuries. In the first part of the century George Catlin traveled around the United States and painted Indians of different tribes, assembling his "Indian Gallery" of paintings that permitted viewers to compare indigenous peoples' features and costumes; in search of the financial reward that eluded him, Catlin took a troupe of Indians to Europe, where they danced for French and British royalty before the show went bankrupt. Before and after 1900 native exhibitions were a part of world's fairs, with the Smithsonian Institute helping to import people for Americans to gawk at.

William Mariner in native Tongan dress.

Oceanians cornered—and sometimes kidnapped—Europeans, too. Kamehameha was not the only island ruler to do so when he held Davis and Young against their will. In 1806, on Tongatapu, Finau 'Ulukálala II detained William Mariner, who served as his advisor and successfully organized his military forces before escaping and returning to London in 1811. (With the help of a physician—yet another mediator in the network linking island societies to literate Europeans—Mariner wrote a narrative of his years in Tonga that was greatly admired by Chamisso.) Melville fictionalized his own experience of captivity in the Marquesas in his first novel, *Typee*.[4]

Bougainville took a native back to France, a young man named Ahutoru whom Ereti, a chief, urged the French to take with them as they departed. The surgeon on board the *Étoile*, a plainspoken and reliable witness named François Vivez, reported that for the first few days as they sailed away from Tahiti, Ahutoru wanted to guide them by the stars to an island with attractive women, for "he knew very well that that was our weakness." Ahutoru frustrated his hosts by proving unable to remember or pronounce more than a few words of French. Commerson, who noted almost nothing about him in his journal, later thought that this inability proved the youth's superiority, writing in his famous letter that Ahutoru was refusing to descend from the perfect clarity of his language to the muddled complexity of a European tongue. It severely limited, however, his usefulness as an informant. The voyagers made only a few comments about him in their journals for the rest of the trip. There is one illuminating entry by Bougainville from September 3–7, 1768, when the ship called at the Dutch settlement on the island of Buru in the Moluccas (today part of Indonesia):

I should say a word regarding the impression that the sight of this European settlement made on our Cytherean. He must have been greatly surprised, as one can imagine, to see men of our color, houses, gardens, great numbers and varieties of domestic animals, and an open and familiar display of hospitality. He comported himself energetically with the Dutch. He began by making it clear to them that in his country he was a chief who was traveling for pleasure with his friends. On his visits, on his walks and while eating he tried to copy us exactly. I didn't take him along on my first visit. He thought this was because he has knock-knees and insisted on being carried by sailors to compensate for this. He asked us if Paris was as beautiful as this trading station.

One would like to know how Bougainville knew that Ahutoru was embarrassed about the bend of his knees. Did he point to them? Did he ask to cover them? Was it his knees or something else he had in mind? Was the word "knee" in the small vocabulary that they had mastered of one another's languages? Question marks hang over the knock-knees, never to be resolved. It is easier to imagine most of the rest: Ahutoru annoyed that he was not invited to go on shore right away; his insistence on precedence over the sailors; his surprise at all he saw; his self-confidence and quickness to imitate the manners of his hosts. Gestures would have sufficed to convey Ahutoru's firm sense of social superiority.[5]

Bougainville proudly paraded Ahutoru around Versailles and Paris after the ship's return in March 1769. He took him along for audiences with the Duc de Choiseul and with the Duc de Praslin. When the king received Bougainville, it was with Ahutoru at his side. Mme de Choiseul adopted Ahutoru as her special favorite and befriended him for the rest of his eleven-month stay in France. Bougainville brought him along for a visit with Buffon at the Royal Garden; philosophes like D'Alembert, Diderot, and Holbach had their chance to see him; so did Commerson's friend and patron, Lalande. Charles-Marie de La Condamine, a famous scientific traveler in his own right and an insatiable curiosity-seeker, took a great interest in Ahutoru and twice dropped in on Bougainville at home in order to spend time with the young visitor. La Condamine brought along Jacob-Rodrigue Pereire, a royal interpreter known for his ability to tutor the congenitally deaf in the art of speaking. The interviews lasted fifteen minutes each, since a longer examination would try Ahutoru's patience. La Condamine wrote down a precise physical description of Ahutoru. They showed him a picture of a near-naked Venus, and he repeated after his teachers the French names of the different body parts, pointing toward the one that was hidden and softly intoning "eros, eros." La Condamine called him a "savage" and Bougainville protested, leading to an argument over the Tahitians' degree of civilization. La Condamine tested whether Ahutoru could comprehend the effects of a horn and glasses on hearing and vision and, satisfied with the result, concluded, "He seems to be intelligent" *(il paraît avoir de la pénétration)*. The scientists discussed a Tahitian expression for blessing one who has sneezed and tested his French pronunciation. It was agreed that Pereire would write up observations on the Tahitian's ability to articulate for inclusion in Bougainville's voyage account. Rousseau's call for accurate reporting by the leading scientists of the day came a little closer to fulfillment.[6]

Two outsiders made notes on Ahutoru that help round out our knowledge of what contemporaries could learn from him. Baron Godefroy Van Swieten, an Austrian diplomat posted in Paris, wrote, "His buttocks bear marks of nobility that are stamped on in that country with a hot iron, as one does in our part of the world to horses. It is hard to convince him to wear clothes precisely because that hides his distinguished origins, and he thinks people will have less respect for him." Louis Petit de Bachaumont, a man of letters with a dislike for Bougainville, noted in his memoirs that Bougainville was making the rounds with his "savage." While he did not find

Ahutoru remarkable-looking in any way, he did not have a bad impression of him: "He is strong and well built, he isn't at all lacking in intelligence, he still expresses himself poorly in French and mixes his language with the latter." Ahutoru, he continued, had no appreciation for the palace of Versailles, liked French food, ate and drank "with great presence of mind," and did not mind getting tipsy. But "his great passion is women, whom he mingles with indiscriminately. The same is true for his countrymen."[7]

A few consistent impressions run through these reports. One is Ahutoru's interest in women. One has to consider the effects of a meeting of minds on this point, as Vivez's journal makes clear: did Ahutoru want to stop off on an island with attractive women for his own sake? Or rather, as Vivez suggested, because he thought it would please his hosts? A second note is Ahutoru's deeply entrenched conviction of his own high social rank and personal worth. One wonders to what extent the French preoccupation with rank heightened this feature in the accounts, exaggerating his behavior and their perceptions of it. Exaggerated or not, it carried him through one trial after another. He left Paris in March 1770 and died of smallpox on November 6, 1771, during the return passage via Mauritius and Réunion to Tahiti.[8]

Bougainville leaned on Ahutoru for his analysis of Tahiti in his voyage account. Ahutoru named European fruits and vegetables that Bougainville passed in front of him after their return. He described how the Tahitians warred with the inhabitants of neighboring islands, killing all the men and male children and taking the wives and daughters back to their own beds. Bougainville questioned him closely about his religion and was able to determine that the Tahitians were (in his view) very superstitious; that priests had great authority among them; that they worshipped more than one deity, "some beneficent, others mischievous"; and that they sacrificed human victims during a certain phase of the moon. Yet the whole subject of religion had to be approached skeptically, cautioned Bougainville, "as there is no subject in which it is more easy to be deceived by appearances." He was on firmer ground when it came to discussing the social order on Tahiti. While the voyagers were on the island, wrote Bougainville,

> We took them to be almost equal in rank amongst themselves; or at last enjoying a liberty, which was only subject to the laws established for their common happiness. I was mistaken; the distinction of ranks is very great at Taiti, and the disproportion very tyrannical. The kings and grandees have power of life and death over their servants and slaves, and I am inclined to believe, they have the same barbarous prerogative with regard to the common people, whom they call *Tata-einou,* vile men; so much is certain, that the victims for human sacrifices are taken from this class of people. Flesh and fish are reserved for the tables of the great; the commonalty live upon mere fruits and pulse [legumes].[9]

Even if language remained a barrier to the end of Bougainville's acquaintance with Ahutoru, he was able to make a leap beyond Commerson's understanding of the island. Bougainville's account of Tahiti turned at this point into an education in disillusionment. "Natural man," even on this blessed island that Bougainville continued to praise, was not a natural democrat, but inhabited a society that had its own social divisions.

Bougainville, aided by the Tahitian's own quest for knowledge, brought back Ahutoru in a spirit of serious scientific inquiry—in the spirit, one might say, of Rousseau's call for a better class of travelers and more reliable observations. He may have returned with a Tahitian in part because he could guess the sensation it would make, but he also put great effort into taking care of him and, if we can believe his own testimony, spent a third of his personal fortune to pay for his unsuccessful return to Tahiti. Despite all the costs of transporting him, Bougainville and his philosophe friends seem to have had no inkling at all of the effect of taking an isolated individual from one environment and setting him down in another, unfamiliar one. That a culture is inseparable from its time, place, and social setting, that a single individual cannot carry it as a kind of nimbus to another place, that an individual and his appearance and actions change in changed circumstances—considerations like these seem to have been completely alien to the milieu of the salons. For this reason there is always an undercurrent of frustration in the reports about Ahutoru. The voyagers claimed to have visited New Cythera, but before them was an ordinary human being. They had brought back a piece of Tahiti—but at their door it changed like Cinderella's carriage into something everyday. La Condamine did his best to study Ahutoru as an object of scientific investigation. But the object of the "experiment" seems in retrospect to have been less Ahutoru than the philosophes' own conception of culture.

Tupaia, Mai, Mahine

When George Forster reflected back on his voyage experiences, he gave his readers a careful account of the sources for his descriptions of island societies. Two Tahitian men stood for the extremes of local expertise and entertainment value that one could obtain from native informants: Tupaia and Mai. With a third, Mahine, he developed the mixture of friendship and mutual interest that quickens insight into a foreign culture.

Tupaia was a Raiatean priest encountered by Cook whom Forster knew only from hearsay of Cook's first circumnavigation. The priest boarded the *Endeavour* in June 1769. Cook at first refused to take him, thinking the government would never support him, but Banks offered to care for him at his own expense. He wrote in his diary, "Thank heaven I have a sufficiency & I do not know why I may not keep him as a curiosity, as well as some of my neighbours do lions & tygers at a larger expence than he will probably ever put me to; the amusement I shall have in his future conversation & the benefit he will be of to this ship, as well as what he may be if another should be sent into these seas, will I think fully repay me." Several Tahitians offered to go with them, but the voyagers had already gotten to know Tupaia well enough to have confidence in his usefulness. "We found him to be a very intelligent person," noted Cook in his journal despite his previous doubts about the wisdom of taking him along, "and to know more of the Geography of the Islands situated in these seas, their produce and the religion laws and customs of the inhabitants than any one we had met with and was the likeliest person to answer our purpose." Banks and Cook chose well; Tupaia had traveled widely in Polynesia and was a bearer of Tahitian geographic and navigational knowledge. He provided Cook with an account of almost 130 islands and set down a chart with 74, including locations in Tuamotu, the Marquesas, Tonga, and New Zealand. Cook also valued him as a guide to Tahitian politics and religion. Tupaia was supposed to go with the *Endeavour* back to England, but was a victim of the epidemic diseases that carried away many of the ship's European passengers too during their stay in Batavia. Although George Forster did not have the opportunity to meet him, he saw a copy of the famous chart, which was reproduced as well in his father's voyage report. Tupaia also remained a presence for Forster and the other *Resolution* voyagers as islanders who remembered him from the previous voyage asked after him.[10]

A more famous informant whom George Forster did know from his own voyage was Mai. Like Ahutoru, he became a European celebrity. Lieutenant Tobias Furneaux took him on board the *Resolution*'s consort ship, the *Adventure*. Cook had a rather modest opinion of his intelligence and noted that he came from the lowest social stratum. During Mai's visit of two years, Furneaux took him to the Admiralty; Banks took him for an audience with King George; the Earl of Sandwich entertained him. Mai did not master very much English, but like Ahutoru he was quick to adopt European manners and knew how to please his exalted hosts. Cook's third circumnavigation, departing in July 1776, returned him to the Society Islands. Forster delivered a balanced judgment of Mai. He thought it unfortunate that such a plain and unremarkable person became Tahiti's representative to England, but enumerated his limitations without disparaging him: "The qualities of his heart and head resembled those of his countrymen in general; he was not an extraordinary genius like Tupaia, but he was warm in his affections, grateful, and humane; he was polite, intelligent, lively, and volatile." Forster's preface blamed the frivolousness of high society for amusing Mai without improving him in any way or making him beneficial to Tahitian society.[11]

The Forsters had a chance to do better with Mahine, a young man from Bora Bora who joined the *Resolution* in mid-September 1773 and returned to the Society Islands in June 1774. There was something luminous and winning about him from the moment he came on board. He entered their company as they were visiting Raiatea, their last stop before sailing away from Tahiti and its neighbors. "A very handsome youth, about seventeen years of age, who went by the name of O-Hedeedee, and who appeared to be of the better sort of people by his complexion and good garments, addressed himself to me, expressing a desire to embark for England," recalled George Forster. George tried to dissuade him, pointing out the cold and hardships he would have to endure, but the handsome youth was not to be deterred, and Cook granted his permission too. Who can speak for Mahine's real motives? Forster adds that "a number of his friends joined with him to desire his admittance into our ship." Was it a personal decision or a collective interest in advancing an alliance with the Englanders that landed him on board? Departure was difficult, with "O-Hedeedee" and his friends shedding tears. Nonetheless, observed Lieutenant Charles Clerke, "the good Lad adher'd to his resolution with a manly and commendable perseverance and attended us with an aching heart but apparently a chearfull spirit." However difficult the departure was, he gained the universal respect and admiration of his shipmates. Born Mahine, he had exchanged his name (a regular Society Island practice to affirm friendships or alliances) for "Hedeedee" or "Odiddy," but the Forsters preferred the original. He was not just a person of rank and good looks, but had an intelligence that made him a valuable informant and mediator for their nine months' journey together.[12]

Mahine won over George Forster with his unaffected moral sensibility. In New Zealand on November 23, 1773, a group of officers went on shore and saw Maoris with the dismembered parts of a recently killed boy. One of the officers, Lieutenant Richard Pickersgill, bought the head and brought it back onto the ship. A piece of flesh had been cut out, broiled, and eaten in the officers' presence. When Cook walked onto the scene, he suppressed his own horror and indignation, and—to settle the question of whether such a thing really took place—ordered that another piece of flesh be cooked, and the Maoris "repeated the experiment once more in his presence." Some of the Europeans were amused; others were so incensed that they were ready to open fire; others vomited; the rest lamented what they had witnessed. "But the sensibility of Mahine . . . shone out with superior lustre among us. Born and bred in a country where the inhabitants have already emerged from the darkness of barbarism, and are united by the bonds of society, this scene filled his mind with horror."

His eyes brimmed with tears and he retreated into the cabin, where he grieved for hours. "As soon as he saw us, he expressed his concern for the unhappy parents of the victim. This turn which his reflections had taken, gave us infinite pleasure; it spoke a human heart, filled with the warmest sentiments of social affection, and habituated to sympathize with its fellow-creatures." (Forster himself did not demonize the Maoris; over the course of several pages he educated his readers in the severely confined circumstances of acts of Maori cannibalism and reminded them of Europeans' more calculated and deliberate capacity for cruelty.) Mahine burst into tears on another occasion too, in the Marquesas Islands on April 8, 1774. The *Resolution* had barely arrived when an islander made off with an iron stanchion, provoking an officer who had just come up to the deck to shoot the man through the head. Forster thought that Mahine's spontaneous show of feeling should "put those civilized Europeans to the blush, who have humanity so often on their lips, and so seldom in their hearts." On Easter Island Mahine enjoyed bargaining for small carved human figures, which he thought would be highly valued when he got back to Tahiti. He pronounced the people good despite the poverty of their country, stimulating Forster once again to praise his humane feelings and sound judgment.[13]

Forster relied heavily on gesture and display of feeling for his portrayal of Mahine. He never gives us a clear description of the exchanges that took place: how sustained their conversations were, how communication improved over the months they spent together, when he came up against limits of vocabulary or understanding, or when he became aware of errors. The transparency of Mahine's emotions in New Zealand and the Marquesas, with or without words, made for an easy contrast to the artificiality and concealment of motives that Forster wished to criticize in European behavior.

A process of learning was certainly taking place, however. The

Forsters had set out for Tahiti much better informed than Bougainville: they had vocabularies from the first Cook voyage, they had veterans of that voyage who could give them some link to the spoken language, and they had Bougainville's own list of Tahitian words. Even though George Forster does not give a detailed account of his relationship with Mahine, he does relate one important stage. As the *Resolution* headed south toward the Antarctic in December 1773, George and his father worked with Mahine to revise and improve on their previous knowledge of Tahitian and to gather information that could prepare them for further inquiries on their return visit. Cook's journal is more informative and makes it clear that even before December, the voyagers could have substantial discussions with him. In October Cook asked him whether it was true, as Bougainville maintained, that Tahitians could freely take fruit from trees or houses, and Mahine replied that anyone who did so would be put to death; so much for the Commersonian illusion of a communist society. In the same month Cook made interesting observations about what Mahine did *not* know. He could not understand a single sentence in Tongan. The barrier was not so much vocabulary as pronunciation, they discovered, and with some application the Europeans could understand more than he could. Cook was thoughtful enough to reflect that Mahine had never been beyond the Society Islands before and lacked the experience to make the transition to an unknown dialect. By March 1774, though, Cook, jotting down impressions of Easter Island, reported that Mahine "understood their language (tho' but very imperfectly) much better than any of us." Initially skeptical about the value of taking him along, Cook testified in his journal to the value of having a Polynesian collaborator on board.[14]

By the time of their return to Tahiti, Mahine was an indispensable interpreter for conversation with the islanders. Even so, as they parted both sides had to exercise their ingenuity. "Just as he was go-

ing out of the Ship he ask'd me to Tattaow some Parou for him in order to Shew to any other Europeans who might touch here, I readily
complied with his request by giving him a Certificate of his good
behaviour, the time and were he had been with us and recommended
him to the Notice of those who might come to these isles after me."
"The meaning" of the Tahitian-English phrase, notes Cook's editor,
"is obvious: mark some speech or words—write him a testimonial, in
fact." It was obvious to those who had dedicated many months to
learning to speak to one another, but strange to anyone less studious,
less skilled. Cook's sentence repays a careful reading, especially as his
written English has become a little strange and reminds us in its own
way of the work of translation between people of different times as
well as different places. The narratives of Cook and the Forsters are
already a long way off from the mutual incomprehension of Ahutoru
and the philosophes.[15]

Elliot de Castro, Marin, Kadu

Chamisso depended on two Europeans to serve as his guides into
Hawaiian culture. Neither had emerged from the Anglo-American
community of foreigners, however; instead they came from an entirely different source, the Hispanic diaspora scattered around the
Pacific. During their stay in San Francisco in October 1816 the *Rurik*
voyagers agreed to take on board several prisoners of the Spanish,
including three deserters from the Russian-American Company
and John Elliot de Castro, who had served as a commercial agent
aboard a Russian-American smuggling ship. He springs to life from
Chamisso's pages like some fantastic creation of his literary friends—
and indeed Chamisso compares this tiny man to a figure in a story
by the Romantic novelist Jean Paul. To read Chamisso's description
of Elliot de Castro and his odyssey is to glimpse the circulation of

people around the Pacific: "of mixed English and Portuguese ancestry . . . a devoted Catholic . . . married in Rio-Janeiro and employed as a surgeon in a hospital there." Elliot was obsessed with making money, Chamisso tells us, and this obsession had driven him across the seas to Hawaii. Before leaving to enter the service of the fur traders, he had spent two years there fishing for pearls in the Pearl River in Oahu. During this time he had also become personal physician to Kamehameha, who had given him some land. He was now hoping to resume his life in Hawaii. During the three weeks' journey to Hawaii after their departure from California on November 1, he became Chamisso's language teacher. Chamisso eloquently described what it meant to make the leap from written information to personal introduction to another culture:

> My discussions with our guest on the voyage across were incalculably instructive to me. To be sure, I had read what was written about the Sandwich Islands and had collected a good deal of data about their present condition, especially with regard to the commerce for which they have become a center. But there I had an O-Waihian (*Naja haore* [*nai'a haole*], porpoise of the white men) before me who had lived with and among the people, who had belonged to a definite caste and from whom I could hear the language and learn about the customs. I used the opportunity industriously, and I was really well prepared, and even not completely ignorant of the childlike language, to visit the residence of this engaging people, at that time still not deprived of its natural character. To his benevolent teacher, Mr. John Elliot de Castro, his willing pupil gladly and cordially extends his gratitude.[16]

Chamisso's second teacher was Don Francisco de Paula Marin, whom he met on his very first day in Honolulu, November 28, 1816. As a boy Marin had brought some fruit and vegetables to a ship in port (in San Francisco, thought Chamisso); the sailors had given him alcohol, he had fallen asleep, and by the time he awoke the ship was at sea. He went ashore on the Hawaiian Islands, where he became a "chief of high repute," a planter and a merchant supplier for the ships that landed there. He had no time for Chamisso when ships were in harbor and did not fulfill his promise to write a memorandum for Chamisso between the *Rurik*'s first and second visit. But Chamisso found him helpful and perspicacious in the time they could share. He relied on Marin for his understanding of the social system of the islands.[17] Instead of having to proceed from guesswork based on visual impressions of islander behavior, Chamisso could rely on the informed testimony of an insider. With Elliot and Marin to serve as mediators, his visit to Hawaii had a different character from Commerson's or Forster's visits to Tahiti. It was anything but an immediate "encounter" between the scientist and a new world; thanks to these informants he was tutored in local lore. The aid of mediators raised his reporting to an altogether different plane from his predecessors', helping him to avoid their speculative fantasies and grounding him deeper in the motives of the people he met. To be tutored was not to be wholly free of fantasy or homegrown prejudice, but it did help him to observe precisely and well during his short stay. Elliot de Castro and Marin are reminders that northern Europeans did not confront a radically new world in the Pacific, but moved into a region of age-old Spanish, Dutch, and Portuguese settlements that benefited their more recent explorations.

Micronesian waters were farther removed from Spanish settlement—and yet here, too, an earlier history of exchange came to Chamisso's aid. On February 23, 1817, the *Rurik* was steering in the direction of Aur, an atoll in the Marshall Islands, when several native boats approached them and islanders came on board the ship. Along with them were two men from the Caroline Islands, to the west, who had settled in the Radak island group. One of them, Kadu, suddenly declared his intention to stay on the *Rurik,* hoping that it would eventually drop him off closer to home. The Rurikers took him on board—not a small concession for the captain, who had to think carefully about the space and provisions available on a small ship. Kadu accompanied them from tropical Radak all the way to their northern goal of Unalaska, from there to Hawaii and finally, at the beginning of November 1817, back to the Radak islands, where he decided to stay.[18]

Chamisso named Kadu "one of the finest characters I have met in my life, one of the people I have loved most." He was not the only one to be so taken by this guest aboard the *Rurik.* "Where is he? What is he doing? Is he still alive? Surely he sometimes thinks of us! It is sad to think that there is a being you love but will *never* see again." So, after the voyage, wrote the ship's artist, Choris, to Chamisso. His portrait of Kadu, one of his best illustrations, became the frontispiece to one of the volumes of Kotzebue's account of the world voyage; it sparkles with Kadu's alert intelligence. Chamisso devoted a chapter to him in his first account of the voyage. Like George Forster with Mahine, the *Rurik* travelers managed to build a bridge across cultures with Kadu, starting from a point of near-inability to converse and ending with a shared language and mutual affection.[19]

Kadu came from Ulea, one of the Caroline Islands, south of Guam. He was not of noble birth, wrote Chamisso, but won the confidence of his "king" Toua, who sent him on journeys to other islands. In 1804 an English sailor settled on Ulea for a time, and Kadu met him before the Englishman and his native wife and child left on a visiting European ship. A storm blew Kadu's boat off course on one of his journeys, and after many months at sea he finally reached the Radak atolls. Kadu was hardly less cosmopolitan than Chamisso and Choris; he too had learned to settle among a foreign people and establish a position of esteem among them. He had heard much about

Kadu in European dress. Drawing by Choris. Otto von
Kotzebue, *Entdeckungs-Reise in die Süd-See und nach der
Berings-Strasse* (1821).

Europeans, and one of their ships had visited Ulea during one of his
periods of absence. On the strange world of the ship he adapted skill-
fully, at first making the mistake of imitating the captain and treating
the sailors as slaves, but quickly catching his own errors and taking
his place among the officers and gentlemen. Although he learned
to enjoy wine, he was careful to drink in moderation after observing drunken behavior on the Aleutian island of Unalaska. He had,
wrote Chamisso, "Gemüt, Verstand, Witz" (feeling, intelligence, wit).
The Rurikers were unable, even though he was curious, to teach him
how to read. He was open to instruction about the social order in Eu-

rope, its habits, customs, and arts; he was also a close observer of the new world of nature that the northward journey opened up to him. Chamisso underlined two features of his character: his revulsion toward bloodshed, although he had fought for his Radak friends and was ready to take up arms to help the Rurikers, and his delicacy toward women. Kadu's sense of humor, and the underlying kindness that accompanied his jests, made him a favorite on board the ship. He was able, noted Chamisso with approval, to appreciate the Rurikers' efforts to add to the flora and fauna of the islands they visited, and they returned him to Radak with a shovel in hand, determined to care for the plants and animals they left behind.[20]

Chamisso acknowledged Kadu's role as a "scientific authority" who became his teacher for Radak and the Caroline Islands. He left a detailed description of their cooperation. On the trip from Radak to Unalaska, teacher and questioner struggled to understand each other. First they had to piece together a linguistic core from some shared Polynesian and Oceanian words. Soon they could relate factual questions and answers—but to make the leap from there to a spontaneous, elastic conversation, in which Kadu freely related what he knew, was more difficult. Kadu's answers did not go beyond Chamisso's questions. Chamisso used the description of the Caroline Islands from the account of an early-eighteenth-century missionary to question his friend more closely. Pleased and astonished by what Chamisso could ask, Kadu confirmed, corrected, and added comments that served as the starting point for new questions. Serendipity as well as system added to the sum of Chamisso's knowledge. Once when Chamisso was talking to Eschscholtz, the ship's doctor, in the polyglot language of the ship, they started counting in Spanish; Kadu, who they thought was asleep next to them, spontaneously started counting in Spanish too, correctly and with a good accent. Kadu sang a song of a country called Waghal, a land of iron and rivers and high mountains, inhabited by Europeans and visited by Caroline Islanders; it remained a puzzle until they landed on Waghal itself, which the Europeans knew as Guam, and an acquaintance there instantly recognized the song. Every spring a convoy of boats from Kadu's native Ulea made the journey to Guam in order to trade. A Spaniard on Guam whom Chamisso later met, Don Luis de Torres—yet another of those Spanish mediators so critical to Chamisso's ethnography—made a visit to Ulea in 1804 to win their confidence, learn their language, and preside over a traffic that was still flourishing at the time of the *Rurik* voyage.[21]

At first sight, then, Kadu appeared to come from a completely foreign world; in the end it turned out that he came from an island that was unusual within the Carolines for its contact with the Spanish-speaking world and was altogether more worldly than the Marshall Islanders, who were farther east and more removed from seagoing traffic with outsiders. Chamisso was the beneficiary of Don Luis de Torres: Kadu greeted the *Rurik* fearlessly at their first meeting because this earlier relationship had familiarized him with Europeans, in contrast to his companions from Aur, who (Chamisso later learned) thought the *Rurik* travelers were cannibals. It was hard going for Chamisso and Kadu to work up their level of communication, but they were starting from well-cultivated common ground.

Kadu exemplifies changes in the informer–ethnographer relationship that had taken place since the time of Ahutoru. In the 1760s there was no common vocabulary to work from; by the time of the *Rurik* voyage fifty years later, the Pacific had become a widely trafficked basin with a circulation of beachcombers, merchants, and sailors on the move from place to place, doing the work of knitting together alien cultures. While few travelers were as reflective as Chamisso, there was nonetheless a body of ethnographic lore that enhanced his skill at working with his informant. A circulation of travelers and body of knowledge had sprung up that enriched the possibilities for conversation.

Ali'i and Kings

While Europeans clearly dominated the informants they took on board, they had to approach island leaders with circumspection. Tahiti and Hawaii in particular had robust elites with their own deeply entrenched social protocols; Europeans had to defer to them in some measure if they wished to get a landing-place for repairs and refreshment. How Polynesians and Europeans perceived each other was strongly conditioned by the fit between their social expectations.

One of the most powerful social groups in Polynesian societies was that which Hawaiians called the *ali'i* and the Tahitians *ari'i*, which had its counterparts throughout the vast island region. These were the chiefs (the usual translation) or aristocrats or nobles or lords—every equivalent has its own charms and distortions—at the top of the social hierarchy. In these highly status-conscious societies, *ali'i* and their variants throughout Polynesia claimed descent from the gods; sacred status was pervasive; bloodlines established rank. At the end of the nineteenth century Augustin Krämer, a German naval physician turned anthropologist who took the trouble to find out about these things in Samoa, transcribed chants memorializing genealogies of many centuries.[22] Polynesian societies were *hierarchies* in the original Greek sense of the word: a sacred order in which ascending stages grew purer and more divine. Endowed with religious as well as social superiority, the *ali'i* were mysterious and truly "other" or different from common mortals: filled with divine power and separated by prohibitions that kept commoners from getting too close. Tahiti and Hawaii were the most hierarchical of all Polynesian societies, and their *ali'i* occupied ranks of corresponding grandeur. Real-life social relations, though, did not correspond neatly to this exalted conception of the social order. Genealogical lines always allow for interpretation and reinterpretation, and in practice intense social jockeying took place as lesser men and women battled their way up the social scale and those on top struggled to stay in place. *Ali'i* were made as well as born.[23]

Europeans in the late eighteenth and early nineteenth centuries were approaching societies intriguingly similar and strangely different from what they knew from home. Their societies, too, were hierarchical. Before 1789 the legal ranking of continental Europeans gave the social order its structure. There were basic differences: noble leadership was not pervasively sacred in Europe, and it was guaranteed by written documentation, two among many distinctions that should make us cautious about analogies between distant worlds. Nonetheless European visitors could soon make out the outlines of Polynesian social hierarchies, and they provoked commentary and cooperation. Polynesians could say the same thing: their elites were quick to discern the hierarchy on the navy vessels and to align themselves with the officers and captains.

Both elites were experiencing challenges and transformations. On the European side, overturning legal hierarchy was the central achievement of the French Revolution, and rescuing what one could of hierarchy—as social status, even if no longer as legally inscribed privilege—was the dominant ambition of conservative political leaders after 1815. Nobles scrambled to survive, with the clever and flexible rising to new positions of prominence while others lost out. Visitors to Polynesia came with highly charged beliefs about hierarchy and could hardly avoid judging places like Tahiti and Hawaii without relying on the experiences they brought from home. At the same time, by intruding on these societies they began to transform them. Agile families of Polynesian rank profited from European weapons and commerce at the expense of their less adept rivals. This complicated meeting of elites offered plenty of opportunity for character development on either side. Whatever impressions made it to the printed page of travelers' accounts were the outcome of a many-sided, many-layered encounter.[24]

From the European vocabulary of hierarchy, kingship was especially pertinent to Polynesia. By the late eighteenth century, European monarchies were both traditional and modernizing. They grounded their legitimacy in genealogy and religion, but also declared themselves to be the supreme patrons of scientific enterprise. Captains and naturalists depended, sometimes directly, on their sovereigns' review of their planning and results. As this interest in the sciences suggests, these monarchs were aggressive entrepreneurs in competition with other heads of state and were challenged, despite their political pretensions to sovereignty, by headstrong aristocrats, the wealthy, the educated, and the rebellious members of popular classes. The term "enlightened absolutism" used to describe Continental monarchies of the late eighteenth century contains a bundle of contradictions, for enlightened monarchies were using critical reason to support obedience to traditional authority. From our postrevolutionary perspective, we tend to think of these monarchies as dying institutions, about to give way to a new democratic order. Yet in the late eighteenth century the autocracies of Frederick the Great, Catherine the Great, and Joseph II of Austria were anything but feeble; on the contrary, they were remarkably successful at forcing through "revolution from above," in the famous Prussian phrase. The right blend of traditional and modern elements provided social cohesion as they fired up their economies and expanded their territories. Captains on naval vessels imitated their monarchs with the precision of a map and the brutality of a whip.[25]

In Polynesia, monarchy was a European instrument of power that had local counterparts. Ambitious island leaders were quick to translate European conceptions of monarchy into their own idiom. The establishment of a monarchy depended on many things beyond any individual's control, beginning with Europeans interested in introducing it, local leaders skilled at collaborating and appropriating it, and favorable local political conditions. Monarchy-building was especially successful in the Tongan Islands. In the early nineteenth century visitors had to contend with the conflicts of local leaders vying for tribute, warfare that could be dangerous or profitable for outsiders. During the 1820s, Wesleyan Methodist missionaries attached themselves to the paramount chief of Ha'apai, Tāufa'āhau, hoping he would be their agent for a policy of conversion from the elite down. By doing so, they set in motion a policy that one recent scholar has aptly summarized as a transition from kinship to kingship.[26] Centralization of political and sacred authority cut through older webs of kin group competition and alliance and created newly efficient engines of power. Under the name of George I, Tāufa'āhau became the founder of a dynasty that has outlasted most of its European counterparts and continues to the present day.

Tonga was not the only place where local leaders successfully transformed kingship from a European into a Polynesian political institution. In Tahiti and Hawaii too, Europeans and ambitious local leaders successfully collaborated to create local monarchies. These monarchies in turn had an impact on European public opinion: both visitors and readers of travel reports were fascinated by the royal families, who came to stand for the greatness and flaws of their peoples.

Kingship in Tahiti: The Pomares

Tahiti has special importance as the place where Captain Cook and his successors first crafted the British policy in Oceania of inventing local monarchies. Cook visited Tahiti on all three of his circumnavigations. On the first voyage Joseph Banks encouraged a playful classicizing of the breathtaking landscape and the impressive men that they met, whom the visitors gave names, recorded in Cook's journal entry of April 13, 1769, like Hercules and Lycurgus. Cook also gave more serious consideration to the kind of political order he was facing. In his systematic account of the polity of Tahiti, dated July 1769, he wrote that the island was divided into two districts or "kingdoms" frequently at war with each other, each presided over by a leader "whome we call a King"—but he was quick to note too that this figure "may be reverenced as a father but he is neither fear'd nor respected as a Monarch." Cook left the first voyage using European terms as a convenience, but aware that he was trying to puzzle out a different kind of polity.[27]

During his second world voyage Cook crystallized an ideology of native monarchy. On his second visit to Tahiti during this voyage, he anchored in Matavai Bay on April 22, 1774. Cook landed not with the intention of staying long, but "to know the error of the Watch from the known Longitude of this place." His friend "Otou the King" (later Pomare I), attended by many chiefs, came on board the *Resolution* two days later, presenting "Ten or a Dozn Hogs which made them exceeding welcome" and receiving presents in their turn. After receiving the hogs, Cook began to revise his plans to leave soon, noting buildings and canoes that had not been there eight months before, with "several large hogs near every house and every other Sign of a rising state." So he decided to settle in for a while, using Matavai Bay as a welcome spot to repair his ships.[28]

After this auspicious beginning came a fresh revelation of his hosts' majesty. On the morning of Tuesday, April 26, he set out for nearby "Oparre" with the Forsters and some officers "to pay Otoo a formal Viset by appointment." As they approached Pare in one of their small boats, they observed a fleet of canoes: to their surprise, "upwards of three-hundred of them all ranged in good order for some distance along the Shore all Compleatly equip'd and Man'd and a vast Crowd of Men on the Shore."[29]

They landed briefly, but not seeing Otoo they went out to sea again, where they got a fuller look at the fleet. The departure of Mahine made it difficult to converse with Tahitians, but even without his help they could not fail to be awed by the sight. They counted 160 large double canoes, "decorated with Flags, Streamers &c so that the whole made a grand and Noble appearance such as was never seen before in this Sea." There were also 170 smaller double canoes. In all, Cook estimated that there were no less than 7,760 fighting men. They were assembling, he learned later, for an expedition against Moorea, "whose Chief had revolted from Otou his Lawfull Sovereign." By now, as his biographer noted, Cook was assuming an English-style relationship of dependence between monarch and nobility that did not exist on the island. A model was emerging of Tahiti as a single, unified monarchy. Yet it was not just Cook who was imposing this design on the Tahitians. "Otoo" invited him to stay, encouraged his patronage, and impressed him with his authority. The Tahitian dynasty collaborated from the start.[30]

Cook's published account of these days further fashioned the ideology of monarchy. For the most part it followed the journal rather closely. But Cook went beyond it in language his readers would easily and eagerly apprehend. He regretted how little he knew about Tahitian political organization beyond its broadest outlines. This did not stop him, however, from asserting that the island was formerly one kingdom that had only recently divided, fitting into an obvious European parallel: "We, however, are sure that it is of the feudal kind; and, if we may judge from what we have seen, it has sufficient stability, and is by no means badly constructed." He topped his observations with a startling advertisement for Tahitian government:

Notwithstanding this kind of kingly establishment, there was very little about Otoo's person or court, by which a stranger could distinguish the king from the subject. I seldom saw him dressed in any thing but a common piece of cloth wrapped round his loins; so that he seemed to avoid all unnecessary pomp, and even to demean himself more than any other of the *Earees.* I have seen him work at a paddle, in coming to and going from the ship, in common with the other paddlers; and even when some of his *Toutous* sat looking on. All have free access to him, and speak to him wherever they see him, without the least ceremony: such is the easy freedom which every individual of this happy isle enjoys. I have observed that the chiefs of these isles are more beloved by the bulk of the people, than feared. May we not from hence conclude, that the government is mild and equitable?

Cook was dressing up the Tahitian government as enlightened monarchy. Government was "mild" and "equitable"; the prince ruled for his people; like Frederick the Great, he seemed to be nothing more than their first servant. The enlightened paternalism of the European regimes that sent out eighteenth-century voyages had its counterpart in the benevolent Tahitian regime.[31]

How naturally the ideology of Tahitian monarchy came to Europeans can be seen from the reactions of George Forster. Radical republican though he was, he never for a moment doubted the reality of kingship on the island. As the *Resolution* approached Matavai Bay for the first time, Pomare I stood out from the crowd that greeted them from the shore as the one person whose shoulders were covered; Forster announced him to his readers as "O-Too, the king of the O-Taheitee-Nue (the Greater Taheitee)." His account of the next day described him as a regal figure:

O-Too was the tallest man whom we saw on the whole island which he governs, measuring six feet and three inches in height. His whole body was proportionately strong and well-made, without any tendency to corpulence. His head, notwithstanding a certain gloominess which seemed to express a fearful disposition, had a majestic and intelligent air, and there was great expression in his full black eyes. He wore strong whiskers, which with his beard, and a prodigious growth of curled hair, were all of a jetty black.

The same day Forster was a witness to a strange sight that only strengthened his belief that monarchy was a native Tahitian political institution. Tu's father bared his shoulders in the presence of his son. Forster was aware from Hawkesworth's account of the first Cook voyage that in Tahiti, eldest sons immediately succeeded on birth to their fathers' social status. This gesture of parental deference nevertheless startled him and inspired a political comment: "Thus, the ideas universally annexed to consanguinity, are suppressed in order to give greater weight to the regal dignity, and I cannot help thinking that such a sacrifice to political authority, argues a greater degree of civilization than has been allowed to the Taheitians by our former navigators." The oddness of this Tahitian custom, then, was well founded in reason, for it reinforced the primacy of the public order. Forster had numerous other opportunities to observe Tu during the first and second stay in Tahiti without ever challenging his regal status. He realized that the term "Aree" *(ari'i)* applied to many chiefs outside the "royal family," but this still did not shake his confidence that it applied especially to the Pomare family.[32]

Vancouver enhanced the status of the Pomares after his ship, the *Discovery,* anchored in Matavai Bay on Friday, December 30, 1791. A joyous welcome awaited them. Canoes laden with local goods swarmed around the ship; "the natives, with every assurance of friendship, and with expressions of the greatest joy at our arrival, were crowding on board." A friendly crowd—but as Vancouver knew, also potentially a pickpocketing crowd whose exuberance on board could turn from jubilant to menacing. The local authorities, however, provided for order; one or two natives, "although not principal chiefs," kept too many people from coming on board, "as that would be the best means to prevent thefts, and insure that amity and good fellowship which they appeared very solicitous to establish and support." Thus in Vancouver's recounting a mutual understanding united the elites, who knew how to establish friendship and do their business while controlling the masses.[33]

Once Vancouver and his party went on shore, the mechanisms of royalty went into play—though with a few unexpected twists. Pomare I, whom Vancouver had met with Cook in 1777, had removed himself to Moorea, "leaving his eldest son the supreme authority over this, and all the neighbouring islands." Vancouver and his co-commander, Lieutenant Broughton, then accepted an invitation "to pay our respects to his Otaheitean majesty." The new "king," the young "Otoo," was by now a boy of about nine or ten years old (guessed Vancouver) who was carried about on the shoulders of a man. He was "clothed in a piece of English red cloth, with ornaments of pigeons' feathers hanging over his shoulders." At their meeting, wrote Vancouver, a "ratification of peace and mutual friendship" was acknowledged on both sides.[34]

Vancouver's original intention was just one of getting fresh water and provisions, but like Cook before him, he began to enjoy the warmth of an invitation to stay longer, thought of wintering there before heading to America, and started arranging for repairs to his consort ship, the *Chatham*. A small boat took him to "Pomurrey" (Pomare I) on Moorea; there Vancouver exchanged gifts, receiving "cloth, hogs, fowls and vegetables," and distributing his gifts, "agreeably to the rank and situation of each individual." The old friends then went back to the *Discovery* for dinner, where Vancouver noted the Tahitians' alacrity "to adopt our manners and customs, and the avidity with which they sought spirituous liquors." In fact "Pomur-rey" managed to get rip-roaring drunk, downing a bottle of brandy which threw him into such violent convulsions that four strong men had to hold him down.[35]

This mixture of the dignified and the grotesque continued to characterize the meetings of British officers and the Tahitian "royal family." On Sunday, January 15, 1792, came the news that Matooara Mahow (Mahu), one of the elders of the family, had died, and Vancouver was invited to attend the funeral, with priests chanting prayers and the royal ladies screaming in lamentation and scratching themselves with shark's teeth. Afterward some "very young girls" performed a dance "in the wanton manner of the country." At one point a young man broke in and added his own "obscene though ludicrous" behavior, although, Vancouver tells us, when his "gentlemen" registered their disapproval, the girls finished their parts without exposing themselves below the waist. Menzies, Vancouver's naturalist, told the story differently: the man who jumped in during the dance amused his countrymen by exposing a large hernia. When the Europeans said they were disgusted, "the girls then went on & performd the part by exposing themselves below the waist." For his part Pomare I had to tolerate Vancouver's outbursts of rage and lashing of two Tahitians. Whatever the lapses in gentlemanly behavior on both sides, he and Vancouver were able to part as friends, with Pomare I aware that the British had the means to satisfy his growing political ambitions and Vancouver full of praise for a character who had seemed timid before but had grown into the character of a king, majestic and intelligent.[36]

William Bligh penetrated more deeply into the nature of the Tahitian political order. We remember him today for the mutiny on the *Bounty*, but he was also an acute ethnographer.[37] He first visited Tahiti as master on Cook's third circumnavigation, an uneventful stop that gave him firsthand familiarity with the society before he returned as the *Bounty's* commander. After his return to England from the disastrous expedition, Bligh admired the Tahitians' "perfect easiness of manners, equally free from forwardness and formality," despite their strict attention to hierarchy.[38] Bligh had plenty of reason, if he had been so inclined, to exaggerate the faults of the Tahitians for his readers. His best explanation for the behavior of Fletcher Christian and the other mutineers was that they had been tempted away from their duty by the allure of Tahitian women and the good life of the South Seas. Yet in his observations on the Tahitians, he insisted on the relaxed but effective deference governing their class relations.

Backed by his patron Joseph Banks, Bligh returned to Tahiti a few years later to complete his mission of transporting breadfruit to the Caribbean. This time he was successful. His two ships arrived April 9, 1792, and after a leisurely, orderly visit departed on July 17, a stay of over three months. He left with 2,126 breadfruits, 472 other plants, and 36 so-called curiosity plants.[39] Although his overriding concern was gathering the breadfruits, he could never have fulfilled it without political and diplomatic skills that ingratiated him with local rulers and made it worth their while to let him accumulate his huge store of foodstuffs. ·

Bligh puzzled in his logbook over his intimate glimpses of life in Tahiti. On this visit he was treated to a close-up look at the relationship between power and religion in a Polynesian polity, a subject that pervades the observations in his logbook. Early on the morning of Wednesday, April 11, 1792, he went from his landing point to nearby Pare to make his first visit with the future Pomare II, who had assumed from his father the name Tu, while his father, Pomare I, took the name Tina (Tynah). They met in a mood of mutual respect and friendship: "He was overjoyed to see me. When I was here in the Bounty he was rather an ill looking Boy, but he is now grown a fine

Youth.—None of the ceremony took place between us that did then, he was very familiar and always kept hold of my hand, altho carried on a Mans Shoulder where he rode as on a horse, and carried a Switch with which he beat back the Crowds." Tu had a transparent motive for courting Bligh's friendship at this moment. He was involved in a conflict with the residents of Matavai Bay and asked Bligh for help against his enemies, an invitation to get caught up in the internal quarrels of the Tahitians that Bligh, wiser than the *Bounty* mutineers, turned down. This did not lessen Tu's courtship of Bligh's favor, for he sought out the captain again on April 20:

> I had another Visit from the Young King and made some presents to him.—I could do nothing to induce him to come on board, or to get off his Man's Shoulders, where he rides as easy as any of us would do upon a Horse—About 20 or 30 Young Men attended him, and he shifts from one to the other without the least inconvenience as they become tired.—I cannot get Tynah, or any one to tell me the exact time when he will be permitted to Walk (any other way) than by saying when he is a Man.—At Home he runs about as other Boys.[40]

What Bligh was confronting here was both familiar and strange, a mixture of hierarchical conceptions he could easily deduce and deviations from European experience, nobility's claims to deference and the unusual status of firstborn sons.[41]

Bligh also became aware of another unfamiliar prerogative of high social rank, human sacrifice. "Cannibalism," real or imagined, played a large part in Europeans' discourse on Polynesian societies, usually characterizing it either as demonic behavior or as the pardonable excess of a warrior code. Bligh recorded the following ceremony in his log entry of April 20, 1792: "Whatever Men are taken in their Wars, are kiled.—They share the same Fate with those who fall in the Battle, and remain on the Field.—their Eyes are taken out—one is presented to their God Oro, and the other to the Erreeāhigh, and the Man is then put into a Grave and buried.—In presenting the Eye to the King, it is put on a leaf, and the person who presents it, on being near him, calls aloud Hammāmah my—The King then Gapes wide, and the Ceremony ends. He does not even touch the Eye, much less to eat, or smell to it."[42] This was, then, a symbolic offering, not a literal ingestion but a mimesis that affirmed the presence of the god and the godlike status of the officiating noble family.

At just that time and place there was a fortuitous convergence of religious-political wares that permitted the sacrifice to take place. In order to pray to 'Oro, god of war, one needed three things: a human sacrifice offered through one of four or five title-holders empowered to officiate—Ari'i Rahi (Great Ari'i) or Ari'i Maro 'Ura (Red-girdled Ari'i); one of the red-feathered belts signifying the title; and a special idol of the god. Pomare I had by marriage inherited the title and acquired the sacred objects.[43] He was therefore in a position of unusual sacred authority when Cook landed for the first time in Matavai Bay and turned it into the base of English operations on the island.

Pomare II integrated his British friends, soon to be his protectors, into his prayers. Bligh witnessed this as early as April 28, when he was treated to another sacrificial ceremony, complete with a body that emitted a "violent stench" after the sun began to rise, a long repetitious prayer by the priests, and Pomare II "carried about on a Man's Shoulders talking to us & playing his tricks during the whole time of the devotion." Before the ceremony ended, the priest "pronounced another Prayer, which was in favor of King George, myself and all the People who were with me in the Ships." The priests were inviting an alliance of rulers, and Bligh made the most of it. He arranged for magnificent ceremonies to celebrate his sovereign's birthday, with marines firing volleys and twenty-one-gun salutes from the ships, liquor freely distributed, and a dozen skyrockets set off and two small balloons floated in the evening, to general satisfaction all around. "Mahannah no Erree Brettànee King George.—The King of Englands Birth Day—King George, was repeated every minute by Men Women and Children." Bligh assembled the chiefs around himself to drink to His Majesty's good health and eat with him. (Tina got drunk; the other chiefs were more restrained.) Thus each side made the other familiar with some of their native rituals of kingship.[44]

We have no way of knowing what the residents of Matavai Bay thought of King George. Bligh for his part left us with a written record of his conclusions about the state of "monarchy" on Tahiti. He wrestled over the exact number of political divisions on the island, introducing a note of ethnographic caution that bears repeating: "To know the exact state of the Government of the Island it would require a person to be some time in each part of it—a just conclusion might then be formed; but the information of any one party is doubtful, and the Strangers who visit us are cautious to give intelligence that may offend."[45] Still, he was willing to reach some tentative conclusions. The "Great Peninsula of Otaheite" was divided into four grand divisions as well as districts, counties, towns, and villages. Tu, his informants agreed, had succeeded his father to enjoy a singular status.[46] Bligh believed they had an exalted conception of leadership, but he was more careful than Cook to understand it as a non-European institution. Through his actions, as much as anything he said, he knew how to build on local politics and religion to create a centralized Tahitian political authority where none had been before.

Kingship in Hawaii: Kamehameha

When Cook happened on the Hawaiian islands and established contact with Europeans in 1778, Kamehameha, the future ruler and dynastic founder, impressed the visitors as a particularly forbidding-looking warrior. Vancouver, then a young officer, was wounded in the melee that led to Cook's death. Despite this unpromising beginning, he and Kamehameha I together crafted the pact that led to a unified Sandwich Kingdom.

The two men made careful displays of goodwill and power in their initial meeting on the island of Hawaii during Vancouver's visit of February 1793. Kamehameha approached Vancouver's ship in "a very large canoe," accompanied by his favorite wife, Ka'ahumanu—later one of the founders of the Hawaiian state as well—and the sailor-turned-advisor John Young. Vancouver later wrote that he found Kamehameha's features softened and admired the public affection that the king and queen showed each other. The royal party avoided asking for any presents and showed a decorum and restraint that impressed Vancouver. The captain then volunteered to distribute to the Hawaiians "presents suitable to their respective ranks and situations." Kamehameha himself received a scarlet cloak and a mirror so that he could see himself, presents that "filled him with rapture, and so delighted him that the cabin could scarcely contain him"; he went outside to strut in front of his compatriots and enjoy their admiration. Later the same day Vancouver visited Kamehameha's home, where the king received him magnificently, coming in from a large canoe with eighteen rowers on each side and wearing a printed linen gown that Cook had given to an earlier ruler of the island and a feathered cloak with brilliant yellow feathers reaching from his shoulders to the ground. His canoe advanced toward the ship, with a parade of ten following it, all in a strict order, with a precision and dignity that Vancouver admired. Kamehameha's paddlers swept alongside the ship, then suddenly stopped. "He instantly ascended the side of the ship, and taking hold of my hand, demanded, if we were sincerely his friends? To this I answered in the affirmative; he then said, that he understood we belonged to King George, and asked it [*sic*] he was likewise his friend? On receiving a satisfactory answer to this question, he declared that he was our firm good friend" and "according to the custom of the country" they touched noses. Kamehameha then presented him with "four very handsome feathered helmets" and ordered the ten large canoes alongside the ship to unload a profusion of hogs and vegetables. Thus the decisive meeting between the two men of state. The potential for violence simmered on both sides: Kamehameha was surrounded by *ali'i* who resented his special share of attention and by commoners who might be tempted to theft or violence; Vancouver had his own worries with sailors and midshipmen who were eager for riotous days on the islands after the rigors of military command in northern waters. The two leaders conferred on means of discipline and threats to contain their unruly followers. When Vancouver came back a third time, they strained themselves once again to build up their pact of friendship, with such success that Kamehameha agreed to a formal British protectorate.[47]

If the collaboration looked smooth in Vancouver's narrative, it took some hidden bullying on his part to make it work. When Vancouver returned to Hawaii in January 1794 he first tried to land in Hilo Bay, but the inhospitable winds there made him decide instead to sail for Kealakekua. Kamehameha, who went out to greet him, told him that he could not meet him there because New Year ceremonies required that he remain in the district where the ceremonies began. When Vancouver insisted, Kamehameha finally sent his half-brother to obtain a dispensation from the priests. Vancouver portrayed this as a disagreement between friends, but in fact, one of his men reported, he threatened to go at once to Kamehameha's rival on the island of Maui, and only in response to this did Kamehameha relent.[48] To the meeting for ratification of the pact between their two countries, Vancouver invited a chief who was held to be responsible for the massacre of an American crew. Some of Vancouver's men, including Menzies, were outraged by this inclusion of a man they considered an unpunished murderer; but Vancouver wanted political considerations—the need for the chief's support—to prevail. There was an ongoing tension between public theater—which continued, and advanced, in the official account—and the dissenting voices that found expression in the privacy of unpublished journals.

If we move forward to the time of Kotzebue in 1816 and 1817, we find Kamehameha still the ruler of his kingdom with a practiced touch on the means to convey his authority. As the *Rurik* visitors noticed, the political unity of the Sandwich Islands was deeply troubled, for the great *ali'i* retained much of their power and were biding their time until Kamehameha's death to make their next move. In this unsettled situation, with the unity of the kingdom uncertain from day to day, the *Rurik* voyagers arrived in suspicious circumstances. They became the witnesses to—and almost the victims of—a drama between Kamehameha and a Russian naturalist-spy.

The plot leading up to this critical moment had its beginnings years before in the colonial ambitions of the director of the Russian-American Company's trading post at Sitka, Alaska. Alexander Baranov, commander of the company's eastern post in 1799, had created the fur-trading empire that was notorious for its kidnapping and enslavement of Aleut men, used as hunters. In desperate need of food for his colony, Baranov sent a first expedition to the Sandwich Islands in 1808 to seek out sites for a Russian settlement. In 1815 he tried again, sending Georg Anton Schäffer, a German surgeon, to the island of Hawaii, where he landed on October 17. Schäffer advertised himself to Kamehameha as a botanist, and indeed both he and Baranov seem to have had real hopes for glory from his plant collecting. He ingratiated himself to the monarch by treating him for heart trouble and, he claimed, curing the king's wife Ka'ahumanu of yellow fever. The monarch set him up with land and a house, apparently hoping to add another advisor like Davis and Young. Instead, on his land in Oahu Schäffer began constructing a fort and alarmed Young by raising a Russian flag. Expelled in April 1816, Schäffer went to Kauai, the outermost of the Sandwich Islands, whose ruler, Kaumuali'i, was virtually independent of the centralizing monarchy. He and Schäffer plotted to place the island under Russian protectorship and built a sturdy fort in Waimea, but the alliance fizzled out as it became clear that the Russian government, which did not wish to damage its relations with Britain for such a small prize, refused to back the scheme. Kaumuali'i expelled Schäffer by June 1817.[49]

When the *Rurik* arrived on the morning of November 24, 1816,

The folkloric North: an Aleut man and woman. From Choris, *Voyage pittoresque autour du monde* (1822).

Kotzebue had to persuade Kamehameha of the tsar's goodwill despite Schäffer's subversive behavior. Four hundred troops were waiting for the *Rurik* voyagers when they landed on Hawaii.[50] Kamehameha, once forced by Vancouver to meet at an inconvenient place, now made Kotzebue travel over land to the village of Kealakekua for an audience. When they met, Kamehameha first greeted him coldly, but Kotzebue's disavowal of Schäffer and insistence that he was an isolated adventurer won him over. The ruler had steadily balanced his special relationship with Britain and a policy of openness to all nations; he had commerce to gain, and little to fear, from accepting his visitor's words at face value. Kotzebue's account spreads a romantic haze over the Hawaiian visit—for factual political reporting one does better to turn to Chamisso—but had its own importance as a public relations piece. He admired the background scenery of "wildness and cultivation" in the place, with its steep mountain rising behind them and the mixture of straw and European-style stone houses in the village. The people, too, mixed native and exotic features:

> I now stood at the side of the celebrated Tamaahmaah [Kamehameha], who had attracted the attention of all Europe, and who inspired me with the greatest confidence by his unreserved and friendly behaviour. He conducted me to his straw palace, which, according to the custom of the country, consisted only of one spacious apartment, and, like all the houses here, afforded a free draught both to the land and sea breezes, which alleviates the oppressive heat. They offered us European chairs, very neatly made, placed a mahogany table before us, and we were then in possession of all the furniture of the palace. Though the king has houses built of stone in the European fashion, he prefers this simple dwelling, not to forsake the customs of his country; he imitates every thing he knows to be useful and tries to introduce it among his

people; palaces built of stone appeared to him superfluous, as the straw houses are convenient, and as he only wishes to increase the happiness, and not the wants of his subjects.

Kotzebue used the language of the Enlightenment here, judging and approving according to the use-value of Kamehameha's actions, advertising his avoidance of luxury and concern for the welfare of his people. He was not alone in his view. It was the same kind of affirmation of paternalistic, enlightened government that had guided the judgment of Cook and George Forster on Tahiti decades earlier.[51]

Under the impact of revolution and Napoleonic wars, there was also a new twist to Kotzebue's account that had no precedent in the travel writings of the late eighteenth century. Kotzebue wrote as an agent of Restoration-era politics who admired Kamehameha for getting the right balance between tradition and modernization. He had already, reported the Russian captain, begun to prepare for the transition of power to his son, who was beginning to observe important religious obligations (above all, not to be seen by day; *ali'i* were supposed to be invisible to ordinary mortals). "Tamaahmaah has ordered this from political motives," commented Kotzebue, "that no *revolution* may arise after his death." Unlike the precipitous Schäffer, he also appreciated the importance for all Europe of supporting Kamehameha's work and even his compact with Britain:

Tamaahmaah, who, by his wise government, has acquired permanent glory, and has laid the foundation for the civilization and improvement of his people, ought to have a successor capable of prosecuting with zeal and judgment the work which he has begun. It would be very important for navigation, if the Sandwich Islands were on a level with Europe in civilization; and the English, who have taken these islands under their protection, should take care that, after Tamaahmaah's death, a sensible man may succeed, and every revolution be avoided.

Avoid revolution: in the aftermath of Napoleon statesmen everywhere could agree to this. Even if local customs differed, one could respect the conservative function of tradition and custom when one met them: Kotzebue quotes Kamehameha as saying, "These are our gods, whom I worship; whether I do right or wrong, I do not know; but I follow my faith, which cannot be wicked, as it commands me never to do wrong." Kotzebue was moved. "This declaration from a savage," he observed, "who had raised himself by his own native strength of mind to this degree of civilization, indicated much sound sense, and inspired me with a certain emotion." Could tsars do better? Here was a corresponding member of the Holy Alliance who appreciated how much religion could do to shore up kingdoms threatened worldwide by revolution.[52]

Impassioned liberal though he was, Chamisso was no less admiring of Kamehameha. His wealth, his cannons, his ships, and his skill in choosing foreign advisors and maintaining their loyalty all impressed the European.[53] When he wrote his second account of the voyage, the Hawaiian ruler came to symbolize monarchy itself. Like Chateaubriand recalling the old regime or Proust remembering the aristocrats of the *belle époque,* Chamisso recalled the majesty of the great *ali'i* at their first interview:

Our captain had arrived. The old warrior received him with cordiality. He understood protocol very well and knew how to act magnificently, impressively, and easily . . . He did not conceal his anger at the Russian [Schäffer] who had rewarded his royal hospitality with such base ingratitude, but in us, who had nothing to do with them and had been sent out on an expedition of discovery, he would not see Russians, but sons and descendants of Cook and his friend Vancouver. We were not

merchants, and he would not be one toward us. He would care for all
our needs completely free of charge. We did not have to give the king a
present, unless we wished. Thus was Tameiameia, king of the Sandwich Islands.[54]

From Cook to Chamisso the conception of monarchy was completely turned around. At the time of Cook it was a European import, a conception that he and other visitors brought to places like
Tahiti, Tonga, and Hawaii. Local power-holders made the most of the
gift. They had highly stratified societies that at the suggestion of European patrons rather easily made the transition to centralized exercise of authority, and Europeans provided the weaponry that permitted ascendant families to triumph over their rivals in a way that had
never before been possible. By the time Chamisso arrived, the European monarchs and nobles who provided the model for this centralization had been menaced or toppled. He looked to Kamehameha as
a vestige of authentic aristocracy who could teach Europeans what it
had once been on their own soil.

Who created the image of Hawaiian monarchy: the visitors or the
monarch? We can see the interplay between the two in the negotiations of Louis Choris, the artist on the *Rurik,* to make Kamehameha's
portrait. When Chamisso, Elliot, Eschscholtz, and Choris first went
ashore to meet the king, they found him sitting on a raised terrace
in front of his residence, a black tapa mantle covering his shoulders. When Choris asked to paint his portrait Kamehameha agreed,
but changed into his European clothes, a shirt and a red vest. He refused Choris's request that he change back into his Hawaiian dress.
Choris honored his wish, and it was the image of the red-vested Kamehameha that became one of the illustrations in the Kotzebue voyage narrative. Chamisso relates that the fame of this picture spread
even before then, for Choris made several copies of the portrait

Native monarchy: Kamehameha I. From Choris, *Voyage pittoresque autour du monde* (1822).

that American merchants took to China, where they were copied in painting factories; reproductions greeted the *Rurik* travelers by the time they reached Manila the following year.[55] Later Choris re-nativized him: in the beautiful volume of lithographs that he put out on his own, he restored the black tapa mantle to his shoulders.

Kamehameha could not, then, entirely leave behind the fate of being a "native." Not that this was entirely alien to Kamehameha, with his insistence on maintaining the tabus, the calendar, and the rituals of the priests. He was artful at manipulating the two sides of his regime, the traditional and the modernizing. The Kamehameha that we can still see today was the outcome of a Hawaiian and a European collaboration.[56]

Collaborators and collaborations came in many forms. Islanders included a broad spectrum of figures who made it their business to work with the newcomers, from a modest man like Kadu to the imposing Kamehameha. Among the Europeans there was a wide span of figures too, from a little person like Choris to the royal naval captains. Entrepreneurs, missionaries, socially ambitious islanders, ordinary sailors, beachcombers turned local advisors—all could play mediating roles; rather than a polarity of opposites, the collision of European and Polynesian worlds left a jumbled crowd of interest-seekers. The high degree of social stratification in Hawaii provided opportunities for specialists on many levels of society, on both sides, to market their skills and knowledge.[57] The richest ethnographies profited from this wide range of interpreters. A master recorder of foreign cultures like Chamisso did not simply "observe." He gathered insights from a community of fellow observers who like him were eager to survive and profit from a newly forming world.

CHAPTER 4

Philosophers

Travelers returned and wrote up their impressions of what they had experienced abroad, but their network of knowledge did not end there. How their reports got read, interpreted, used, and reused depended on their public, which could take their writings in very different directions from the one originally intended. As we have seen in the reception of Ahutoru and Mai, Europeans in the late eighteenth and early nineteenth centuries often took a rather frivolous approach to exotic visitors, regarding them more as a source of amusing anecdotes than as a subject for serious reflection. The irreverent use of "natives" did not end in the eighteenth century. Chamisso was outraged that a reviewer who should have known better, the geographer Malte-Brun, called Kadu a "cannibal" in a review of Choris's visual account of the *Rurik* voyage. "Once something palpably tasteless is put down on paper," observed Chamisso, "it rolls on incessantly from book to book, and it is the first thing the professional writers of such books reach for." When Kamehameha's son Liholiho (Kamehameha II) visited England in 1824, he received a most dignified diplomatic and social reception, but a gross lampooning in the press. Intellectuals in Europe brought their own preconceptions to bear on travel accounts, and how they read them was as complicated and contested as the relationship between patrons and travelers or travelers and informants.[1]

Leading thinkers of the late eighteenth and early nineteenth centuries took a serious interest in travelers' reports that went beyond salon chatter and its literary equivalents; Rousseau was not alone in his hunger for more accurate, more penetrating accounts. The more serious and self-critical they were, the deeper were the questions they raised about what Europe could comprehend of other cultures. Philosophically inclined readers came to travel accounts with strongly defined hypotheses about the nature of society and man; how much they could absorb from them depended on the nature of those philosophies and on presuppositions of the Enlightenment and Romantic eras. They in turn had something to offer the travelers, for full-

Popular derision is expressed in *Robeing royalty, a treat for the Sandwichers, at the sign of the Hog in Armour.* Print by Samuel W. Fores (1824).

time intellectuals could be sharp cross-examiners who brought their education, their scientific knowledge, their powers of conceptualization, and their critical skills to bear on travel accounts. If travel accounts were not revelations but products of a highly elaborate process of production, then they had to submit to a process of critique along the way to being admitted into the European world of knowledge.

Here we can once again observe the transformation of ethnographic knowledge as it made its way from node to node on its network. Travelers culled information from different sources and synthesized their observations into texts; their texts were material for philosophers who wrote for different ends. We can sample three major philosophers' use of travel writings not just as reminders of how deeply travel writings entered into European culture, but as examples of how the knowledge of foreign cultures underwent a further process of selection and reworking.

Diderot and the Shock of Tahiti

Denis Diderot, critic of many arts and sciences, and coeditor of the *Encyclopedia* that was a summation of the Enlightenment's world of knowledge, had a long-standing interest in non-European societies. Like his contemporaries, he assessed his own society by comparing it with alternatives from other parts of the world. At the time he was working on the *Encyclopedia* he was not unaware that non-Europeans might have qualities deserving of European admiration, or that he could contrast their attributes to the deficiencies of European society; his *Encyclopedia* article on Scythians declared his preference for the barbaric fierceness of this ancient people over the civilized lassitude of the Greeks. On the whole, however, Diderot took an antisentimental and antinostalgic approach to tribal societies, experimenting with different evaluations but not thinking of them as desirable alternatives.[2]

He turned to Bougainville with the professional expertise of a contributor to Guillaume-Thomas Raynal's famous *History of the Two Indies*. "There has never been an event as interesting," declared the work's opening lines, "for the human species in general and for the peoples of Europe in particular, as the discovery of the New World and the passage to the Indies by way of the Cape of Good Hope. It began a revolution in commerce, in the power of nations, in the culture, industry and government of all peoples." If Gibbons examined the fate of empires and Voltaire took as his theme the ennobling eras of high culture, Raynal was turning to a theme equally important, the history of exploration and discovery. The *History of the Two Indies* was one of the works that announced a new radical tone to the European public, cataloguing the errors of French foreign policy, denouncing the evils of slavery, and calling for freedom from despotism. First published in 1770, it went through numerous printings and two revised editions. Diderot began collaborating with Raynal on the project in 1769 and had a hand in changing the third edition of 1780 into an aggressive, polemical work. After it was condemned by the parlement of Paris in 1781 for its attacks on state and clerical authority, Raynal went into exile, while rumors circulated of Diderot's involvement.[3]

The compendium that took shape under Raynal's name was a product of courage and far-reaching research. It was not, however, the kind of historical scholarship that entered into the distinctive culture of the peoples it studied. Raynal's Canadian Indians were men of reason and natural virtue in their primitive state of equality, in contrast to the corruption of hierarchized European society.[4] By the time Raynal published the expanded 1780 edition of his work, Cook had completed the third of his circumnavigations; the British voyager's painstaking effort at recording and understanding native peoples was in striking contrast to Raynal's clichéd counters to civilization.

Diderot's reflections on Bougainville overlapped with his work on the *History of the Two Indies*. He reviewed Bougainville's voyage account in the year it was published, 1771. As for Diderot's famous essay, *Supplement to Bougainville's Voyage,* he finished it by October of the following year, although he continued to revise the text, inserting some new material in 1778 or 1779.[5] Unlike his anonymous contributions to Raynal's encyclopedic work, the *Supplement* announced Diderot's views in his own name.

Diderot wrote his 1771 review of Bougainville for the journal *La Correspondence Littéraire* (a manuscript journal for a small number of subscribers edited by his friend Melchior Grimm), but it did not appear there and was not published in his lifetime. It began with praise for Bougainville and emphasized Bougainville's empirical veracity, which reached right into the scientist-captain's style: "It is written without bombast, with the sole aim of serving truth and simplicity." He admired Bougainville's description of the expulsion of the Jesuits from Paraguay (where the religious order had established theocratic rule over the indigenous Amerindians, which they had to abandon when the Jesuit order itself was dissolved in 1773). He commended Bougainville's truthful account of the Patagonians as neither giants nor men of special wisdom. Bougainville encountered "savages" too stupid, according to Diderot, to be astonished by anything, whether the wonders of nature or human artifices (he seems to have had European ships in mind).[6]

So far Diderot presented Bougainville as a scientific hero, in keeping with the kind of praise that had become a convention for talking about Cook. At this point, however, his review turned to a conflicting perspective: "O Monsieur de Bougainville, remove your ship from the shores of these innocent and blessed Tahitians; they are happy and you can only destroy their happiness. They follow nature's instinct, and you are going to erase its high and sacred mark." Bougainville and his expedition were introducing European conceptions of love and property that would destroy this paradise, wrote Diderot, who also asked how Bougainville could claim this island as the property of France except by use of force. The voyagers killed a Tahitian who had been seduced by the glitter of European trinkets, and the Tahitians retreated in horror and fear. The Tahitians should weep over the day Europeans came, not (as Bougainville related) the day they departed; one day the visitors would impose their behavior and their unhappiness on the islanders. Diderot did not end with this condemnation of the latest chapter of European colonialism, but returned to the voyage's anecdotes (including the story of Jeanne Barret) and achievements. Near the end he added a personal reflection on the effect of reading Bougainville: "This is the only voyage account that whets my appetite for another country than my own. Until now the ultimate result of my reflections has always been that people are nowhere better off than at home."[7]

Diderot's judgment of Bougainville was thus many-sided. It was part of the colonial history that he helped to survey and condemn in Raynal's work; but it was also the revelation of a world truly different from his own, not a fiction like the myth of sage Patagonian giants but a real place and people witnessed by a traveler of unimpeachable reliability. Diderot was a skeptical reader, respectful of Bougainville's intelligence, but able to pierce through it to reveal the destruction of another society, and an unusually admirable one, beneath the surface of a friendly and humanitarian visit. Not that Diderot himself was entirely scrupulous in his reportage: having battled with government censors over the publication of the *Encyclopedia*, he suppressed details of Bougainville's account that did not suit his own ideological purposes. There was no mention of Bougainville's admission that Tahiti, far from being the utopia he had momentarily imagined, had tyrannical rulers and deep social divisions. Like the *History of the Two Indies*, Diderot's review touched up its "savages" to fit its conceptions of man in a state of nature.[8]

His review echoed the shock of Tahiti that the voyagers had experienced firsthand: that a well-ordered society could also be a place of public and pervasive erotic freedom. The travelers attested to this seeming paradox in their journal entries as well as in Commerson's and Bougainville's published accounts of it. Diderot registered the impact of this "discovery" when he wrote about the voyage's effect on his imagination. He reflected on it again, in greater depth, in his *Supplement to Bougainville's Voyage*, which was circulated as the third of three tales in Melchior Grimm's *Correspondance littéraire* and not published for the general public until 1796, when it appeared without its companion stories.[9] Only in 1969 did scholars rediscover its original context, and since then they have pointed out that the preceding stories are inseparable from the *Supplement*'s meaning.[10]

The stories deal with love in French society and pose a problem, the general unhappiness of relations between the sexes, to which the *Supplement* offers a solution.[11] "This Is Not a Story," the first of the three tales, examines male and female deceitfulness in love. A tale within the tale relates the kind of wandering life and ultimate misfortune that sometimes befell naturalist voyagers. It tells of a young man named Tanié who goes abroad to satisfy the appetite of his lover, Madame Reymer, for wealth. First he spends time in the French colony of Saint Domingue (Haiti), where he makes a modest fortune and returns home to a quiet and happy life with Madame Reymer. Then Maurepas, the secretary of the navy, summons him and tells him he is planning a new commercial enterprise in the north. Will Tanié agree to go? Reluctant, he follows his lover's advice to add to their wealth; within four days of his arrival in St. Petersburg, he has died of a fever. The second mini-tale shows that men can be just as bad as women: a Monsieur Gardeil seduces a woman, exploits her erudition, and abandons her, a betrayal from which her frail character never recovers. This tale moves from individual egoism to a critique of the rottenness of public morals: in front of family and friends a proud woman extracts a promise from her future husband that he will never be unfaithful. When she discovers an incriminating sheath of letters years later, she assembles the same company, confronts him, leaves him, and refuses any reconciliation. Happy marriage gives way to separation, inner withering, and early deaths. Was the aggrieved wife right or wrong to act as she did? Would it have been better to forgive and endure the inevitable relapses? Diderot ultimately blames his society for supporting a moral order at odds with human nature. "I have my own ideas," states the storyteller, "which may be correct but are certainly eccentric, on certain actions which I regard less as vices in mankind than as the consequences of our absurd laws—themselves the source of equally absurd ethical conventions and of what I would like to call an *artificial* depravity. I am not making myself very clear, but perhaps I could do better another time."[12]

That "other time" is the third of the three tales, the *Supplement to Bougainville's Voyage*. It takes the form of an imaginary dialogue between two anonymous Frenchmen ("A" and "B"). In the opening scene speaker B makes admiring remarks about the polymath Bougainville that incorporate Diderot's own words from the review: "He's a true Frenchman, balancing a treatise of integral and differential calculus on one side, with a voyage round the world on the other." The conversation turns to historical and demographic questions: how did the islanders get there? If they keep multiplying, how will they fit on a small island? And to questions of civic order: the speakers put the remark in Bougainville's mouth that "the savage is innocent and gentle whenever his peace and security are left undisturbed," and blame all wars on "conflicting claims to the same property." Ahutoru, they tell us, is unable to learn French because of the limited number of sounds in his own language and will not have the words to describe the complexities of French society when he returns home. Europeans may have a more complex society, but it is not morally advanced; in the cyclical philosophy of history Diderot expounds through the dialogue partners, "the Tahitian is close to the origins of the world and the European near its old age." Weary of their European world, the protagonists prepare the reader for something different, perhaps something better, from the Tahitians.[13]

The first part of the dialogue celebrates exploration and discovery in the same way that Bougainville and Cook were publicly celebrated for expanding scientific knowledge. The story shifts to a native point of view as A and B turn to the manuscript account of a speech by an old Tahitian. The tone shifts, too, from complacency to an indictment of Bougainville. The old man is a prophetic figure. He accuses the Europeans of evil and predicts the destruction of the Tahitians, telling them to weep, and calling Bougainville a ruffian. Their crime: to have destroyed the innocence, the naturalness of the Tahitians' reproducing their own kind in the light of day; to have poisoned their blood with venereal disease. "Wretched man. You must bear guilt," says the old man to Bougainville, "either for the ravages that will follow the deadly caresses of your people, or for the murders we shall commit to arrest the poison."[14] The speech functions as a comeuppance: carried to this point by the traveler's self-serving account, the reader suddenly discovers the fatal cost of the voyage for the hosts. Now we hear from the other side that contact with Europeans sets off a history of catastrophe for the Tahitians. The terrible doubt, whispered and then checked by Cook and Forster, about whether voyagers may not be responsible for bringing venereal disease to a new part of the world, here recurs as certainty.

The tone and scene switch again to a dialogue within the dialogue, the story of a fictive ship chaplain. A Tahitian named Orou offers the chaplain his wife and three daughters. After making protests (incomprehensible to the Tahitians) about how his religion won't permit it, the chaplain spends the night with the youngest daughter. Diderot intends more than anticlerical ribaldry here (though that is certainly part of the story): a dialogue afterward between the chaplain and the Tahitian reveals that European restraints on sexuality are contrary to nature and bring about disorder and human misery. Orou's island is not a new Cythera where natives abandon themselves to sexual pleasure for its own sake, which European visitors can then dress up in their reports as a libertine paradise. Rather, Diderot's Tahitians are strict utilitarians.[15] They reproduce in order to increase the strength and wealth of their country. All forms of procreative sex are permitted; there is no prohibition against incest, no value to fidelity, no sanction against amorous adventure. But boys and girls are strictly guarded until they are sexually mature, while women past menopause wear a black veil and women having their period wear a gray veil to mark them off as undesirables. (All this was Diderot's invention, not historical fact or Bougainville's version.) There is no altruism in this society, no "marital tenderness and paternal care," which are European illusions that mask human beings' real motivating sentiment: "In their place we've another which is altogether more general, energetic and durable: self-interest." To drive home the utilitarian ethic he is proposing, Diderot returns the reader to A and B, who draw general conclusions from what they have learned about Tahiti. There are three codes of law, natural, civil, and religious. The second and third make everything awful; the first strictly follows the logic of the pleasure–pain calculus: "We have no more in common with other human beings at birth than an organic similarity of form, the same need, an attraction to the same pleasures and a shared aversion to the same pains." Keeping women as property limits the natural attraction of the sexes, finds expression in legal prohibitions, and results in human misery. He prefers the "anarchy" of Calabria in southern Italy to state order, declares one of the dialogue partners, but then pulls back from this extreme position to one of reform: "We must speak out against senseless laws until they're reformed and, in the meanwhile, abide by them . . . Let's follow the good chaplain's example and be monks in France and savages in Tahiti." The dialogue ends with a clear vision of a state of nature in which there would be no conflict between physical desire and social convention. Even if such a world is not theirs to enjoy in Europe, they have gained intellectual clarity that can serve as a starting point for correcting Europe's sexual misery.[16]

Diderot's Tahiti was a utopia. "Dialogue between A and B on the inappropriateness of attaching moral ideas to certain physical actions that do not accord with them," reads the subtitle to the dialogue, which sketches out the kind of place where there would no longer be discord between "certain physical actions" and the moral order imposed by society. To make a model of such a place Diderot could not remain within the confines of history, for he was perfectly aware that it did not exist, even in the South Pacific; instead he needed to construct a theoretical island that could follow the logic of reproduction to its natural conclusion. What remained of the real Tahiti, the one reported on by Bougainville, the one to which Ahutoru tried to return? In one sense, not very much; Bougainville's visit is the occasion for Diderot to subtract and add as many details as he needs in order to make it complete. But at the same time Diderot shows us how the voyages of discovery opened up a utopian space in the European imagination. Tahiti's sexual ethic was genuinely unsettling, and the radical intellectual tried to tease out the fullest consequences of this "discovery." Even if it was not Tahiti, the island described in the dialogue takes the real Tahiti as its point of departure; the completely different erotic arrangements made it possible for Diderot to imagine real alternatives to the dissembling and destruction of the European lovers in his first two tales. Philosophy had gained a foothold in a foreign place and a starting point for critical reflection.

Kant and George Forster

Although he never left his native town of Königsberg, Immanuel Kant was well read in the travel literature of his time, which he was using for his lectures as early as the mid-1750s. Much later in life, the mature philosopher stated in his occasional writings his interest in the reports streaming into Europe. Like Rousseau, he regretted their unreliability and wished that "someone with a head for historical criticism" would go through them and order them to compare the contradictory ones. As it was, he wrote in 1785, one could prove that "true Mongolians" were bearded or unbearded, that Americans and Negroes were inferior or equal to other portions of humanity; any system built on such shaky foundations looked like a tumble-down affair.[17]

Despite his doubts about the reliability of travel writing, Kant turned his attention to it in more systematic published form, questioning what it could add to an understanding of the nature of man. He began his published reflections on the idea of "race" by stating that his essay was a response to the stimulus of the new travel literature; he wanted to give direction to the ensuing discussions. Kant was an admiring reader of Rousseau and could hardly fail to be aware of the importance of one's understanding of indigenous peoples for discussions of human nature. In keeping with the universal scope of his thinking, he devoted a considerable amount of attention to non-European peoples, and his treatment of them was systematically connected to the rest of his political thought as he scanned forward from the diversity and conflict of peoples visible in the world of his time to hope for their ultimate reconciliation.[18]

Kant's view of indigenous peoples was firmly grounded in his belief that the different races of man constitute a single species descended from a single ancestry. Discussion of the unified or diverse origins of humanity was a subject of widespread Enlightenment debate. The major thinkers of the Enlightenment were by no means uniformly on the side of unity, for the debate was mixed up in an untidy way with the era's critique of organized religion. Since Christianity dogmatically asserted the unity of the human species, Enlightenment thinkers, interested in promoting a naturalistic view of man, toyed with possibilities of human diversity. In particular Voltaire and Diderot, in the course of their attacks on organized religion, took a certain gleeful pleasure in arguing for the different origins and inferiority of some peoples. The philosophers had no single or obvious view on the subject of race.[19]

Kant stands out, by contrast, for the clarity of his assertion of humanity's unity. Even though he was not free of racial prejudices, this was his fundamental view and the one that fit his philosophy. His own position, he took care to point out, was not based on sentimentalism or speculation, but was a careful hypothesis based on whatever empirical evidence travelers' reports afforded and on the same rules of inquiry one would apply to any other scientific question. All human beings, wrote Kant, belong to the same species, for they are able to produce children capable of further reproduction, the definition of a species throughout nature. Beyond this, he compared the races that in his view had migrated in a distant eon to the different corners of the earth and reproduced among themselves. There they developed their distinctive features from the common pool of human characteristics that enabled them to adapt to their local climates and soils. Once an accommodation between environment and people took place, imagined Kant, the genetic material changed too and resisted alteration; hence if a people subsequently removed itself to a new place, as he believed American Indians had done by crossing over from Asia, they did not continuously undergo change. He viewed with skepticism reports that members of different races could change their skin color if transported to a different environment; Africans remained dark in Europe, Europeans remained light-skinned in Africa. Yet these were superficial differences within a single human family.[20]

Kant's theory combined heredity and environment to account for the ultimate unity of the species. Like many Enlightenment contemporaries, he attributed a profound importance to climate in the formation of character. Indeed in lecture notes published after his death, he adopted the truism of the age that inhabitants of the temperate zone, by which he meant primarily Europeans, were the most physically attractive human beings and throughout history had demonstrated the superiority of their cultural achievements. He also accepted travelers' reports that the "savages" of North America had the feral characteristics of a special odor and especially keen eyesight. Even in these lectures, though, he rejected the notion of different origins, or that view's religious-mythical counterpart with regard to Africans, a curse on the dark-skinned children of Ham. His published essays excluded these myths and legends and dismissed the arguments for anything less than full equality among the different kinds of human beings. Against the notion of multiple origins of the human species (supposedly originating in different places yet capable of interbreeding), Kant stated that this idea was an unnecessary complication of presuppositions; the rules of scientific practice instead called for the simpler thesis of one place of origin.[21]

Kant also argued against another kind of late-eighteenth-century understanding of race, according to which the human species had derived from a single ancestry, but an ancestry that resembled modern Europeans. Other races, according to this view, were an imperfect falling away from this original type. This kind of degenerationism was associated in the Germany of Kant's time with Johann Friedrich Blumenbach. Within the debates of the late Enlightenment, Blumenbach's position was actually a qualified defense of the unity of humanity against the polygenism—the belief that members of different races were descended from different original ancestors—associated in Germany with the writings of Samuel Thomas Soemmerring. Nonetheless, Blumenbach's position was an ambivalent one that asserted an original unity of the species but also guaranteed that Europeans remained the human norm. Kant was opposed to Blumenbach's model as well as to more radical assertions like Soemmerring's of European racial superiority. He noted that there was not the slightest bit of evidence to support such a hypothesis. Kant's essay defining the concept of a human race concluded: "It is therefore impossible now to deduce how the original human line (according to skin color) may have been created; even the character of the whites is only the development of one of the original potentials that, along with others, one might have encountered in the original." Racial differences amounted in any case to no more than a superficial response to environment, while human powers of understanding and reason were everywhere the same.[22]

This conception of the unity of the human species was Kant's application of his critical philosophy to the problem of how to reconcile the visible diversity of human appearances with the underlying unity of human nature. At the same time, Kant's vision of society and history contained its own difficulties; it achieved its unity only by creating a division between savage and civil freedom. This division ran through one of his central political essays, "On Eternal Peace" (1795–96). Writing amid the ideological wars unleashed by the

French Revolution, at a moment of European-wide conflict between the agents of reason and of tradition, he asked his readers to step back from the passions of his time and to consider whether the world could ever reach a condition of peace: not the false peace brought about by oppression, but the lasting peace of justice and human contentment.

Kant proposed three principles as the foundations of such a lasting peace. The first was that the constitution of each state should be republican, that is, some form of representative constitutional government. The second principle was federalism: Kant looked forward to a confederation of free states (and not a universal monarchy, which Kant thought would end in chaos or despotism). The third principle was the universal right of hospitality: visitors or temporary residents had a right not to be treated in a hostile fashion (an important provision, he thought, for the regulation of borders).[23] These three principles would ground government in universal human reason, would provide checks to the human appetite for power, and would peacefully regulate the points of overlap between peoples. Indigenous peoples occasionally showed up in this overview. His first mention of "savages" came in his remarks on federalism. He brought them in to drive home to Europeans how far beneath their own claims to civilization it was when their rulers behaved like autocrats who exploited their subjects for their own power-political ends. "Savages," he wrote, preferred their lawless freedom to lawful order and thus provoked the contempt of humanity, but by the same logic morally decent peoples should be hurrying to move from a similarly debased anarchy to union with one another.[24] According to reason states have no choice in their mutual relations, he added, "than that they, like individual human beings, give up their savage (lawless) freedom" and lead the way to a confederation of peoples that will eventually encompass the whole world.[25] Kant pressed "savages" here into the service of a moral philosophy contrasting lawless freedom to legally regulated freedom, which he extended in this writing to international politics. As in the ethical behavior of individuals, so in the behavior of states an unrestricted license to all man's selfish impulses must give way, under the rule of reason, to a consideration of the interests of the whole and their reconciliation in a harmonious system.

The same work compared Europeans with American "savages."[26] The comparison allows us to localize Kant's discussion, placing it in the long history of European observations about American Indians and their "savage" freedom compared with European civilization. Throughout the eighteenth century travelers and philosophes had debated the value of European civilization by comparing it with the condition of American Indians, with opinions ranging from contemptuous to praiseful. Kant's analysis of lawless freedom also merits comparison with Rousseau's description of the savage state in his *Discourse on Inequality*. Here, too, society begins in a state of anarchy; indeed, Rousseau asks us to consider an initial state of absolute individual freedom as a premise for his analysis of man's irreversible movement toward social organization. For Rousseau, the "savage" state, once universal and still to be observed among indigenous peoples, is not the original state of nature, but rather a moment of modest social organization regulated by the family. It was, he thinks, the moment best suited to man's nature—not a moment of complete happiness, but one of stability and satisfaction before the technological and political transformations that brought human beings to their present state of civilized unhappiness. Kant used a similar model of movement from anarchy to order, but without Rousseau's skepticism toward civilization; while aware of its imperfections, he was convinced of its superiority to earlier, more lawless epochs. In one sense, though, Kant's philosophy of history diminished the distance between "savages" and civilized Europeans. Kant meant exactly what he said when he called European rulers "savage" on account of their refusal to accept limitations on their sovereignty; their anarchic behavior was synonymous with his category for the noncivilized.

Even though he ranked human societies in a hierarchy from "savage" to civilized, Kant condemned Europe's exploitation of non-European peoples in "On Eternal Peace." His discussion of the right of hospitality pointed out how Europeans had violated this right again and again through their behavior as guests in the countries of other peoples: "If we take for comparison the behavior of the decent, primarily commercial states of our part of the world, the extent of their acts of injustice while visiting foreign peoples and places (a matter of indifference to them while conquering the latter) is horrifying. America, the countries inhabited by Negroes, the spice islands, the Cape, etc., to them belonged to nobody when they discovered them, for the inhabitants in their eyes counted for nothing." He recalled how Europeans had brought all the evils of warfare on India and sympathized with the restrictions that China and Japan set on their Western visitors. Finally he turned to the greatest evil of all, the European regime in the sugar colonies, "this seat of the most horrible and systematic slavery." His belief in a moral law whose application was worldwide made him an uncompromising critic of lawless behavior toward non-European peoples.[27]

Kant's 1785 essay "Definition of the Concept of a Human Race" irritated George Forster, who by this time was very much under the influence of Soemmerring's views on race. They had first met when Soemmerring, whose dissertation had just been approved, traveled to London in 1778 and ended up spending a good bit of time in the Forster household. After Forster started working in Kassel in April 1779, he proposed Soemmerring's name for a position, which he was offered, beginning work in October. They were there together until Forster left for Vilna in April 1784 and Soemmerring departed the same year for a professorship in anatomy and physiology in Mainz. When Soemmerring's *On the Physical Difference of Mohrs and Europeans* argued for the racial inferiority of Negroes in a new edition in 1785, it was with a dedication to Forster, who admired his theory and thanked him for the dedication. After Kant's 1785 essay reached him in mid-1786, he wrote to Soemmerring with the news that he was preparing a reply. "It would be good," he commented, "if the shoemaker would stick to his own craft! Kant is such a fine thinker but he too yields to the hopeless paradox of the professional philosopher who has to redo nature to fit his logical distinctions. The booty is more harmful than useful." Forster's response, "Another Word about Human Races," appeared in October and November of 1786. It was a piece he took pride in, and he shared it with important thinkers such as Johann Gottfried Herder and Georg Christoph Lichtenberg as well as Soemmerring, while awaiting its publication.[28]

Forster began his essay with a general defense of empiricism and a caution that the philosopher, in his search for concepts, could lose sight of the lessons of experience. If he followed a false principle, the philosopher was less reliable than the unprejudiced bystander who simply reported faithfully on what he had observed. "Who would not prefer the few observations of a mere, yet acute and reliable empiricist to the many dandified observations of a partial system-builder? Besides, the open eyes of the former tend to notice important things that are never apparent to someone always on the lookout for the signs that confirm his own hypotheses." Forster asked his readers to consider the value of modern travelers according to these standards, for they included a large number of "credible men whose observations are irreproachably exact, detailed and therefore usable" when it came to the subject of race. If Kant complained that there was not yet any clarity about the color of South Sea islanders, Forster, the specialist, paraded some of the descriptions from Cook, Bougainville, and other travelers to show that they had given a detailed and differentiated color map. With no less confidence Forster turned to the question of the permanence of color. It was well known, he stated, that Negro children were not born "black" but "red" and then in response to the atmosphere turned "black" after several days. In general, it was the influence of climate that created a human color spectrum from tropics to north, black to white; Europeans who remained in southern climates over several generations, wrote Forster, turned darker. Asking his readers for a manly facing up to the facts, even monstrous ones, Forster, relying on Soemmerring, then went on to argue that beyond skin color there were important physiological differences between Europeans and Africans that made them closely related but not identical. Taking up the question of whether they shared a common ancestry or had different genealogies, he declared himself agnostic and argued that it was wrong for Kant to pretend to have an answer to the question. Kant's arguments, according to Forster, were moralistic, dictating what ought to be out of fear of the consequences of admitting the possibility that Europeans and Africans had different racial origins. But what, he asked, was the consequence of admitting this possibility for the subject of slavery? Forster doubted whether the teaching of common ancestry had ever reduced at all the tyranny and cruelty of bondage. His proposal was a different one: to instill in Europeans a sense of paternalism, calling on an imaginary audience of slaveowners to take pride in elevating their chattel.[29]

Forster was taken aback by the force of Kant's response. In his 1788 essay "On the Use of Teleological Principles in Philosophy," Kant dismissed Forster's attempted distinction between philosophers and travelers by noting that conceptualization was always the condition for scientific observation; only with the guidance of an idea did one graduate from mere description of nature to causally linked natural

history. He then repeated many of the arguments he had made before in favor of monogenism. For a discussion of the unity or diversity of the human race, superficial distinctions such as skin color
were unimportant. Inability to reproduce was the sure sign of different origin, whereas it was not possible to point to any hindrance
to common descent so long as reproduction between individuals
of different population groups could take place. Forster, following
Soemmerring's lead, imagined a separate genealogy for Negroes, but
it was simpler to posit one human origin rather than two; it was just
bad scientific logic to complicate one's explanation by imagining two
separate creations of the human species on different parts of the
globe. Kant hypothesized as he had before that humanity had a single
origin with a great capacity for diversification, which had permitted
it to spread out and occupy different portions of the globe. With remarkable clear-sightedness, even in the absence of a scientific understanding of the mechanisms of species diversification, he set down
the monogenetic outlines of human prehistory.[30]

It was not a proud moment in Forster's intellectual biography. The
subsequent exchange with Kant made it bitterly clear to Forster that
he had no philosophical training and had not understood Kant's
clear and straightforward arguments for the definition of humanity
as a single race. Despite his feeling that he was still right on the subject of race and despite his previous plan of writing more on the subject, he let it drop.[31] In the introduction to his 1777 *Voyage round the
World,* he had actually come much closer to a Kantian methodology
of scientific observation when he argued that travel writers had to
know what they were looking for and make it meaningful by applying concepts to their empirical material. By contrast his criticism of
Kant fell back on a rather flat empiricism and for its evidence relied
heavily on Soemmerring. Forster had also shifted his loyalties: if he
had returned from the Cook voyage as an advocate for non-Europe-

ans, by the late 1780s he had turned into a partisan of the Enlightenment with a missionary vision of bringing European standards of reason and industry to the rest of the world.[32]

The debate between Kant and Forster captured some of the strengths and weaknesses of European thinkers' categories for comprehending the diversity of peoples and cultures around the world. Kant was not always generous or understanding toward non-Europeans, but he exposed the underlying unity of humanity and affirmed that there was no contradiction between the unity of rational beings descended from a common ancestry and the diversity of their physical appearance and cultures. It was a coherent theory that subsequent thinkers rarely emulated, preferring instead to err either on the side of a cultural or racial particularism that fell apart into mutually exclusive nationalities or a universalism that sought a single human nature or elevated one civilization to the status of human norm for judging all others.

There were limitations to Kant's position too; while he dealt expertly with physical diversity, he did not begin to address the significance of the different languages and cultural forms through which human beings exercised their rationality. This task, though not incompatible with his philosophy, was simply beyond the horizon of his own universal philosophical principles. During the French Revolution and the Napoleonic era, the consequences of applying abstract principles to society mattered not just to peoples in distant points on the globe like the South Pacific but to Europeans themselves; the Jacobin Terror and the march of revolutionary armies across the Continent taught European intellectuals a new appreciation for the value of historical, particular cultures. After 1789 new philosophies of culture, which looked back to the eighteenth century but had greater immediacy and applicability than ever before, could enhance Europeans' insight into their new worlds. The network of knowledge depended not only on what reports travelers brought back home, but on the historical maturity and contemporary experience that permitted thinkers to imagine a common yet radically differentiated humanity.

Wilhelm von Humboldt on Linguistic Diversity

Wilhelm von Humboldt, who died in 1835, takes us into a different era. Diderot wrote on the Tahitians at a late Enlightenment moment to clarify his conception of natural social behavior; Kant defined race in order to extend his conception of human reason. Humboldt began his intellectual career as they were ending theirs and wrote his mature philosophical reflections many decades later, at a cultural moment defined by the revolutionary transformations in European society and politics.

Born in 1767, Wilhelm was educated in the Enlightenment culture that preceded the French Revolution. He was slow to determine where his originality lay and to set his ideas down in print, however, and absorbed new impulses from Romantic philosophy and literature in the turbulent decades from the end of the old regime to the establishment of a new European order after 1815. His subsequent essays on language are a tortuous rethinking of cultural difference in the setting of a historical philosophy of language. Not that he ever became a proponent of particular cultures released from universal categories of human understanding: rather, a recurring theme of his late writings was the tension between particularity and universality, the insistence that each language was an intrinsically valuable revelation of the human spirit and at the same time that all the partial revelations of different languages belong together in a single developmental scheme. Precisely the meditative, incomplete, and essayistic quality of Humboldt's writings, his recurring exploration of particularity and universality without a one-sided resolution, makes of them a résumé of the revolutionary era's complex conversations. Even if it belonged to a different cultural era from Diderot's and Kant's, Humboldt's mature thought did not fit the conventional boxes of Enlightenment and Romanticism. Indeed it reminds us of the limits of labels that are too often taken as mutually exclusive alternatives. What is more striking over the decades from the late eighteenth to the early nineteenth century is how often intellectuals and artists synthesized tendencies that we tend to assign either to Romanticism or to Enlightenment neoclassicism, when the era drew much of its creativity from its broad embrace; for many it was a moment of classical romanticism. It was also a moment of simultaneous positivism and hermeneutics, fascination with Gall's "science" of reading skulls to determine racial character and newly heightened sensitivity to the difficulty of overcoming one's own cultural limitations. Although the early nineteenth century is sometimes portrayed as a moment of rising disenchantment with exotic cultures, it was far too rich, and at times contradictory, to conform to a single intellectual paradigm.

Humboldt's biography begins in a highly privileged Berlin household. His father was a courtier to Frederick the Great, his mother a wealthy Huguenot heiress; the parents took great care to provide him and his brother Alexander with a French tutor who exposed them at an early age to the ideas of the French Enlightenment. His first experience of cultural difference was the Jewish salons of Berlin: at a time when Jews were subject to legal disability and cultural prejudice, Wilhelm briefly fell in love with the famous salon host Henriette Herz. Like Chamisso, he got a firsthand education in what it meant to cross lines of class and confession in a Jewish Berlin household, not an easy experience to acquire, and certainly not a universal one, for highborn members of the old regime. Humboldt's later letters reveal crude resentment toward Jews; nonetheless the partial disintegration

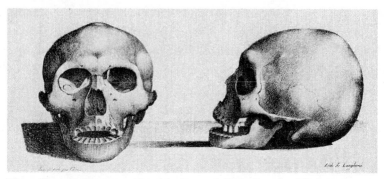

These Aleut skulls were analyzed by Franz Gall, the founder of phrenology, in Choris, *Voyage pittoresque autour du monde* (1822).

of ancient lines of social division, and his own youthful crossing of them, briefly exposed him to a different world.

Humboldt's friendship with George Forster widened his horizons beyond Europe. Wilhelm von Humboldt met him and his wife Therese when he was a twenty-one-year-old in the summer of 1788. Humboldt was then a student in Göttingen; Forster was a celebrated man in his mid-thirties. Soon after the Forsters' move to Mainz, Wilhelm von Humboldt visited them there for three or four days in October 1788; among other topics, they seem to have talked about Forster's essay on race, which he had written not long before. Humboldt noted in his diary that Forster was surely the only person who could write something valuable in this field, given his experiences and philosophical talents. After Humboldt's return to Göttingen they began a lively correspondence, and he visited the Forsters again in Mainz in September 1789, staying with them for over two weeks. The relationship that Humboldt had pursued with such fervor was soon abandoned. He disapproved of Forster's plunge into radical democratic politics, and after Forster's death in Paris at the beginning of 1794 he made no attempt to preserve the memory of his former host and friend. Soon afterward he moved to Jena, where he came under the influence of Schiller and Goethe, who also disapproved of Forster's political adventures. The relationship had become an embarrassment to him. Years later, when Therese Huber-Forster asked him to contribute letters to an edition of George's letters in the late 1820s, Humboldt was very reluctant to do so, and only let her make a limited selection after receiving a stinging rebuke from her. After Therese's death he wrote to a friend: "In the time in which I knew him and when I myself was very young, I had a very high opinion of him; afterward however I realized that he really, both as scholar and writer, had a greater name than his abilities and knowledge entitled him to." However strongly Humboldt later felt the need to repudiate him, Forster had served as a mentor to an entire generation of Germans. Friedrich Schlegel wrote in an essay praising Forster's worldly experience as a new model of self-cultivation for Germans: "No other German prose writer of distinction remotely approaches him: for cosmopolitanism, for sociability." Humboldt was one of Forster's pupils. The world traveler's example was a context for his own yearning to travel in the 1790s and 1800s, and the influence persisted in his post-1800 travel writing, which followed Forster's delineation of climate and other local conditions as the formative factors in the creation of national character.[33]

Humboldt was born in the same year as August Wilhelm Schlegel. Their relationship went back to their student days in Göttingen in 1788–89, where both of them studied classical philology with Christian Gottlob Heyne, George Forster's father-in-law. They came together again in Jena, where Schlegel started teaching in fall 1796 and Humboldt stayed in the winter of 1796–97. By then Schlegel had already staked out his own intellectual program as one of the young Romantics and was writing widely regarded reviews in literary journals. The two men overlapped a third time when Humboldt was

Prussian envoy *(Ministerresident)* in Rome; Schlegel arrived there in February 1805 as the companion of Germaine de Staël and frequently visited Humboldt's house, a meeting place for German visitors. Finally, intellectual interests drew them together at a later stage of their lives. Schlegel, following his brother Friedrich's lead, became a scholar of Sanskrit, while Humboldt was deeply interested in Sanskrit for his linguistic theorizing.[34] The significance of the brothers Schlegel for Wilhelm von Humboldt went beyond Sanskrit studies alone, however. Their conception of a comparative study of world literature was an important part of their Romantic program, which August Wilhelm Schlegel had popularized first in lectures in Berlin and later in Vienna. So was translation, which Schlegel defended as an original, creative act—indeed part of the very definition of cultural activity—and, against cultural nationalists, upheld as part of Germany's distinctive character: "Universalism, cosmopolitanism is the truly distinctive German character."[35] A translation such as August Wilhelm Schlegel's famous rendering of Shakespeare into German demonstrated that cultural creativity did not have to be indigenous, but could be an act of importation, an issue that would later occupy Wilhelm von Humboldt. In the Rome period and in their correspondence of the 1820s, Humboldt treated him with a touch of condescension, perhaps in part because of Schlegel's notorious vanity, in part because he seemed the more conventional talent in comparison with his brother Friedrich.[36] Yet both of the Schlegels changed the landscape of German literary culture and opened up areas that Humboldt further explored.

Many factors in Wilhelm von Humboldt's education prepared his receptiveness to cultural diversity, including the Berlin Jewish salons, the contact with George Forster, and the burgeoning of early German Romanticism. A travel experience gave him firsthand knowledge of a different culture: his trip of 1801 through Basque country. It was a

Romantic journey to a country which, though geographically part of Europe, seemed singularly autochthonous and undamaged by the civilizing influence of outside conquerors. Protected by mountains and the sea, the Basques had preserved, he wrote in an unpublished essay completed in 1805, their national character and their love of freedom: "Intermingling with none of their neighbors they have remained, despite all the progress of luxury and cultivation surrounding them, in a condition of original simplicity of manners, and still have their distinctive national character, and above all have preserved the old spirit of freedom and independence that Greek and Roman writers already praised in them." The Basque language was the living embodiment of their primitive virtues. Not yet a literary or scientific language, it still had the vigor and immediacy of a language close to the people. This plea for the value of Basque was an example of what would later be called salvation anthropology—part of that broad program of efforts throughout the nineteenth and twentieth centuries to rescue folk cultures around the world before they were corrupted or destroyed by modernization. His praise for the Basques' spirited and freedom-loving character followed his era's established convention of praising rude republican virtue, whether among Highland Scots or the Iroquois. At the same time his Basque journey gave him his own formative experience of cultural diversity that went beyond the literary offerings of the time.[37]

The essay on the Basques that he actually published in 1812, one of the bits of his reflections on language that he released for public view before the 1820s, continued this focus on the people as an object of study. Humboldt proposed a study of national character in the natural historical tradition going back to the Forsters: he imagined human beings as formed by a variety of circumstances, including common descent, the soil, climate, and natural barriers, into separate ethnic groups and nations. The task of world history, he wrote, was to bring these separate groups together in ever new, creative combinations; the task of the researcher, to narrate their relations to one another. It was a cosmopolitan conception starting from the diversity of history and pointing it in the direction of unity: "The preparations for a world history must be made in various ways, above all through exact, detailed and faithful descriptions of individual peoples, of a kind that hardly exists today."[38] Humboldt's conception of ethnography was in equal parts devoted to its subject and to a larger conception of humanity.

Humboldt's Basque studies remained incomplete, a fragment, like many of the other projects he undertook, that never cohered into a larger, published whole. They were remarkable nonetheless as documents in the development of a thinker strongly drawn to the humanist vision of ancient Greece as the cultural norm for all time and all mankind. He had intensively pursued the study of classical Greek, and it never lost its hold on his imagination. Yet he also felt a powerful pull in another direction, toward the primitive vitality of a "barbarian" people who had held off the conquerors of classical antiquity and preserved their own language and national community. His turn to the Basques was remarkable in another way, too: Humboldt had grown up as a child of exceptional privilege, having little contact at any time with people outside the highest social strata. Yet he conceived of his Basque studies as a concerted effort to overcome the separation between educated and uneducated, and to locate the source of human creativity in the conversations of the people that moved from mouth to mouth. This justification for studying the Basques could be used for studying any people on earth. It was folklore with a cosmopolitan intent.

Humboldt's views on cultural diversity were furthered by his ambivalent relationship to the modern state. In December 1791 he wrote an important essay, later much admired by John Stuart Mill, on the limits of state power, in which he argued that the personal autonomy of the individual was the highest end of social life, and that the state should be nothing more than a guardian guaranteeing collective safety with a minimum of intervention in the affairs of its citizens.[39] As a young man he briefly entered public service and then retreated into the privacy of family life, self-cultivation, and intellectual friendships. The crisis of the Prussian state after its defeat by Napoleon in 1807 created a new situation in which he could no longer cherish personal autonomy above all else. When Baron Stein, the political reformer who envisioned a revived Prussia that would be motivated by an ethos of citizenship and personal freedom, asked him to rejoin state service, he did not refuse. One of his most important achievements was to set down the guiding principles for the University of Berlin, which was founded in 1810. His conception balanced personal development and public responsibility, envisioning the modern university as an institution that would thrive on autonomy and the absence of prescribed practical ends for its work, although scientific advances in the end would benefit society and state. Humboldt remained in state service until 1820, a period of twelve years in which he rarely had time for literature and learning. Public life did not turn him into an uncritical admirer of the state; he maintained his suspicion toward it and concern for the vitality of national culture under modern conditions.

Absent from his writings was anything like the celebration of the state in Hegel's political philosophy and in the writings of subsequent generations of German professors. Hegel, a professor at the University of Berlin, published his lectures on political philosophy as *The Philosophy of Right* in 1821, the year after Humboldt left state service.[40] It was the Restoration moment when the disturbances of the French Revolution and the Napoleonic years had been capped and the Prussian monarchy was firmly reestablished on the throne, its reform program a success at rebuilding the state and unleashing the energies of economy and society. Hegel himself was not an uncritical admirer of the Prussian state and was certainly not an opponent of the principles of 1789: he saw his task as one of reconstruction, uniting freedom for the individual and for civil society with sensitivity to the older differences of rank and authority of the monarchy that could guarantee political stability and the welfare of all parts of society. His lectures delineated the family's ethical nurturing of the individual, the individual's drive to a mature adulthood of independence from the family and freedom in civil society, and the need, in turn, for constraints on the conflict of individuals in civil society and the reintegration of the individual in a rational whole with claims on his loyalty, the state. Ultimately, however, after these elaborate mediations, Hegel's philosophy was a justification of the state as the embodiment of reason in history, with its civil servants the agents of reason who rose above the particular interests of different parts of society and governed for the sake of the social whole.

During the same moment Hegel was offering the world his philosophy of society and the state, Humboldt, freed of his ministerial duties, returned to his investigations into the nature of language. In their own, indirect way his writings reflected on the relationship between state power and human freedom. Obligation forced them out of him: as a member of the Prussian Academy of Sciences he was required to give reports on his work. The first of these papers, read to the academy on June 29, 1820, and published in 1822, was a moment of breakthrough that finally defined language as his object of study; it was followed by other published and unpublished papers culminating in his monograph, incomplete at the time of his death, on the Kawi language of Malaya, with an introduction attempting a final summation of his philosophy of language.

The first principle of this new phase of his productivity was the primacy of language for the analysis of human societies. Humboldt was a linguist as Durkheim was later a sociologist, asking how the group identity of human beings could be grounded in the phenomenon that he had chosen as his object of study. In an unpublished essay of the later 1820s he wrote: "The great unities that determine the movement of human history are defined solely or mainly through language." From this standpoint he criticized racial theories. It is obvious, he wrote in the same essay, that language groups and racial groups do not correspond to each other, and that speakers of a common language do not necessarily share a common descent. The accidents of history can give peoples of different ethnic origin a common language and, vice versa, common language speakers may have different origins. He was equally dismissive toward the idea that physical characteristics such as size, color, build, or facial features had in any way influenced the formation of languages. Ideas of this kind came from apologists for slavery or ridiculous pride in skin color, for language expressed man's spiritual nature and was not dependent on these accidents of human beings' physical makeup.[41]

Humboldt's essays included extensive deliberations on "savage" or "barbaric" nations in which he defended the importance of studying their languages. The so-called crude or barbaric languages, he wrote in his academy address of 1820, have everything they need for full power of speech. They can also absorb any idea one wishes to import into them. He criticized the practice (routine in travel accounts) of breaking down languages into lists of words and grammatical peculiarities. "The speech of even the crudest nation is too noble a work of nature to break into accidental parts and represent in fragmentary form. It is an organic entity and must be treated as such." The first rule of comparative linguistic studies was "to study every known language with regard for its inner coherence" and only thereafter to go on to comparison between languages. Moreover, Humboldt added a motive for studying every known tongue: languages were not just arbitrary signs linked to sounds: rather each one was a creative principle, an original way of grasping the world that provided unique insight into it. A so-called barbaric language was not an inferior means of expression, but a unique complement to all other languages.[42]

In his 1822 talk to the academy, however, Humboldt also introduced a significant distinction between European and other languages. Titled "On the Origins of Grammatical Forms, and Their Influence on the Development of Ideas," the essay took up a question which had long preoccupied theorists of language: whether the grammatical forms of a given language limited or encouraged the intellectual life of its speakers. Did ancient Greek and Latin or modern European languages predispose their users to the development of higher ideas of science and religion? Did the speakers of non-European languages have a more muddled linguistic structure and, as a result, a more limited grasp of the world? Humboldt asserted that all languages have grammatical forms capable of clear intellectual comprehension; he pointed in particular to American Indians for finely differentiated languages among "savage" peoples. But his opinion altered when he turned from the question of what *could* be expressed in a language—that is, what could be translated into it—to the issue of its spontaneous power of developing ideas. Following the lead of Friedrich Schlegel's philosophy of language, he introduced a hierarchy: the clear articulation of logical categories in Greek and Latin gave them an advantage over most other languages in the articulation of ideas. Humboldt puzzled over the case of Chinese, which had developed a literature over thousands of years despite its lack of a highly differentiated grammar; nonetheless he thought it was plain to see that a language like Greek permitted a clear and supple exchange of views in spoken debate. While Humboldt took pains to impress on his readers the dignity and worthiness for study of any language, he was also reluctant to give up the notion of an intrinsic superiority of European languages and their nearest relatives.[43]

The ambiguity of Humboldt's views on language recurs in his final, great work, his unfinished introduction to his study of Kawi. Overall the essay subscribes to the notion of a hierarchy of languages rising according to the complexity of their grammatical forms. At the top are the so-called inflected languages such as Sanskrit and Greek, which in Humboldt's view exhibit the fullest perfection in the articulation of logical categories. Below them are other inflected languages such as Hebrew and Arabic (the "Semitic" languages), and still lower are the "agglutinative" languages, which are stuck together without any kind of internal logic. Humboldt was drawn to the idea of a single, universal language that could be a perfect vehicle of logical thought; though no language completely realized this idea, he thought Sanskrit came closest, followed in diminishing degrees by the lower orders of the linguistic hierarchy. Yet this universalism contradicted his own Romantic impulse toward appreciation of diversity and particularity, which had led him to study the most diverse and peripheral languages in order to further the widest possible conception of humanity. Humboldt's love of linguistic diversity pulses through the work. It is the tension between the universalist and particularist directions of his thought that give it an internal drama, which is not so much resolved as exposed, an ongoing, incomplete struggle between two different views of language and the human communities that speak them.

Humboldt was in some critical respects more cosmopolitan than Herder, who is often cited as a starting point for the modern study of culture. A contemporary of George Forster's, Herder challenged the notion of a single, universal culture and envisaged the course of history instead as the gradual unfolding of a multiplicity of cultures, each intrinsically valuable, each a contribution to the universal definition of humanity. There was another side to Herder's thought that could make it a starting point for cultural insularity: Herder emphasized the rootedness of each culture in its particular climate and soil; he had no theory of the formation of one culture through interaction with others. His thought could be used by others to sanction a xenophobic politics of authenticity that raised ethnicity and nationality to the status of sacred absolutes; it could rail against Jews and other peoples uprooted from their original soil. The main impact of Herder on his own time and subsequent generations, however, was to turn away from the utopia of a single, universal civilization and conceive of a humanity ever enriched and renewed by the multiplicity of its cultural expressions.

Humboldt was an inheritor and beneficiary of Herder's critique of monocultures that crush local diversity. But Herder's organic ideology had no place in his thought; instead his philosophy of language emphasized the formation of language through borrowing. Kawi interested him as a case of cultural synthesis. He spoke of it as the ancient sacred language of "Malaya," by which he meant a cultural region centering on present-day Indonesia—mainly Java and Sumatra—but more broadly a language area extending from the Philippines to New Guinea. He turned to Kawi for his final work because Malayans had assimilated Indian culture without losing their independence; Kawi exemplified the marrying of foreign and indigenous cultures. On this issue Humboldt was opposed to Herder's cultural insularity (and Jacob and Wilhelm Grimm's collection of German language and fairy tales in search of unadulterated German origins). Humboldt was engaged in a different kind of scholarly inquiry, the study of creativity through linguistic interaction. The Kawi language demonstrated how an infusion of foreign vocabulary and ideas may result in a new and beautiful and even sacred synthesis.[44]

Differences between peoples were part of man's natural condition:

both physical and linguistic variation was a given. He mentioned these differences, but only as the changing, timebound means of human expression: "The division of the human race into peoples and tribes and the differences among its languages and kinds of speech are immediately related to one another but also connected and subordinated to a third, higher phenomenon, the engendering of human creativity in always new and often heightened form . . . This . . . revelation of human creativity is the highest end of all cultural change, the ultimate idea toward which world history clearly permits us to strive." The task of comparative and historical linguistic studies was to observe this gradual revelation of the human spirit. The study of language as Humboldt imagined it was a successor to the study of sacred texts: instead of the particular revelation set down in Christian scripture, language itself was everywhere a revelation of a higher spirit, everywhere meriting examination. To assert as did the ethnic purists that languages were isolated from one another would for Humboldt have meant denying the movement of history through the meeting and mixture of different languages. Humboldt used the example of the decline of the Roman Empire and the rebirth of modern Europe with its newly formed languages to remind his readers that this process of mixture and renewal was part of their own linguistic history.[45]

There was a worrisome contrast, thought Humboldt, between these historical cases of linguistic transmission and the linguistic and cultural diffusion of his own time. In Europe, and in India and Indonesia of millennia past, change had taken place so gradually that the spirit of an invading culture, along with its forms, accompanied its spread to new languages and peoples. Humboldt observed a different process in modern times, when European conquest of non-Europeans was rapid and destructive. To be sure, an unprecedented spread of civilization from Europe was taking place, and with it Europe's esteem for the dignity of the individual. Nonetheless, Humboldt was filled with doubts about this process. He prized *Bildung*, often translated as education or self-cultivation, but for him more specifically the individual's spontaneous power of shaping the world into a meaningful whole: "When we in our language say *Bildung*, we mean something simultaneously higher and finer, namely the way our knowledge and our entire cultural and moral striving come together in a sensuous, spontaneous harmony to nurture our sensibility and character." The spread of modern civilization seemed to bring about something very different—indeed the opposite of *Bildung:* "thus under our influence the nations become more homogeneous and the formation of distinctive national character is often nipped in the bud where it might have taken place." The outward drive of modern European civilization only brought about the death of older cultures and was too rapid and overwhelming to permit the growth of a new culture in their place.[46]

Humboldt's meditations on language derived from the linguistic and philosophical speculations of his age, but also from its travel culture, including his contact with George Forster, his trip to the Basque country, and the travels of his brother. In the end his mature writing absorbed the cosmopolitan influences streaming into Europe in a different way from the writings of Diderot and Kant. While the late-eighteenth-century thinkers certainly took travel writing seriously, and considered the significance of its reports on unfamiliar societies for their philosophical systems, they absorbed them into their existing conceptions of nature and reason rather than reconsidering them. Wilhelm von Humboldt takes us into a different style of thinking. He turned to the particularity and diversity of existing languages, made the study of them crucial to his own enterprise, and explored how to retain them in his philosophy.

Both Humboldt and Chamisso lived and worked in Berlin, leading parallel if rather distant lives. From 1820 to the mid-1830s Humboldt was free of his state duties and could turn to his linguistic researches; during the same period of time Chamisso, who had returned from his voyage in 1818, pursued his literary and scientific activities. Humboldt, privately wealthy, a retired minister of state, moved among the great men and women of the capital. Chamisso was a more ambiguous figure, his status complicated as always; he was employed as a lowly curator of the royal botanical garden, but also worked as an influential editor and man of letters. No matter how far apart their lives, Chamisso was already aware of Humboldt's linguistic studies when he prepared his naturalist's report for the Kotzebue voyage account and was eager later to share his own work with Humboldt.[47] At the Prussian Academy of Sciences, where Wilhelm had spoken on his linguistic researches, Chamisso presented the results of his study of Hawaiian. In his lecture of January 12, 1837, he offered his own work as a continuation of his predecessor's, and declared his intention of preparing a Hawaiian grammar and vocabulary, which he hoped to compare with other Polynesian languages.[48] Humboldt provided a philosophical framework for his task. At that moment, travel and philosophy, experience and conceptualization for the world of learning, came together.

Humboldt's linguistic ruminations are fragments, difficult to compose into a larger order, and certainly not written with a wide audience in mind. Yet they exerted a key influence on later thinkers who wrestled with the issues of universalism and particularity in the study of language and culture. He is widely viewed as the founder of the study of "linguistic relativity," that is, the degree to which the human capacity for thought is conditioned by the specific grammatical forms and other linguistic attributes of any single language. This school of thought has been much disputed, especially since it has retained the ambiguity, already built into Humboldt's work, of resolving itself into a hierarchy in which claims are made for the superiority of some languages over others as vehicles of rational thinking or some other valued intellectual capacity. Nonetheless, historians of linguistic theory and culture have traced a continuity from Humboldt to Franz Boas, the German immigrant to the United States who became the key founder of American cultural anthropology, and Boas's student, the famous linguistic anthropologist Edward Sapir.[49] Humboldt's theory marks the historical origin of a new kind of relationship between travel account and scientific reception. No longer, in Humboldt, did a travel account fit into a ready-made receptacle, or serve simply as evidence for or against its correctness; instead he demanded that the scientific theory itself recognize the specific features of its subject, explore its intrinsic logic, and confront its effect on prior assumptions. In his essays on language, the reports of travelers like Chamisso found a welcome home—and modern cultural sciences had one of their most fruitful starting points.

CHAPTER 5

Missions

Scientific travelers and philosophers may have argued with each other, but they belonged to a common culture and a common world of learning. Diderot and Bougainville were men of the Enlightenment; so were Kant and George Forster; Chamisso and Wilhelm von Humboldt spanned two eras, blending Enlightenment and Romantic values. Scientific expeditions from the 1820s to the 1840s were their direct descendants; their captains and scientists continued in the tradition of Cook to gather the widest assortment of knowledge, including knowledge of human beings, on voyages that combined scientific curiosity with the imperial aims of their home countries. Russia, France, and Britain all continued to send out major expeditions. So did the United States, which had an interest in expeditions going back to Thomas Jefferson's sponsorship of Lewis and Clark's overland journey of 1804–1806, and which sponsored an ambitious voyage to the Pacific, commanded by Charles Wilkes, from 1838 to 1842.[1] These nations' voyage aims continued to have the typical mixture, dating back to the eighteenth century, of imperial rivalry and scientific community.

The official accounts that followed from these later voyages show a high standard of professionalism. They are also the work of a successor generation following a fixed paradigm, skilled at filling in details of the cartographic and ethnographic picture but with little in the way of original insight into the peoples of the Pacific or other parts of the world; they stereotype what was already known rather than deepening understanding. If captains and scientists turned to a handbook of scientific exploration like the one the astronomer John Herschel prepared for the British navy in 1849, the quality of its individual contributions could not have been higher: Charles Darwin wrote the chapter on geology, and the leading exponent of monogenism, James Prichard, wrote the chapter on ethnology. Yet naturalists learned from Herschel how to add new facts to the established paradigms of scientific travel rather than risk an original idea. A voyage like the Wilkes expedition was lavishly outfitted by the United States, and Wilkes in time produced a multivolume voyage account, but it is remarkable only for its dullness, its absence of insight into the peoples Wilkes visited, and its suppression of the conflicts that led to his court-martialing. The disappointing results of expeditions like this one help to explain anthropology's later disdain of "travelers": theoretical innovation and richer ethnography had to crack through the conventions of scientific expeditions that had lost their creative impulse.[2]

Dumont d'Urville and the Triumph of Racial Science

As one of the most intelligent navigators of the Restoration era, Jules Dumont d'Urville exemplifies the outermost achievements as well as the limitations of exploration after 1815. From a distinguished Norman family, he combined classical learning and technical aptitude with the fervent ambition to rival the achievements of Cook. Assigned to charting duties on a Mediterranean cruise in 1819, he recognized the aesthetic value of the statue uncovered by a peasant on the island of Melos and made the arrangements for transporting the Venus de Milo to France, an achievement that earned him an honor and a promotion. He commanded two expeditions to the Pacific, the first from 1826 to 1829, the second from 1837 to 1840. His arrogance and liberal politics made him plenty of enemies, although he had his admirers too. D'Urville and Chamisso, liberal aristocrats who greeted the July Monarchy of Louis Philippe as the beginning of a new age, met at least once in Paris in 1825, and the normally dour d'Urville wrote a warm note after failing to find his friend at home ("Dear Sir, I stopped by your house to have the honor or rather the pleasure of seeing you once more before your departure . . .)." Alexander von Humboldt and Adam von Krusenstern, too, admired d'Urville and supported his second circumnavigation. So did the Geographic Society of Paris, which after his death in a train accident in 1842 collected money for a memorial statue. None of the captains of the era dating back to Cook sailed with a stronger or more justified self-confidence in his scientific abilities, which made d'Urville fully the equal of the *savants* of the metropolis.[3]

D'Urville did not limit his scientific investigations to technical questions; he took a strong personal interest in the ethnography of the Pacific. Responding to a prize question from the Paris Geographic Society he wrote an essay, published in 1832, outlining a fourfold division among the islanders of the Pacific into the categories of Polynesian, Melanesian, Micronesian, and Malaysian. These types derived from his strict color hierarchy of "white," "yellow," and "black" races. Disdaining to enter into the debate over monogenism or polygenism, he simply declared that the "races" were differently endowed by nature, with whites the conquering race and blacks the natural subordinates. His description of Oceania allied the Polynesians with whites, for while he questioned whether the islanders were descended from Hindus, he thought that they and Hindus were descended from a common ancestor.[4] D'Urville praised all the Polynesians for their high level of civilization, noting that before the arrival of Europeans they had formed nations with genealogies, social ranks, and in a few cases even monarchies. His favorites were the Maoris, whom he compared to northern Europeans: like the French, British, and Germans of an earlier era, they might look uncouth, but with exposure to higher civilization would bound past their neighbors living in sunnier climates.

D'Urville was a hard man who responded with a deep note of admiration to the warrior ethos of the Maoris. At the lower end of his hierarchy were, predictably, Melanasians, "natural enemies of whites," who had shown such a consistent dislike of travelers and extended none of the hospitality Cook, Bougainville, and their successors had enjoyed among Polynesians; at the very bottom were the Australians and Tasmanians. D'Urville was a devotee of phrenology (even though he made allowance for its sometimes speculative assertions) and successfully pleaded with Louis Philippe to have a phrenologist added to the scientific contingent of his second voyage. D'Urville's verbal descriptions and the magnificent atlas for the second voyage put character on visual display, ennobling and degrading different peoples according to their supposed merits (although the portrayals of Maoris range from "savage" to lofty-looking). The French navigator's writings repeat a paradox of the writings of George Forster later in his life as he entered his Jacobin phase: it was perfectly possible to combine liberal and republican ideals for European politics with hierarchical judgments on the extra-European world. D'Urville's writings come at the end of an age: they are a compendium of the racial speculation of the preceding half century, served up for an audience that was increasingly confident of its right to exterminate entire peoples as the cost of European "progress." To be sure, d'Urville's writ-

The master race: Rangui, a chief from New Zealand.
From Jules Dumont d'Urville, *Voyage de la corvette
L'Astrolabe* (1833).

ings shimmered with ambiguities. His vision of the decline and fall
of peoples oddly echoed his fear that his own expedition could van-
ish in the wastelands of the South and his own name fail to make
its mark in the annals of discovery. Scientifically precise, d'Urville's
work was also a transition to the civilizing mission of the high age of
nineteenth-century European imperialism.[5]

In its own time d'Urville's hierarchy of the "races" of the Pacific
could be regarded as a triumph of the naturalist network of knowledge. His ability to visit islands far and wide across the Pacific depended on the measuring and mapping techniques of his predeces-

sors; his ethnography was no less dependent on their reports, and he specifically mentioned "the immortal Forster" (probably a reference to Johann Reinhold), Chamisso, Cook, and "the celebrated Malte-Brun" (the Danish geographer prominent in French geographic circles) as authorities in the sweeping survey of Oceania that he published in the journal of the Geographic Society. The network of knowledge had thickened and settled; in his article, scientific knowledge of the peoples of this vast region seemed to have arrived at a definitive form and content.

Sex, Speech, and Prophecy in Tahiti

At the very moment in the late 1820s when the naturalist's ethnographic survey seemed to be complete, a second, largely independent network had arisen and threatened to displace it. Missionaries constructed an independent world of knowledge with its own patrons, its own informants, and its own audience. At an intellectual level, too, missionaries challenged the naturalists, for they had their own conception of what it meant to "know" another culture, diminishing the aesthetic and racial categories so important to the naturalists and replacing them with ethical and religious canons for understanding another world. Christian missionary work had preceded by centuries the scientific expeditions of the eighteenth and nineteenth centuries. The Anglo-American missions to Oceania were not directly indebted to older missions, however. Rather, their evangelical founders devised new organizations to carry Christianity to islands halfway around the world. They succeeded in building an independent machinery to disseminate their own faith abroad and bring back their own ethnographic vision of the island peoples they wished to convert.[6]

Much of the writing about missionaries in the Pacific has taken the form of polemics for and against them and their work. Understandably so, for they dramatically toppled old systems of belief while working to install colonial rule and capitalist commerce. From the beginning they were controversial. Polemics can and probably should continue; but there are other ways, too, of viewing their story. Missionary sources are extraordinarily rich and, when one turns to them from secular sources, they seem to contain many unexamined stories. A historical approach would ask not, "were they right?" but rather, "what did they know, and how?" C. A. Bayly in *Intelligence and Empire*, which examines the British failure to anticipate India's Great Rebellion of 1857–1859, remarks that the British in mid-nineteenth-century India lacked three great sources of intelligence: marriage, landholding, and religion. His model provides a starting point for comparing naturalists and missionaries in Polynesia. One can begin to comprehend the role of the missionaries by asking about their behavior in at least two of these three areas, marriage (including the overlapping categories of kinship and sexual exchange) and religion.

On August 4, 1797, the *Duff*, a ship specially commissioned for the task, left a missionary community of thirty at Matavai Bay, Tahiti. It was the first of the many European religious missions to Oceania that would follow during the nineteenth century. "We are now situated," states their diary entry for that day, "in one of the most delightful countries in the world; here the cares and anxieties, which possess the poor man's breast, with respect to the maintenance of his family, require not a thought." The London Missionary Society issued a reassuring report on the Tahitians' character soon after the return of the *Duff* to England: "Their manners are affable and engaging; their step easy, firm and graceful; their behaviour free and unguarded; always boundless in generosity to each other, and to strangers; their tempers mild, gentle, and unaffected; slow to take offense, easily pacified, and seldom retaining resentment or revenge, whatever provocation they may have received." In their own way the missionaries looked forward to working in a tropical paradise where they could carry out their work in comfort.[7]

In its intellectual origins the missionary project was far removed from the scientific travelers. The great evangelical revival of John Wesley and others in the late eighteenth century was a reaction to the urbane skepticism of the upper classes in Britain and an attempt to return to a faith that relied on feeling and personal experience. The first missionaries were evangelicals and "godly mechanics": craftsmen and others from the lower end of the respectable classes who combined heartfelt religiosity with a yearning to separate themselves from the lowest social orders and improve their own social status. Repentance for sins and a conversion experience were inseparable from strict self-discipline and the exercise of practical work skills.[8]

When the official account of Cook's first voyage was published and reports circulated about the travelers' Tahiti experience, evangelicals were appalled by the descriptions of Polynesian mores; Wesley himself refused to credit the stories of people openly copulating in broad daylight.[9] Nonetheless the tales of a Polynesian paradise intrigued them no less than their contemporaries. As evangelicals began to dream of a great new missionary endeavor in the wider world, their thoughts quickly turned to Tahiti as an ideal site for their work. When the London Missionary Society (LMS) was officially founded in September 1795, its leaders quickly organized an expedition to Tahiti, which offered an irresistible mixture of material comfort and a people in need of moral uplift.

No matter how great their initial dislike of the scientific travelers' accounts, the LMS directors did not hesitate to make use of them to guide their own planning. For the best possible intelligence they turned to the master authority himself, Joseph Banks. Thomas Haweis, the main founder of the missionary society, introduced himself to Sir

Joseph as the directors were forming their plans and asked if Banks would "be so obliging as to give him some hints, how Persons, who may be left at Otaheite may be serviceably employed, whilst instructing the natives, in any attempt that may be of use to ourselves, and future investigators who may call there. Mr H[aweis] understands Capta[in] Bligh will breakfast with Sir Joseph tomorrow, and he [Haweis] will then knock at his Door." Afterward Haweis wrote in the name of the LMS directors to thank Banks for his advice and to offer aid to the African Society if it sought cooperation with the missionaries.[10]

Another LMS spokesman, Joseph Hardcastle, wrote a letter to Banks demonstrating that their objectives were not as far apart as they might seem at first sight. The more conservative LMS members were deeply Tory in their views, with a conception of the Georgian monarchy that bordered on sacred kingship and a dedication to British imperial interests that did not lag behind Banks's own. Their conception of Christianity itself could converge with Enlightenment notions of commerce and science. Hardcastle hoped that the LMS, in addition to spreading Christianity, would "subserve also the Interests of Science, enlarge the sphere of our acquaintances with the productions of Nature, and ultimately extend the operations of Commerce—we hope therefore our Institution will prove honourable to our Country whose Renown is as much founded in the superior excellence of its moral principles and conduct, as in its acquisitions and science, or its extended commerce, Wealth or power." This description of the directors' aims was rather disingenuous. They did not make any direct effort to promote science in their initial missions to the Pacific; there were no promises to collect plants, survey land, or report to Banks on native societies. Although the LMS was an ecumenical organization, the dominant strand was an emotional evangelicalism that combined Calvinist asceticism with a suspicion of education. Nonetheless they were not hostile toward useful learning that could promote their religious ends, and they made a serious attempt to learn what they could about Tahiti by consulting with the reigning scientific experts.[11]

Outfitted with scientific intelligence, the LMS directors expected islanders to receive their emissaries with unqualified gratitude. The missionaries were to explain to the chiefs the advantages of their residence so that their stay would be the result of the chiefs' "earnest desire"; the chiefs were to give them full title to the land that they might need and to respect their laws, customs, and religion while guaranteeing their safety; and the missionaries' presents "should not be considered as payments, but as gratuities, the expressions and pledges of our goodwill."[12] Perhaps the missionaries themselves, by the time they reached Matavai Bay, were less certain they would receive such a submissive welcome. Even the record of the first day reveals their anxiety about being stranded so far from home:

> Still we have our troubles and anxieties, when we consider our critical situation, upon a small Island, many thousands of miles distant from our native country, and surrounded by an uncivilized people. We have, it is true, received from them kind treatment, greatly surpassing what we expected; but, from our knowledge of human nature, we have cause to apprehend, that much deceit and covetousness may be mingled with their actions, as well as professions of kindness; and are therefore taught the necessity of some degree of caution in our transactions with them.[13]

Their "knowledge of human nature" was grounded in a Calvinist sectarianism that taught them that human appearances hid a heart of darkness, which was inconstant and unreliable even among Christians and was bound to contain evil in an un-Christian and, as they wrote, "uncivilized" land. Their suspicions were soon confirmed. Visitors like Cook and Bligh had guns and cannons to enforce a cautious civility. Even they could barely enforce their "friendship" with islanders. The missionaries had no such armaments and were that much more exposed to island ambition, greed, and politics. By August 23 they were reporting thefts from the blacksmith's shop—hardly surprising, since iron was a valuable military commodity—and suffered from constant fear of theft and plundering. They were receiving painful lessons in the insufficiency of their initial intelligence, grounded as it was in the misleading security of naval expeditions and the LMS directors' own fanciful underestimation of the difficulties that awaited them.

They now began receiving information from another, better-informed source: the beachcombers. Even before the missionaries left they had made use of beachcomber knowledge, drawing while still in England on the Tahitian vocabulary compiled by James Morrison, one of the sailors who survived the *Bounty* mutiny and his subsequent trial in England. Once the religious emissaries landed in Tahiti their well-being and perhaps their lives depended on the castaways who could mediate between them and their hosts. Two Swedes were living on the island: Andrew Lind, who had survived a shipwreck and lived there since 1792, and Peter Haggerstein, who had been left on Tahiti by his ship captain.[14] Peter the Swede, as the missionaries called him in their diary, was particularly helpful—indeed one wonders whether their mission would have outlasted its initial days at all without his help. Beachcombers like Peter belonged to a class found too on mainlands and islands in other parts of the world: the first settlers. They did not have the glory of the explorers who claim "discoveries" or the scientists who mapped them and wrote them up; but they initiated the mediation between cultures. Another group that fits the same description is the *coureurs de bois* of New France, who were often the first Europeans to mix with Indians in the arc that stretches from Canada and the Great Lakes to the Mississippi Valley. In both cases these were largely male adventurers who could not expect much recognition from missionaries and explorers. Yet the more respectable settlers often depended on the first arrivals' painfully acquired local knowledge.

Peter saved the missionaries from their own paranoia. On their second day the missionaries thought that Pomare I's mother ("the most powerful person upon the island") was planning to plunder them on the sabbath. She for her part was alarmed by their behavior and sent Peter "to inform us that we were quite mistaken in our conceptions." Later when missionaries Henry Bicknell and Thomas Lewis wanted to do some ethnographic fieldwork, they turned to Peter; Lewis hoped "to obtain from an old priest, the father of the woman with whom Peter cohabits, some historic account of the origin of the Otaheiteans." We continue to hear of Peter in 1799. He brought the missionaries "a large baked fish"; he warned them of the danger of warfare between their district and a neighbor; he cooled down a conflict between the Tahitians and a visiting merchant ship. Peter had linguistic and diplomatic skills that the newly arrived missionaries badly needed. Even Peter, however, was not saved from the depredations of a society breaking down under the impact of European weapons and disease; when war broke out later the same year his house was burned down by unknown arsonists, a frightening event for the missionaries, who feared that their own houses might be next.[15]

Peter at this time had the benefit of one of Bayly's critical intelligence sources: a local wife. Though they benefited from the relationship, the missionaries were not about to condone cohabiting with local women—at least not openly. When John Cock (together with Peter) came to his fellows and asked whether he might marry a young native woman, he was refused and was reminded that "the church had already determined such conduct, in any of her members, to be a departure from the faith. The same day Peter made his own request: "Peter the Swede asked the society, if the woman he lived with, and whom he called Mary, might be baptized, and he married to her? The answer made was in the negative." Yet who could resist, and how many did resist, of those who did not bring their wives with them to Tahiti? They had intruded on a society that was open to alliances, and indeed proposed alliances when they seemed to offer visible advantages. It was the missionaries who were behaving in a way that by island standards was bizarre. "Even Christian converts . . . ," writes Neil Gunson in his history of the Pacific missions, "were intensely suspicious of persons of more mature years who were either unmarried or not living with a woman." The Tahitians suspected the Westerners of sleeping with their daughters or each other. The absence of kinship networks was not just a blank spot on the social map, but a refusal of social relations that disrupted customary civilities well before the Tahitians could make sense out of the missionaries' religious motives. Later Claude Lévi-Strauss would interpret kinship relations as a system of gift exchanges that bound together the different household units of society; the Tahitians were fully competent anthropologists who did not need to wait for modern anthropology in order to draw their own conclusions about this strange withdrawal from normal social relationships.[16]

The conflict between religion and sex was intolerable for many of the single missionaries; in fact many did have relations with local women, leading to an atmosphere of mutual suspicion and recrimination.[17] Thomas Lewis, one of the group's four ordained missionaries, repeatedly attended church service with an unnamed woman in June and July of 1799 while arguing with the community about whether the relationship was compatible with church membership. Finally on July 17 he was excommunicated and left the missionaries' settlement to live with her. On October 17 they learned that he was dead: whether by suicide or by murder they could not determine. His wife told them that he had continued to pray morning and night. Looking at the bloodstained rock he had fallen on, and listening to the malicious gossip of yet another beachcomber named Michael Donald and the jeers of natives gathered around Lewis's coffin, the missionaries were too depressed for words. Not just individuals, but the community as a whole was nearly destroyed by their prohibition on local marriages.[18] Their refusal of marriage alliances deprived them of their best chance for access to knowledge and power in Tahitian society.

Religious difference was just as destructive as the missionaries' refusal of kinship relations. They were stymied, of course, by their ignorance of Tahitian; in a nonlettered society whose language they did not know, it was difficult to convey the meaning of a written system of belief. To the extent that they could make themselves understood, their religious conceptions were so peculiar to the Tahitians that they only had the effect of angering them. The record of those years—which they submitted to the directors, and which they with admirable frankness saw into print—is one of intruders rebuffed by islanders with their own sophisticated religious life.

The spread of European epidemic diseases, too, poisoned their dialogue with the islanders. Some were venereal disorders, while others seemed to have different causes. There was general agreement that by the time the missionaries arrived, Tahiti had undergone drastic depopulation. When the missionaries could begin to make themselves understood they promised eternal salvation, but what their listeners observed in their wake was biological catastrophe. The diary reported this argument from a tour of 1803:

We have seen a considerable number of sick persons, who all tell us, and very often in a provoking manner, that all their diseases come from us: but we can hardly think that they believe their diseases are from England, though some perhaps do believe it. They say, that Captain Cook brought the intermitting fever, the crooked backs, and the scrophula, which breaks out in their necks, breasts, groins, and armpits. That Vancouver brought a bloody flux, that in a few months killed a great number, and then abated; but it is still among them. They are agreed, that all their mortal diseases are from the ships; but they are not agreed what ships brought particular diseases. Some say, that Captain Bligh brought the scrofula. We generally tell them, that they have got no disease from England but the venereal, and that, through their own women going on board of ships.

The missionaries were unwilling to confront a reality that was perfectly obvious to the Tahitians but, if they had admitted it, would have undermined the moral legitimacy of their own position on the island: as Diderot predicted in his *Supplement to Bougainville,* European visitors—the English among them—had from their earliest arrival brought deadly illnesses. The missionaries could try to blame the spread of venereal disease on the Tahitians themselves and view their suffering as divine retribution, but the Tahitians were skeptical.[19]

The Tahitians did not need a Diderot to speak for them; they were clear and eloquent in their responses to their visitors' preaching. Their "bodily afflictions," reported the diary, "irritate them against the gospel, and they frequently address us in some such words as these—'You tell us of salvation, and behold we are dying.' When we tell them it is the salvation of their souls from the wrath of God we preach to them about, and not the salvation of their bodies from sickness and death in this world, they still misconceive thereof, and sometimes some will say—'We want no other salvation than to live in this world.'"[20] Diderot was prescient, but his eloquence fell short of the Tahitians'. With their passionate will to life and health, and their conviction that Europeans had poisoned the source of generation, they listened testily to their visitors' gospel of an afterlife. Hecklers confronted the missionaries when they made their tours around the island, where they gathered large crowds but no converts.

The legitimacy of the missionaries' work did not increase when they began trying in late 1803 to educate children by teaching them the alphabet and a short catechism. By June 1804 the experiment was clearly a failure: it was hard to collect the children in one place and to find convenient times when they were not fishing, looking in the mountains for plantains, gathering breadfruit, making ovens, or playing. Adults did their best to undermine the missionaries' work, never letting the children out of their sight and ridiculing the teachers as they spoke. "Another considerable obstacle," noted the missionary diary, "is the notion both among old and young that we are their debtors, or ought to give them great things if they attend on our instructions." After six years they found themselves a tolerated nuisance who were taking the children away from their work without offering anything in return.[21]

Native prophets abounded, as the missionaries found out in their evangelizing around the island. When they went into one valley and began a friendly conversation with a group of men building a house to hold canoes for the war god 'Oro, a man came up and in a heightened state of excitement gave them directions for building the canoes. On another tour, a prophet denounced them in front of a crowd, asking when their "*parrow* or speech" had ever saved anyone, and finished, "We will hear our own gods: they will kill you!" Complaining in 1805 that the natives were as hardened against the gospel as they had been three years before, the diary related one story of the wife of a priest who was considered dead for several days and then revived. She gave a long account of "the Po, or other world; which, notwithstanding its absurdity, her deluded countrymen seem to receive with a strong persuasion of its reality." The missionaries could denounce native prophecy as superstition and satanism, but they knew that they had failed to make a dent in its hold on the Tahitians. They faced a cohesive, intellectualized, and ritualized religious system that did not easily yield to outsiders.[22]

The islanders repudiated a religious conception that seemed to them to be intolerably one-sided. From the missionaries' point of view, it was they who had done—or facilitated—all the giving. They had given up all the comforts of home, family, and friends to bring the gospel to Tahiti, yet the Tahitians treated them as unwelcome intruders. Their Calvinist deity gave the gift of grace as an entirely one-sided act, uninfluenced by human entreaty or will, yet the Tahitians made it clear that they viewed the relationship very differently. As they saw it, the missionaries were uninvited guests, a material burden on an island already suffering from European invasion. By 1803 the missionaries had few supplies left for gift-exchange; meanwhile visiting ships stripped the island of much of its surplus food, leaving very little for its residents. In their relationship with the gods, the Tahitians expected a two-way exchange that was both symbolic and material: "When Brother Nott asks, 'Who is the true atonement for sins?' they sometimes reply, 'Hogs and pearls.' Some have told us since we left Matavai, that they never knew before that the Son of God is the atonement for sin; but that they always thought it was hogs." The missionaries came bearing neither pearls nor swine, but disease and death, a grim caricature of exchange. To advertise the benefits of their religion as purely otherworldly and immaterial only heightened the Tahitians' incredulousness toward a religious system that asked them to give—to grant the missionaries their time, their patience, and their produce—while receiving nothing in return.[23]

The disavowal of kinship relations and failure to introduce an alien religious system nearly destroyed the Tahitian mission. It did, however, have one important source of strength that eventually turned it into a lasting presence in Tahitian society: the patronage of the Pomares. When it came to the self-made "royal" family, the missionaries were able to build on the work of their predecessors. Cook, Bligh, and Vancouver had effectively picked out the family and declared it to be the monarchy of the island—an interpretation they effectively imposed on island politics, with Pomare I quickly learning to play along. The missionaries learned in turn to cooperate with Pomare I and Pomare II. In the end it was this patronage that permitted an exchange between native social systems and European technologies.

An exchange of linguistic knowledge was the starting point. By April 1806 the missionaries could report real progress in learning Tahitian—and a new understanding of the complexity of the language:

In the afternoon had a meeting to read our Taheitean English Vocabulary. It is proper to observe, that our meetings for the purpose of collecting, in alphabetical order, all known Taheitean words, commenced in March 1805; from that time we have in general met twice a week. We have paid a native for attending our meetings, in order to ascertain the proper pronunciation of every word which we have written down, according to our new alphabet, as also its corresponding English, and its various significations. We have now gone through the alphabet in that manner, and to-day began to read what is put down, for the purpose of farther correction.

Our present collection amounts to 2,100 words, exclusive of 500 names of trees, plants, fishes, birds, insects, &c. It appears that the Taheitean language has been much mistaken by Europeans in general; all the vocabularies we have seen are essentially deficient and erroneous, not only in the spelling and signification of words, but in all the fundamental principles of the language. It has been represented as uncommonly easy of attainment; but we know the contrary, by long experience. In respect to some of the common occurrences of life, we allow that an European of ordinary capacity may soon make himself understood; but in respect to such a knowledge of the language as is necessary to convey instruction, it is far otherwise.

A bricklayer like Henry Nott was not a linguistic virtuoso like the Forsters and Joseph Banks; but he and his fellow mechanics had also learned lessons of a kind that were unavailable in universities and learned academies. They had shed the illusion of a transparent foreign language and culture. If gentlemanly naturalists emphasized the ease of learning Tahitian and, by implication, of grasping their culture, the missionaries knew better after years of hardship. Their diary goes on to note that Tahitian might not have words for European arts, science, law, trade, commerce, and theology, but was "full and copious" for the natives' world; it was difficult, they came to realize, to distinguish "the vast number of words that are nearly the same in pronunciation, but widely different in sense." Respect accompanied growing linguistic competence.[24]

The missionaries' advancing sophistication was matched by a new Tahitian interest in the knowledge they had to offer. When the missionaries first arrived, they settled under the protection of Pomare I. He was the patron who tolerated their presence and gave them a foothold in Tahitian society. In return he expected gifts. "Pomére and Edéa [his mother]," recorded the diary entry of April 2, 1798, "seem insatiable: they range from apartment to apartment night and day, and carry away great quantities of all kinds of articles that they find." At the time of Pomare I's death in 1803 the missionaries reckoned him to have been a moral disaster, who had built hundreds of *marais* (temples) and offered profuse sacrifices of hogs and fish, and, they estimated, hundreds of human sacrifices; an "oppressive" governor, he had always been friendly toward the missionaries because he could extract wealth from them. They formed a different kind of relationship with his son, tempestuous and frustrating, but intimate, too, and ultimately rewarding. Pomare II had a large appetite for sex and alcohol that the missionaries were never able to restrain, but he was also determined to learn English, seeking both to read and to write. The diary entry of March 11, 1806, records a letter that he wrote in Tahitian (which the missionaries translated into English) blessing the missionaries and promising to banish the war god 'Oro to Raiatea; from them he requested men, women, children, property, cloth, and "plenty of muskets and powder" as well as "paper ink, and pens." The letter documented a newly emerging relationship in which the ruler acknowledged the special powers of the missionaries, who were not just a source of material goods and claimants of a special deity but also possessors of a powerful technology of knowledge. The missionaries and Pomare II stuck together through a time of crisis in 1808 when the paramount chief, harassed by rivals, fled Tahiti for Moorea; in 1811 he returned to Tahiti determined to convert to Christianity. Popular conversions followed, the beginnings of christianization of the island.[25]

The patronage relationship turned into a stable and powerful one at several levels. On a political level the missionaries proved themselves to be reliable allies of the Pomare family in bad times as well as good, a testing that had taken place over more than one lifetime; precisely because they had no other island connections, they had little choice but to stand by Pomare II. The missionaries had not arrived in a gunship and in the early years there was little evidence of state power behind them; perhaps islanders were nonetheless careful not to harm them as one potential avenue of access to the armed ships from overseas. This attribute would never have sufficed to make them interesting to an island ruler, however, for merchant ships were selling munitions. Rather, the relationship worked through language and alphabet. Language alone was not the missionaries' prerogative; Peter the Swede, too, had made some progress in learning Tahitian.

The missionaries, however, created a native alphabet and gave it to the Tahitians. To bring writing to a nonlettered culture was a two-sided act of empowerment that gave both foreigners and islanders a means of domination. Religious unity followed on literacy: in 1819 Pomare II was finally baptized, and in 1821 the regular use of native missionaries began. Once the breakthrough to alphabetization of the Tahitian language took place, both sides could rapidly work toward the establishment of a sacred monarchy combining propagation of Christianity and rule of written law.[26] The missionaries' lessons from their Tahitian tutors—and their tutoring in turn of the Tahitians in reading and writing—became the painstakingly assembled conduits of a new network of knowledge.

Native Missionaries, New Englanders, and Kapus in Hawaii

If we turn from the LMS on Tahiti to the American mission on Hawaii, then from the start the tone of the undertaking looks different. It appears closer to the self-assured manner of Perry Miller's Puritans than to its rather hapless English contemporaries. The American mission began as a striking success. Although there were many reasons for the relative ease of the Americans' initial religious conquest of the Sandwich Islands—including extraordinary luck as their arrival coincided with a revolution in native politics and religion—there is an instructive contrast in their network of knowledge, which they laid out with care at home, and stronger links abroad.

The mission originated in New England's colleges and seminaries. It went back to Williamstown, Massachusetts, home of Williams College, "where in 1806 a dozen young college students, led by Samuel J. Mills, were pouring out to one another and to God the sorrow of their hearts over the moral darkness of Asia." Two years later they formed a small group called the Brethren and carried their dream of missionizing to Andover Seminary (newly founded in Andover, Massachusetts), where they met students who had come from other colleges, including Brown, Harvard, and Union College in Schenectady, New York. By 1810 the budding evangelists were ready to make a public appeal; on June 28 they addressed a conference of a recently formed organization, the General Association of Massachusetts Proper, a conservative Congregationalist group formed eight years earlier. The association voted the next day to approve the plan for the formation of a missionary society and also planned to invite its counterpart in Connecticut to join in the new undertaking. On September 5 the newly formed missionary society, the American Board of Commissioners for Foreign Missions (ABCFM), held its first meeting in Farmington, Connecticut, formed an executive committee, and voted to send one of its members to London to confer with the LMS about possibilities for creating a joint mission. The leaders of the LMS were unwilling to coordinate joint efforts at such a distance, but they encouraged the board to act on its own. At its second meeting of September 1811, the board appointed four missionaries and tentatively adopted two more while waiting for them to complete their theological studies at Andover.[27]

The American missionary organization had some important affinities with the LMS. Like their London brethren, the Americans belonged to a revivalist movement that was a reaction against the growing influence of the Enlightenment and religious indifference in their own society. American Congregationalism was, however, a different denomination from the emotional evangelicalism that predominated among the London mission leaders. The Congregationalists were heirs to the Calvinism of the Massachusetts Bay Colony. Unlike in England, the value of education was never questioned by these New World congregants. Theology gave organization and direction to their religious and practical life; New England revivalism of the early nineteenth century had a strong emotional dimension, but in the missionary society it never implied a conflict with higher education or skepticism about the authority of the educated as leaders and participants in a mission. Whereas the LMS missionaries were "godly mechanics," lower-middle-class aspirants to higher social status who trumpeted their religiosity as a substitute for their lack of education and social polish, the Americans were from the beginning dominated by college men with an intellectual cast that carried over into rigorous organizational efficiency. The anti-intellectualism of the LMS was a great hindrance to its early missions; its religion of the heart nurtured an emotional instability that could be swayed in different directions under the impact of travel to a foreign culture. The American missionaries had their own difficulties, but they rarely doubted and rarely strayed from their straightforward task of educating, christianizing, and policing Hawaiian society. In a sense the Americans bore the same relationship to the LMS missionaries as Humboldt did to previous voyagers: nothing they accomplished was wholly unprecedented, but they prepared their trip with such systematic care that it amounted to a different kind of voyaging.

One innovation was their schooling of native missionaries. At the time the American Board was forming, a few Hawaiians were beginning to show up in the ports of New England, and the would-be missionaries were quick to recruit them. By 1816 one author wrote that at least ten "heathen youths" from the island of Hawaii were living in New England. As it was they were homeless and fell into bad company. "Let them be placed in religious families," wrote the anonymous author as part of his plea for training native aides, "under the care of persons who shall stand in the relation of parents, and to their instructions shall add their example and their prayers"; they could then become "instruments of salvation to their benighted countrymen." He cited their many advantages over foreign missionaries:

they knew their home "manners and customs"; "they will be free from suspicions"; will have "ties of blood and affection"; "their constitution is suited to the climates" of home countries; they knew the language of their countrymen. Like the LMS directors, the author appreciated the value of practical training, but his ambition reached further: "Christianity and civilization go hand and hand, and ever have been and ever will be mutual helps to each other. This being the case, it is indispensable that many of these youths should be instructed in the arts of mechanism, agriculture, and commerce. It is also highly important, that a considerable number should be educated as Physicians." A higher education could thus be the equipment not just of Anglo-Americans but also of the native assistants.[28]

Especially significant for the development of the missionary movement was the career of a young Hawaiian named Henry Opukahaia (called "Obookiah" by contemporaries). In 1809 Captain Brinthal of New Haven, Connecticut, spent some time in Hawaii and planned to take back a son of Kamehameha I; this plan fell through, but two commoners who were to have been his servants, Opukahaia and Thomas Hopo, did board the ship and landed in New Haven in spring 1810. Captain Brinthal first took them into his own house, but then gave them into the care of some students, who promised to educate Henry. Samuel J. Mills, who had led the original group of Williams students four years earlier, placed Henry with his father, a minister in Torrington, Connecticut. Henry earned his own keep there, working on the senior Mills's farm while beginning his education; he then joined the younger Mills in Andover, spending two years working and studying there. Henry continued moving from place to place as he worked while continuing his studies of grammar, geography, and arithmetic, spending some time in Litchfield, Connecticut, before returning to the Mills farm. By July 1816 the *Missionary Herald* could report that he was making good progress in his studies, teaching himself Hebrew and translating portions of the Hebrew Bible into his own language. He met with the approval of his teachers as a young man of genuine piety and intelligence who worked to uplift his fellow native Hawaiian students. Despite their enthusiasm for their work and their tireless optimism, the New England evangelicals were skeptics when it came to religious conviction; they did not expect every recruit to undergo inner conversion and valued frank statements about one's own and others' shortcomings. Henry impressed them as a novice on the path to his own and his people's christianization. After his illness from typhus and death in 1818, he took on the new role of tragic witness to Christianity:

> From yonder barbarous clime, where Moloch sways his blood stained iron sceptre, and trains his savage slaves to violence and death, a noble youth escaped. Conducted by an unseen arm, he came to the land of Christian freedom, and safely entered the city of God. The daughter of Zion beheld the stranger with wonder and with pity. She rejoiced in his happy escape and unexpected arrival, and welcomed him to her bosom. She adopted him for a son, and trained him in the nurture of the Lord as a favorite son.

In their literature his life had followed a course from native depravity, through a period of wandering, to Christian vocation. Accounts of the death of Opukahaia helped raise an outpouring of enthusiasm—and donations—for the Hawaiian mission.[29]

The American Board did more, however, than just recruit individuals; it actually organized a missionary school for the training of native aides. The London Missionary Society provided a forerunner: by 1802 it had begun educating a few Tahitians in London and formed a Missionary Seminary at Gosport with eight students. The board, however, had larger designs. At its meeting on October 19, 1816, at the

(OBOOKIAH.)

A NATIVE OF OWHYHEE.

Hero of the American mission to Hawaii: Henry Opukahaia.

house of the Reverend Edwin Welles Dwight in New Haven, a constitution was adopted for a school for educating "heathen youth." The
board members aimed to educate a cadre of foreign aides who would
be fully armed with intellectual and professional skills: "The object
of the school shall be the education of heathen youth in such a manner, as that with future professional studies, they may be qualified to
become missionaries, schoolmasters, interpreters, physicians, or surgeons, among heathen nations, and to communicate such information in agriculture and the arts, as shall tend to promote Christianity and civilization." The school opened the next year in the town
of Cornwall, Connecticut, which donated its old public schoolhouse
for the seminary, and Opukahaia and other Hawaiians were among
its first students. By September 1822 the school had nine students
from the Sandwich Islands, one New Zealander, one Malayan, fifteen
American Indians from different tribes, one Portuguese, three Chinese, two Greek Islanders, one Jew, and three "young men of our
own country." The board's annual report was frank about the linguistic difficulties of bringing together such a diverse student body:
students from the same country stuck together, and as a result they
did not learn much English. During the nine years the Cornwall
school was open, nineteen students from the Sandwich Islands attended. Among them two were demoted to printer and shoemaker;
one was dismissed for chronic depression; one died of consumption;
one "remained a religious skeptic"; and six returned to the islands as
assistants to the mission. The school leaders were self-satisfied masters whose idea of fun in 1821 was to have the students ridicule their
native cultures. After taking their examinations in May, the Cherokees would hold a "war council" and the Society Islanders, if an idol
from home arrived in time, "will go through with mock worship
or something of that kind for the entertainment of the audience."
Nonetheless the school set in motion an everyday experience of liv-

ing side by side between evangelicals and Hawaiians; the American Board developed a program of practical education which, beyond just providing its members with native intermediaries, gave them a preliminary idea of the difficulties they would encounter when they went abroad. The school closed in 1826, in part because of the high costs of running it, in part because the townspeople rioted over two proposed intermarriages between wealthy Cherokees and local girls. While it lasted, it was a remarkable experience in mutual education and was of special importance for the Hawaiian mission.[30]

The American Board had enormous financial support. On January 27, 1812, years before it was ready to send out a full-scale mission, it voted to send four missionaries on a ship about to depart for India. In response to a public appeal money poured in, and in February they departed, two from Salem, Massachusetts, and two from Philadelphia, fully outfitted and with a year's advance salary in their pockets. Before the first expedition of missionaries set out from Boston on October 23, 1819, the September edition of the *Missionary Herald* included a call to honor the memory of Henry Opukahaia and a booming appeal for contributions. Outfitting the vessels, providing for a voyage of five or six months, furnishing the missionaries with their needs on arrival—the frame for a small house, medicines, farming implements, mechanical tools, books, a printing press, and stationary—would be expensive. "But what is all this expense, in its utmost estimate," wrote the corresponding secretary of the board's governing committee, "compared with the object?" Charitable giving was best thought of as a celestial investment: "Friends of man and of the Redeemer of man, is it not a rare opportunity—presenting itself at a moment when your store-houses, and barns, and fields, are demanding from you a grateful offering to the bountiful Parent of all?—The object is before you—the bringing of many thousands of fellow beings to light and to glory—GOD LOVETH A CHEERFUL GIVER."

Compared with the meager outfitting of the early Tahitian missionaries and the stingy responses to their desperate appeals for more
funding, the early Hawaiian expeditions seemed to tap into an inex-
haustible American enthusiasm for their work and readiness to back
up that enthusiasm with donations. The long list of donors in 1819–
20 came from across New England and represented a broad cross-
section of society, as one can see from their prolific gifts in kind
marked for the Sandwich Islands (which streamed in alongside cash
donations).[31]

A small sampling suggests the diversity of donors. From Boston:
"From a young physician, a set of amputating and trepanning instruments"; and "Mr. John Homes, sundry articles of hard ware:
braids, tacks, and carpenter's and mason's tools." From Cambridge,
Massachusetts: "Two maps of the stars, by Mr. William Croswell,
the author." From Charlestown, Massachusetts: "Mr. Daniel Gregg, a
smith's vice, carpenter's tools, and 93 lb. of medicines." From Chelsea,
Vermont: "Asenath Hatch, a box of sundry articles, principally from
students in her school." From the Connecticut Bible Society: "100
Bibles . . . by H. Hudson, Esq." From New Haven: "A box containing
hardware, and books, (200 vols.) presented by students of Yale College, by Col. Charles Sherman." Philanthropists of tools and books,
craft and intellect, worked side by side to aid the mission.[32] This kind
of financial support also set the mission apart from the scientific
voyages. While the latter were objects of patronage, a thin thread that
could snap under the impact of a change of policies or a patron's
whim, the missions were the outcome of a broad-based movement
linked to churches, colleges, and a generation's religious enthusiasm.

If the mission's donors spread like a net across New England society, the board members were prominent representatives of learning
and politics. A list of forty members, past and present, compiled in
1821, was made up of names from Maine, New Hampshire, Massa-

chusetts, Connecticut, New York, and New Jersey, including the Reverend William Allen, president of Bowdoin College; John Langdon, former governor of New Hampshire; William Phillips, lieutenant governor of Massachusetts; Reverend Zephaniah Swift Moore, president of Williams College; William Jones, former governor of Rhode Island; Jeremiah Day, president of Yale; Ashbel Green, president of Princeton; and John Jay, the former chief justice of the Supreme Court.[33] They brought tremendous confidence and energy to the board, which by 1820 was receiving reports from missions in Bombay, Ceylon, and American missions to Cherokees and Choctaws as well as the Sandwich Islands. Their skills for managing a worldwide empire rivaled those of a Joseph Banks. They operated a different kind of net, however, woven from the materials of a different society. Banks worked a narrow world of government and personal contacts; hundreds of private individuals across the eastern seaboard, whether they were employed as judges, college presidents, professionals, housewives, schoolteachers, farmers, or schoolchildren, bankrolled and outfitted the ABCFM's early missions.

When the missionaries of the first expedition arrived on the Sandwich Islands, they discovered a situation that could only seem providential. Liholiho, or Kamehameha II, son and successor of the great unifier of the islands, had voluntarily begun the destruction of the old religion by eating in the presence of women and thereby violating the old kapu regulations. Kapus ("taboos") were not just prohibitions; they signified places and things that were sanctified and filled with the being and power of the gods. To abandon the kapu system was not just to lift a series of restrictions, but also to secularize the former sites of divine presence in Hawaii. The vacuum of faith seemed to invite the missionaries to rush in. There was indeed a crisis of the monarchy and a remarkable opportunity for the missionaries to play the role of advisors and promulgators of a new faith. For years the leading men of the islands had chafed under the rule of Kamehameha I and had in fact reduced him to first among equals, his actual monarchical powers constrained; after his death they might have torn the kingdom apart but instead adopted a more politic strategy, watching and waiting as the succession to his rule took place and European powers weighed in with advice. The recommendations began with the French naval captain Louis de Freycinet, who pressured the Hawaiians to avoid a civil war.[34]

Although the island kingdom held together, a profound demoralization was taking place in Hawaiian society. The *ali'i* enjoyed unprecedented opportunities for personal display as they profited from the sandalwood trade, which stripped the islands of the wood that was then shipped to China to be burned as incense. The ordinary people worked as forced laborers to remove the wood and load it

Queen Ka'ahumanu. From Choris, *Voyage pittoresque autour du monde* (1822).

onto ships. All Hawaiians, high and low, suffered from epidemic diseases, which here, as in Tahiti, terribly reduced the overall population of the islands and undermined the indigenous people's belief in the efficacy of the old gods. The missionaries formed an alliance with Kamehameha's widow, Ka'ahumanu, regent and the real political power in the royal household. She became their fierce advocate, fully their equal in her determination to destroy the old religion and establish Christianity in its place. By 1822 Ka'ahumanu was helping the missionaries to burn carvings of the gods, and in December 1825 she was admitted into their church as a relentless enemy of native worship and rival Catholic missionaries.[35]

While new networks of knowledge were fashioned, old ones were discarded or ignored. The same Marin who for Chamisso was a valued informant was for the missionaries a curmudgeon, very put out when the missionaries pushed into his economic territory. "This morning," stated the missionary journal of October 16, 1821,

> it was found that Mr. Marin was highly offended on account of the intended gift of cattle and horses to the mission. He urged that he had brought them here and was keeping them for the king, and he wanted to increase their number. If the missionaries wanted cattle, said he then why did they not bring them from America. This reasoning together with what has been said by others has probably put a stop to the intended present. Mr. Marin makes no use of the cattle himself. The cows have never been milked. The horses of which it is said there are more than fifty on this island have never been harnessed. They are only used to carry persons occasionally on their backs.[36]

The journal's rationalization of the missionaries' demand for the cattle fit in with the well-established Puritan justification for taking land from natives, the utilitarian argument that they would employ the cattle profitably and therefore had the right to take them away from their current owner. It was an illogical argument in this case, because Marin had made clear to the newcomers that he was a capitalist strategically planning for the cattle commodity's long-term accumulation.[37] The missionaries, however, were unable to conceive of "Mr. Marin" as someone who might have valuable knowledge about the islands and could only view him as a competitor for business and Hawaiian royal patronage. The different reactions to Marin suggest the different perspectives of the Romantic scientist with his enthusiasm for local culture and the missionaries working to secure their authority.

The missionaries' view of Hawaiian culture was more mixed than it might appear at first sight. They left home with unchallenged assumptions about a culture in need of redemption. Their homegrown belief in their providential calling seemed to find clear outward confirmation in Kamehameha II's abandonment of the kapu system just before their arrival. They arrived with many advantages over the Tahitian missionaries—their relative prosperity, their education, their careful years of preparation, their regular contact with the missionary community at home, and their good fortune at walking into a wealthy society that was far more politically unified but faced a moment of crisis; their advantages buffered them against the kind of shock experienced by their LMS counterparts. Yet their early journal entries show that they were taken aback by a self-confident elite whose displays of power and magnificence they recorded. Their journal of May 10, 1823, began by mentioning that the missionaries had set aside the day for fasting and prayer "to seek divine guidance in concerting measures for the more extensive & vigorous prosecution of the work of the mission—to endeavor especially to have our hearts prepared to follow the leadings of Providence & cheerfully to do or to suffer whatever the Lord may appoint." While they were making their preparations, Hawaiian processions were marching through Honolulu; the songs and shouts reached them in their mission house. An ethnographic impulse to record "an ancient national custom which may soon be entirely laid aside" took hold of the journal author as ladies passed by in gowns of sixty or seventy yards of silk and a lord was carried in a whale boat on the shoulders of seventy or eighty men. The author reacted uneasily:

> In these exhibitions & on other occasions among the people, there is a most singular combination of the grand with the ludicrous, the beautiful with the ugly, the admirable with the disgusting—order with confusion, splendor with debasement—such as could scarcely be found in any other part of the world—as for instance, a company of stately warriors with the superb *mahiole*, or lofty feather helmets on their heads, long splendid feather cloaks hanging from their shoulders to their feet, contrasted with a group of females patroling the ramparts armed with muskets—the grand imposing kahiles [*kahilis*, or feather standards] & canopies attending the chiefs of the nation in their best attire, mounted on a moving scaffold, which a group of half naked, noisy dirty servants throng their way:—the king riding an unmanageable pony, & his guard running in disorder to keep near him:—the show of the hudahuda [hulahula]—with the filthiness of their songs & conversation: these are some of the points of contrast in which the motley group might be viewed.[38]

Charles Stewart, one of the missionaries of the second expedition, wrote letters home that repeatedly registered similar expectations of the islands against the unexpected realities, and expressed his uncertainty over whether to be attracted or repelled. As their ship approached the island of Hawaii, canoes drew up to them and the voyagers observed the islanders for the first time:

> The first view of these wretched creatures was, especially to the females, almost overwhelming. Their rude canoes—naked persons, wild but interesting countenances—their whole appearance in fact, struck

them as *half man* and *half beast*; and produced an involuntary burst of tears, and they were obliged to retire to their births, before they could recover sufficient composure and fortitude to go on deck to see them.

They remained an hour or two, disposing of fish and watermelons, bananas, and sweet-potatoes, and greatly commended themselves to our commiseration and sympathy, by the artlessness and simplicity of their manners, and an apparent sprightliness and intelligence of mind. They seemed greatly rejoiced to know that more missionaries had come.

The landscape had the same double effect: as they sailed past the northern end of the island "everything seemed burnt up by the sun" and the houses scattered along the beach "looked more like pigstyes and dog kennels, than the abodes of human beings." This, added Stewart, was how he had imagined Hawaii when he had first thought of serving as a missionary in the islands. But on closer approach he saw that "there is much beauty and fertility, visible between and underneath the precipices and mountains."[39]

After they arrived in Honolulu on May 23, Stewart had similarly divided impressions of Liholiho. When they first met he was recovering from a "drunken frolic" following four or five days of celebrating the death of the old king and his own accession. Naked except for a piece of chintz around the waist, fanned by attendants and receiving tea from one of his queens, he looked "almost disgusting and brutish." Seeing the king again after he had recovered, Stewart found him well dressed and dignified.[40] His first impressions of the islands were dizzying for him, again and again leaving him uncertain whether they were in a nightmare kingdom or a place receptive to the task of civilization and conversion. The greatest surprise was Ka'ahumanu:

To speak candidly, I do not think I ever saw any lady enter a room with more real majesty than she did. Her walk was stately, and look and manners really elegant. She was in the *native female* dress: it consisted of several large and graceful folds of the richest yellow satin, falling from the waist to a little below the knee, fastened by a large and negligent beau in front; and of a large mantle of purple satin, of the same quality, containing perhaps twenty yards, passing under one arm and over the other shoulder, and flowing on the ground far behind her. Her hair was handsomely dressed and ornamented with a double coronet of the exquisite feathers, so often mentioned in accounts of these islands; colours bright yellow, crimson, and bluish green. She appears about 40 years of age, is large and fleshy, and has an expression of greater sternness and hauteur than most others.[41]

The journal entries and letters waver between their civilizing mission and their aesthetic response to the *ali'i*.[42] The Americans were much firmer and less addled than the LMS missionaries. Yet even in this case of forceful outsiders entering a weakened culture, the islanders could put on a show to awe the newcomers.

As with earlier Puritan movements, moral repression set off protest. Disagreement about observance of the sabbath was a flashpoint for the larger conflict over island morals. In 1825, at the urging of the missionaries, the king and chiefs placed a kapu on card playing and on prostitution in the ports of Honolulu and Lahaina (on Maui). One party of chiefs resented and resisted the new order; so did Europeans living in Honolulu and ship captains visiting the islands. In a firm and clear hand, one of the leading missionaries, Levi Chamberlain, wrote a somber assessment of the mission's task:

Neither the Chiefs nor the people are yet sufficiently enlightened to adopt on rational principles a code of civil regulations to be enforced by severe penalties. The pleasure of the king and of the chiefs has heretofore been the only law and it would be easy to see that the dark minds and depraved hearts of despots, who hold the common people in the most absolute subjection, would lead them to institute rules of duty for their subjects at variance with the plainest rules of right. It will be difficult for the chiefs to free themselves from their old notions and professions and if they should concede that their former principles were wrong, they could not easily be made to feel the force of new principles, and to act with promptness & energy in enforcing them. Savages do not view crimes in the light that civilized nations view them. And as this people have not been in the habit of viewing murder, adultery, incest, sorcery, theft, treachery, and numerous other vices allied to them, as crimes, in the light in which Christians view them, it would not be a matter of surprise if persons acting in the new capacity of magistrates should be lax in enforcing penalties against such crimes.

Battle fatigue colored the mood of Chamberlain's pronouncement. During the 1820s the missionaries maintained their alliance with the Kamehameha dynasty, established a standardized written Hawaiian language, and set up schools for thousands of native Hawaiians. Yet they were unable in the end to control the economic forces that were reshaping island society and politics. The proselytizers were fighting stubborn enemies: on the one side against the chiefs and the old religion; on the other side against sailors who rioted when they tried to limit the sex trade in Honolulu. Hawaii, repeating the history of the New England they had left behind, was becoming not a theocracy but a hub of commercial empires.[43]

From Berlin Chamisso took note. In his first talk to the Berlin Academy of Sciences, delivered on January 12, 1837, he declared his intention of using his last strength to research the Hawaiian language. At the time of his visit two decades before, no one had yet begun to commit the language to writing; in the meantime it had become a written language, and enough books had reached him—he listed thirty-one—to form the basis of a grammar and a vocabulary. Most of them were Bible translations or other religious books, a few were elementary schoolbooks. Not one was dedicated to preserving knowledge of ancient Hawaiian culture. Social conditions, customs, histories, myths, religion: all were in danger of disappearing from human memory. "Shouldn't we remind these pious missionaries: the thirst for knowledge, which separates men from beasts, also comes from God. It is not a sin if man longs to look back at his own history, in which God progressively reveals himself. But too late! Before the New has taken shape, the Old has already vanished."[44] Two confessions stood side by side. One was Chamisso's: the doctrine of the sanctity of culture, a revelation that, as Chamisso wrote, progressively unfolded in the course of human history. This doctrine was a historical faith in its own right within which Polynesian culture was a precious good, a chapter to be preserved as fully as possible before it vanished under the impact of European commerce. With their Christian vision of history, the missionaries took no more than irregular note of the culture that was rapidly disintegrating. The network of scientific knowledge came up against an outer limit, a different network and a different set of values with little overlap or opportunity for conversation about the appreciation of alien cultures.

Science and Religion in Conflict

During the 1820s and 1830s travelers argued over whether missionaries were saving or destroying the island kingdoms of Tahiti and Hawaii. William Ellis, the bluff, energetic genius of the second generation of LMS missionaries, a candle manufacturer and gardener before he followed his religious calling, worked in Moorea and Huahine in the Society Islands before joining the young American mission on Oahu in 1823–24. His *Polynesian Researches,* still valued today as an ethnographic source, defended his coworkers as the epitome of lower-middle-class virtue. "Their family connexions," he wrote of the missionaries, "may not indeed have been of the highest class, neither may the individuals themselves have enjoyed the advantages of a very liberal education, nor possessed any very extensive acquaintance with the world." The advantages of the privileged classes, however, were not the best qualifications for missionary work in the Pacific:

> They were not perhaps distinguished by brilliancy of genius, or loftiness of intellect; but in uncompromising sternness of principle, unaffected piety, ardour of devotedness, uncomplaining endurance of privations, not easily comprehended by those who have always remained at home, or visited only civilized portions of foreign climes, in undeviating perseverance in exertion under discouragements the most protracted and depressing, and in plain and honest detail of their endeavours and success, they have been inferior to few who have been honoured to labour in the Missionary field.

His fellow missionaries were the kind of practical men and women who came to grips with the horrors of paganism and replaced it with pious respectability. They also worked hard at self-improvement, and their "philological and other manuscripts" showed "they were far from being unqualified for their work." Brilliant—no; dedicated to their calling—yes: the missionaries' actions were a sufficient reply to their genteel critics.[45]

The critics did not give up their doubts or their contempt. Frederick W. Beechey, scion of a prominent British navy family, visited Tahiti in 1826 as commander of a scientific expedition to the Pacific. Ellis's account of his missionary work in Tahiti, he wrote, exaggerated the improvements in the Tahitians' moral condition and degree of civilization. The missionaries did their best to suppress innocent amusements of the people and in this way diminished their own influence. Beechey and his officers got a sample of this when they accepted an invitation of the "queen regent," mother of Pomare III (then six years old), to spend an evening at her house in Papiete. By the light of the moon Beechey and his companions walked to a romantic spot about a mile from their ship. There they made their way into a large house with bamboo partitions. After a little bit of stumbling around they reached "the royal saloon, which we found illuminated by a yellow and melancholy light proceeding from a rag hung over the edge of a broken cocoa-nut shell half filled with oil." A number of "atheletic [*sic*] men, her majesty's favourites," were waking up from a nap, and lying around her on mats were "several interesting young females." On the arrival of their guests, the queen decided to produce some dancing, even though this was strictly prohibited by law, under severe penalties, and had to be done quietly so as not to attract the attention of "an aava, or policemen, who was parading the beach, in a soldier's jacket, with a rusty sword." The dance was harmless, and indeed disappointing compared with one of the pictures he knew from one of the Cook narratives. Meanwhile, amusement was going on in the background "which must have convinced the greatest sceptic of the thoroughly immoral condition of the people." Beechey concluded that their contact with Europeans "had tended to debase rather than to exalt their condition" and that "they were wilfully violating and deriding laws which they considered ridiculously severe." Beechey made fun of the queen and her entourage, but his main message was one of sympathy toward them and dislike of the missionaries for suppressing a pleasant way of life in a romantic setting.[46]

Another critic of the missionaries was Otto von Kotzebue. Commissioned to command a second Pacific voyage, the former commander of the *Rurik* expedition visited Tahiti from March 14 to March 24, 1824. As an experienced Pacific commander he could write about the Tahitians with an authority that few of his contemporaries could match. His assessment of them was highly positive, though written with the superficiality that Chamisso had criticized. After reviewing the impressions of Cook and other early travelers, he wrote: "The disposition of the Tahaitians is gentle, benevolent, open, gay, and peaceable, although some of them show scars of wounds received in war, which prove that they are not deficient in courage. To hatred and revenge they are wholly strangers." As Kotzebue portrayed them, the Tahitians were lazy children who easily showed their feelings and were incapable of concentrating, although they produced attractive crafts. Whatever their deficiencies, he added that they were "particularly distinguished by their superior civilization from all other savages, among whom indeed they scarcely deserve to be ranked." He set up his readers to enjoy an altogether civilized tropical vacation as generations of voyagers going back to Cook and Bougainville had done before him.[47]

When his ship first anchored in Matavai Bay, it enjoyed a welcome that was a reprise from the days of Cook and Bougainville: a joyful greeting sounded from the shore, boats came up with all kinds of fruit and provision, and Tahitian men came on board and chose *tayos*, or partner-friends, with whom they exchanged gifts. In contrast to the early years there were no women visitors and no incidents of theft. The next day there was brilliant sunshine, but to the astonishment of the visitors not a person was in sight. By the missionaries' calendar (which was one day off), it was the sabbath. "The inhabitants of Tahiti were celebrating the Sunday, on which account they did not leave their houses, where they lay on their bellies reading the Bible and howling aloud; laying aside every species of occupation, they devoted, as they said, the whole day to prayer." Kotzebue and his entourage went on shore to visit Charles Wilson, one of the leading missionaries. Wilson made a good impression with his "neat and simple dwelling" and his wife and two children. He "was originally a common sailor," observed Kotzebue, "but has zealously devoted himself to theology, and is honest and good-natured." Kotzebue had little good to say, however, about Wilson's works. He was amazed by the native Tahitians who were being trained and sent out to missionize on neighboring islands: "Besides these English Missionaries, some native Tahaitians, after receiving a suitable education, are sent to spread Christianity among the islands of the dangerous Archipelago. In Russia, a careful education and diligent study at schools and universities is necessary to qualify any one to be a teacher of religion. The London Missionary Society is more easily satisfied; a half savage, confused by the dogmas of an uneducated sailor, is, according to them, perfectly fitted for the sacred office." It was a remark provoked by conflicting conceptions of empire building. For the representative of Russian autocracy, religion was supposed to be under careful church and state control; teachers of religion were guardians of correct ritual and doctrine. The LMS missionaries represented a British tradition of religious voluntarism that looked casual by comparison. Each side during the 1820s could have pointed to evidence of the rightness of its approach. Christianity did percolate remarkably quickly through different strata of Tahitian society, but by the end of the decade native prophetic movements were challenging the European missionaries' authority. It was simply a different world from the one that Kotzebue knew from home or, for that matter, from the priestly Hawaii of Kamehameha, with its strict regulation of the calendar and religious prohibitions.[48]

A religious service left him with like impressions. He acknowledged "the seriousness and devotion apparent among the Tahaitians." Nonetheless, he added, "it is almost impossible for an European, seeing them for the first time in their Sunday attire, to refrain from laughter." The Tahitians vied with one another to show off their European clothing, but since a whole suit was too expensive for them they would wear a single article, often torn, and almost nothing else. "Let any one imagine such an assembly, perfectly satisfied of the propriety of their costume, and wearing, to complete the comic effect, a most ultra-serious expression of countenance, and he will easily believe that it was impossible for me to be very devout in their presence." Kotzebue did not look into the Tahitians' personal piety; he wanted order, neatness, a unified style, and a dignified presence.[49]

What disturbed him more than missionary religion was the decline of the Polynesian culture he had known just a few years earlier on Hawaii: the Tahitians hardly knew how to make their maps or their tapa, the once-great navy was no more, the flute was silent, and dancing, mock-fights, and plays had disappeared. Beauty and joy had vanished from the island. Kotzebue blamed it on the missionaries, and to account for it he told the story of a missionary war that had transformed Tahiti. As he told it, beginning in 1797 the missionaries had sided with one King Tajo, who had become a fanatical proselyte and conducted a war of annihilation against "whole races" that clung to their "ancient faith." Finally "a young warrior, Pomareh, King of the little island of Tabua, took the field against him." Pomare in this account was a peacemaker who let his subjects practice their new religion, yielded late to Nott's entreaties to adopt it, and was universally loved and esteemed by his subjects. The damage of religious warfare had been done, however: "it was, therefore, the bloody persecution instigated by the Missionaries which performed the office of a desolating infection." The story was a founding myth that blamed the missionaries for all the shortcomings of Tahitian society while eliding other factors—venereal disease, other epidemic illnesses, the introduction of new and more deadly forms of warfare, and world commerce—that were inseparable from the scientific expeditions of Cook, Bougainville, and their successors. It was easier to indulge in anticlericalism than to keep in view all the consequences of contact with Europe.[50]

There is no reason to think that Kotzebue was anything less than sincere in his denunciation of missionary rule. His account culminated in a reckoning of the lost opportunity to institute a different kind of order on the island:

> A religion which consists in the eternal repetition of prescribed prayers, which forbids every innocent pleasure, and cramps or annihilates every mental power, is a libel on the Divine Founder of Christianity, the benign Friend of human-kind. It is true, that the religion of the Missionaries has, with a great deal of evil, effected some good. It has abolished heathen superstitions, and an irrational worship, but it has introduced new errors in their stead. It has restrained the vices of theft and incontinence, but it has given birth to bigotry, hypocrisy, and a hatred and contempt of all other modes of faith, which was once foreign to the open and benevolent character of the Tahaitian. It has put an end to avowed human sacrifices, but many more human beings have been actually sacrificed to it, than ever were to their heathen gods.[51]

From his visit to Hawaii on the voyage of the *Rurik* he knew a contrasting model of modernization. Kamehameha I had established an orderly and generous regime that, as Kotzebue viewed it, was dedicated to the enlightenment of its people. He had synthesized native majesty and modernization.

Kotzebue's critique outraged missionary spokesmen. Among them were two travelers, Daniel Tyerman and George Bennet, whom the London Missionary Society commissioned to visit its growing number of stations around the world, starting in the South Seas. To turn from Kotzebue to the published report on Tahiti compiled from their journals is to see the world upside-down. Before the glorious revolution wrought by the Christian gospel, Tahiti had been a satanic realm in which (they assured their readers) three-fourths of the children were murdered as soon as they were born and vengefulness and cruelty were commonplace.[52]

By the time their deputation arrived on September 25, 1821, Tahiti had been transformed into a peaceable Christian kingdom. Gone were the Arioi, "a kind of strolling players," a "vagabond race" of "chartered libertines." Their talented recitations had disappeared, but so too had the "licentious dancers and the "barbarous cock-fightings." The world travelers' language carried overtones of class conflict in England, with the respectable middle class carrying on its campaign for morality against the barbarous amusements of its social superiors and inferiors. Not that the deputation had anything against rank and hierarchy as such. On the contrary, their account placed heavy emphasis on the authority and role of the king as the agent of moral transformation in Tahiti, exemplified by his own progress from "gross idolator" to discerning Christian monarch. They also noted with satisfaction that Tahitians respected their social superiors; signs of social status were visible everywhere.[53]

Tyerman and Bennet were on the island when Kotzebue arrived. He met them in Wilson's house, and later he saw them in church, glowering at a girl who was tittering and flirting with him. They had observations to make about him, too. On November 29 Nott had a long conversation with Kotzebue about the relationship of the Society Islands to England, for the missionaries suspected Russia of having designs on them. While the Tahitians were strictly keeping the sabbath, the Russians held a perfunctory service and then used the day "disgracefully" by going about their normal business. It was rather unfriendly of Kotzebue, they added, not to invite them on board his ship. When he took leave of them at the end of his stay on Tahiti, he made it clear that he did not think the missionaries had improved the island, "though," they noted tartly, "he had every reason to be satisfied with the general behavior and conduct of the people."[54]

The editor of the American edition of their journal was outraged by Kotzebue's polemic. Writing from Boston, he confronted the conflicting claims to truthful reporting. Tyerman and Bennet had returned with a work of impressive volume and impartiality. "The candid reader," he wrote, "will perceive so much evidence of conscientious integrity running through these pages, that he will seldom be tempted to incredulity." The missionaries had good reason to be ethnographers; it was important to preserve as much as possible of rapidly disappearing heathen ways so that one could appreciate the effects of true religion. To distinguish fiction from truth about the islands was "necessary at the present time, when the grossest fictions are invented, industriously circulated, and in some instances eagerly received—to bring the missionaries and their labors into contempt." The arch foe of religion was Kotzebue, who, the editor wrote, "has thought proper to assert as historical facts things which never happened under the sun, and to express sentiments, concerning the missionaries and their converts, which no man could entertain who was not under strong prejudice, if not actual delusion." Kotzebue's story of the convert king Tajo was an absurd invention; his simple historical facts were unreliable.[55]

William Ellis was deeply disturbed by Kotzebue and Beechey's attacks on the Pacific missions, and with good reason. Their criticisms carried all the authority of their class and rank: as captains on royal naval vessels they had the legitimacy of impartial witnesses who were the best guides for the political classes in Europe. There was an additional weight to their words because they commanded scientific expeditions. Such reports as theirs of damaged native cultures were a real threat to the missionaries' public standing. Ellis threw himself into making the case for the defense, replying with a pamphlet that singled out Kotzebue for criticism but blasted Chamisso and Beechey too. To win over the public he had to beat them at their own game; he had to show that he was the more reliable observer and—with an appeal to morality—the better gentleman.

He pummeled away at Kotzebue's account with a point-by-point attack on its accuracy, thereby demonstrating the superiority of his own learning and immersion in Polynesian culture. "In the essential point of *accuracy*" he had correction after correction to make. According to Ellis, even though Kotzebue was traveling under the auspices of Krusenstern, the Russian circumnavigator (who had published an atlas of the Pacific in 1827), his map of the village and bay of Matavai was inaccurate; so was his account of the tides; he misnamed rocks of the interior as granite; and the story of Tajo was ridiculous. As to the native teachers, wrote Ellis, none had "received a university education," but they were all literate and familiar with the "mechanical arts"; and they were noble, dedicated, and persevering. Since Kotzebue had stayed on the island only ten days, it was ridiculous for him to pass judgment on them. "Had he resided some time among the people, and understood their language; or had he derived his information from those whose own piety and means of observation had enabled them to have imparted it—his testimony might have been entitled to regard," but from his position of ignorance he should have kept quiet. Ellis countered Kotzebue's account of a lower-middle-class dystopia with the image of a fallen society reborn: the Tahitians, their lower classes "plundered and oppressed," their women the slaves of the men, a fiendish nation "filled with wickedness, covetousness, maliciousness, envy, malignity, and murder," had become a pious people with a New Testament in every home, where their true state now was one of hard work, generosity, education, honesty, and temperance. Turning to the Sandwich Islands, Ellis denounced Kotzebue as an "apologist for paganism." Kamehameha I, whom he so admired, "about the year 1806, sacrificed three men to propitiate the gods when his queen was ill." (This was a neat exemption of Ka'ahumanu, pious patron of the missionaries, from any culpability for the misdeeds of the old regime.) Chamisso too came in for reprimand for comparing human sacrifice on Hawaii to the workings of justice in Europe. Ellis delivered his criticisms of Beechey more gingerly; it was one thing to deride a Russian captain's report, another to oppose the word of a British commander. "I have no hesitation in stating my own conviction, that his sense of justice would not have permitted Captain Beechey to pass so sweeping and indefensible a judgment against the virtue of the female population of the island, had his means of evidence been more extended and better chosen." As for what he had seen—the behavior of a court—European readers knew all about that from home: "We need not go to the South Sea Islands, to learn the degree of influence which a profligate court is capable of exerting over those who are exposed to it." Beechey had not seen any of the women of the Christian community and had placed "a too great confidence in the sources of his information" when he regretted the suppression of pagan amusements and "lascivious dancing." Ellis's vindication worked to win the authority of truthful ethnography for the missionaries; he, not the representatives of science, knew the islands and islanders, while his opponents relied on superficial eyewitness and shoddy sources.[56]

Ellis's picture of peaceable islands was fanciful in its own way, but his criticisms hit their mark often enough to be a serious challenge to the captains and the naturalist Chamisso and, by extension, the naturalist tradition of reporting reaching back to Cook. The missionaries had suffered from the inadequacies of naturalists' reporting from the time they first came to Tahiti three decades before, whereas Ellis by the early 1830s could draw on decades of continuous fieldwork. Yet in the end Ellis's service was different from the one he intended. The authority of the missionaries could never go as far as they wished; islanders, beachcombers, naval captains, and merchants all contested it. And his scientific authority was transparently damaged from the start by his partiality; his propagandistic ends distorted his considerable learning and experience. The rise of a missionary network had instead the effect of relativizing any one network of knowledge. Neither missionaries, nor naturalists, nor any other outside observer could claim superior authority as ethnographers; instead all of them became interpreters of cultures.[57]

CHAPTER 6

Darwin, Melville, and the End of a World

The great missionary conflict deserves a central place in our intellectual history of the first half of the nineteenth century, if only because it shaped the social vision of two travelers who are still very much part of our own conversation today, Charles Darwin and Herman Melville. Both of them traveled to the Pacific, and their voyaging turned them into global thinkers. Both impressed their contemporaries (and subsequent generations) with their observations of native peoples, ethnographies that took shape in response to the debate between the missionaries and their critics. Darwin defended the missionaries, Melville deplored them; the two men's differences mark the breakdown of a unified travelers' world.

Darwin and the "More Cheerful View"

We remember Darwin today primarily for his theory of evolution and associate the *Beagle* voyage above all with its stop at the Galápagos Islands and the stimulus it gave to his thinking about the mutation of species. Darwin was also, however, a curious and precise observer of human societies who publicized his impressions in his

Journal of Researches, the account of the voyage that he published in 1839. Darwin as travel writer was an immediate literary success two decades before his study of the origin of species. His account brought him a congratulatory letter from his hero Alexander von Humboldt; made his scientific name among his British contemporaries; and confirmed his decision to spend his life as a gentleman naturalist. A vivid narrative intimately linked to the discourse of its predecessors reaching back to Cook, it can stand in its own right, apart from its author's later fame, as a notable event in the history of travel writing.

Charles Darwin embarked on the scientific voyage of the *Beagle* as a supernumerary, a guest whose function was to be a gentlemanly companion to Captain Robert FitzRoy. Such a position was a prize opportunity for a young man, and it had not come to Darwin by chance; he was the beneficiary of social and scientific networks. As a wealthy grandson of Erasmus Darwin and of the famous pottery manufacturer Josiah Wedgwood on his mother's side, Darwin grew up surrounded by privilege. The two families were a network in their own right, warm, loyal, and ready to support an indecisive young man's search for the right calling. Darwin's father paid his way for a voyage that lasted over five years—a circumstance that put him in the small company of wealthy fellow naturalists such as Joseph Banks and Alexander von Humboldt and that set him apart from the many roving naturalists without means. The family's gentry status made Darwin a suitable companion for his aristocratic captain, as did his self-confidence and good manners, which saw him through more than one tense moment in their relationship. The second set of relationships that brought him into FitzRoy's proximity was the Cambridge network. It was Darwin's professors who introduced him to Humboldt's narrative of his American voyage, which stimulated his desire to travel; provided him with field experience; and recommended him for the voyage. Once under way Darwin benefited from yet another network, the local elites in places like Brazil and Chile as well as in missionary settlements in Tahiti and New Zealand, which could provide aid for his work, some of the atmosphere of home, and material comforts.[1] Once they were under way FitzRoy was an indulgent captain who went out of his way to assist Darwin's observations and collecting (as a supernumerary Darwin was allowed to keep his own collections and write his own voyage account). The official voyage naturalist, Robert McCormick, was so disgusted by FitzRoy's favoritism toward Darwin that he exited the ship at Rio de Janeiro and returned to England in June 1832. McCormick was a peevish man, but he had also struggled, as the son of a navy surgeon who had died in a shipwreck in 1811, to get an education that would qualify him for naturalist duty on a scientific expedition. Darwin's dismissive reaction in a letter to his sister Caroline ("He is no loss") is a reminder that he took for granted opportunities beyond the reach of the usual voyage naturalist.[2]

The ship departed from Plymouth on December 27, 1831, at the end of the same year in which William Ellis published his *Vindication of the South Sea Missions;* Kotzebue's *New Voyage round the World* had appeared in English the year before. The main task of the *Beagle* expedition was to make an accurate survey of Tierra del Fuego; FitzRoy was an expert surveyor and could be counted on to improve the existing charts of the extreme South American land mass. At the same time the *Beagle* voyagers were to aid in establishing a missionary station. They carried with them Fuegians who had been christianized; these were to be returned to their homes together with a missionary who could use them as intermediaries. FitzRoy was pious and serious in his religious beliefs, in contrast to Beechey or Kotzebue, and stood behind the goal of setting up the new mission station. Darwin was also sympathetic to their religious mission. His first publication, coauthored with FitzRoy, was a defense of the LMS mission to South Africa.

The arrival of the *Beagle* in Tierra del Fuego was not the gentle disembarkment of civilization that the voyagers expected. At first, on December 17, 1832, Darwin and his companions met an attractive group of Fuegians who matched the lore of a tall people, around six feet, he estimated. To describe them he turned to the imagery of literary Romanticism, comparing them to the devil figures in Carl Maria von Weber's opera *Der Freischütz*. According to Darwin, these Fuegian "demoniacs" could barely speak and instead had exaggerated powers of mimicry. The country matched the people: climbing his way through a swampy wood, up a height for an hour, Darwin "was amply repaid by the grandeur of the scene. The gloomy depth of the ravine well accorded with the universal signs of violence . . . [I]n these still solitudes, Death, instead of Life, seemed the predominant spirit." On December 25 the *Beagle* met another group of Fuegians, six of them in a canoe: "These," he wrote, "were the most abject and miserable creatures I any where beheld." "Quite naked" in rain and sleet, they had hideous faces, discordant voices, violent gestures, and hardly seemed to be fellow creatures. According to Darwin their lives were marked by famine, cannibalism, and parricide. Again the natural surroundings matched their personalities: "Their country is a broken mass of wild rock, lofty hills, and useless forests: and these are viewed through mists and endless storms." These people were, he concluded, "savages of the lowest grade." Within the history of travel writing the integration of people and landscape corresponded to the beliefs of Alexander von Humboldt, and behind him the Forsters, in the climatological formation of human character and appearance.[3]

The encounter with the Fuegians was a fateful one for Darwin's anthropology. To his Cambridge teacher J. S. Henslow he wrote on April 11, 1833:

The Fuegians are in a more miserable state of barbarism, than I had expected ever to have seen a human being.—In this inclement country, they are absolutely naked, & their temporary houses are like what children make in summer, with boughs of trees.—I do not think any spectacle can be more interesting, than the first sight of Man in his primitive wildness.—It is an interest, which cannot well be imagined, until it is experienced. I shall never forget, when entering Good Success Bay, the yell with which a party received us. They were seated on a rocky point, surrounded by the dark forest of beech; as they threw their arms wildly round their heads & their long hair streaming they seemed the troubled spirits of another world.[4]

Natural man in his purest state, devoid of clothing, the starting point not yet moderated by the upward descent toward civilization: this is what Darwin thought he had seen in Tierra del Fuego. The notion was of a piece with the long history of travelers dating back to those of the sixteenth century who thought that they had seen natural man in the New World and could now declaim on his qualities, good or bad.[5] This early impression haunted Darwin for decades to come and continued to serve as a point of reference for his mature work. Almost forty years later in *The Descent of Man,* his extension of his theory of natural selection to human societies, he still turned to the Fuegians as an example of the "lowest barbarians."[6]

Darwin presented his reaction to the Fuegians as an immediate impression, untempered by history or circumstance, yet his record of the meetings had a specific setting that must have influenced his feelings. He was writing in the context of the missionary venture: the Fuegians were hostile to the missionary left on their shores, whom FitzRoy later had to pick up, and as for the "civilized" Fuegians the voyagers had brought with them, they preferred staying with their relatives to returning to Britain. Like religious missionaries, Darwin resorted to the language of the demonic to explain the appearance and behavior of human beings he found abhorrent and unwilling to yield to the wishes of European travelers, certifying their demonic

Darwin's lowest grade on the human hierarchy: a Fuegian at Portrait Cove. From Robert FitzRoy, *Narrative of the Surveying Voyages of His Majesty's Ships Adventure and Beagle* (1839).

character by proving to his own satisfaction that they were cannibals (an assertion denied by later researchers; it seems more probable either that Darwin misunderstood his interlocutors, or that they told him what he wanted to hear). Darwin demonized the Fuegians with a light touch (and a Romantic inflection) by referring the reader to Weber's opera, but he had mentioned the idea in a more serious tone in his letter to Henslow. He had to look no further than Ellis's *Polynesian Researches,* a copy of which was in the library of several hundred volumes aboard the *Beagle,* for a missionary account of demonic possession.[7]

The *Beagle* anchored in Matavai Bay on November 15, 1835, three years and ten months after its departure from England, and eleven years after Kotzebue and the missionary deputation crossed paths in Tahiti. The FitzRoy expedition stayed on Tahiti for eleven days. Darwin wrote that he was especially eager to see and judge the missionary regime on Tahiti for himself. He had read Kotzebue, Beechey, and *Polynesian Researches;* the contrast between the missionary and the captains' point of view had whetted his curiosity. The appearance of the Tahitians pleased him right away: "There is a mildness in the expression of their countenances, which at once banishes the idea of a savage; and an intelligence, which shows they are advancing in civilization." The contrast to the Fuegians was unmistakable; Darwin had traveled from inferno to idyll. The mixture of modes of dress that Kotzebue found grotesque he thought had settled into an acceptable blend of the European and the native, and while a little disappointed in the appearance of the women he praised the athletic, graceful bodies and movements of the men.[8]

He got a favorable impression of their religiosity when he took an overnight hike up a steeply ascending slope behind Matavai Bay with the help of native guides. The Tahitians insisted on saying grace before meals, and one of them made a prayer before going to sleep at night that Darwin found to be a convincing demonstration of spontaneous religious fervor. "Those travellers," he wrote, "who think that a Tahitian prays only when the eyes of the missionary are fixed on him, should have slept with us that night on the mountain-side." Attention in the church service he attended was disappointing, but people were neat and clean, and the hymns were well sung. There was a paradisic theme here carried over from Humboldt: "I felt the force of the observation, that man, at least savage man, with his reasoning powers only partly developed, is the child of the tropics." As in his description of Tierra del Fuego, Darwin's prose artfully blended bodies and landscape, the pleasing islanders and their island, recalling how they looked as he wound down a mountainside with his guides after a botanical excursion: "The Tahitians, with their naked, tattooed bodies, their heads ornamented with flowers, and seen in the dark shade of the woods, would have formed a fine picture of man, inhabiting some primeval forest." Decisive for Darwin's judgment, however, was the transformation of their moral condition. He accepted Ellis's view of their earlier condition as one marked by human sacrifice, infanticide, cruel wars, and "a system of profligacy unparalleled in the world," and contrasted it to the people he now saw, cheerful, pious, not perfect, but much improved. They had not become a "gloomy race" as Beechey and Kotzebue had led him to fear; when it came to the prohibition on flute playing and dancing, and the strict regulation of the sabbath, he deferred to the judgment of the missionaries who had long lived among them.[9]

New Zealand, the *Beagle*'s next stop, was also the subject of a controversy about the work of British missionaries. This time the criticisms came from someone Darwin knew, for the author, Augustus Earle, had served as artist aboard the *Beagle*. Earle came from an American loyalist family that had resettled in London at the time of his birth in 1793; he received a good artistic education before he embarked on a restless life of travel around the world from 1815 to 1830, and he had a half-brother in the navy who afforded him some patronage. In 1827 he visited Sydney; in October of the same year he continued on to New Zealand, returning to Sydney in May of the following year. By August 1830 he was back in England and accepted an offer to serve as personal draftsman to FitzRoy on the *Beagle*. Ill health forced him to separate from the *Beagle* in August 1832, and he made his way back to England again, where he exhibited in the Royal Academy in 1837 and again in 1838 before his death in the same year. Earle was not a lowly draftsman like Choris, but an artist with a public and good social connections who had chosen a life of bohemian wandering.[10]

Earle stirred public debate with his criticisms of the Anglican missionaries in and around the Bay of Islands in New Zealand. He arrived at the end of October 1827, already favorably disposed toward the Maoris from the ones he had met in Sydney. Soon after he witnessed the remains of a human body which had been roasted. While he looked on, "hogs and dogs were snarling and feasting upon it." The slave boy of a chief had neglected the field of *kumara* or sweet potatoes he was supposed to be watching, and when his master came upon him he killed him with a hatchet, ordering a fire to be made and the body dragged into it.[11] Nonetheless Earle remained an admirer of the Maoris, impressed by "the frugality and industry of these savages" and appreciative of the carving and ornamentation of their storehouses and the paintings and sculptures on their houses and canoes. On their way to the missionary settlement at Kerikeri he and his party observed jarring contrasts:

> We had travelled all day through a country in which every object we saw was of a character that reminded us forcibly of the savage community we were with. Occasionally we met groups of naked men, trotting

along under immense loads, and screaming their barbarous songs of recognition; sometimes we beheld an uncouthly carved figure, daubed over with red ochre, and fixed in the ground, to give notice that one side of the road was tabooed. An extraordinary contrast was now presented to our view, for we came suddenly in front of a complete little English village. Wreaths of white smoke were rising from the chimneys, of neat weather-boarded houses. The glazed windows reflected the brilliant glow from the rays of the setting sun, while herds of fat cattle were winding down the hills, lowing as they leisurely bent their steps towards the farm-yard.

Earle was not disturbed by the appearance of the Maoris, nor was he relieved to find himself suddenly in a virtual England. As they approached the farmhouse they were greeted by a group of New Zealand boys who were living with the missionaries. He was disgusted to find them dressed in crude European clothing, either too tight or too loose for their forms, their hair cropped close. The missionaries, he wrote, had "no taste for the picturesque" and "had obscured the finest human forms under a seaman's huge clothing." The incendiary point in his book came when he criticized one of the missionaries, Henry Williams, for receiving him coldly; he went on to criticize the missionaries for trying to teach incomprehensible theology instead of useful crafts and to contrast their inhospitality with his warm welcome among his "savage friends." Earle was a gentleman-adventurer with an artist's eye for the aesthetic qualities of Maori life and an unperturbable affection for human contrasts. He did not try to ennoble his Maori subjects; if anything he seemed to enjoy shocking his readers.[12]

Darwin was infuriated. Earle was said to have consorted with a native woman; the Reverend William Williams explained in a letter to Darwin that for this reason he and his brother did not wish to take him into their house. Darwin's own published account of the natives and missionaries in New Zealand reads like a refutation of Earle's. He found the Maoris fearsome ("there is a twinkling in the eye, which cannot indicate any thing but cunning and ferocity"), rough, and dirty. Part of what disturbed him was the independence of the Maoris, who seemed to have little regard for social rank or social forms to regulate the relationship between freemen and slaves. He noted approvingly that Tahitians had formerly been required to bare themselves to the waist in the presence of their "king." Even when Europeans first met them they had had, he thought, more government and "complex formalities" to regulate the relationship between social orders. The antidemocratic political undercurrent steadily fed Darwin's anthropological musings. Concluding his observations on the Fuegians, he ranked them, the Tahitians, and the Maoris according to their degree of political hierarchy:

> The perfect equality among the individuals composing these tribes [the Fuegians], must for a long time retard their civilization. As we see those animals, whose instinct compels them to live in society and obey a chief, are most capable of improvement, so is it with the races of mankind. Whether we look at it as a cause or a consequence, the more civilized always have the most artificial governments. For instance, the inhabitants of Otaheite, who, when first discovered, were governed by hereditary kings, had arrived at a far higher grade than another branch of the same people, the New Zealanders—who although benefited by being compelled to turn their attention to agriculture, were republicans in the most absolute sense.

No matter how steeped in republican disorder Maori society was, it was not beyond redemption, for Darwin saw with his own eyes at the settlement of Waimate, which he reached in December 1835, that "the lesson of the missionary is the enchanter's wand." Three large farmhouses and an abundance of fruits and vegetables, "pigs and poultry"; a mill that powdered the Maori miller "white with flour, like his brother miller in England"; young men redeemed from slavery who dressed in shirts and trousers and played cricket; tidy-looking Maori servant girls; a Christmas-day party of merry children; all this the missionaries had brought about "in the centre of the land of cannibalism, murder, and all atrocious crimes!" Darwin did not like New Zealand, but he was hopeful that the missionaries of Waimate would improve "the moral state of the people." Whereas Earle wrote as an aesthete with an eye for the human form, art, and diversity of experience, Darwin was an eloquent and persuasive advocate of conventional morality.[13]

Darwin's account of foreign peoples in the *Journal of Researches* belongs to a different world from the one visited by Commerson, the Forsters, or Chamisso. Unlike earlier generations of Pacific travelers, Darwin wrote with the comfortable distance of a voyager who enjoyed an almost complete physical superiority to the peoples he met in Tierra del Fuego, Tahiti, New Zealand, and Australia. There was no need to beg for their hospitality or entreat them to exchange foodstuffs; the economy of dependence that had sharpened the insights of earlier travelers was gone. There was no need to question them for directions; the travelers came with maps. British hegemony on the seas was so clearly established that the voyage instead had the altogether different character in these places of a cruise, perhaps with larger strategic purposes as part of the continuous policing of the world which was necessary to hold together the empire, but a cruise nonetheless for a voyager who was never challenged in his assumptions of moral superiority to the natives he met.[14]

Darwin's firsthand impressions of Pacific peoples left a deep mark on his thinking. Fuegians and islanders still populate his imaginary map of the human world in *The Descent of Man,* published in 1871. It belonged to a different age and returned to the places of Darwin's earlier colonial encounters for different purposes. Darwin published his account of the *Beagle* voyage as a young man attached to family, church, and the example of Alexander von Humboldt; he wrote the later work as the world-famous author of *Origin of Species*, which since its publication twelve years earlier had had a revolutionary effect on the world of learning. *The Descent of Man* promised to take the conclusions of evolutionary theory and apply them to the history of humankind. Whereas the *Journal* was a travel account and altogether conformed to the conventions of travel narrative, reporting on things seen and fitting them into a typology, the later work was the application of a theory: individual peoples and places mattered only for the bits and pieces of evidence that fitted into or modified it. *The Descent of Man* takes the form of an analysis: what unfolds across its many hundreds of pages is not a chronicle as in the travel account, but an enormous accumulation of evidence for logical steps that carry Darwin's case from beginning to end. Yet we can see in the later work how the travel experiences of the 1830s, grounded in conventions and debates reaching back to the second half of the eighteenth century, informed Darwin's mature views. Darwin's general outlook and his specific use of Fuegians and Polynesians in *The Descent of Man* had evolved out of the world of travelers from Commerson to Chamisso even as he developed a different kind of global catalogue of peoples.

In the long-standing debate between monogenists and polygenists, *The Descent of Man* came down emphatically on the monogenist side. The historical terms of the debate and the logic of Darwin's argument conditioned his choice. Polygenism had functioned as an alternative to the biblical account of humankind's Adamic descent, but it was also associated with an eighteenth-century view of creation as a static event bringing forth a limited variety of species that were arranged at different points around the globe. In such a view there was no need to introduce change over time in order to explain human diversity. A monogenist hypothesis of a single human stock, in contrast, required historical explanation; the evolutionary naturalist would need to introduce a process by which diversity had emerged out of original unity. Darwin's monogenism differed from the monogenism of Blumenbach and other predecessors, for their degenerationism, the notion of decline from a normative human type, gave way to a "more cheerful" theory: "To believe that man was aboriginally civilised and then suffered utter degradation in so many regions, is to take a pitiably low view of human nature. It is apparently a truer and more cheerful view that progress has been much more general than retrogression; that man has risen, though by slow and interrupted steps, from a lowly condition to the highest standard as yet attained by him in knowledge, morals and religion." The underlying theory was neither cheerful nor pessimistic, but simply the general formula of an evolutionary movement from simpler to more complex living beings that had a greater probability of survival and reproduction. Once Darwin applied his theory to human beings, however, it was nonetheless a significant break with earlier generations' ethnological assumptions, for as Darwin himself suggested, it posited a real and unambivalent advance in their degree of civilization.[15]

The peoples Darwin had encountered in his world voyage entered *The Descent of Man* as material evidence for his evolutionary hypothesis. He carefully positioned them so that they were members of the same species, yet far removed from northern Europeans, who must therefore have advanced far beyond them in historical time. He turned back more than once to the Fuegians as his prime document of what original, natural man was, the starting point from which to measure the zenith of civilization represented by modern England. There was no essential difference, he wrote, between a Newton or Shakespeare and the beings who would murder a child for dropping a basket. He pointed out how much progress toward civilization the Fuegians could make under English tutelage, recalling how even tiny gestures of the natives who were his companions on board the *Beagle* resembled the movements of their English guardians. At the close of the entire work his thoughts returned again to his encounter with the Fuegians: "The main conclusion arrived at in this work, namely that man is descended from some lowly organized form, will, I regret to think, be highly distasteful to many. But there can hardly be a doubt that we are descended from barbarians. The astonishment which I felt on first seeing a party of Fuegians on a wild and broken shore will never be forgotten by me, for the reflection at once rushed into my mind—such were our ancestors." Thus he connected his mature theory to the shock of his youthful encounter.[16]

The Descent of Man used evidence from Polynesia for further contemplation of the vestiges of man in a state remote from modern civilization. Darwin was more convinced than ever of a point he had already made in the *Journal*, that contact between "savage" and "civilized" human beings usually resulted in a swift destruction of the "savages." After citing the examples of New Zealand and non-Polynesian Tasmania, he turned to the Sandwich Islands, where the availability of statistics helped him to make his case. He accepted an estimate that when Cook discovered the islands in 1779, their population was about 300,000; by 1872 it had dropped to 53,531. While recognizing effects of so-called female profligacy, wars, labor exploitation, and new diseases, he attributed the reduction above all to declining fertility of parents and the weakening constitution of children. Darwin speculated that changing conditions of life were fatal to peoples "who must have been long exposed to nearly uniform conditions." All wild animals adjusted poorly to environmental change; civilized people were more like domesticated animals in their ability to adapt.[17]

In *The Descent of Man* Darwin was convinced that aristocratic Europeans were more beautiful because their males had chosen the most beautiful women for themselves; he worried about the effects of noneugenic breeding on the rest of the European population and contemplated the drastic population decline and extinction of native peoples as the satisfactory working out of natural mechanisms.[18] This way of thinking was a far remove from the era when Cook and the Forsters were horrified by the possibility that Europeans had introduced venereal disease into Tahiti. These earlier voyagers saw themselves in the trail of a different history: the invasion of the conquistadors and the extermination of the peoples of the Americas. Concern over the fate of native peoples and the legitimacy of European overseas exploration had given way to Darwin's annoyance toward writers who sentimentalized the moral capacity of "savages."[19]

Melville and the Casket Ships

Whereas Darwin enjoyed the support of a wealthy and loving family, and owed his position on the *Beagle* to the recommendation of his Cambridge botany professor, Melville had neither money nor education; he came from a down-at-the-heels genteel family and did not go to college. Born in 1819, he crossed the seas as an ordinary seaman aboard the whaling ship *Acushnet*, captained by Valentine Pease, a Nantucketer. Like Augustus Earle—and contrary to Darwin—Herman Melville traveled as a gentleman bohemian who took up an attitude of sympathy toward "natives" and hostility toward missionaries.

Departing from Fairhaven, Massachusetts, on January 3, 1841, the whaler rounded Cape Horn in mid-April, continued up the coast of Chile, viewed the Galápagos, and reached the Marquesas Islands in late June. Melville and a friend named Richard Tobias Greene took their leave in Nukuhiva Bay and did not return, instead crossing over the mountains into the valley of the Taipis, arriving there July 13. On August 9 an Australian whaler short of hands, the *Lucy Ann*, picked up Melville and made its way to Tahiti. Melville joined a group of dissatisfied sailors who stayed on shore; he and the ship's doctor, John Troy, ended up raising sweet potatoes on neighboring Moorea. In early November Melville joined the *Charles and Henry*, which dropped him off in early May on Maui; from there he made his way to Honolulu, boarded an American warship, the *United States*, and after stops in Nukuhiva and Tahiti returned to Boston on October 3, 1844. For the purpose of chronicling the political and cultural history of the Pacific his timing was very good. He left when whalers were sweeping across the Pacific; he arrived in the Marquesas, Tahiti, and the Sandwich Islands at just the right time to observe political crises in all three places as the age of semiautonomous native kingdoms gave way to colonial rule; he could compare Nukuhivans exposed to and sheltered from contact with Euro-Americans. Melville came near the end of an era, making his voyage just when he could catch the older world of sailing ships, whalers, and missionaries before it was swept away by industrialization, a global economy, and the high imperialism of the late nineteenth century.[20]

Melville claimed that *Typee* (1846), his first book, was a factual account of his stay in the valley of the Taipis. It is usually called a novel, and it certainly was a fictionalized reworking of his adventures, but we simplify it by confining it to a single genre; its author was a daredevil talent who crossed and mixed up literary divisions. The story moves step by step through the simplest kind of adventure story: desertion on Nukuhiva, flight into a cannibal valley, captivity and escape. It was the stuff of literary convention, but Melville turned convention inside out, exposing its holes and seams. He wrote in the context of a legendary earlier American visitor, the naval captain David Porter, who in 1813 landed his frigate, the *Essex*, on the Happah tribe's side of Nukuhiva, took a native mistress, declared the island to be an American colony, and tried to conquer the Taipis. After they beat back his men, Porter took his revenge by leaving a trail of fire as his troops retreated across the island. Later Porter justified his Marquesan campaign as his attempt to bring civilization to a barbaric people whom he admired.[21]

When Melville arrived, the Taipis had still staved off would-be civilizers. His narrative is structured to subvert his era's typical opposition of civilization and savagery. He does not merely reverse this confrontation—but plies it from all sides, playful with his reader and doing what he can to bring us to a closer observation of the Marquesans. He and Toby are terrified by the Typees, who have a fearsome reputation as cannibals. They *are* cannibals, but they are also human beings of unexpected kindness and grace. Typee Valley has the look of a paradise—and, as he and Toby approach it from a mountain height, a kind of Venus stretched out before his eyes, at that—but after a soaking night of rain the narrator thinks that young men in search of paradise ought to bring along their umbrellas. Melville has his Fayaway, his beautiful island girl, but amid his courtship of her he meets Marnoo, a "Polynesian Apollo" whose "cheek was of a feminine softness," an exalted, mediating figure, free to wander between the island's warring tribes, who later arranges for his rescue.[22] Satire spreads far and wide across the book whenever Melville meets figures of authority, though he treats the Typee chief Marhevee gently and reserves his worst ridicule for Abel Dupetit-Thouars, the French captain who just as Melville arrived was in the process of seizing the Marquesas for France. With the antiauthoritarian twists and turns of its commentary, it is not a book to please puritans of any generation or ideology.

As in his later works Melville alternated between comedy and earnest critique. Petty traders, he wrote, trailed from island to island committing atrocities that never came to light; missionaries invented exaggerated stories of cannibalism as if "human victims are daily cooked and served up upon the altars"; scientists listened to "retired old South-Sea rovers" for their native horror stories. Implicit in the entire book, with its affectionate portrayal of Marquesan daily life, was a rebuke of the missionaries. There were none on the Marquesas: a brief, ABCFM-sponsored settlement came in 1833 only to leave in less than a year, traumatized by thieving, sex, and cannibal threats. Having none to criticize on Nukuhiva, Melville went out of his way to report on the outcome of missionary rule in the Sandwich kingdom: a loutish Kamehameha III adored in the publications of the "republican missionaries of Oahu"; the division of the native Hawaiians into the opulent chiefs and impoverished people; the dispossession of the people from the land. In Honolulu he saw the natives "evangelized into beasts of burden" who were harnessed to the carriages of their evangelical masters. It was one thing, he wrote, to read the missionary accounts of their hardships and triumphs, another to see their pretty villas alongside native misery. Melville was not writing for missionary superiors, military superiors, or any other corporate master. An outsider to the established networks of knowledge, his position was closer to the American journalists of the 1840s writing exposés of slavery; outside the lines of patronage and piety he tried to appeal directly to a democratic reading public.[23]

"A strange, graceful, most readable book . . . As a book to hold in one's hand and pore dreamily over of a summer day, it is unsurpassed," wrote Walt Whitman about *Typee* in the Brooklyn *Eagle*. Other reviewers agreed, a few placing him in the discourse of travel writing. *Robinson Crusoe* was a natural comparison—especially for writers who wished to question the authenticity of Melville's adventures; but one reviewer compared him favorably to the eighteenth-century classics: "*Typee* . . . is a very curious and interesting narrative of savage life, and well deserving perusal. It reminds us of those delightful volumes of our boyhood, the voyages of Cook, Carteret, Byron and Anson, over the plates and pages of which we so loved to linger. This residence at Typee lacks nothing but the plates to be as attractive as either of these voyages." British and American reviewers were fully alive to the freshness, zest, and humor of Melville's writing as well as its intimate ethnography of the Marquesans; even hostile critics conceded its captivating qualities as a work of literature. Many, including sympathetic reviewers, recognized right away that it was not a factual voyage account and speculated on how much was based on personal experience and how much on fantasy. Melville himself had raised the issue of empirical veracity, and complicated it, through his own idiosyncratic mixture of fact and fiction. *Typee* jumbled together a real-life story, his fictional embellishments, and the reporting of a muckraking journalist, all between the covers of a purported factual voyage account.[24]

Melville's second novel, *Omoo,* takes up his story after a whaling vessel short of sailors rescues him from the valley. Like *Typee* the sequel mixes journalism and fiction, the revelations of the investigative reporter and the symbol-laden tales of the habitual storyteller. Amid its amusing vignettes and picaresque adventures, Melville once again took on the controversies of the day concerning European destruction of Polynesian cultures and missionary regimes to regenerate them. Although the tone is comic—grandly so in this work written in the aftermath of the earlier novel's success—decay and death haunt the destinies of both Europeans and Tahitians.

The narrator brings the reader on board the *Little Julia* with a rollicking but also carefully observed description of life aboard a whaler. The *Little Julia,* he tells us, was built as an American ship for the War of 1812, lived out its American life and was sold to British interests in Sydney. The ship is half-rotten, and its crew is as much in tatters as its sails: a third of the men have already deserted and most of the rest are sick, including the captain, who is also a coward. The crew is an ingathering of humanity (as would later be the crew of the *Pequod* in *Moby-Dick*): it includes a "Mowhree," a Dane, a Finn, an ex-slave from Baltimore, the shabby-genteel narrator, and English sailors. There is also the narrator's friend Dr. Long Ghost, a down-at-the-heels physician who is still comfortable at a table set with fine wine and owns a few tattered books.

The would-be whalers drift to Tahiti. The captain and mate try to keep the men on their floating prison while the sickly captain himself goes on shore. The men are on the edge of mutiny; with some effort the narrator and Long Ghost manage to stave off open rebellion. Instead they compromise on the less dangerous action of a sit-down strike. The English consul, a friend of the captain's, comes on board and tries to cow them into going back to work, which only makes them more determined than ever to be set on shore. Finally they are turned out of the ship and marched off to the "Calabooza Beretanee," the British clink. This turns out to be the house of a friendly Tahitian, Captain Bob, who has no love for the consul. He lets them wander off and get their fill of fruit from a neighboring orange grove. An Irish priest takes notice of them and makes sure that they have fresh bread. There is no getting them back on board the *Little Julia,* and before long they are waving good-bye to the ship, which gives up on the deserters and heads out to sea stocked with an assortment of sailors from the local beachcomber crowd.

Melville records the decay of the Tahiti that once was: a special South Sea kind of decay, not the Gothic rot of the damp foggy north, but something quite different. It is the decay of those great Homeric canoes that had once greeted Forster and Cook. (Their counterpart is the leaky tubs that take Melville a-whaling around the Pacific and embody the decay of the once-great whaling trade.) On Tahiti the native vessel of Melville's time is Captain Bob's canoe. Bob is, after all, a "captain" too, the comic reduced successor to those commanders of native fleets, his floating vessel nothing more than a hollowed-out log. Wood, wood, and more wood recurs in Melville's story as the symbol of Tahiti's fallen majesty. Wood it is that has brought a new pestilence to the valley of Martair on Eimeo (Moorea), where Melville and Long Ghost end up after they escape the Calabooza. The valley should be a paradise of a getaway, still untainted by the missionaries, but a whaling captain with some sort of grudge against the natives took care of that by towing a rotten old water-cask ashore and leaving it in a damp taro patch. There its mosquitoes multiplied and became the curse of the place. The rotting wood breeds a pestilence that fills the air. A valley of death: Melville slips in this idea so neatly that one hardly notices it amid all the comedy and misadventure. He and Long Ghost go on "a hunting ramble." As they misfire at some wild boars and trudge back home, they come to an open space. Here they see a wall of stones in ruins, "an almost forgotten burial-place, of great antiquity," unkempt since the christianization of the islanders. They pass the site of a deserted village. Their informant, Tonoi, was born here, in this place that is only a heap of stones today. Going down into the plain they see a tree, the *ati*, that Melville describes as truly regal: "In Tahiti, I was shown a narrow, polished plank fit to make a cabinet for a king." But the valley, too, is a ruin, of a natural kind. Melville's native informant tells him that in the war of conversion in the time of the first Pomare, a war party came and destroyed "entire groves of these invaluable trees" by girdling them. The inhabitants driven out of valleys like these are now "natives" who do no work and earn the contempt of Zeke, the Yankee entrepreneur.[25]

More wood: the narrator and the doctor go to the beach to get away from the mosquitoes. There they discover an old warship, still on the blocks on which it had been built, forgotten perhaps before it was ever launched. It is, Melville tells us, "crumbling to dust." Earlier, on the hunting ramble, they saw the trees once used to build the canoes, the trunks shooting over seventy feet high. Now they make out the traces of paint, the high prow, the carving; and Long Ghost thinks that on the stern he sees "the arms of the royal House of Pomaree." This is a vessel of the great fleet, a remnant of the workmanship that has decayed throughout the island. Melville was adding a new phase to the history of monarchy in the Society Islands. Once a project of Cook and his successors, then a collaboration of Pomares and missionaries, now the remnant of monarchy signified the decline of the people and the land.[26]

If Melville was a fictionalist, it was—as every reader of *Moby-Dick* knows from its catalogue of the natural history of whales—with a naturalist's gusto for fact collecting. It was also with a passion for political and social polemic. *Omoo*'s chapter on "Tahiti as it is" abandoned fiction to deliver Melville's assessment of the effects of missionary rule. He turned to Kotzebue, Beechey, and missionary sources in order to assess the pros and cons of the case before reaching his judgment that the missionaries had worsened the islanders' moral condition. They could no longer make tapa (cloth from mulberry bark), their tools, or their objects of everyday use. He noted their drastic decline in population and observed that all the wars and other evils of earlier times "were nothing" compared with the smallpox, the alcoholism, and above all the venereal disease brought by Europeans and not mitigated by the missionaries. The outcome of the missionaries' labors was the extinction of the Tahitians.[27]

Reviewers returned to Melville as a famous writer, his name a familiar one to readers; they marveled again over his freshness, inventiveness, and gift for bringing characters to life. About Melville's factual accuracy there was still a certain bubbling of controversy going back to the preceding book; about the theme of death hanging over the book little was said; about Melville's stinging anti-imperialism there was little excitement, for it was directed in this book, as in *Typee,* against the French, hardly a choice to set off demurral from British or American reviewers; even about Melville's randy sailor jokes and stories about one-legged cocks and googoo-eyed Pacific maidens nonreligious reviewers did not make much fuss. If "Omoo" according to Melville meant "wanderer" in the language of the Marquesans, a broad international public enjoyed the romp.

Religious readers of the two books were a different story. Indignation blazed from their reviews. The reviewer of *Typee* wrote in the New York *Evangelist:* "The book abounds in praises of the life of nature, *alias* savageism, and in slurs and flings against missionaries and civilization. When the author alludes to, or touches matters of fact at the Sandwich Islands, he shows the sheerest ignorance, and utter disregard of truth." The *Critic* of London thought it was "despicable and mischievous" of Melville to ridicule the missionaries whenever he could, but to excuse himself in the preface; the London writer warned readers not to be taken in by Melville's "tone of mock respect." From Boston the *Christian Observatory* (in a review of *Typee* wonderfully alert to Melville's disguised sexual innuendoes) felt obliged to attack a book wrapped in an aura of respectability by its dedication to the Chief Justice of the state of Massachusetts, Lemuel Shaw (Melville's father-in-law) and circulating in influential families. Another defender of the missionaries, William O. Bourne, imagined Melville as a depraved adventurer, "the shameless herald of his own wantonness, and the pertinacious traducer of loftier and better men," and cited Darwin's dismissal of such immoralists. Bourne's reaction was a continuation of the outrage over Pacific sensuality that dated all the way back to Banks's boasts over his conquests in Tahiti. Melville's genteel family connections provided him with some protection, but left him more vulnerable to destructive criticism than an English or a Russian naval captain.[28]

A London reviewer of *Typee* went beyond admiration for the storyteller or anger toward the traducer of missions. Instead he linked Melville to a German and American tradition of young men educating themselves through travel.[29] This was the expanded notion of *Bildung* or education that Friedrich Schlegel had recognized in George Forster, a traveler's education that would take young Germans from the narrowness of their studies into the wider world. It was the same impulse that made Alexander von Humboldt a national hero to educated Germans. This wanderlust was most clearly conceptualized in German culture, yet travelers from other places shared it: Melville was the latest in the succession of educated wanderers stretching back to Chamisso, the Forsters, and Commerson. There was of course a different, European tradition of the Grand Tour, which was travel from northern Europe to Italy. But that was a journey into the European past; by traveling to Venice, Rome, and Naples, English, German, and other travelers imbibed the sources of their own culture from the Renaissance and classical antiquity. Melville spoke for the world travelers who embarked on a different kind of journey, one that went beyond the old world and introduced them to an enlarged humanity.

Conclusion

The travelers' world had a beginning, a middle, and an end. It began gradually, bit by bit, sometime in the early eighteenth century, as France and England sent out organized scientific expeditions. Scientific bodies like the Royal Society and the Paris Academy of Sciences drew up their goals, sponsored improved instruments of navigation, and planned the voyages in collaboration with naval ministries. Monarchs looked to the expeditions for prestige and profits. Officers and naturalists joined them in the hope of a glorious naval or scientific career as their reward. In the 1760s the travelers' world took on its mature form: the Bougainville and Cook voyages announced a new scientific mastery of travel with well-defined routes and securely located islands across the Pacific. Subsequent travelers retraced the routes, filled in the shorelines, added islands and atolls, searched for a Northern Passage to link the Pacific and Atlantic, promoted island kingdoms, and expanded the fur trade. And then this world in turn eroded as nautical adventure gave way to routine, sail to steam, and encounter to European domination.

Travelers as Interpreters

Travelers' encounters with island peoples from the 1760s to the 1840s were a cumulative education. Within this time span several generations of travelers went from Europe to the Pacific. Each reflected on the experience of its predecessors while adding its own reflections on understanding foreign cultures. The dialectic of European politics during the same period matured travelers' thinking too, as Enlightenment ideas about human nature entered society and Europeans lived through revolution, Jacobin terror, Napoleonic wars, and post-Napoleonic conservative restoration. Experiences at home and abroad during this turbulent era further intensified a rethinking of Enlightenment assumptions and the formation of a new understanding of culture. This post-1815 perspective remained true to the Enlightenment belief in a unified human nature, but gave more serious attention to humanity's diverse forms of expression and the need to translate between them.

If we try to retrace this evolution toward translation as the model for the study of cultures, Rousseau may be taken as the travelers' starting point: his *Discourse on Inequality* gave classic formulation to the Enlightenment's impatience for scientific travel narratives. He announced what was, in effect, a double task that voyagers gradually called into question. It should be possible, he thought, for an educated traveler to bring back straightforward truths about foreign places: to go, look, and report with empirical veracity. At the same time, exotic cultures held the promise of revealing truths about human nature: of showing what human beings were like at an earlier stage of their development, one irretrievable for Europeans but possibly more suitable to human happiness than later, more advanced states of civilization. The *Discourse on Inequality* captured a widespread Enlightenment confidence—shared by Kant, for example—in the possibility of accumulating accurate and valuable ethnographic knowledge by sending out scientific expeditions. What travelers instead discovered over the course of the late eighteenth and early nineteenth centuries was something else: that the appearance and workings of foreign societies were anything but transparent—and in fact were muddled beyond the comprehension of any single eyewitness; the task of conveying information, so straightforward to the faraway theorist, turned out in practice to be impossible. The knowledge that the travelers acquired offered no single pattern of human nature, but rather an irreducible multiplicity of cultures. The lesson veered toward the opposite of the expected one: instead of a coherent human nature, an ever greater variety of forms of sex, politics, language, and every other human institution expanded their definition of humanity. The travelers and their readers did not abandon the idea of human nature, but they had to reconcile it with a greatly enlarged inventory of human possibilities.

The principal travelers studied in this book—Commerson, George Forster, and Chamisso—exemplify this process of education. Philippe Commerson started out with a belief, strongly influenced by Rousseau, in a state of nature that was the point of departure for the development of more powerful and corrupt modern civilizations. Commerson's letter, with its claims for the radical transparency of Tahitian culture, explored the thesis that one could indeed go to a distant place, comprehend it, and find in it a utopia. He had no sensitivity to the danger of confusing immediate perception with valid social observation. Instead he wrote with the clarity and conviction of one who had seen the truth of another society, who had indeed observed human nature in its uncorrupted original state. From the moment his letter was published, his description enchanted and met with the skepticism of his contemporaries. George Forster's narrative was more self-critical; it recorded the moments when his expectations or first impressions gave way to a deeper understanding of social institutions, as when the spectacle of an *ari'i* being stuffed with food ended his illusion of Tahitian egalitarianism. The drama of Forster's narrative was built around the tension between the author's ongoing belief in a generalized human nature and his discovery everywhere of differences between cultures. Notions like friendship, sensitivity to cruelty, and hospitality served as universals that could mediate between islanders and Europeans, serving to establish a common humanity that transcended baser motives and misunderstandings. Chamisso spoke for a different era. He was a member of the early Romantic generation that was schooled in the ideals of the Enlightenment but exposed to the turmoil of the Terror, Napoleonic France's imperialism, and the countermovement among intellectuals and peoples of Europe to preserve their cultural autonomy. Skepticism about the possibility of communication between cultures pervaded his travel narrative. Wilhelm von Humboldt demonstrated a similar movement from Enlightenment universalism to a philosophy of language encompassing both the universal human capacity for reason and the particularity of linguistic expression.

The early missionaries to Tahiti and Hawaii complemented Chamisso's and Wilhelm von Humboldt's critique of the Enlightenment when they discovered that a brief acquaintance with a radically foreign culture was a superficial acquaintance. The early LMS missionaries left England expecting Tahitians to welcome them as friends, treat them as guests, and embrace a new religion. They quickly found that it was not enough just to land on Tahiti and spend a few weeks visiting the place; mastering the language and unraveling the structures of kinship, politics, and religion were the work of years, and even at that an unending labor. The shock of their early trials and their dependence on their Tahitian allies made them acutely aware of their initial overconfidence. The American missionaries to Hawaii never experienced a comparable assault on their expectations, but even they were taken aback by the self-confident *ali'i* and had to learn Hawaiian in order to carry out their missionary work. The missionaries to Tahiti, Hawaii, and other Pacific islands turned into close, sometimes sympathetic observers of native cultures. The great controversy over the early missions underlined the point: if even observers as talented and conscientious as Darwin and Melville could come to opposite conclusions, then understanding cultures was something far trickier than Enlightenment philosophes had imagined.

The movement from a naive to an interpretive method, from seeming transparency to more accurate translation, was part of the era's larger exploration of the role of interpretation in the human sciences, whether in biblical criticism, legal studies, or the writing of history. The growing sophistication of travelers joined a larger revolution in scholarship that was widespread in Europe but most deeply at home in Germany. Thinkers like Friedrich and August Wilhelm Schlegel expanded the European literary canon across time and space, teaching a new appreciation of European traditions since the Middle Ages and of Sanskrit as a repository of wisdom equaling that of ancient Greek. Chamisso was one of the makers of this early Romantic revolution, expanding the horizons of diversity still further when he reported on the islanders of Hawaii and Micronesia. His travels and writing exemplify the newly defined idea of translation as a creative mediation between cultures.[1]

Travelers as Mediators

Travelers' interpretations of foreign cultures were just one moment in the global production of ethnographic knowledge. The travelers themselves had only a limited comprehension of this social formation of their studies, for they viewed each station of their journey as an outlet for scientific investigation, without regard for the social and psychological cross-currents that conditioned their work wherever they went. However sensitive they may have been to cultural difference, they assumed that their control over the process of production could remain continuously intact. In this unsociological conception of their work, the initial guarantee of their truth-in-reporting was their own devotion to empirical veracity; their patrons' job was to further science; their informants offered up facts to take back home; and the scientific and literary public advanced a rational exchange of ideas. If the system had worked thus, then they could indeed have hunted out their intellectual game in exotic places, bagged it, and brought it home for domestic use. After all, this is what they were supposedly doing when they collected plants, pickled tarantulas, and brought back animals dead or alive.[2]

Transporting ideas about human beings was intrinsically more difficult. When it came to foreign languages, polities, personalities, and histories, taking information back to Europe inevitably modified it, sometimes with tragic consequences.

Both egoistic calculation and emotion worked against sealing information abroad and opening it untampered at home. The process of shaping started, even before the voyagers set out, with the patrons who made demands that were at odds with reality, like the LMS directors who imagined that Tahitians would gratefully cede land to the missionaries. In general, patrons, radically underestimating the complexity of the tasks they set, expected travelers to be able to gather whatever intelligence they needed in short visits to foreign societies. For their part the travelers were not impersonal instruments of their masters' will; they viewed foreign places with feelings of gratitude, anxiety, and resentment toward their patrons that inevitably shaped their writings.

When they went to island societies, visitors praised locals as friends or denounced them as demons according to their homegrown religious, aesthetic, and political predilections. Even sophisticated visitors like George Forster and Chamisso were too beholden to their belief in friendship between hosts and guests to ask or discern when their informants were withholding, partially disclosing, disguising, or prettifying their words and behavior. Kamehameha's show of majesty covered the fragility of his hold on power when the *Rurik* voyagers met him in 1816 and 1817; Chamisso was charmed by the gentle Marshall Islanders and praised their peaceableness, but failed to observe the sexual tyranny of the chiefs over their subjects. If travelers had systematically thought of their friendships as power relationships from which they were trying to extract a scarce commodity—knowledge—and locals were dispensing it with an eye to maximizing their return, they might have come to different conclusions about the information they were getting.

The travelers were more aware of the loss of control that took place when they returned to Europe, as they confronted real or perceived dangers of censorship and restrictions on their ability to publish their findings. When travel accounts entered the public sphere, they spun further out of their authors' control. Philosophers like Kant and Diderot, who lacked any personal experience with radical cultural difference, domesticated travelers' tales by inserting them into existing conceptions of human society; the general reading public was inclined to gross lampooning of tropical islanders no matter how hard travelers tried to correct European preconceptions. Travelers resented these distortions without recognizing that their work was from the beginning a cooperative venture.

At the far end of their journeys, they had occasionally met like-minded travelers whose cooperation they were happy to acknowledge: Tupaia, Mahine, and Kadu, for example. Melville fashioned one memorable image of these convergences. It is the meeting in *Typee* of Tommo, Melville's fictional self, and Marnoo, the mediator between warring tribes. Marnoo's broken English and Tommo's broken Marquesan are all they have to work with. Using their patchwork languages, Marnoo arranges for Tommo's rescue from the Typees. Tommo for his part cannot save Marnoo and the Marquesans from whalers and colonizers; he can only write down what he has gathered of their story. After his return, Melville endured his own difficult fate of being first celebrated, then forgotten, by his public.

This story is a reminder that travel was never far removed from danger. Outcomes could be disastrous for individuals and for entire island peoples. Travelers were risk-takers who created mutual comprehension where at first there was none: adventurers in newly opened realms of space and spirit.

Chronology

1727   *November 18.* Philibert Commerson born in Châtillon-les-Dombes.

1728   *October 10.* James Cook born in Marton, Yorkshire.

1729   Louis Antoine de Bougainville born in Paris.
October 22. Johann Reinhold Forster born in Dirschau.

1735   Linnaeus, *Systema naturae,* first edition.
La Condamine sails to South America.

1739   Buffon is made intendant of the Jardin du Roi, a position he holds until 1788.

1740   *July 27.* Jeanne Barret born in Burgundy.

1743   (?) Pomare I born in Tahiti.
February 13. Joseph Banks born in London.

1744   *August 25.* Johann Gottfried Herder born in Mohrungen, East Prussia.

1749   Buffon, *Histoire naturelle,* first volumes published (completed 1767).

1750   (?) Ahutoru born in Tahiti.

1751   Linnaeus, *Philosophia botanica.*

Encyclopédie, volume 1, is published, with Diderot and Jean Le Rond d'Alembert as coeditors.

1752   (?) Kamehameha I born in Kohala, Hawaii.

1753   Mai (Omai) born in Raiatea, Society Islands.

1754   *April 3.* Nikolai P. Rumiantsev born.
November 5. Alejandro Malaspina born in Mulazzo, northern Italy.
November 27. George Forster born in Nassenhuben near Danzig.

1755   Rousseau, *Discourse on Inequality.*

1756   Seven Years' War begins.

1758   Franz Gall, founder of phrenology, born in Tiefenbrunn, southwest Germany.

1761   August von Kotzebue born in Weimar.

1763   Treaty of Paris ends Seven Years' War.

1766   *November 15.* Bougainville departs in *La Boudeuse,* with consort ship *L'Étoile* to follow.

1767   *June 18.* Wallis reaches Tahiti.
June 22. Wilhelm von Humboldt born in Berlin.

1768   (?) Ka'ahumanu born on the island of Hawaii.
April 6. Bougainville arrives in Tahiti.
August 26. First Cook voyage departs in *Endeavour.*

1769   *March 16.* Return of Bougainville voyage to St.-Mâlo.
April 13. Cook voyagers arrive in Tahiti, stay three months.
September 14. Alexander von Humboldt born in Berlin.

1770   Raynal, *History of the Two Indies.*
November 8. Adam von Krusenstern born in Hagudi, Estonia.

1771   Bougainville, *Voyage autour du monde.*
July 12. First Cook voyage returns.
November 6. Ahutoru dies on return voyage from France to Tahiti.

1772   Diderot composes his *Supplément;* it is circulated, changed, and first published posthumously in 1796.

July 13. Departure of second Cook voyage in the *Resolution*, with consort ship *Adventure*.

1773   *March 13.* Commerson dies on Mauritius.
August 15. Cook sights Tahiti.
September 17–June 4, 1774. Mahine travels with the *Resolution*.

1774   Henry Nott, later an LMS missionary to Tahiti, born in Birmingham, England.

1775   Blumenbach, *On the Natural Variety of Mankind.*

1776   *July 12.* Cook departs on third voyage in the *Resolution*, with consort ship *Discovery*.

1777   George Forster, *A Voyage round the World.*
August. Mai, sailing with Cook on the *Resolution*, returns to Tahiti.

1778   Banks made president of Royal Society.
January 10. Death of Linnaeus.

1779   *February 14.* Cook killed on Kealakekua Bay, Hawaii.

1781   *January 30.* Adelbert von Chamisso (Louis Charles Adélaïde de Chamisso) born in Château Boncourt, Champagne.

1782   (?) Pomare II born in Tahiti.

1787   *December 30.* Otto von Kotzebue born in Reval (today Tallin), Estonia.

1788   African Association founded in London.

1789   Erasmus Darwin, *The Botanical Garden.*
Outbreak of the French Revolution. July 14, storming of the Bastille; August 4, abolition of serfdom.
July 30. Malaspina departs in *Descubierta*, with consort ship *Atravida*, from Cádiz.

1790   *March 25–June 11.* George Forster and Alexander von Humboldt travel from Mainz to Holland, England, and France.

1791   Chateaubriand travels to North America (returns to France on January 2, 1792).

April 1. Vancouver departs in *Discovery*, with consort ship *Chatham*.

1793   *June 10.* Transformation of the Jardin du Roi into the Museum of Natural History.
September. Reign of Terror begins in France.

1794   *January 10.* George Forster dies in Paris.
July 27 (9 Thermidor). Overthrow of Robespierre.
September 1. Return of Malaspina expedition to Cádiz.

1795   Kamehameha conquers Oahu.
London Missionary Society is founded.
French constitution of 1795; rule of the moderate Directory.
October 25. Creation of the Institut National.
May 22. Louis (Ludovik, Ludwig) Choris born in Dniepropetrovsk, Ukraine.

1797   Great Mutinies of 1797 shake British navy.
August 4. LMS missionaries depart on the *Duff* for Tahiti.

1798   Napoleon's Egyptian expedition, 1798–99.
Kant, *Anthropology from a Pragmatic Point of View.*
December 9. J. R. Forster dies in Halle.

1799   Russian-American Company gets monopoly charter from Tsar Paul.
June 5. Beginning of Humboldt's and Bonpland's voyage to the Americas.
November 9–10 (18 Brumaire). Coup d'état in Paris; Napoleon becomes First Consul.

1803   *August 7.* Krusenstern departs in the *Nadeshda*, with consort ship *Neva*.
September 3. Death of Pomare I, followed by endemic war on Tahiti.

1804   *February 2.* Kant dies in Königsberg.
May 14. Meriwether Lewis and William Clark begin their trans–North American expedition in St. Louis.
December 12. Napoleon crowns himself emperor.

1805   Publication of Alexander von Humboldt's travel account, *Voyage aux régions équinoxiales* (continues to appear until 1834).

July 29. Alexis de Tocqueville born in Paris.

1806 Holy Roman Empire, the traditional confederation of Central European states, is dissolved.
August 19. Krusenstern voyage returns to Baltic.
September 26. Lewis and Clark expedition returns to St. Louis.

1807 *August 5.* Jeanne Barret dies in Sainte-Aulaye.
September 24. Confiscation of *De l'Allemagne*. Mme de Staël moves to Coppet, near Geneva, a center of intellectual life until 1810.

1808 Alexander von Humboldt, *Views of Nature.*

1809 Malte-Brun begins to edit the journal *Annales des Voyages.*
February 12. Charles Darwin born in Shrewsbury, England.

1810 *Spring.* Henry Opukahaia and Thomas Hopu arrive in New Haven, Connecticut, from Hawaii.
September 5. First meeting of the American Board of Commissioners for Foreign Missions in Farmington, Connecticut.

1811 *August 20.* Death of Bougainville, who is buried in the Panthéon.

1812 Kamehameha I cedes control of government to *ali'i* oligarchy.
Defeat of Napoleon's army in Russia.

1813 *October 25.* The American David Porter on the *Essex* visits and occupies Nukuhiva, in the Marquesas Islands, until December 13.

1814 Chamisso, *The Amazing Story of Peter Schlemihl.*
March. Congress of Vienna opens.
April 6. Napoleon abdicates as emperor.

1815 *June 9.* Congress of Vienna concludes.
August 17. Rurik, with Otto von Kotzebue as captain, departs from Copenhagen.

1817 Freycinet voyage until 1820.

1818 *Late September. Rurik* arrives in St. Petersburg.

1819 Malte-Brun founds the journal *Nouvelles Annales des Voyages.*
Playwright August von Kotzebue, father of Otto, assassinated by the German student Karl Sand.

May 8. Kamehameha I dies at Kailua, Hawaii.
May 19. Pomare II is baptized.
August 1. Herman Melville born in New York.
October 23. Seventeen ABCFM missionaries depart from Boston in Thaddeus for the Sandwich Islands.

1820   Revolution in Naples and Sicily, repressed by Austria, 1820–21.
Carl Ritter becomes professor of geography at the University of Berlin (until 1859).
March 30. Thaddeus arrives on coast of the island of Hawaii.
June 19. Joseph Banks dies in London.

1821   Otto von Kotzebue, *Voyage of Discovery.*
Greek war of independence begins (lasts until 1829).
December 15. Geographic Society founded in Paris.

1822   Choris, *Voyage pittoresque autour du monde.*
January. Death of Pomare II.

1824   Death of Tsar Alexander I.

1826   Choris, *Vues et paysages.*
January 3. Rumiantsev dies in St. Petersburg.

1827   Krusenstern, *Atlas of the South Sea.*
May 12. Alexander von Humboldt moves back to Berlin.

1828   *March 21.* Choris is murdered on the road to Jalapa, Mexico.
April. Founding of the Berlin Geographic Society.

1829   Alexander von Humboldt voyages to Siberia.
Abrupt collapse of sandalwood trade in Hawaii.

1830   "July Revolution" brings liberal Louis-Philippe to the throne in France.
Otto von Kotzebue, *New Voyage round the World.*
Royal Geographical Society founded.

1831   *May.* Alexis de Tocqueville and his traveling companion, Gustave de Beaumont, arrive in North America; stay until February 1832.
January. Jules Dumont d'Urville, "Sur les îles du grand océan," defines four Oceanic "races."
December 27. Beagle departs from Plymouth.

1832   First Reform Bill passed in British Parliament.
           June 5. Ka'ahumanu dies in Hawaii.

1833   Slavery outlawed in British Empire.

1835   Wilhelm von Humboldt dies in Berlin.

1836   Wilhelm von Humboldt, *On the Kawi Language*, published
           posthumously.
           October 2. Beagle returns to England.

1838   United States Exploring Expedition, the first American scientific
           naval expedition, commanded by Charles Wilkes (until 1842).
           August 21. Chamisso dies in Berlin.

1839   Darwin, *Journal of Researches.*

1841   *January 3.* Herman Melville sails with the whaling ship *Acushnet.*

1846   Melville, *Typee.*
           Death of Otto von Kotzebue in Reval.

1847   Melville, *Omoo.*

1848   Liberal revolutions, ending in failure, across continental Europe.

1858   *July 9.* Franz Boas born in Minden, Westphalia.

1859   Darwin, *On the Origin of Species.*
           May 6. Alexander von Humboldt dies.

1871   Darwin, *The Descent of Man.*

1872   *May 10.* Marcel Mauss born in Bischwiller, in Alsace.

1891   *September 28.* Melville dies in New York.

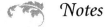 *Notes*

Abbreviations

ABF *Archives Biographiques Françaises* [microfiche] (Munich: Sauer Verlag, 1993).

Chamisso, *Werke* Adelbert von Chamisso, *Sämtliche Werke in zwei Bänden* (Munich: Carl Hanser Verlag, 1982).

Chamisso, *Voyage around the World* Adelbert von Chamisso, *A Voyage around the World with the Romanzov Exploring Expedition in the Years 1815–1818 in the Brig Rurik, Captain Otto von Kotzebue,* translated and edited by Henry Kratz (Honolulu: University of Hawaii Press, 1986).

Cook, *Journals* James Cook, *The Journals of Captain James Cook on His Voyages of Discovery,* 3 vols., edited by J. C. Beaglehole [Hakluyt Society, extra series, vols. 34–36] (Cambridge: Cambridge University Press, 1955–1967).

DNB Stephen, Leslie, and Sidney Lee, eds., *Dictionary of National Biography,* 22 vols. (London: Smith, Elder and Co., 1908–1909).

Forster,   George Forster, *A Voyage round the World, in His*
Voyage round the World   *Britannic Majesty's Sloop, Resolution, commanded*
                               by Capt. James Cook, during the Years 1772, 3, 4,
                               and 5 (London: White; Robson; Elmsly; and
                               Robinson, 1777).

Forster, *Werke*   George Forster, *Werke: Sämtliche Schriften,*
                               Tagebücher, Briefe, edited by Gerhard Steiner
                               (Berlin: Akademie-Verlag, 1965–1982).

Michaud   Joseph and Louis Michaud, *Biographie*
                               Universelle, Ancienne et Moderne, Nouvelle
                               Édition (Paris: Desplaces, 1843–1865).

Introduction

1. See John Gascoigne, *Science in the Service of Empire: Joseph Banks, the British State, and the Uses of Science in the Age of Revolution* (Cambridge: Cambridge University Press, 1998).
2. Marshall Sahlins, "Captain James Cook; or, The Dying God," in Sahlins, *Islands of History* (Chicago: University of Chicago Press, 1985), 104–135; Greg Dening, *Mr. Bligh's Bad Language: Passion, Power, and Theatre on the Bounty* (Cambridge: Cambridge University Press, 1992).
3. For related approaches that deal with travelers as mediators and networks of knowledge, see Mary Louise Pratt, *Imperial Eyes: Travel Writing and Transculturation* (London: Routledge, 1992); Hans Erich Boedeker, "'Sehen, hören, sammeln und schreiben.' Gelehrte Reisen im Kommunikationssystem der Gelehrtenrepublik," *Paedagogica Historica* 38 (2002): 1–30; Tony Ballantyne, *Orientalism and Race: Aryanism in the British Empire* (Basingstoke: Palgrave, 2002); and Neil F. Safier, "Writing the Andes, Reading the Amazon: Voyages of Exploration and the Itineraries of Scientific Knowledge in the Eighteenth Century" (Ph.D. diss., Johns Hopkins University, 2003); and cf. C. A. Bayly, *Empire and Information: Intelligence Gathering and Social Communication in India, 1780–1870* (Cambridge: Cambridge University Press, 1996). For a survey of recent network theory and empirical analysis, see Peter R. Monge and Noshir S. Contractor, *Theories of Communication Networks* (Oxford: Oxford University Press, 2003).

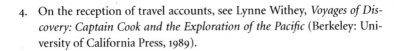

4. On the reception of travel accounts, see Lynne Withey, *Voyages of Discovery: Captain Cook and the Exploration of the Pacific* (Berkeley: University of California Press, 1989).

1. Travelers

1. James L. Larson, *Interpreting Nature: The Science of Living Form from Linnaeus to Kant* (Baltimore: Johns Hopkins University Press, 1994), 10–17; Daniel Mornet, *Les Sciences de la nature en France, au 18. siècle: Un chapitre de l'histoire des idées* (Paris: Armand Colin, 1911), 2–12, 108–121, 183–189; Jacques Roger, *Buffon: A Life in Natural History*, trans. Sarah Lucille Bonnefoi, ed. L. Pearce Williams (1989; Ithaca, N.Y.: Cornell University Press, 1997), 46. Cf. David Elliston Allen, *The Naturalist in Britain: A Social History* (1976; Princeton, N.J.: Princeton University Press, 1994).

2. On Linnaeus' primitivist style, see Lisbet Koerner, *Linnaeus: Nature and Nation* (Cambridge, Mass.: Harvard University Press, 1999), 64. On his writing style, see H. C. Artmann, Afterword, in Carl von Linné, *Lappländische Reise*, trans. H. C. Artmann (Frankfurt am Main: Insel, 1975), 231–234.

3. Maurice Cranston, *Jean-Jacques: The Early Life and Work of Jean-Jacques Rousseau, 1712–1754* (New York: Norton, 1983), 292–293. Jean Starobinski provides an admirable guide to Rousseau's thought in *Jean-Jacques Rousseau: Transparency and Obstruction*, trans. Arthur Goldhammer, introd. Robert J. Morrissey (1971; Chicago: University of Chicago Press, 1988). Rousseau's critics from his time to ours have accused him of a more simplified primitivism. See the critique of this misreading in Arthur O. Lovejoy, "The Supposed Primitivism of Rousseau's Discourse on Inequality" (1923) in Lovejoy, *Essays in the History of Ideas* (1948; reprint, New York: George Braziller, 1955), 14–37.

4. Jean-Jacques Rousseau, *A Discourse on Inequality*, trans. and ed. Maurice Cranston (London: Penguin, 1984), 155–158 (note "J"). The *Oxford English Dictionary* states that "pongo" was "a name in early writers of a large anthropoid African ape: variously identified with the Chimpanzee, and the Gorilla." Later it was further confused with the orangutan. For a discussion of Rousseau's views on human kinship with apes and their place in eighteenth-century thought, see

Lovejoy, "Monboddo and Rousseau," in *Essays in the History of Ideas,* 43–54.

5. Rousseau, *Discourse on Inequality,* 154–155, 160–161, quotation at 161.

6. There was an affinity between Linnaean plant collecting and Rousseau's call for a clear understanding of the structures of nature, whether in the ordering of plants or the evolution of society. On Rousseau's relationship to Linnaeus, see Albert Jansen, *Jean-Jacques Rousseau als Botaniker* (Berlin: Georg Reimer, 1885); Jean-Jacques Rousseau, *Confessions,* ed. Patrick Coleman, trans. Angela Scholar (Oxford: Oxford University Press, 2000), 623–627; and Jean-Jacques Rousseau to Carl Linnaeus, 21 September 1771, in *Correspondance complète,* ed. R. A. Leigh, vol. 38 (April 1770–December 1771) (Oxford: Voltaire Foundation, 1981), 267. For Rousseau's botanical guide, which took the form of letters to the daughter of an aristocratic friend, see *Oeuvres complètes,* vol. 14: *Mélanges,* part 4 (Lyon, n.p., 1796); for background, see Rousseau, *Lettres inédites de Jean-Jacques Rousseau à Mmes Boy de la Tour et Delessert comprenant les Lettres sur la Botanique. Publiées pour la première fois d'après le texte original,* ed. Philippe Godet and Maurice Boy de la Tour (Paris: Plon, 1911), i–v; and Rousseau, *Oeuvres complètes,* vol. 4: *Émile—Éducation—Morale—Botanique,* ed. Bernard Gagnebin and Marcel Raymond (Paris: Gallimard, 1969), 1808. See also Rousseau, *Confessions,* 629.

7. Recent historians of this navy have superseded the older view that these sea vessels were miniature totalitarian societies in which a degrading discipline guided every movement and have emphasized how they functioned rather as compressed versions of the society at home with special differences created by the conditions of life and work on board. See N. A. M. Rodger, *The Wooden World: An Anatomy of the Georgian Navy* (London: Collins, 1986); and Brian Lavery, ed., *Shipboard Life and Organisation, 1731–1815* (Aldershot: Ashgate, 1998). On the midshipmen, see Lavery, *Shipboard Life and Organisation,* 76, 111–112, 129.

8. Cf. David Cordingly, *Heroines and Harlots: Women at Sea in the Great Age of Sail* (New York: Random House, 2001), 54–56, 63. So far as one can judge from the scarce evidence, homosexuality was rare. See Lavery, ed., *Shipboard Life and Organisation,* 372; Rodger, *Wooden World,* 80. There is also little written evidence of homosexuality aboard whalers. See Briton C. Busch, *"Whaling Will Never Do for Me": The*

American Whaleman in the Nineteenth Century (Lexington: University Press of Kentucky, 1994), 147.

9. Philibert Commerson to Louis Gérard, 15 December 1757, in Paul-Antoine Cap, *Philibert Commerson, naturaliste voyageur: Étude biographique* (Paris: Victor Masson, 1861), 67, 68–69. See also Anon., "Commerson, Philibert," in Hoefer, *Nouvelle biographie générale* (Paris: Didot, 1855), 11, cols. 345–347, hereafter cited as Hoefer; C. J. Dufay, "Commerson, Philippe," in *Dictionnaire biographique des personnage notables . . . de l'Ain. Galerie civile . . .* (1882), 319–321; J. I. Depery, "Commerson, Philibert," *Biographie des hommes célèbres du département de l'Ain*, 2 vols. (1835), in ABF, 307–312; Dupetit-Thouars, "Commerson, Philibert," in Michaud, 8:688–689; and Alfred Role, "Commerson, Philibert," *L'Academie des sciences d'outre-mer: Hommes et destins*, 7 vols. (1975–1986), in ABF, 322–324.

10. Commerson to Curé Beau, 20 October 1766, in Cap, *Commerson*, 83. James L. Larson, *Reason and Experience: The Representation of Natural Order in the Work of Carl von Linné* (Berkeley: University of California Press, 1971), 59, dates Bernard de Jussieu's support of Linnaeus from 1739. For the story of Jeanne Barret, see Carole Christinat, "Une femme globe-trotter avec Bougainville: Jeanne Barret (1740–1807)," *Revue française d'histoire d'outre-mer* 83 (1996): 83–95; this article is also a valuable source of information on Commerson. See also Henriette Dussourd, *Jeanne Baret (1740–1816): Première femme autour du monde* (Moulins: Imprimerie Pottier, 1987).

11. Commerson to Beau, 17 November, 23 December 1766, in Cap, *Commerson*, 90, 94–95.

12. Christinat, "Une femme globe-trotter," 88–89.

13. Commerson to Beau, 28 May, 7 September 1767, in Cap, *Commerson*, 99, 101; Commerson to Georges-Marie Commerson, 30 November 1768, ibid., 107.

14. Commerson to Georges-Marie Commerson, 30 November 1768, ibid., 106–107. For the dates of the Tahiti stay, see John Dunmore, *Who's Who in Pacific Navigation* (Honolulu: University of Hawaii Press, 1991), 36. For Commerson's belief that they were the first European visitors, see his journal entry in Étienne Taillemite, ed., *Bougainville et ses compagnons autour du monde 1766–1769: Journaux de navigation*, 2 vols. (Paris: Imprimerie Nationale, 1977), 2:498. On Wallis, see Lynne

Withey, *Voyages of Discovery: Captain Cook and the Exploration of the Pacific* (Berkeley: University of California Press, 1989), 60–74.

15. Taillemite, ed., *Bougainville et ses compagnons*, 496, 497–498.

16. For a biographical overview, see the editor's introduction to Pierre Poivre, *Reisen eines Philosophen, 1768*, trans. and ed. Jürgen Osterhammel (Sigmaringen: Jan Thorbecke Verlag, 1997), 7–40.

17. Yves Laissus, "Catalogue des manuscrits de Philibert Commerson," *Revue d'histoire des sciences* 31 (1978): 133–134, 139, quotation at 134; Anon., "Commerson," in Hoefer, 346–347; and Dupetit-Thouars, "Commerson," 689.

18. Philippe Commerson, "Academia politica, sive universalis, aliter Respublica academica seu litteraria," ms. 1904, dossier 3, Bibliothèque Centrale du Muséum d'Histoire Naturelle, Paris.

19. Cf. Richard H. Grove, *Green Imperialism: Colonial Expansion, Tropical Island Edens, and the Origins of Environmentalism, 1600–1860* (Cambridge: Cambridge University Press, 1995), 216–247, especially for Commerson's Mauritius context.

20. "*Testament Singulier* de M. Commerson, docteur en médicine, médecin-botaniste et naturaliste du roi, fait le 14 et le 15 Décembre 1766," in Cap, *Commerson*, 44.

21. "Post-scriptum sur l'île de Taïti ou Nouvelle-Cythère," in F.-B. de Montessus, *Martyrologe et biographie de Commerson* [Extrait des Bulletins de la Société des Sciences Naturelles de Saône et Loire, vol. 3 (1885)] (Châlon-sur-Saône, 1889), 135. Nicholas Thomas discusses the similar scene observed by the voyagers on Cook's first visit to Tahiti on May 14, 1769. He points out that later visitors never observed a public display of this kind and hypothesizes that the Tahitians organized it to parody the behavior of their European visitors. Thomas, *Cook: The Extraordinary Voyages of Captain James Cook* (New York: Walker, 2003), 155–159.

22. Commerson, "Post-scriptum sur l'île de Taïti," 135, 136.

23. Ibid., 137, 139.

24. Philibert Commerson to Curé Beau, 16 February 1772, in Montessus, *Martyrologe*, 233.

25. "Although I am not a pupil of Linnaeus, however I know his method and reckon myself to be a kind of Linnaean *being*." J. R. Forster to Thomas Pennant, 17 September 1768, MH-100, Peabody-Essex Museum, Salem, Mass.

26. On the search for the southern continent, see editor's introduction in Cook, *Journals*, 1: *1768–1771*, ed. J. C. Beaglehole, lxxviii–lxxix. For the history of geographic speculation about the Terra Australis and the Dutch and other pre-Enlightenment explorers of Oceania, see William Eisler, *The Furthest Shore: Images of Terra Australis from the Middle Ages to Captain Cook* (Cambridge: Cambridge University Press, 1995). Eisler points out that much of the geographic knowledge gathered by the Dutch was not available to Cook and his companions in English translation. Banks in particular lamented his limited access to an account of Abel Tasman's discoveries. Ibid., 148, 154. On the instructions for the second voyage, see "The Instructions," in Cook, *Journals*, 2: *The Voyage of the Resolution and Adventure*, clxvii–clxix.

27. Forster, *Voyage round the World*, 1:x–xi (quote), 12. According to Michael Hoare, Forster relied on his father's journal while writing his account. Nonetheless George Forster shaped the voyage materials into a work with its own intellectual and artistic integrity and with its place in his own intellectual biography. Cf. editor's introduction, J. R. Forster, *The Resolution Journal of Johann Reinhold Forster, 1772–1775*, ed. Michael E. Hoare (London: Hakluyt Society, 1982), 1:68. On Hawkesworth, see Withey, *Voyages of Discovery*, 175–176, 185–187. Cf. John Hawkesworth, comp., *An Account of the Voyages undertaken by the Order of His present Majesty for making discoveries in the Southern Hemisphere . . .* , 3 vols. (London: Strahan and Cadell, 1773).

28. The remark about Rousseau comes in the context of the Cook voyagers' first visit to Vanuatu. See Forster, *Voyage round the World*, 1:xi (on Enlightenment thinkers), 1:xii (on the traveler's intellectual penetration), 2:207.

29. Ibid., 1:xii, 3–4. On providentialism, see Jonathan Lamb, *Preserving the Self in the South Seas, 1680–1840* (Chicago: University of Chicago Press, 2001), 103–104.

30. Forster, *Voyage round the World*, 1:335, 2:325.

31. Ibid., 1:510, 2:324. See also the description of tyrannical male behavior toward women on New Caledonia, 2:414–415.

32. Ibid., 1:488, 535, 536, 2:420.

33. Ibid., 1:176–177, 177–178, 178–179, 179, 523.

34. Ibid., 238–239, 239–240 (quote).

35. Ibid., 2:347, 347–348, 349–350, 351, 352–353. On the elegy, see Theodore

Ziolkowski, *The Classical German Elegy, 1795–1950* (Princeton, N.J.: Princeton University Press, 1980).

36. Forster, *Voyage round the World,* 1:253, 254, 255.

37. Ibid., 1:256, 258–260.

38. Ibid., 1:270, 271, 276–279.

39. Ibid., 1:295–296, 312, 321.

40. Ibid., 1:337, 363.

41. Ibid., 1:366, 367.

42. Rousseau, *Discourse on Inequality,* 131–135. On the history of the republican tradition, see J. G. A. Pocock, *The Machiavellian Moment: Florentine Political Thought and the Atlantic Republican Tradition* (Princeton, N.J.: Princeton University Press, 1975).

43. Forster, *Voyager round the World,* 1:367–368; Patrick V. Kirch and Marshall Sahlins, *Anahulu: The Anthropology of History in the Kingdom of Hawaii,* vol. 1: *Historical Ethnography,* by Marshall Sahlins with the assistance of Dorothy B. Barrière (Chicago: University of Chicago Press, 1992).

44. Forster, *Voyage round the World,* 1:431–432.

45. Ibid., 1:363.

46. Ibid., 1:xvi; Forster, "Reply to Mr. Wales's Remarks," *Werke,* 4: *Streitschriften und Fragmente zur Weltreise . . . ,* 23–24.

47. See Forster's discussion of sites for colonization in New Zealand and Vanuatu, Forster, *Voyage round the World,* 1:523, 2:243, 550–551 (quote).

48. Ibid., 2:606.

49. See the editors' introduction to Forster, *Werke,* 5: *Kleine Schriften zur Völker- und Länderkunde,* ed. Horst Fiedler, Klaus-Georg Popp, Annerose Schneider, and Christian Suckow, 727–734, 737.

50. Forster, "Cook der Entdecker," in Forster, *Werke,* 5:193, 280–281.

51. Ibid., 281, 291–292.

52. Timothy Tackett, *Becoming a Revolutionary: The Deputies of the French National Assembly and the Emergence of a Revolutionary Culture (1789–1790)* (Princeton, N.J.: Princeton University Press, 1996).

53. The preceding information is taken from the chronology in Adelbert von Chamisso, *Sämtliche Werke,* ed. Volker Hoffmann, 2 vols. (Munich: Winkler Verlag, 1975), 2:655.

54. Ibid.; see also Georges Clause, "En guise d'introduction: Adelbert de Chamisso, le déraciné," in Centre d'Études Argonnais, *Chamisso:*

Actes des journées franco-allemandes des 30. et 31. mai 1981 (Sainte-Menehould: n.p., 1982), 11.

55. Clause, "En guise d'introduction," 11. On the early German Romantics, see Rudolf Haym, *Die Romantische Schule: Ein Beitrag zur Geschichte des deutschen Geistes*, 5th ed., ed. Oskar Walzel (Berlin: Weidmann, 1928).

56. Chamisso, *Voyage around the World*, 11.

57. Hitzig introduced Chamisso and Hoffmann in 1807; see editor's note, Chamisso, *Werke*, 2:696.

58. Ewert von Krusenstjern, *Weltumsegler und Wissenschaftler: Adam Johann von Krusenstern, 1770–1846. Ein Lebensbericht* (Gernsbach: Casimir Katz Verlag, 1991), 188.

59. Adelbert von Chamisso to Hippolyte de Chamisso, 17 March 1821, cited in editor's note, Chamisso, *Werke*, 2:695.

60. Chamisso, "Peter Schlemihls wundersame Geschichte," in Chamisso, *Werke*, 2:74–75.

61. Ibid., 2:117.

62. Ibid., 2:116.

63. Paul Hiepko, "Der Naturwissenschaftler Adelbert von Chamisso und das Herbarium am Botanische Museum in Schöneberg," in Klaus Bździach, ed., *Mit den Augen des Fremden: Adelbert von Chamiso— Dichter, Naturwissenschaftler, Weltreisender* (Berlin: Gesellschaft für interregionalen Kulturaustausch/Kreuzberg Museum, 1984), 110–113.

64. Adelbert von Chamisso, "Bemerkungen und Ansichten," in Otto von Kotzebue, *Entdeckungsreise in die Sued-See und nach der Berings-Strasse zur Erforschung einer nordoestlichen Durchfahrt: Unternommen in den Jahren 1815, 1816, 1817 und 1818, auf Kosten Sr. Erlaucht des Herrn Reichs-Kanzlers Grafen Rumanzoff auf dem Schiffe Rurick unter dem Befehle des Lieutenants der Russisch-Kaiserlichen Marine Otto von Kotzebue*, 3 vols. (Weimar: Gebrüder Hoffmann, 1821), 3:15, 16.

65. Chamisso, *Voyage around the World*, 242–243 (quote), 243–245; Chamisso, *Werke*, 2:467, 470, 638.

66. On the shift from equality to freedom as a preoccupation of travelers, see Harry Liebersohn, "Discovering Indigenous Nobility: Tocqueville, Chamisso, and Romantic Travel Writing," *American Historical Review* 99 (June 1994): 746–766; and Liebersohn, "Scientific Ethnography and Travel, 1750–1850," in *The Cambridge History of Science*, vol. 7: The

Modern Social Sciences, ed. Theodore M. Porter and Dorothy Ross (Cambridge: Cambridge University Press, 2003), 100–112.

67. Chamisso, *Werke,* 2:594–595; Chamisso, *Voyage around the World,* 308. On the decline of the Sandwich Kingdom and its native elite, see Sahlins, *Anahulu.*

68. Chamisso, *Voyage around the World,* 8.

69. Ibid., 116, 126, 189. On European perceptions of native nobility, see Liebersohn, "Discovering Indigenous Nobility."

70. Chamisso, *Voyage around the World,* 121.

71. See Valèrio Valeri, *Kingship and Sacrifice: Ritual and Society in Ancient Hawaii,* trans. Paula Wissing (Chicago: University of Chicago, 1985), chap. 7, esp. 217–220.

72. Chamisso, *Voyage around the World,* 122, 123.

73. Ibid., 125.

2. Patrons

1. Bernard Cohen analyzes British rulers' incomprehension of their Mughal predecessors' gift-giving practices and the damaging consequences for their own legitimacy in "Representing Authority in Victorian India," in *The Invention of Tradition,* ed. Eric Hobsbawm and Terence Ranger (Cambridge: Cambridge University Press, 1983), 168–173.

2. For discussions of patronage and the tensions between autonomy and dependence in the late eighteenth and early nineteenth centuries, see Maynard Solomon, *Beethoven* (New York: Schirmer Books, 1977), 62–63; Tia DeNora, *Beethoven and the Construction of Genius: Musical Politics in Vienna, 1792–1803* (Berkeley: University of California, 1995); Christopher M. S. Johns, *Antonio Canova and the Politics of Patronage in Revolutionary and Napoleonic Europe* (Berkeley: University of California Press, 1998); Brian W. Dippie, *Catlin and His Contemporaries: The Politics of Patronage* (Lincoln: University of Nebraska, 1990); and Martin S. Staum, *Minerva's Message: Stabilizing the French Revolution* (Montreal: McGill-Queen's University Press, 1996), 9.

3. See Donald Cutter, "Introduction," lxxv–lxxvi, and the other introductory essays in Alejandro Malaspina, *The Malaspina Expedition 1789–1794: Journal of the Voyage by Alejandro Malaspina,* vol. 1: *Cádiz to Pan-*

ama, ed. Andrew David et al., introd. Donald C. Cutter (London: The Hakluyt Society, in association with the Museo Naval, Madrid, 2001).

4. One notable exception is Richard Drayton, *Nature's Government: Science, Imperial Britain, and the 'Improvement' of the World* (New Haven, Conn.: Yale University Press, 2000), 109–110, which points out how often the French were ahead of the British in the organization of scientific travel expeditions.

5. On the early history of French scientific expeditions, see Jordan Kellman, "Discovery and Enlightenment at Sea: Maritime Exploration and Observation in the Eighteenth-Century French Scientific Community (Ph.D. diss., Department of History, Princeton University, January 1998). For an introduction to French exploration in the Enlightenment and its political context, see Yves Laissus, "Les Naturalistes français en Amérique du Sud au 18. siècle: Les conditions et les résultats," 65–78, and E. Taillemite, "Conclusions," in M. Mollat and E. Taillemite, eds., *L'Importance de l'exploration maritime au siècle des lumières (A propos du voyage de Bougainville)* (Paris: Éditions du Centre National de la Recherche Scientifique, 1982), 177–180. For the early nineteenth century, see Jean-Paul Faivre, *L'Expansion française dans le pacifique de 1800 à 1842* (Paris: Nouvelles Éditions Latines, 1953).

6. Charles C. Gillispie, *Science and Polity in France at the End of the Old Regime* (Princeton, N.J.: Princeton University Press, 1980), 81–83.

7. Jacques Roger, *Buffon: A Life in Natural History*, trans. Sarah Lucille Bonnefoi, ed. L. Pearce Williams (1989; Ithaca, N.Y.: Cornell University Press, 1997), xvi, 21–22, 44.

8. On Commerson, see "Commerson, Philibert," in Hoefer, *Nouvelle Biographie Générale* (Paris: Didot, 1855), 11: cols. 345–347, and Abel Dupetit-Thouars, "Commerson, Philibert," in Michaud, 8:688–689. On Poivre, see the editor's introduction in Pierre Poivre, *Reisen eines Philosophen, 1768*, ed. and trans. Jürgen Osterhammel (Sigmaringen: Jan Thorbecke Verlag, 1997), esp. 12–23.

9. Michèle Duchet, "Bougainville, Louis-Antoine de," *Dictionnaire de Diderot*, ed. Roland Mortier and Raymond Trousson (Paris: Champion, 1999), 87–89; René de Kerallain, *La Jeunesse de Bougainville* (Paris: n.p., 1896), 34, 36; Mary Kimbrough, *Louis-Antoine de Bougainville 1729–1811: A Study in French Naval History and Politics* (Lewiston: Edwin Mellen, 1990), 3–6; Jean Lefranc, *Bougainville et ses campagnons*

(Paris: Albin Michel, 1929). On Bougainville in North America, see Louis Antoine de Bougainville, *Adventure in the Wilderness: The American Journals of Louis Antoine de Bougainville, 1756–1760*, trans. and ed. Edward P. Hamilton (Norman: University of Oklahoma Press, 1964).

10. See "Memoir since November 15, 1756," in Bougainville, *Adventure in the Wilderness*, 328–329.

11. Jean-Étienne Martin-Allanic, *Bougainville, navigateur, et les découvertes de son temps*, 2 vols. (Paris: Presses Universitaires de France, 1964), 1:70–72. On Bougainville and Choiseul, see Étienne Taillemite, ed., *Bougainville et ses compagnons autour du monde 1766–1769: Journaux de navigation*, 2 vols. (Paris: Imprimerie Nationale, 1977), 1:11, 13–14.

12. Martin-Allanic, *Bougainville*, 243, 273, 298, 311–313; Kimbrough, *Bougainville*, 25–48, 211.

13. Editor's introduction, Jean-François de La Pérouse, *The Journal of Jean-François de Galaup de la Pérouse, 1785–1788*, trans. and ed. John Dunmore, 2 vols. (London: Hakluyt Society, 1994), 1:xx–xxiv, xxvii–xxix, xxx, lxxxiv–xciv, xcvii–xcviii, cv; and Kellman, "Discovery and Enlightenment," 392–393. The National Assembly also funded a voyage that departed in 1791 to search for the missing voyagers. Kellman, "Discovery and Enlightenment," 412.

14. On the connection between science and the state, see Nicole and Jean Dhombres, *Naissance d'un pouvoir: Sciences et savants en France (1793–1824)* (Paris: Payot, 1989). They portray this as a movement from a world of disengaged *érudits* to one of applied scientists acting in state service. I find here less a revolution than a Tocquevillian intensification of older traditions of state direction of society. On merging elites and network building, see Louis Bergeron, *France under Napoleon*, trans. R. R. Palmer (Princeton, N.J.: Princeton University Press, 1981).

15. Faivre, *L'Expansion française*, 258. The Academy of Sciences was dissolved in 1793 but reconvened in 1795, with many of the same professors, as the First Section of the newly created Institut National. It regained the name Academy of Sciences in 1816. See Christiane Demeulenaere-Douyère, "De l'Institut national à la réforme de 1976: l'Academie des sciences aux XIXe et XXe siècles," in Éric Brian and Christiane Demeulenaere-Douyère, eds., *Histoire et mémoire de l'Academie des sciences* (Paris: Technique & Documentation, 1996), 33–35.

16. On Dumont d'Urville's commission, see Faivre, *L'Expansion française*,

258–261. Dumont d'Urville wrote to Louis-Philippe on 7 May 1831 asking for better compensation for himself and his men: Dumont d'Urville, Collection of holograph letters, etc., regarding the *Astrolabe*, 1826–1846, Letters to King, C175, State Library of New South Wales, Sydney; and the dismissive critique of d'Urville's achievements from 1838 by Beautemps-Beaupré, the French naval minister, in the Nan Kivell collection, ms. 4222, National Library of Australia, Canberra. Cf. the editor's introduction to Jules Dumont d'Urville, *An Account in Two Volumes of Two Voyages to the South Seas . . .* , 2 vols., trans. and ed. Helen Rosenman (Hawaii: University of Hawaii Press, 1988), 1: *Astrolabe, 1826–1829*, xlix.

17. Richard W. Burkhardt, Jr., "Naturalists' Practices and Nature's Empire: Paris and the Platypus, 1815–1833," *Pacific Science* 55 (2001): 328.

18. On Thouin and on French natural history in the Royal Garden, see E. C. Spary, *Utopia's Garden: French Natural History from Old Regime to Revolution* (Chicago: University of Chicago, 2000), 13, 20, 39, 49–98.

19. Burkhardt, "Naturalists' Practices," 331, 333, 335.

20. On the founders' belief in the society's importance, see *Bulletin* de la Société de Géographie 1 (1822): 1–2. On the society's foundation and organization, see Jules Girard, "La Société de Géographie: Sa vie et ses Oeuvres pendant un siècle, 1821–1921," "Ressources financières," and "Organisation" in carton 494, Gu-Gr, Société de Géographie, Cartes et plans, Bibliothèque Nationale, Paris. See also *Bulletin* de la Société de Géographie 1:10, 12–24. On leadership of prominent scientists, see Report on meeting of the Society's Central Commission of 18 January 1822, in *Bulletin* de la Société de Géographie, 1:27. On the Société de Géographie generally, see Dominique Lejeune, *Les Sociétés de géographie en France et l'expansion coloniale au XIX. siècle* (Paris: Albin Michel, 1993); and Anne Marie Claire Godlewska, *Geography Unbound: French Geographic Science from Cassini to Humboldt* (Chicago: University of Chicago Press, 1999). Malte-Brun had founded a predecessor, *Annales des Voyages,* which ceased publication in 1814. It continued in 1819 under the name *Nouvelles Annales des Voyages,* coedited by Malte-Brun and Eyriès. See "Eyries, Jean-Baptiste-Benoît," in Michaud, 13:240–245; and "Malte-Brun, Conrad," ibid., 6:6–10. On Malte-Brun, see also Godlewska, *Geography Unbound,* 90–110. On the state traditions that preceded the formation of a voluntary association, see Numa

Broc, *La Géographie des philosophes: Géographes et voyageurs français au xviiie siècle* (Paris: Ophrys, 1975), 481–482.

21. On hopes for bold missions, see the report on the meeting of the Society's Central Commission of 18 January 1822, in *Bulletin* de la Société de Géographie, 1:152, 154. On the trip to Vietnam, see Girard, "La Société de Géographie," "Explorations." On the strengths and weaknesses of French geography in this period, see Godlewska, *Geography Unbound*.

22. Liebersohn, "Zur Kunst der Ethnographie: Zwei Briefe von Louis Choris an Adelbert von Chamisso," *Historische Anthropologie* 6 (1998): 486; Choris to Chamisso, 3 April 1820, ibid., 486–487; Louis Choris, *Voyage pittoresque autour du monde avec des portraits de sauvages d'Amérique, d'Asie, d'Afrique, et des îles du grand océan; des paysages, des vues maritimes, et plusieurs objets d'histoire naturelle: Accompagné de descriptions par M. le Baron Cuvier, et A. de Chamisso, et d'Observations sur les crânes humains par M. le Docteur Gall* (Paris: Didot, 1822); Conrad Malte-Brun, "Voyage pittoresque autour du monde," *Journal des Débats*, 6 November 1821, offprint in Chamisso Nachlass, K.26 N.52, Deutsche Staatsbibliothek, Berlin.

23. Choris to Chamisso, 10 October 1822, in Liebersohn, "Zur Kunst der Ethnographie," 489–490; Séance de la commission centrale, 6 September 1822, Société de Géographie, colis nr. 18 (2921), Bibliothèque Nationale; *Bulletin* de la Société de Géographie, 1:139.

24. Jomard, "Questions de Mr Jomard sur l'Amérique pour Mr. Choris," Société de Géographie, colis nr. 3 bis (1628), Bibliothèque Nationale.

25. Minister of the Marine and the Colonies, to Jomard, President of the Central Commission of the Geographic Society, 27 August 1827, Société de Géographie, colis nr. 19 bis (3186), Bibliothèque Nationale; John P. Gosy, Secretary for Foreign Affairs, Medico-Botanical Society of London, to Jomard, 14 November 1827, Société de Géographie, colis nr. 19 bis (3211), Bibliothèque Nationale; meeting of the professors of the Museum of Natural History, 25 September 1827, AJ15/127, Archives Nationales; Louis Choris to Georges Cuvier, 28 December 1827, nr. 1986, tome 3, 355, Bibliothèque Centrale du Muséum d'Histoire Naturelle, Paris.

26. Louis Choris to Georges Cuvier, 28 December 1827, nr. 1986, tome 3, 355, Bibliothèque Centrale du Muséum d'Histoire Naturelle, Paris;

meeting of 30 April 1828, AJ15/127, Archives Nationales; meeting of 18 June 1828, ibid.; meeting of 27 August 1828, ibid. Cf. the official attestation relating the circumstances of Choris's death reprinted in Louis Choris, *Journal des Malers Ludwig York Choris*, ed. Niklaus R. Schweizer (Bern: Peter Lang, 1999), 23–25, and also the editor's introduction, ibid., 12–13. Deciphering Choris's difficult-to-read script, this edition of Choris's diary makes available to readers one of the era's most interesting travel documents.

27. On the distinction between voluntary and state-sponsored societies, see James E. McClellan III, *Science Reorganized: Scientific Societies in the Eighteenth Century* (New York: Columbia, 1985), 13–15.

28. On Banks and the relationship between scientific exploration and state patronage, see John Gascoigne, *Science in the Service of Empire: Joseph Banks, the British State, and the Uses of Science in the Age of Revolution* (Cambridge: Cambridge University Press, 1998). Application cited (from the Royal Society Council Minutes of 9 June 1768) in J. C. Beaglehole, *The Life of Captain James Cook* (Stanford: Stanford University Press, 1974), 144.

29. Beaglehole, *Life*, 273–274.

30. Michael E. Hoare, *The Tactless Philosopher: Johann Reinhold Forster (1729–98)* (Melbourne: Hawthorn Press, 1976), 72–75.

31. The preceding description is drawn in part from the editor's introduction to J. R. Forster, *The Resolution Journal of Johann Reinhold Forster, 1772–1775*, vol. 1, ed. Michael E. Hoare (London: Hakluyt Society, 1982), 1–30 (phrase quoted from ibid., 28), and from Hoare, *Tactless Philosopher*, 67–75, 160–162.

32. Hoare, *Tactless Philosopher*, 69, 72–76, 162–163, 179–180, 190–197, 330.

33. On the worldwide destinations of Linnaeus's students, see Lisbet Koerner, *Linnaeus: Nature and Nation* (Cambridge, Mass.: Harvard University Press, 1999), 113; and Lisbet Koerner, "Purposes of Linnaean Travel: A Preliminary Research Report," in David P. Miller and Peter H. Reill, eds., *Visions of Empire: Voyages, Botany, and Representations of Nature* (Cambridge: Cambridge University Press, 1996), 117–152, esp. 119, 125, and 136.

34. Gascoigne, *Science in the Service of Empire*, 27, 124; David Mackay, *In the Wake of Cook: Exploration, Science, and Empire, 1780–1801* (London: Croom Helm, 1985), 99, 60–69.

35. Gascoigne emphasizes Banks's dependence on government patrons in *Science in the Service of Empire,* 37, 44, 124–125; see also Mackay, *In the Wake of Cook,* 106.

36. Gascoigne, *Science in the Service of Empire,* 130; Mackay, *In the Wake of Cook,* 146–151.

37. David Mabberley, "Foreword," and Neil Chambers, "Editorial Principles," in Joseph Banks, *The Letters of Sir Joseph Banks: A Selection, 1768–1820,* ed. Neil Chambers, introd. Harold Carter (London: Imperial College Press, 2000), xi, xvii. Mabberley calls the correspondence a "network permeating the society of its day," ibid., xi. The best existing overview of Banks's correspondence is Warren R. Dawson, ed., *The Banks Letters: A Calendar of the Manuscript Correspondence of Sir Joseph Banks, Preserved in the British Museum, The British Museum (Natural History) and Other Collections in Great Britain* (London: Trustees of the British Museum, 1958). The Dawson edition's summaries treat the reader to a panorama of personalities linked to Banks and his many projects. Since Dawson compiled his calendar, Banks researchers have assembled many more of the letters, which after his death were auctioned and widely dispersed; see the commentaries in Banks, *Letters,* ed. Chambers, for details of subsequent scholarship.

38. Banks's involvement with wool-breeding began in 1781; the riots took place in 1799. See Harold B. Carter, *Sir Joseph Banks, 1743–1820* (London: British Museum [Natural History], 1988), 227–231, 311–312. George Augustus Pollen to Banks, 23 February 1804, Banks Letters, 2:287–288, Royal Botanic Gardens, Kew, England; Banks to Pollen, 29 March 1804, ibid., 2:290. The letters are summarized in *Calendar,* ed. Dawson, 678–679; I have relied on Dawson's transcription of Banks's hard-to-read scrawl. Sigismund Bacstrom to Banks, 28 June 1786, Banks Letters, 1:222, Royal Botanic Gardens, Kew, England; for Bacstrom's later adventures see *Calendar,* ed. Dawson, 26–27. John Knox Laughton, "Flinders, Matthew," DNB 7:325–329; *Calendar,* ed. Dawson, 328–332.

39. Joseph Banks to William Townsend Aiton, 7 June 1814, in Banks, *Letters,* ed. Chambers, 313.

40. Ibid., editor's note, 314; copy of a letter from James Bowie and Allan Cunningham to William Aiton, 29 March 1815, Botanical Gardens 1:16, Sutro Library, California State Library, San Francisco; Joseph Banks to Allan Cunningham, 13 February 1817, Botanical Gardens, 1:39, Sutro Li-

brary; Alan Macquarie to Joseph Banks, 18 December 1817, Botanical Gardens 1:45, Sutro Library; Banks to [Macquarie], July 1818, Sutro Library, 1:48; Banks to James Bowie, undated, Sutro Library, 1:64. Cf. the description of Cunningham's and Bowies's travels in Carter, *Sir Joseph Banks*, 475–482.

41. Joseph Banks to Jacques Houttou de La Billardière, 9 June 1796, in Banks, *Letters*, ed. Chambers, 171, cf. 172; Joseph Banks to Jean Charretié, 18 March 1797, ibid., 188, cf. 364; Pierre Broussonet to Joseph Banks, 25 July 1794, in Dawson, ed., *Calendar*, 169. Sergius Plescheyeff to Joseph Banks, 30 July 1795, Joseph Banks Papers, Ru 1:17, Sutro Library.

42. Editor's introduction, George Vancouver, *A Voyage of Discovery to the North Pacific Ocean and round the World, 1791–1795*, 4 vols., ed. and introd. W. Kaye Lamb (London: Hakluyt Society, 1984), 23–24; Greg Dening, *Mr. Bligh's Bad Language: Passion, Power, and Theatre on the Bounty* (Cambridge: Cambridge University Press, 1992), 114.

43. Editor's introduction, Vancouver, *Voyage of Discovery*, 1:30–31; Archibald Menzies, *Hawaii Nei 128 Years Ago*, ed. W. F. Wilson (Honolulu: n.p., 1920); Menzies to Banks, 14 September 1795, in *Calendar*, ed. Dawson, 607.

44. Vancouver, *Voyage of Discovery*, 1:272, 416, 418–419; Menzies, *Hawaii Nei*, 32–33.

45. J. D. Hooker, "A Sketch of the Life and Labours of Sir William Jackson Hooker," *Annals of Botany* 16 (1902): ix–xxii, xxviii, lv; Appendix C, "List of Some of Sir W. J. Hooker's Chief Correspondents (1808–65)," ibid., clxxxviii; cf. Drayton, *Nature's Government*, 145, 170, and more generally chaps. 5–6. On Banks's early influence on the elder Hooker, see Mea Allan, *The Hookers of Kew, 1785–1911* (London: Michael Joseph, 1967), chap. 4. See also F. O. Bower, "Sir William Hooker, 1785–1865," in F. W. Oliver, *Makers of British Botany: A Collection of Biographies by Living Botanists* (Cambridge: Cambridge University Press, 1913), 136–137, 141.

46. Fleming Fergus, *Barrow's Boys* (New York: Atlantic Monthly Press, 1998), 2–8, 11, 276–277.

47. Edward Smith, *The Life of Sir Joseph Banks, President of the Royal Society, with some Notices of his Friends and Contemporaries* (London: John Lane, 1911), 46–47; Hans Plischke, *Johann Friedrich Blumenbachs*

Einfluss auf die Entdeckungsreisenden seiner Zeit (Göttingen: Vandenhoeck & Ruprecht, 1937). On the origins of the Royal Geographical Society, cf. Ian Cameron, *To the Farthest Ends of the Earth: 150 Years of World Exploration by the Royal Geographical Society* (New York: Dutton, 1980), 16.

48. Cameron, *To the Farthest Ends*, 17, app. 3; *Journal* of the Royal Geographical Society 1 (1832): vii–viii, xiii–xix. Cf. the more detailed description of the leadership and membership of the Royal Geographical Society in Harry Liebersohn, "European Geographic Societies and Ethnography (1821–1840)," in Philippe Despoix and Justus Fetscher, eds., with Michael Lackner and Nikola von Merveldt, *Cross-Cultural Encounters and Constructions of Knowledge in the 18th and 19th Century: Non-European and European Travel of Exploration in Comparative Perspective*, Georg-Forster-Studien, Beiheft 2 (Kassel: Kassel University Press, 2004), 145–160.

49. *Journal* of the Royal Geographical Society 1 (1832): x–xi. According to James Buzard, John Murray III published the first "handbook"—a new term at the time—in 1836. See Buzard, *The Beaten Track: European Tourism, Literature, and the Ways to 'Culture', 1800–1918* (Oxford: Clarendon, 1993), 66.

50. Barry M. Gough, *The Royal Navy and the Northwest Coast of North America, 1810–1914: A Study of British Maritime Ascendancy* (Vancouver: University of British Columbia Press, 1971), 8–9.

51. Adam von Krusenstern, *Reise um die Welt in den Jahren 1803, 1804, 1805 und 1806 auf Befehl seiner Kaiserlichen Majestät Alexander des Ersten auf den Schiffen Nadeshda und Newa* (St. Petersburg: Schnoorsche, 1810), 1:xi–xii. On Russian scientific voyages, see Glynn Barratt, *Russia in Pacific Waters, 1715–1825: A Survey of the Origins of Russia's Naval Presence in the North and South Pacific* (Vancouver: University of British Columbia Press, 1981).

52. Krusenstern, *Reise um die Welt*, xiii–xvii.

53. Daniel L. Schlafly, Jr., "Rumiantsev, Nikolai Petrovich," in *The Modern Encyclopedia of Russian and Soviet History*, ed. Joseph L. Wieczynski (Gulf Breeze, Fla.: Academic International Press, 1983), vol. 32, cols. 11–12.

54. Barratt, *Russia in Pacific Waters*, 114–117; John Dunmore, *Who's Who in Pacific Navigation* (Honolulu: University of Hawaii, 1991), 146–147.

55. Barratt, *Russia in Pacific Waters,* 141; Krusenstern, *Reise um die Welt,* xviii; Ewert von Krusenstjern, *Weltumsegler und Wissenschaftler: Adam Johann von Krusenstern, 1770–1846—Ein Lebensbericht* (Gernsbach: Casimir Katz Verlag, 1991), 158–159, 163–168, 175, 203–204, 206–215; Adam von Krusenstern, *Atlas de l'Océan Pacifique* (St. Petersburg: n.p., 1827).

56. F. G. Bellingshausen, *The Voyage of Captain Bellingshausen to the Antarctic Seas 1819–1821,* trans. and ed. Frank Debenham, 2 vols. (London: Hakluyt Society, 1945); V.-M. Golovnin, *Around the World on the Kamchatka, 1817–1819,* trans. and ed. Ella L. Wiswell, fwd. John J. Stephan (Honolulu: University of Hawaii Press, 1979); see also the biographical entries in Dunmore, *Who's Who in Pacific Navigation.* On the creation of a new generation of naval officers, see Barratt, *Russia in Pacific Waters.*

57. Krusenstjern, *Weltumsegler und Wissenschaftler,* 164–166, 180–182, 186–187, 204; Barratt, *Russia in Pacific Waters,* 177–179; Charlotte Bernhardi, *Memoir of the Celebrated Admiral John de Krusenstern, the First Russian Circumnavigator,* ed. Rear-Admiral Sir John Ross (London: Longman, Green, Brown and Longmans, 1856), 29. Bernhardi was Krusenstern's daughter.

58. Krusenstern to Chamisso, 2–14 June 1815, Chamisso Nachlass K.28 N.67, Deutsche Staatsbibliothek, Berlin.

59. On the relation between Chamisso and Kotzebue, see Chamisso's letter to his brother: Adelbert von Chamisso to Hippolyte de Chamisso, 21 May 1816, Chamisso Nachlass, K.17 N.15; cf. Chamisso, *Voyage around the World,* 35. Chamisso, *Voyage around the World,* 113, 125, 173–174. Cf. Liebersohn, "Discovering Indigenous Nobility: Tocqueville, Chamisso, and Romantic Travel Writing," *American Historical Review* 99 (June 1994): 764.

60. Chamisso to Rumiantsev, 3 September 1819, Chamisso Nachlass, K.30 N.22. Copy of a letter from Rumiantsev to Chamisso, 12 November 1819, Stock 1414, "Familie von Krusenstern," series 3, item 23, letters from Rumiantsev to Adam von Krusenstern, 1815–1825, National Archives, Tartu, Estonia. Rumiantsev to Chamisso, 29 January 1820, Chamisso Nachlass, K.30 N.22. Krusenstern to Chamisso, 27 January 1820, Chamisso Nachlass, K.28 N.67.

61. *Neues Magazin für die neuere Geschichte, Erd- und Völkerkunde, als eine*

Fortsetzung des Büschingischen, ed. Friedrich Gottlieb Canzler, der Weltweisheit Doctor und Privatlehrer der historisch- und geographisch-statistischen Wissenschaften zu Göttingen (Leipzig: Jacobäer, 1790), Vorrede, n.p. See also *Literatur und Völkerkunde, Ein periodisches Werk,* ed. Johann Wilhelm von Archenholz, vol. 1 (Dessau, 1782); Georg August von Breitenbauch, *Vorstellung der vornehmsten Völkerschaften der Welt nach ihrer Abstammung, Ausbreitung und Sprachen* (Leipzig: Lange, 1786); *Die Reisenden für Länder- und Völkerkunde,* ed. Cunradi (Nürnberg: Felserksche Buchhandlung, 1788); *Ethnographisches Archiv,* vol. 1 (Jena: August Schmid, 1818); *Denkwürdigkeiten für die Länder- und Völkerkunde,* ed. Friedrich Karl Gottlob Hirsching, Doctor und Professor der Philosophie in Erlangen, und verschiedener gelehrten Gesellschaften Mitglied, Erster Teil (Leipzig, 1792); *Magazin der Erd- und Völkerkunde,* vol. 1 (Giessen, 1783).

62. "Kenntnis des Nahrungsstandes": *Allgemeines Archiv für die Länder und Völkerkunde,* ed. Friedrich Carl Gottlob Hirsching, vol. 1 (Leipzig: Hilscher, 1791), Vorerinnerungen, n.p. The anonymous editor of a magazine for geography and anthropology, introducing his new enterprise in April 1782, makes similar claims, announcing that he was attempting to provide a complete compendium or "system" of geographic knowledge, which, he added, had never been put forth before: *Magazin der Erd- und Völkerkunde* 1: Vorrede, n.p.

63. Joh. Jos. Polt, *Die Biene: Merkwürdigkeiten aus der Länder- und Völkerkunde. Ein sehr unterhaltendes und belehrendes Lesebuch für alle Klassen von Lesern, welches, wegen seines mannigfaltigen und pikanten Inhalts, den angenehmsten Zeitvertreib gewährt; Stoff in gesellschaftlichen Kreisen zu Gesprächen liefert, und insbesondere für Reisende, einsame Spaziergänger, leichte Kranke u.s.w., zur Aufheiterung gegeben ist* (Prague: C. W. Enders, 1824). Cf. Anon., *Ährenlese: Sammlung von Bruchstücken zur älteren und neueren Geschichte, Literatur und Völkerkunde* (Vienna: Anton Strauss, 1819). Two contemporaneous books filled with anthropological information for children, the first a factual compilation, the second in the form of fiction, are Joh. Matth. Trefzer, *Kurze Charakteristik der vorzüglichsten fremden Völker und Nationen nach den neusten Entdeckungen und Beobachtungen entworfen; und für Freunde der Geographie und Völkerkunde* (Pforzheim: Katz, 1818); and Anon., *Julius merkwürdige Abentheuer auf*

seinen Reisen in fremde Welttheile: Ein Buch zur Beförderung der Länder- und Völkerkunde unter der Jugend, vom Verfasser der Erzählungen für das erste Kindesalter (Nuremberg: Bieling, 1813).

64. German travelers had gone overseas and brought back reports of new worlds since the early days of European discovery. Cf. William Eisler, *The Furthest Shore: Images of Terra Australis from the Middle Ages to Captain Cook* (Cambridge: Cambridge University Press, 1995), 20, 39. See also the story of Maria Sibylla Merian by Lucas Wütherich in *Allgemeine Deutsche Biographie* (1875–1912; Berlin: Duncker & Humblot, 1969), 21:425–427; and in Natalie Z. Davis, *Women on the Margins: Three Seventeenth-Century Lives* (Cambridge, Mass.: Harvard University Press, 1995).

65. Carsten E. Carstens, "Niebuhr, Carsten N.," in *Allgemeine Deutsche Biographie*, 23:661–662; Jonathan Sheehan, *The Enlightenment Bible: Translation, Scholarship, Culture* (Princeton, N.J.: Princeton University Press, 2005), 186–199.

66. Christa Riedl-Dorn, *Das Haus der Wunder: Zur Geschichte des Naturhistorischen Museums in Wien* (Vienna: Verlag Holzhausen, 1998), 26–36 (quote from 29), 44–49.

67. Ibid., 54, 91, 101–102.

68. F. W. P. Dougherty, *Commercium Epistolicum J. F. Blumenbachii: Aus einem Briefwechsel des klassischen Zeitalters der Naturgeschichte. Katalog zur Ausstellung in Foyer der Niedersächsischen Staats- und Universitätsbibliothek Göttingen 1. Juni–21. Juni 1984* (Göttingen: n.p., 1984), 21–34.

69. Joseph Banks to J. F. Blumenbach, 18 July 1789; Banks to Blumenbach, 6 February 1794, both Blumenbach Nachlass, part 3 (correspondence), Niedersächsische Staats- und Universitätsbibliothek, Göttingen.

70. Dougherty, *Commercium Epistolicum*, 219. J. F. Blumenbach to E. Ash, 4 September 1792. Blumenbach Nachlass, part 3, Niedersächsische Staats- und Universitätsbibliothek. Plischke *Blumenbachs Einfluss*, 15. Cf. Gascoigne, *Science in the Service of Empire*, 179–182.

71. On the history of exploration and anthropology in late-nineteenth-century Germany, see H. Glenn Penny, *Objects of Culture: Ethnology and Ethnographic Museums in Imperial Germany* (Chapel Hill: University of North Carolina Press, 2002); and Matti Bunzl and H. Glenn Penny, *Worldly Provincialism: German Anthropology in the Age of Em-*

pire, ed. H. Glenn Penny and Matti Bunzl (Ann Arbor: University of Michigan Press, 2003).

72. On the Seehandlung, see Johann Friedrich Meuss, *Die Unternehmungen des Königlichen Seehandlungs-Instituts zur Emporbringung des preussischen Handels zur See: Ein Beitrag zur Geschichte der Seehandlung (Preussische Staatsbank) und des Seewesens in Preussen in der ersten Hälfte des 19. Jahrhunderts* (Berlin: Mittler, 1913). See also Heinz Burmeister, *Weltumsegelung unter Preussens Flagge: Die Königliche Preussische Seehandlung und ihre Schiffe* (Hamburg: Ernst Kabel, 1988); P. Bellardi, "Wann umsegelten deutsche Handelsschiffe zum ersten Male die Erde?" *Deutsche Allgemeine Zeitung,* 18 March 1922, copy in Geschichte des Seehandels, I./109.2508, Geheimes Staatsarchiv, Preussischer Kulturbesitz, Dahlem-Berlin; article by Dr. Rolf Keller, Wirtschaftsblatt der *Deutschen Allgemeinen Zeitung,* Morgen-Ausgabe, 24 April 1940, copy, ibid.; J. F. Meuss, "Friedrich der Grosse und die Gründung der Seehandlung," *Marine-Rundschau,* Feb. 1912, 220–231, copy, ibid.

73. List prepared by F. J. F. Meyen, Wissenschaftliche Reisen des Dr. Meyen 1832, I.HA Rep. 89 (2.2.1) Nr. 21361, Geheimes Staatsarchiv.

74. Altenstein to Friedrich Wilhelm III, 25 October 1832, Wissenschaftliche Reisen des Dr. Meyen 1832, I.HA Rep. 89 (2.2.1) Nr. 21361, Geheimes Staatsarchiv; F. J. F. Meyen, *Reise um die Erde: Ausgeführt auf dem königlich preussischen Seehandlungs-Schiffe Prinzess Louise, commandirt von Capitain W. Wendt, in den Jahren 1830, 1831 und 1832,* 2 vols. (Berlin: Sander'schen Buchhandlung, 1834).

75. Carl Ritter to anonymous government recipient, 8 December 1822, Die Gesellschaft f. Erdkunde, Rep. 76 Vc. Sekt.1. Tit.XI. 6. Abteilung XI, Teil I, Bd. I, 1822–1878, Geheimes Staatsarchiv.

76. Carl Ritter, *Erste jährliche Übersicht der Thätigkeit der Gesellschaft für Erdkunde in Berlin, nach dem ersten Lustrum des Vereines für das Jahr 1833 (4.Mai) bis 1834,* 4, 6–8.

77. H. Lichtenstein in *Vierte jährliche Übersicht der Thätigkeit der Gesellschaft für Erdkunde in Berlin, vom 7. Mai 1836 bis 6. Mai 1837 . . . vorgetragen am 6. Mai 1837,* 14.

78. See the list of participants printed in the Society's *Erste jährliche Übersicht.*

79. Liebersohn, *Aristocratic Encounters,* 129–130, 137–141.

80. This description is drawn from Robert Avé-Lallemant, "Sein Aufenthalt in Paris 1808–1826)," and Julius Löwenberg, "Auf der Höhe seiner Jahre (Berlin 1827–59)," in Karl Bruhns, ed., *Alexander von Humboldt: Eine wissenschaftliche Biographie*, 3 vols. (Leipzig: Brockhaus, 1872), 2:4–5, 23–24, 26–32, 48–51, 55–56, 66–67, 74–75, 99–102, 121–122, 127–128, 130–131.

81. Hoare, *Tactless Philosopher*, 196–197, 213. Forster wrote from Halle to an English friend, Thomas Pennant, on 3 July 1782 that he was "in favour with the King; with whom I spoke on my arrival in 1780 for abt 2 hours about the political system of England. I have since my arrival here had 3 letters from the Kings own hand, & have leave to write to him on any emergency; which I make use of very sparingly." J. R. Forster, Letters to Thomas Pennant, 1768–1786, MH-100, Peabody-Essex Museum, Salem.

82. Forster, *Werke*, 12: *Tagebücher*, ed. Brigitte Leuschner, 121–123.

83. Georg Forster to Joseph II, 1 February 1787, in Forster, *Werke*, 14: *Briefe 1784–Juni 1787*, ed. Brigitte Leuschner, 630; Joseph II to Georg Forster, 27 February 1787, in Forster, *Werke*, 18: *Briefe an Forster*, ed. Brigitte Leuschner, Siegfried Scheibe, Horst Fiedler, Klaus-Georg Popp, and Annerose Schneider, 145. The editorial commentary to the essay "Cook der Entdecker," in Forster, *Werke*, 5: *Kleine Schriften zur Völker- und Länderkunde*, ed. Horst Fiedler, Klaus-Georg Popp, Annerose Schneider, and Christian Suckow, 735, mentions the ring.

84. See Forster, "Promemoria für Katharina II (Entwurf)," 25 December 1787, *Werke*, 15: *Briefe, Juli 1787–1789*, ed. Horst Fiedler, 78–79, 414–415.

85. Heyne to J. Müller, 9 March 1788, ibid., 15:532–533; Heyne to Müller, 12 March 1788, ibid., 15:533; Georg Forster to Johann Georg von Zimmermann, 10 March 1788, ibid., 15:118–119.

86. Heyne to Müller, 9 March 1788, ibid., 15:533.

87. Georg Forster to Friedrich Karl Josef von Erthal, Elector and Bishop of Mainz, 12 August 1788, ibid., 15:178–179.

88. Mit edler Uneigennüzigkeit hat er jede Bezahlung für diese Gegenstände abgelehnt . . .": Uhden to Friedrich Wilhelm III, 30 December 1822, Rep. V f. Litt.C. N.2, Geheimes Staatsarchiv.

89. Alexander von Humboldt to Adelbert von Chamisso, n.d., in Chamisso, *Werke*, vol. 6, ed. Julius Eduard Hitzig (Leipzig: Weidmann, 1839), 94–95.

90. Friedrich Wilhelm IV to Adelbert von Chamisso, 16 May 1836, ibid., 6:93–94.

3. Collaborators

1. For recent discussions of colonial knowledge and power in the writing of Pacific ethnographies, see Vicente M. Diaz, "Native Pacific Cultural Studies on the Edge," *Contemporary Pacific* 13, no. 2 (Fall 2001): 315–341; Teresia K. Teiwa, "L(o)osing the Edge," ibid., 343–357; and Geoffrey M. White and Ty Kawika Tengan, "Disappearing Worlds: Anthropology and Cultural Studies in Hawai'i and the Pacific," ibid., 381–416. An eloquent meditation on crossing culture borders, and the kinds of scholarship that can comprehend it: Greg Dening, *Beach Crossings: Voyaging across Times, Cultures, and Self* (Philadelphia: University of Pennsylvania Press, 2004).

2. Ralph S. Kuykendall, *The Hawaiian Kingdom, 1778–1854: Foundation and Transformation* (Honolulu: University of Hawaii Press, 1947), 22–23, 25, 43.

3. Mason Wade, "French Indian Policies," in *Handbook of North American Indians,* ed. William C. Sturtevant, vol. 4: *History of Indian-White Relations,* ed. Wilcomb E. Washburn (Washington, D.C.: Smithsonian Institution, 1988), 20; Michel de Montaigne, *Essays,* ed. J. M. Cohen (London: Penguin, 1958), 18–19 (editor's introduction), 118–119. "Cultural exchange" has often been by force, as Linda Colley has shown in epic breadth in *Captives: Britain, Empire, and the World, 1600–1850* (New York: Anchor, 2002).

4. On Catlin, see William H. Truettner, *The Natural Man Observed: A Study of Catlin's Indian Gallery* (Washington, D.C.: Smithsonian, 1979); and Brian W. Dippie, *Catlin and His Contemporaries: The Politics of Patronage* (Lincoln: University of Nebraska Press, 1990). On world fairs, see Robert W. Rydell, *All the World's a Fair: Visions of Empire at American International Expositions, 1876–1916* (Chicago: University of Chicago Press, 1984). On William Mariner, see Vanessa Smith's introduction to a selection from his memoir in Jonathan Lamb, Vanessa Smith, and Nicholas Thomas, eds., *Exploration and Exchange: A South Seas Anthology, 1680–1900* (Chicago: University of Chicago Press, 2000), 191–192.

5. Étienne Taillemite, ed., *Bougainville et ses compagnons autour du monde 1766–1769: Journaux de navigation*, 2 vols. (Paris: Imprimerie Nationale, 1977), 2:249, 406 (quote). Hereinafter cited as *Bougainville et ses compagnons*. On Vivez, see the interesting description, ibid., 1:83–85. Commerson briefly mentions that Ahutoru was contemptuous of the residents of New Hebrides when they showed themselves to be afraid of the French. Ibid., 2:478.

6. Jean-Étienne Martin-Allanic, *Bougainville, navigateur, et les découvertes de son temps*, 2 vols. (Paris: Presses Universitaires de France, 1964), 2:889–890, 965–969, 970. Martin-Allanic bases his account of the interviews with La Condamine on a memorandum that La Condamine prepared on April 25, 1769, for Président de Brosses, author of the large work on the southern hemisphere and one of Bougainville's patrons.

7. The quote from Van Swieten comes from an article written by Father O'Reilly in his work *Tahitiens*, cited in *Bougainville et ses compagnons*, 1:93. For de Bachaumont, see ibid., 1:118–119.

8. Martin-Allanic, *Bougainville*, 2:1326.

9. Louis de Bougainville, *A Voyage round the World*, trans. J. R. Forster (London: Nourse and Davies, 1772; repr. New York: Da Capo Press, 1967), 245, 253, 255–256, 269–271.

10. Banks's diary entry cited in Cook, *Journals*, 1:117n4; also quoted in Lynne Withey, *Voyages of Discovery: Captain Cook and the Exploration of the Pacific* (Berkeley: University of California Press, 1989), 124–125. Cf. Cook, *Journals*, 1:117. See Beaglehole's deciphering of the list of names, ibid., 293–294. On Tupaia and the map, see Nicholas Thomas, "Introduction: Tupaia's Map," in *In Oceania: Visions, Artifacts, Histories* (Durham, N.C.: Duke University Press, 1997), 1–20.

11. On Mai, see Withey, *Voyages of Discovery*, 301–307, 342; Forster, *Voyage*, 1:xv–xvi, 389.

12. Forster, *Voyage*, 1:411. For Clerke, see Cook, *Journals*, 2:230n2.

13. Forster, *Voyage*, 1:513–514, 517–518 (comparison with Europeans), 601–602; 2:11, 12.

14. Karl H. Rensch, "Forster's Polynesian Linguistics," in Johann Reinhold Forster, *Observations Made during a Voyage round the World*, ed. Nicholas Thomas, Harriet Guest, and Michael Dettelbach, with a linguistics appendix by Karl H. Rensch (Honolulu: University of Hawaii Press, 1996), 288, 384. Cook, *Journals*, 2:270, 275, 356.

15. Cook, *Journals*, 2:387n6, 426, 426n1.

16. Chamisso, *Voyage around the World*, 106–107, 111–112.

17. Ibid., 120, 185, 309–310.

18. Chamisso, *Werke*, 2:266, 324–327, 490–491, 500.

19. Chamisso, *Voyage around the World*, 129; Louis Choris to Adelbert von Chamisso, 3 April 1820, in Harry Liebersohn, "Zur Kunst der Ethnographie: Zwei Briefe von Louis Choris an Adelbert von Chamisso," *Historische Anthropologie* 6 (1998): 488.

20. Chamisso, *Werke*, 2:324, 491–495, 498, 502.

21. Ibid., 2:237, 275–276, 330–331.

22. Kirch and Green (who use the spelling *ariki*) list the cognate terms for thirty-two places. There is considerable local variation in their meaning. See Patrick V. Kirch and Roger C. Green, *Hawaiki, Ancestral Polynesia: An Essay in Historical Anthropology* (Cambridge: Cambridge University Press, 2001), 227–231. Cf. Augustin Krämer, *Die Samoa-Inseln: Entwurf einer Monographie mit besonderer Berücksichtigung Deutsch-Samoas*, 2 vols. (Stuttgart: Schweizerbartsche Verlagsbuchhandlung [E. Naegele], 1902–1903).

23. For a recent synthesis of scholarship on Polynesian elites, see George E. Marcus, "Chieftainship," in Alan Howard and Robert Borofsky, eds., *Developments in Polynesian Ethnology* (Honolulu: University of Hawaii Press, 1989), 175–209. An interpretation focusing on Hawaii is Valerio Valeri, *Kingship and Sacrifice: Ritual and Society in Ancient Hawaii*, trans. Paula Wissing (Chicago: University of Chicago, 1985).

24. On the situation of European nobility, see Liebersohn, *Aristocratic Encounters: European Travelers and North American Indians* (Cambridge: Cambridge University Press, 1998), 63–64, 116–117.

25. On France and Prussia, cf. the astute, nonanachronistic interpretation in C. B. A. Behrens, *Society, Government, and the Enlightenment: The Experiences of Eighteenth-Century France and Prussia* (New York: Harper & Row, 1985). On the enforcement of hierarchy onboard ship and the significance of whipping, see Greg Dening, *Mr. Bligh's Bad Language: Passion, Power, and Theatre on the Bounty* (Cambridge: Cambridge University Press, 1992), 113–116.

26. Christine Ward Gailey, *Kinship to Kingship: Gender Hierarchy and State Formation in the Tongan Islands* (Austin: University of Texas Press, 1987), 178. William Mariner described the chaotic conditions in pre-

unification Tonga in John Martin, *An Account of the Natives of the Tonga Islands in the South Pacific Ocean, With an Original Grammar and Vocabulary of Their Language, Compiled and Arranged From the Extensive Communications of Mr. William Mariner, Several Years Resident in Those Islands*, 2 vols. (London: John Murray, 1818).

27. Cook, *Journals*, 1:78, 133–134.

28. Ibid., 2:381–383.

29. Ibid., 2:384.

30. Ibid., 384–387 (quotes at 385, 387); see Beaglehole's comments on Cook's misunderstanding of the monarch–nobility relationship, ibid., 387n2.

31. James Cook, *A Voyage towards the South Pole, and round the World, Performed in His Majesty's ships the Resolution and Adventure in the Years 1772, 1773, 1774, and 1755*, 2 vols. (London: Strahan and Cadell, 1777), 1:351.

32. Forster, *Voyage*, 1:326–327, 331, 338.

33. George Vancouver, *A Voyage of Discovery to the North Pacific Ocean and round the World, 1791–1795*, 4 vols., ed. W. Kaye Lamb (London: Hakluyt Society, 1984), 1:393.

34. Ibid., 1:393–395.

35. Ibid., 1:399–400.

36. Ibid., 1:411–412, 413, 413n3, 434–435.

37. See Douglas Oliver, *Return to Tahiti: Bligh's Second Breadfruit Voyage* (Honolulu: University of Hawaii Press, 1988); and Dening, *Mr. Bligh's Bad Language*.

38. William Bligh, "Voyage to the South Seas (1792)" in *A Book of the Bounty*, ed. George Mackaness and introd. Gavin Kennedy (London: Dent, 1981), 60 (November 1788). Cf. ibid., 58 (October 1788): "Among people so free from ostentation as the Otaheiteans, and whose manners are so simple and natural, the strictness with which the punctilios of rank are observed is surprising."

39. See the preface by Lord Mountbatten in William Bligh, *The Log of H.M.S. Providence, 1791–1793* (Guildford, England: Genesis, 1976).

40. Bligh, *Log of H.M.S. Providence,* entries of 11, 16, and 20 April 1792. On the name change, see Withey, *Voyage of Discovery,* 430; and Oliver, *Return to Tahiti,* 47.

41. Cf. Oliver, *Return to Tahiti,* 46.

42. Bligh, *Log of H.M.S. Providence,* entry of 20 April 1792.

43. Oliver, *Return to Tahiti,* 49.

44. Bligh, *Log of H.M.S. Providence,* entry of 28 April and 4 June 1792.

45. Ibid., 26 June 1792.

46. Ibid.

47. Vancouver, *Voyage of Discovery,* 3:807, 809, 811, 812, 1180–1182.

48. Quoted ibid., 1139–1141.

49. Peter R. Mills, *Hawai'i's Russian Adventure: A New Look at Old History* (Honolulu: University of Hawaii Press, 2002), 23–28; Klaus Mehnert, *The Russians in Hawaii, 1804–1819,* in University of Hawaii, *Occasional Papers,* no. 38 (April 1939) [University of Hawaii Bulletin, vol. 18, no. 6], 15–17, 21–23, 26–27, 36–46; editor's introduction and Schäffer to Main Office of the Russian American Company in St. Petersburg, 1 January 1816, in Richard A. Pierce, ed., *Russia's Hawaiian Adventure, 1815–1817* (Berkeley: University of California Press, 1965), 31–32, 42–43, 60–61; Chamisso, *Werke,* 2:219–220, 229, 305–306.

50. Mills, *Hawai'i's Russian Adventure,* 28.

51. Otto von Kotzebue, *A Voyage of Discovery . . . undertaken in the years 1815–1818,* trans. H. E. Lloyd, 3 vols. (London: Longman, 1821), 1:300, 301.

52. Ibid., 1:308–309, 312.

53. Chamisso, *Voyage around the World,* 307.

54. Ibid., 116–117.

55. Ibid., 114–115, 123–124; Louis Choris, *Voyage pittoresque autour du monde avec des portraits de sauvages d'Amérique, d'Asie, d'Afrique, et des îles du grand océan; des paysages, des vues maritimes, et plusieurs objets d'histoire naturelle: Accompagné de descriptions par M. le Baron Cuvier, et A. de Chamisso, et d'Observations sur les crânes humains par M. le Docteur Gall* (Paris: Didot, 1822), "Îles Sandwiches."

56. Cf. Kotzebue, *Voyage of Discovery,* 1:312. On the portraits, see Harry Liebersohn, "Images of Monarchy: Kamehameha I and the Art of Louis Choris," in Nicholas Thomas and Diane Losche, eds., assisted by Jennifer Newell, *Double Vision: Art Histories and Colonial Histories in the Pacific* (Cambridge: Cambridge University Press, 1999), 44–64. On the early European art of Hawaii, with reproductions of Choris paintings of Kamehameha and Ka'ahumanu, see David W. Forbes, *Encounters with Paradise: Views of Hawaii and Its People, 1778–1941* (Honolulu: University of Hawaii Press and Honolulu Academy of Arts, 1992).

57. Cf. Peter R. Monge and Noshir S. Contractor, *Theories of Communication Networks* (Oxford: Oxford University Press, 2003), 143.

4. Philosophers

1. Conrad Malte-Brun, *Journal des Débats*, 6 November 1821, offprint in Chamisso Nachlass, "Zu 'Voyage pittoresque . . . ,'" K.26 N.52, Deutsche Staatsbibliothek, Berlin; Chamisso, *Voyage around the World*, 190. On Liholiho's visit to England, see Ralph S. Kuykendall, *The Hawaiian Kingdom, 1778–1854: Foundation and Transformation* (Honolulu: University of Hawaii Press, 1938), 76–81.

2. Michèle Duchet, *Anthropologie et histoire au siècle des lumières: Buffon, Voltaire, Rousseau, Helvétius, Diderot* (Paris: Maspero, 1971), 408–410, 444–450, 460; Denis Diderot, "Scythes, Thraces, et gètes, philosophie des," in *Oeuvres complètes*, ed. H. Dieckmann and J. Varloot, vol. 4 (letters M–Z), ed. John Lough and Jacques Proust (Paris: Hermann, 1976), 309–312.

3. Guillaume-Thomas Raynal, *Histoire philosophique et politique des établissemens et du commerce des européens dans les deux Indes*, 10 vols. (Geneva: Jean-Leonard Pellet, 1780), 1:1–2. See also Michèle Duchet, *Diderot et l'Histoire des Deux Indes, ou l'Écriture Fragmentaire* (Paris: Nizet, 1978), especially 164–165. On Raynal, see G. Goggi, "Raynal, Guillaume-Thomas," in Roland Mortier and Raymond Trousson, eds., *Dictionnaire de Diderot* (Paris: Champion, 1999), 430–432; Anthony Strugnell, "Raynal, Guillaume-Thomas," in *Encyclopedia of the Enlightenment*, ed. Alan C. Kors (New York: Oxford University Press, 2003), 3:398–399. Denis Diderot, *Political Writings*, trans. and ed. John Hope Mason and Robert Wokler (Cambridge: Cambridge University Press, 1992), xxvii–xxxi, 166–167.

4. Raynal, *Histoire des deux Indes*, 8:35ff.

5. Peter Jimack, *Diderot: Supplément au Voyage de Bougainville* (London: Grant & Cutler, 1988), 11–12.

6. Denis Diderot, "Voyage autour du monde—Par la frégate du roi *La Boudeuse*, la flûte *L'Étoile* en 1766, 1767, 1768, 1769, sous le commandement de M. de Bougainville," in Diderot, *Oeuvres complètes*, vol. 12: *Le Neveu de Rameau (Fiction 4)*, ed. Henri Coulet et al. (Paris: Hermann, 1989), 510–513. See also ibid., editor's introduction, 499.

7. Ibid., 514–518.

8. For Diderot's modern editors' note on some of Diderot's omissions, see ibid., 517n20. P. N. Furbank points out that Diderot belonged to a literary tradition (which included such predecessors as Defoe and Swift) of calling into question the relationship between fact and fiction; editor's introduction, Denis Diderot, *This Is Not a Story and Other Stories*, trans. and introd. P. N. Furbank (Columbia: University of Missouri Press, 1991), 5–8.

9. Editor's introduction and note, Diderot, *This Is Not a Story*, 2, 161, 162.

10. Jimack, *Diderot*, 12–13; cf. editors' introduction, Diderot, *Oeuvres complètes*, 12:504.

11. Jimack, *Diderot*, 12.

12. Diderot, "On the Inconsistency of Public Opinion," in Diderot, *This Is Not a Story*, 58–59.

13. Diderot, "Supplement to the voyage of Bougainville, or dialogue between A and B on the inappropriateness of attaching moral ideas to certain physical actions that do not accord with them," in *Political Writings*, 36, 38, 39, 40.

14. Ibid., 43–44.

15. Herbert Dieckmann makes this argument in his introduction to Denis Diderot, *Supplément au voyage de Bougainville* (Geneva: Droz, 1955), xxxix, xl, xliii.

16. Diderot, "Supplement to the voyage," 60–63, 67, 74.

17. Immanuel Kant, "Rezensionen von J. G. Herders Ideen zur Philosophie der Geschichte der Menschheit. Teil 1.2. (1785)," in *Kleinere Schriften zur Geschichtsphilosophie, Ethik und Politik*, ed. Karl Vorländer (1913; Hamburg: Meiner, 1973), 42. See also editor's introduction, Immanuel Kant, *Anthropology from a Pragmatic Point of View*, trans. Victor L. Dowdell, ed. Frederick P. Van De Pitte (Carbondale: Southern Illinois University Press, 1978), xi.

18. Immanuel Kant, "Bestimmung des Begriffs einer Menschenrasse" (1785), in *Werkausgabe*, vol. 11: *Schriften zur Anthropologie, Geschichtsphilosophie, Politik und Pädagogik*, ed. Wilhelm Weischedel (Frankfurt am Main: Suhrkamp, 1977), 65. For an especially penetrating and clear survey, see Howard Williams, *Kant's Political Philosophy* (New York: St. Martin's, 1983). On the movement from conflict to harmony as the general pattern of Kant's thought, see Hans Saner, *Kants Weg vom Krieg zum Frieden*, vol. 1: *Widerstreit und Einheit: Wege zu Kants politischem*

Denken (Munich: Piper, 1967) ["Kant's Path from War to Peace, vol. 1: Conflict and Unity: Paths to Kant's Political Thought"], rendered into English with the anemic title *Kant's Political Thought: Its Origins and Development*, trans. E. B. Ashton (Chicago: University of Chicago, 1973).

19. See Arthur Hertzberg, *The French Enlightenment and the Jews* (New York: Columbia University, 1968).

20. "Von den verschiedenen Racen der Menschen zur Ankündigung der Vorlesungen der physischen Geographie im Sommerhalbenjahre 1775" (1775, 1777), in Kant, *Werkausgabe*, 11:11, 28–30; "Bestimmung des Begriffs einer Menschenrasse," in Kant, *Werkausgabe*, 11:81–82.

21. "Von den verschiedenen Racen der Menschen," in Kant, *Werkausgabe*, 11:12–13, 17–28; Kant, "Immanuel Kants physische Geographie," ed. Friedrich Theodor Rink, *Kants Werke: Akademie-Textausgabe*, vol. 9: *Logik, Physische Geographie, Pädagogik* (1902; Berlin: de Gruyter, 1968), 311–312, 317–318, 313; Kant, "Bestimmung des Begriffs einer Menschenrasse," *Werkausgabe*, 11:71–73. While this line of reasoning makes good sense to twenty-first-century ears, we should not overmodernize Kant. His views on race derived in part from his teleological understanding of nature: racial differences furthered the spread of the human species across the globe and could therefore be seen as part of nature's providential design. Ibid., "Von den verschiedenen Racen der Menschen (1775)," 11:17–28. For examples of human adaptation, he relied on the science of his time, some of which looks strange today: Africans' "black" skin, he maintained, made it easier for their bodies to rid themselves of phlogiston, which heavily suffused their humid climate. Ibid., "Bestimmung des Begriffs einer Menschenrasse," 11:79. His views on race depended not on his teleology or outdated science, however, but on his more general philosophical and methodological principles.

22. Johann Friedrich Blumenbach, "De Generis Humani Varietate Nativa" ("On the Natural Varieties of Mankind," 3rd ed., 1795) in *The Anthropological Treatises of Johann Friedrich Blumenbach*, trans. and ed. Thomas Bendyshe (1836; New York: Bergman, 1969), 196–200, 264–265. On European debates over monogenism and polygenism, see George W. Stocking, Jr., *Victorian Anthropology* (New York: Free Press, 1987). On Soemmerring, see Frank W. P. Dougherty, "Johann Friedrich Blumenbach und Samuel Thomas Soemmerring: Eine Auseinandersetzung in anthropologischer Hinsicht?" in Gunter Mann and Franz

Dumont, eds., *Samuel Thomas Soemmerring und die Gelehrten der Goethezeit* (Stuttgart: Gustav Fischer Verlag, 1985), 35–56. Kant, "Bestimmung des Begriffs einer Menschenrasse," 82.

23. Immanuel Kant, "Zum ewigen Frieden: Ein philosophischer Entwurf (1795, 1796)," *Kleinere Schriften zur Geschichtsphilosophie*, 128–139.

24. Ibid., 131.

25. "Als dass sie, ebenso wie einzelne Menschen, ihre wilde (gesetzlose) Freiheit aufgeben": ibid., 134.

26. Ibid., 131.

27. Ibid., xxx, 136, 138. On the right to hospitality, cf. Williams, *Kant's Political Philosophy*, 260.

28. George Forster to Soemmerring, 8 June 1786, quoted in editor's comments in Forster, *Werke*, vol. 8: *Kleine Schriften zu Philosophie und Zeitgeschichte*, ed. Siegfried Scheibe (Berlin: Akademie-Verlag, 1974), 400, 399, 403–404. See also Hans Querner, "Samuel Thomas Soemmerring und Johann Georg Forster—eine Freundschaft," in Mann and Dumont, *Samuel Thomas Soemmerring und die Gelehrten der Goethezeit*, 229–234.

29. Georg Forster, "Noch etwas über die Menschenrassen," in Forster, *Werke*, vol. 8: *Kleine Schriften zu Philosophie und Zeitgeschichte*, 133, 134–138, 140–142, 153–156.

30. Immanuel Kant, "Über den Gebrauch teleologischer Prinzipien in der Philosophie (1788)," in *Schriften zur Geschichtsphilosophie*, ed. and introd. Manfred Riedel (Stuttgart: Reclam, 1974), 92, 94–105.

31. Editor's comments in Forster, *Werke*, vol. 8: *Kleine Schriften zu Philosophie und Zeitgeschichte*, 407.

32. George Forster, "Cook der Entdecker (1789)," in Forster, *Werke*, vol. 5: *Kleine Schriften zur Völker- und Länderkunde*, ed. Horst Fiedler, Klaus-Georg Popp, Annerose Schneider, and Christian Suckow (Berlin: Akademie-Verlag, 1985), esp. 280–281, 291–292. For a view of the controversy more sympathetic to Forster's empiricism, see Vanessa Agnew, "Pacific Island Encounters and the German Invention of Race," in Rod Edmond and Vanessa Smith, eds., *Islands in History and Representation* (London: Routledge, 2003), 81–94.

33. Albert Leitzmann, *Georg und Therese Forster und die Brüder Humboldt: Urkunden und Umrisse* (Bonn: Ludwig Roehrscheid, 1936), 3, 9–10, 29, 105, 106, 124–125. Friedrich Schlegel, "Georg Forster: Fragment einer

Charakteristik der deutschen Klassiker," in Schlegel, *Charakteristiken und Kritiken,* vol. 1 (1796–1801), ed. Hans Eichner (Munich: Ferdinand Schöning, 1967), 81, 92.

34. Summarized from the editor's notes to Wilhelm von Humboldt, *Briefwechsel zwischen Wilhelm von Humboldt und August Wilhelm Schlegel,* ed. Albert Leitzmann, introd. B. Delbrueck (Halle: Niemeyer, 1908), 263–264.

35. *A. W. Schlegels Vorlesungen über schöne Litteratur und Kunst,* ed. J. Minor, in *Deutsche Litteraturdenkmale des 18. und 19. Jahrhunderts in Neudrucken,* ed. Bernhard Seuffert, vols. 17–19 (Heilbronn: Henninger, 1884), 33. The quote comes from Schlegel's third cycle of lectures, "Geschichte der romantischen Literatur," which he delivered in Berlin in 1803–1804.

36. Cf. Leitzmann, introduction to Humboldt, *Briefwechsel zwischen Humboldt und Schlegel,* 263–264.

37. Wilhelm von Humboldt, "Die Vasken, oder Bemerkungen auf einer Reise durch Biscaya und das französische Basquenland im Frühling des Jahrs 1801," in Humboldt, *Werke in Fünf Bänden,* ed. Andreas Flitner and Klaus Giel, vol. 2: *Schriften zur Altertumskunde und Ästhetik—Die Vasken* (Stuttgart: Cotta, 1961), 419 (quote), 424. Hereafter cited as Humboldt, *Werke.* On the dating of the essay, see the editorial comments by Wolfgang Ostberg, ibid., 5:431. On the Highland Scots, see Hugh Trevor-Roper, "The Invention of Tradition: The Highland Tradition of Scotland," in Eric Hobsbawm and Terence Ranger, eds., *The Invention of Tradition* (Cambridge: Cambridge University Press, 1992), 15–41; on the Iroquois, see Liebersohn, *Aristocratic Encounters: European Travelers and North American Indians* (Cambridge: Cambridge University Press, 1998), 13–14, 19–22.

38. "Ankündigung einer Schrift über die Vaskische Sprache und Nation, nebst Angabe des Geschichtspunctes und Inhalts derselben," in Humboldt, *Werke,* 5:115.

39. Wilhelm von Humboldt, *Ideen zu einem Versuch, die Grenzen der Wirksamkeit des Staats zu bestimmen* (Leipzig: Reclam, n.d.). Cf. John Stuart Mill, "On Liberty" (1859), in *On Liberty and Other Writings,* ed. Stefan Collini (Cambridge: Cambridge University Press, 1989), 3; Mill, *Autobiography,* ed. Jack Stillinger (1873; Boston: Houghton Mifflin, 1969), 151.

40. G. W. F. Hegel, *Hegel's Philosophy of Right,* trans. and ed. T. M. Knox (1821; Oxford: Oxford University Press, 1967).

41. "Über die Verschiedenheiten des menschlichen Sprachbaues," in Humboldt, *Werke,* 3:237–238, 243, 364–367.

42. "Über das vergleichende Sprachstudium," in Humboldt, *Werke,* 5:2, 8–9, 19–20, 24.

43. "Über das Entstehen der grammatischen Formen, und ihren Einfluss auf die Ideenentwicklung" [Gelesen in der Academie der Wissenschaften am 17. Januar 1822], in Humboldt, *Werke,* 3:32, 34, 41, 48, 49–61. A succinct study placing Humboldt's thinking about linguistic relativity in the history of ideas is Roger Langham Brown, *Wilhelm von Humboldt's Concept of Linguistic Relativity* (The Hague: Mouton, 1967). Humboldt's German-language predecessor was Friedrich Schlegel, *Über die Sprache und Weisheit der Indier: Ein Beitrag zur Begründung der Alterthumskunde,* ed. E. F. K. Koerner (1808; Amsterdam: Benjamins, 1977). One curiosity of Humboldt's admiration for articulated languages is his lack of extensive discussion of English. With its almost complete abandonment of case endings and elaborate verb forms, it would seem to belong among the passive recipients. Humboldt, however, did not take up the question of whether this was so.

44. Humboldt, *Werke,* 3:375–382, 423–424.

45. Ibid., 3:382–383, 392–396.

46. Ibid., 3:401–403.

47. Chamisso, "Bemerkungen und Ansichten," *Werke,* 2:643; editor's notes, ibid., 2:768, 774–775. Chamisso sent Humboldt several copies of an unnamed newspaper that was written in Hawaiian. See the thank-you note from Wilhelm von Humboldt to Adelbert von Chamisso, 13 May 1829, in Chamisso Nachlass K.28 N.38, Deutsche Staatsbibliothek, Berlin.

48. Chamisso, "Über die Hawaiische Sprache," in *Werke,* 2:670–671.

49. See Brown, Wilhelm von Humboldt's *Conception of Linguistic Relativity;* and John A. Lucy, *Language Diversity and Thought: A Reformulation of the Linguistic Relativity Hypothesis* (Cambridge: Cambridge University Press, 1992).

5. Missions

1. For a survey of the voyages of the later period, see C. Hartley Grattan, *The Southwest Pacific to 1900: A Modern History (Australia—New Zea-*

land—*the Islands—Antarctica*) (Ann Arbor: University of Michigan Press, 1963), 184–187.

2. John F. W. Herschel, *A Manual of Scientific Inquiry; Prepared for the Use of Officers in Her Majesty's Navy; and Travelers in General* (1849; London: John Murray, 1859); Charles Wilkes, *Narrative of the U.S. Exploring Expedition, 1838, 1839, 1840, 1841 and 1842*, 5 vols. and Atlas (Philadelphia: Lea and Blanchard, 1845). On the Wilkes expedition, see David B. Tyler, *The Wilkes Expedition: The First United States Exploring Expedition (1838–1842)* (Philadelphia: American Philosophical Society, 1968).

3. Jules Dumont d'Urville to Adelbert von Chamisso, Paris, 15 December 1825, Chamisso Nachlass, K.26 N.69, Deutsche Staatsbibliothek, Berlin. Biographical details are from the editor's introduction, Jules Dumont d'Urville, *An Account in Two Volumes of Two Voyages to the South Seas . . .* , 2 vols., trans. and ed. Helen Rosenman (Hawaii: University of Hawaii Press, 1988), 1: *Astrolabe,* xlii–liii. See also Camille Vergniol, *Dumont D'Urville* (Paris: La Renaissance du Livre, n.d.), which includes a useful description of archival sources. For the references to Humboldt and Krusenstern, see Dumont d'Urville, "Introduction," *An Account in Two Volumes of Two Voyages,* 2:327. For d'Urville's relationship to the Geographic Society, and for the letter of invitation to the unveiling of the Montparnasse Cemetery monument in memory of d'Urville (dated Paris, 25 October 1844), see Société de Géographie, Carton Du-Ey, Cartes et Plans, Bibliothèque Nationale, Paris. Jules Girard, "La Société de Géographie: Sa vie et ses oeuvres pendant un siècle, 1821–1921," carton Gu-Gr, mentions that in 1910, the society bore the expenses of restoring the statue.

4. On the belief that an "Aryan" lineage stretched from Britain to Polynesia, see Tony Ballantyne, *Orientalism and Race: Aryanism in the British Empire* (Basingstoke: Palgrave, 2002).

5. The preceding description summarizes Jules Dumont d'Urville, "Sur les îles du grand océan," *Bulletin de la Société de Géographie* 17 (1832): 1–21; the reference to "ennemis naturels des blancs" is from 11. D'Urville makes many of the same points in his official account of his first circumnavigation, *Voyage de La Corvette L'Astrolabe exécuté par ordre du roi, pendant les années 1826–1827–1828–1829* (Paris: Tastu, 1830), div. 1, vol. 2, part 2. Bernard Smith discusses d'Urville's ideas on the Maoris and the Melanasians, and specifically his prediction of a great future

destiny for the Maoris as Spartans of the south, as well as his observations on less-favored peoples, in *European Vision and the South Pacific,*
2nd ed. (New Haven, Conn.: Yale University Press, 1985), 331–332, 335–
339. For an analysis of d'Urville's racial discourse and the images ac-
companying his texts, see Bronwen Douglas, "Art as Ethno-historical
Text: Science, Representation, and Indigenous Presence in Eighteenth
and Nineteenth Century Oceanic Voyage Literature," in Nicolas
Thomas and Diane Losche, eds., *Double Vision: Art Histories and Colonial Histories in the Pacific* (Cambridge: Cambridge University Press,
1999), 65–99. On the European discourse of extinction, see Patrick
Brantlinger, *Dark Vanishings: Discourse on the Extinction of Primitive
Races, 1800–1930* (Ithaca, N.Y.: Cornell University Press, 2003).

6. On missionaries in the Spanish colonies in the New World, see An-
thony Pagden, *The Fall of Natural Man: The American Indian and the
Origins of Comparative Ethnology* (Cambridge: Cambridge University
Press, 1982); on early modern Asia, see R. Po-chia Hsia, *The World of
Catholic Renewal* (Cambridge: Cambridge University Press, 1998), 154–
177; and on North America, see Liebersohn, *Aristocratic Encounters:
European Travelers and North American Indians* (Cambridge: Cam-
bridge University Press, 1998), 21–22, 78–83.

7. *Transactions of the [London] Missionary Society,* vol. 9: *From its Institution in the Year 1795, to the End of the Year 1802* (London, 1803), 1. Hereafter cited as LMS. London Missionary Society, *A Missionary Voyage to
the South Pacific Ocean, Performed in the Years 1796, 1797, 1798, in the
Ship Duff, commanded by Captain James Wilson* (London: Chapman,
1799), 336.

8. See Neil Gunson, *Messengers of Grace: Evangelical Missionaries in the
South Seas, 1797–1860* (Melbourne: Oxford University Press, 1978). I
have relied on Gunson for the missionaries' first names and other biographical details. See especially Appendix 4, part 1, ibid., 344–351.

9. Lynne Withey, *Voyages of Discovery: Captain Cook and the Exploration
of the Pacific* (Berkeley: University of California Press, 1989), 185.

10. Thomas Haweis to Joseph Banks, n.d., Joseph Banks papers, LMS, 1:2;
Haweis to Banks, 14 June 1796, LMS, 1:3; Haweis to Banks, 22 November
1798, LMS, 1:7; Haweis to Banks, 3 March 1800, LMS, 1:19. All Sutro Library, California State Library, San Francisco.

11. Joseph Hardcastle to Joseph Banks, 7 March 1799, Joseph Banks papers,
LMS, 1:50, Sutro Library. Cf. Gunson, *Messengers of Grace,* chap. 3.

12. LMS, *A Missionary Voyage,* xcix.

13. LMS, 1:1–2.

14. Richard Lovett, *The History of the London Missionary Society, 1795–1895,* 2 vols. (London: Henry Frowde, 1899), 137. On Morrison, see Vanessa Smith's introduction to a selection from his memoir in Jonathan Lamb, Vanessa Smith, and Nicholas Thomas, eds., *Exploration and Exchange: A South Seas Anthology, 1680–1900* (Chicago: University of Chicago Press, 2000), 123–126.

15. LMS, 1:2, 16 (27 November 1797), 104 (7 January 1799), 107–108 (3–4 February 1799), 140–142 (7–11 October 1799).

16. Ibid., 24 (25 January 1798); Gunson, *Messengers of Grace,* 155; Claude Lévi-Strauss, *The Elementary Structures of Kinship,* rev. ed., trans. James Harle Bell, John Richard von Sturmer, and Rodney Needham, ed. (1949; Boston: Beacon Press, 1969).

17. Gunson, *Messengers of Grace,* 155.

18. LMS, 1:122–126 (June 9–July 17, 1799), 143–156 (October 17–November 30, 1799).

19. LMS, 2:349 (21 November 1803). Cf. Gunson, *Messengers of Grace,* 248–249.

20. LMS, 2:286 (26 June 1803).

21. LMS, 2:307 (5 June 1804).

22. LMS, 2:342 (3 November 1803), 345 ("Brothers Bicknell and Youl's Journal Round Tyarrabboo, 1803," 21 November 1803); 2:51 (2 June 1805). Ancient Tahitian religion had its own distinctions between body and soul and believed that the soul left the body during sleep and at other times to inhabit the po or other world. See Douglas Oliver, *Return to Tahiti: Bligh's Second Breadfruit Voyage* (Honolulu: University of Hawaii Press, 1988), 116, 222–223.

23. LMS, 2:58 ("A Journal of Brothers Nott and Elder's Journey round OTAHEITE; Commencing February 26, and Ending April 5, 1802," 4 March 1802), 272 (11 April 1803).

24. LMS, 3:179 (9 April 1806).

25. LMS, 1:44 (April 2, 1798); 2:295–297 (10 September 1803); 3:175–177 (11 March 1806–1 January 1807). Colin Newbury, *Tahiti Nui: Change and Survival in French Polynesia, 1767–1945* (Honolulu: University of Hawaii Press, 1980), 14–58; C. Silvester Horne, *The Story of the L.M.S., 1795–1895,* 2nd ed. (London: London Missionary Society [John Snow & Co.], 1895), 34–37.

26. Cf. Horne, *Story of the L.M.S.*, 35–45.

27. William E. Strong, *The Story of the American Board: An Account of the First Hundred Years of the American Board of Commissioners for Foreign Missions* (Boston: Pilgrim Press [American Board of Commissioners for Foreign Missions], 1910), 3, 7, 10–11. Cf. *The Missionary Herald* 6 (July 1810): 388–390.

28. Anon., "On Educating Heathen Youth in our own Country," *Missionary Herald* 12 (July 1816): 297–298, 299.

29. *Missionary Herald* 12 (July 1816): 300–302; ibid. 14 (April 1818), 191; ibid. 15 (September 1819): 429; Edwin Welles Dwight, *Memoirs of Henry Obookiah, A Native of Owhyee and a Member of the Foreign Missionary School, Who Died at Cornwall, Conn. Feb. 17, 1818, Aged 26 Years*, rev. ed. (New York: American Tract Society, n.d.); David Forbes, ed., *Hawaiian National Bibliography 1780–1900*, vol. 1: *1780–1830* (Honolulu: University of Hawaii Press, 1999), 332–333; Nancy J. Morris, "Hawaiian Missionaries Abroad, 1852–1909" (Ph.D. diss., Department of History, University of Hawaii, 1987), 31; Barbara B. Peterson, "Opukahia," http://www.anb.org/articles/08/08-02166.html: *American National Biography Online*, February 2000.

30. "Introduction," *Transactions of the [London] Missionary Society* 1 (1803): xviii–xx; *Missionary Herald* 13 (February 1817): 80; Morris, "Hawaiian Missionaries," 28, 33–37; ABCFM, *Annual Report*, 14 (1823): 132–134; H. N. Hubbell [principal], Foreign Ministry School in Cornwall, to Eli Ruggles, 10 April 1821, Cornwall Foreign Mission School, Hawaiian Historical Society, Mission Houses Museum Library, Honolulu.

31. Strong, *Story of the American Board*, 13–16; S. Worcester, Corresponding Secretary of Prudential Commission of ABCFM, Boston, August 23, 1819, *Missionary Herald* 5 (September 1819): 430.

32. ABCFM, *Annual Report* 11 (1820): 36, 38.

33. ABCFM, *Annual Report* 12 (1821): 205.

34. See Louis de Freycinet, *Hawai'i in 1819: A Narrative Account*, trans. Ella L. Wiswell, ed. Marion Kelley, *Pacific Anthropological Records*, vol. 26 (Bernice P. Bishop Museum, Department of Anthropology, Honolulu, Hawaii), October 1978; Jacques Arago, *Narrative of a Voyage round the World, in the Uranie and Physicienne Corvettes, commanded by Captain Freycinet, during the years 1817, 1818, 1819, and 1820* (London: Treuttel and Wurtz, 1823).

35. On the crisis of Hawaiian society, see Patrick V. Kirch and Marshall Sahlins, *Anahulu: The Anthropology of History in the Kingdom of Hawaii*, vol. 1: *Historical Ethnography*, by Marshall Sahlins, with the assistance of Dorothy B. Barrère (Chicago: University of Chicago Press, 1992). Demographic figures before and after contact have been a subject of controversy in recent years. Cf. David E. Stannard, *Before the Horror: The Population of Hawai'i on the Eve of Western Contact* (Honolulu: Social Science Research Institute/University of Hawaii, 1989). On island politics in the early missionary years, see Sahlins, *Anahulu;* and Ralph S. Kuykendall, *The Hawaiian Kingdom, 1778–1854: Foundation and Transformation* (1938; Honolulu: University of Hawaii Press, 1947). On Ka'ahumanu, see Hiram Bingham to Jeremiah Evarts, 9 August 1822, ABCFM 19.1: Hawaiian Islands Mission, vol. 1, Houghton Library, Harvard University. See also Kuykendall, *The Hawaiian Kingdom, 1778–1854*, 133.

36. Journal of the Sandwich Island mission, 16 October 1821, ABCFM 19.1, vol. 1, Houghton Library, Harvard University.

37. Cf. William Cronon, *Changes in the Land: Indians, Colonists, and the Ecology of New England* (New York: Hill and Wang, 1983), 56–57.

38. Journal of the Sandwich Island mission, 10 May 1823, ABCFM 19.1, vol. 1, Houghton Library, Harvard University.

39. *Christian Advocate* 2 (July 1824): 320.

40. Ibid., 321–323.

41. Ibid., 322. Stewart left out the first two sentences when he later assembled his letters into a book. Charles S. Stewart, *Journal of a Residence in the Sandwich Islands, during the Years 1823, 1824, and 1825,* ed. and introd. William Ellis (3rd ed., 1830; Honolulu: University of Hawaii Press, 1970), 102.

42. Clifford Geertz discusses this kind of ambivalence in "Found in Translation: On the Social History of the Moral Imagination," in Geertz, *Local Knowledge: Further Essays in Interpretive Anthropology* (New York: Basic Books, 1983), 42.

43. Kuykendall, *The Hawaiian Kingdom, 1778–1854*, 1:122–123; Levi Chamberlain to Jeremiah Evarts, Honolulu, 26 July 1826, ABCFM 19.1, vol. 2, Houghton Library, Harvard University.

44. Adelbert von Chamisso, "Über die Hawaiische Sprache," in Chamisso, *Werke*, 2:670–674. Quotation at 674.

45. William Ellis, *Polynesian Researches, during a Residence of Nearly Six Years in the South Sea Islands . . .*, 2 vols. (1829; London: Dawsons of Pall Mall, 1967 [facsimile reprint]), 1:278–279.

46. F. W. Beechey, *Narrative of a Voyage to the Pacific and Beering's Strait, to Co-Operate with the Polar Expeditions: Performed in His Majesty's Ship Blossom . . . in the Years 1825, 26, 27, 28* (Philadelphia: Carey & Lea, 1832), 174, 176, 182, 183–184, 186.

47. Otto von Kotzebue, *A New Voyage round the World, in the Years 1823, 24, 25, and 26*, 2 vols. (London: Henry Colburn and Richard Bentley, 1830), 1:130, 131, 133.

48. Ibid., 1:146–149, 150, 152, 153–154.

49. Ibid., 1:155, 156–157.

50. Ibid., 1:203, 159, 160, 161–162, 169, 170–174.

51. Ibid., 1:167–169.

52. Daniel Tyerman and George Bennet, *Journal of Voyages and Travels*, compiled by James Montgomery, 3 vols. (Boston: Crocker and Brewster, 1832), 1:53, 55–57.

53. Ibid., 1:70, 63, 72–76, 149, 2:69, 238, 239. For a recent popular account of their tour, see Tom Hiney, *On the Missionary Trail: The Classic Georgian Adventure of Two Englishmen, Sent on a Journey around the World, 1821–29* (London: Vintage, 2001).

54. Kotzebue, *New Voyage*, 1:158; Tyerman and Bennet, *Journal*, 2:216–217.

55. "R.A.," Preface, in Tyerman and Bennet, *Journal*, 1:vi–vii, xiv.

56. William Ellis, *A Vindication of the South Seas Missions from the Misrepresentations of Otto von Kotzebue, Captain in the Russian Navy, with an Appendix* (London: Frederick Westley and A. H. Davis, 1831), 1–10, 22–24, 41–42, 54, 58, 76, 80, 94, 98, 112–113, 147–148, 149, 154.

57. Cf. Clifford Geertz, *The Interpretation of Cultures: Selected Essays* (New York: Basic, 1973).

6. Darwin, Melville, and the End of a World

1. The preceding description, and in particular its emphasis on networks, is drawn from Janet Browne, *Charles Darwin: A Biography*, vol. 1: *Voyaging* (Princeton, N.J.: Princeton University Press, 1995), esp. xii, 133, and 183; and the editors' introduction to Charles Darwin, *Voyage of the Beagle: Charles Darwin's Journal of Researches*, ed. and introd. Janet Browne and Michael Neve (London: Penguin, 1989).

2. Robert McCormick, *Voyages of Discovery in the Arctic and Antarctic Seas, and round the World: Being Personal Narratives of Attempts to Reach the North and South Poles; and of an Open-Boat Expedition up the Wellington Channel in Search of Sir John Franklin and Her Majesty's Boat "Forlorn Hope," under the Command of the Author*, 2 vols. (London: Sampson, Low, Marston, Searle, and Rivington, 1884), 2:183–184, 215–218, 222; John K. Laughton, "McCormick, Robert (1800–1890)," DNB, 12:455; Charles Darwin, to Caroline Darwin, Botofogo Bay, 25–26 April 1832, *The Correspondence of Charles Darwin*, vol. 1 (1821–1836), ed. Frederick Burkhardt and Sydney Smith (Cambridge: Cambridge University Press, 1985), 225; cf. Browne, *Darwin*, 1:199.

3. Darwin, *Voyage of the Beagle*, 175, 177, 178, 181. FitzRoy agreed that the Fuegians were cannibal but civilizable "savages." See Robert FitzRoy, *Narrative of the Surveying Voyage of H.M.S. Adventure and Beagle, between the Years 1826 and 1836*, vol. 1: *Proceedings of the First Expedition, 1826–30, under the Command of Captain P. P. King*, 462, and vol. 2: *Proceedings of the Second Expedition, 1831–36, under the Command of Captain R. FitzRoy* (London: Henry Colburn, 1839), 175, 189, 203.

4. Darwin, *Correspondence*, 1:306–307.

5. Cf. Fernando Cervantes, *The Devil in the New World: The Impact of Diabolism in New Spain* (New Haven, Conn.: Yale University Press, 1994).

6. Charles Darwin, *The Origin of Species by Means of Natural Selection, or the Preservation of Favored Races in the Struggle for Life/The Descent of Man and Selection in Relation to Sex* (1859/1872; New York: Modern Library, n.d.), 445. On the early modern history of demonic imagery, see Bernadette Bucher, *Icon and Conquest: A Structural Analysis of the Illustrations of de Bry's Great Voyages*, trans. Basia M. Gulati (Chicago: University of Chicago Press, 1981).

7. On Darwin's understanding of the Fuegians, see the editors' comments in Darwin, *Correspondence*, 1:306n5. On the ship's library see ibid., app. 4, 560.

8. Darwin, *Voyage of the Beagle*, 298, 301, 293–294.

9. Ibid., 298, 299, 300, 301, 302–303. Darwin's phrase about the Tahitians' profligacy is reminiscent of the Hawkesworth account. On the same page, with regard to the morality of the women, Darwin mentions "the scenes described by Captain Cook and Mr. Banks." While he does not specifically cite the Hawkesworth account, it was available to him in the library of the *Beagle*; see Darwin, *Correspondence*, 1: app. 4, 560.

10. On Earle, see the editor's introduction, Augustus Earle, *Narrative of a Residence in New Zealand—Journal of a Residence in Tristan da Cunha,* ed. E. H. McCormick (1832; Oxford: Clarendon Press, 1966), 1–15.

11. Earle, *Narrative,* 56–57, 60–61. For the New Zealand background, see editor's introduction, ibid., 27–46.

12. Ibid., 56–57, 60–61, 62–64, 73, 74, 85–86.

13. Editor's introduction, Earle, *Narrative,* 22–23; Charles Darwin to Caroline Darwin, 27 December 1835, Bay of Island, New Zealand, Darwin, *Correspondence,* 1:472. Darwin, *Voyage of the Beagle,* 183–184, 306–307, 309, 311, 313, 314, 315–316. The great critic of supernatural explanation seems to have been particularly charmed by the notion of the "enchanter's wand," for he uses the phrase on page 310 as well as on page 311. See also FitzRoy's similar connection between democracy and savagery among the Maoris. FitzRoy, *Narrative,* 2:609.

14. Physical dependence makes for good ethnographers: Karin O. Kuperman makes this straightforward but important point about the history of travel in *Indians and English: Facing Off in Early America* (Ithaca, N.Y.: Cornell University Press, 2000), 13–14.

15. Darwin, *Origin of Species/Descent of Man,* 511, 537. On Darwin's application of his theory to human beings, see, for example, Darwin's interest in determining the "values" of racial differences, his description of the moral sense of "savages," and his belief in the superiority of the English, ibid., 390, 487–488, and 508, respectively.

16. Ibid., 445–446, 539, 919.

17. Ibid., 543, 545–547, 548–550.

18. Ibid., 497–509. According to a writer sympathetic to Darwin, "Darwin's speculative bio-history of humanity, although dark and violent in its account of genesis and tribal warfare, was ultimately predicated within a language of social optimism. As small tribes had been absorbed into larger and larger communities through war and genocide, people's [*sic*] sympathies became broader." Paul Crook, *Darwinism, War, and History: The Debate over the Biology of War from the "Origin of Species" to the First World War* (Cambridge: Cambridge University Press, 1994), 28. For a critical survey of the larger context of this kind of "social optimism" in nineteenth-century intellectual history, see Patrick Brantlinger, *Dark Vanishings: Discourse on the Extinction of Primitive Races, 1800–1930* (Ithaca, N.Y.: Cornell University Press, 2003).

19. Darwin, *Origin of Species/Descent of Man*, 489.

20. The description of Melville's itinerary is taken from Hershel Parker, *Herman Melville: A Biography*, vol. 1 (1819–1851) (Baltimore: Johns Hopkins University Press, 1996), 189–288. On the whaling industry's shift to the Pacific, see Briton Cooper Busch, *"Whaling Will Never Do for Me": The American Whaleman in the Nineteenth Century* (Lexington: University Press of Kentucky, 1994), 2–4; on the changing economy of the Pacific, see Douglas L. Oliver, *The Pacific Islands*, rev. ed. (Honolulu: University of Hawaii Press, 1961), chap. 8.

21. David F. Long, *Nothing Too Daring: A Biography of Commodore David Porter, 1780–1843* (Annapolis, Md.: United States Naval Institute, 1970), 109–135; David Porter, *Journal of a Cruise Made to the Pacific Ocean in the United States Frigate Essex in the Years 1812, 1813, and 1814*, rev. ed., 2 vols. (New York: Wiley & Halsted, 1822), 1:lxvi.

22. Herman Melville, *Typee: A Peep at Polynesian Life* (1846; London: Penguin, 1972), 193. The title of the original London edition was more ambiguous, its first part promising a factual travel account: *Narrative of a Four Months' Residence among the Natives of a Valley of the Marquesas islands; or, A Peep at Polynesian Life.*

23. Ibid., 63, 234–236, 257–258, 265–270. On the failed mission, see T. Walter Herbert, Jr., *Marquesan Encounters: Melville and the Meaning of Civilization* (Cambridge, Mass.: Harvard University Press, 1980), chaps. 2–3. A sailor who visited Honolulu in late 1839 gave a pathetic description of native poverty and missionary indifference. "Their condition is equally as bad if not worse than any slave in the U.S. If the former are the object of an interest, the latter should be of a compassion, that should almost border on agony. But alas 'poor they' their condition is little thought of by those godly men, if they are thought of very little is done to ameliorate their condition, In beholding their degradations and the near approach they make to the beast, is enough to make a person blush and hang his head to think himself a man." William Clark, "Journal, Kept in the U.S. Ship Vincennes, Charles Wilkes Esq. Commander on a Voyage of Discovery & Survey in the Years 1838–1839–1840–1841–1842," 149, Peabody-Essex Museum, Salem.

24. Walt Whitman, Brooklyn *Eagle*, 15 April 1846, reprinted in Brian Higgins and Hershel Parker, *Herman Melville: The Contemporary Reviews*

(Cambridge: Cambridge University Press, 1995), 46. Charleston [S.C.] *Southern Patriot*, 25 April 1846, ibid., 47.

25. The phrase "fallen majesty" is from W. B. Yeats, "Fallen Majesty," in *Selected Poems and Two Plays*, ed. M. L. Rosenthal (n.p.: Collier/ Macmillan, 1962), 47. Herman Melville, *Omoo* (1847; Mineola, N.Y.: Dover, 2000), 201, 202, 203.

26. Melville, *Omoo*, 203–204.

27. Ibid., 174–175, 180. For other examples of expectation that contact with Europeans would result in the extermination of native peoples, see Brantlinger, *Dark Vanishings*; Liebersohn, *Aristocratic Encounters: European Travelers and North American Indians* (Cambridge: Cambridge University Press, 1998), 89, 90–91, 106, 112; and George W. Stocking, Jr., *Victorian Anthropology* (New York: Free Press, 1987), 274–283.

28. H.C., New York *Evangelist*, 9 April 1846, in Higgins and Parker, *Melville: The Contemporary Reviews*, 46. *Critic* [London], 3 (14 March 1846), ibid., 16. *Christian Observatory* [Boston], 1 (May 1847), ibid., 69. W[illiam] O. B[ourne], "Melville's Adventures in the South Seas: *Typee* and *Omoo*," New York *Tribune*, 2 October 1847, ibid., 157 (Bourne quoted a passage from Darwin, *Voyage of the Beagle*, 302). This was a point that Bourne himself made in another review of *Omoo*. Cf. William O. Bourne, "Missionary Operations in Polynesia," *New Englander* [New Haven], 6 (January 1848), in Higgins and Parker, *Melville: The Contemporary Reviews*, 171. Herbert discusses Melville's self-conscious mixture of roles as "gentleman-beachcomber" in *Marquesan Encounters*, 160.

29. *Critic* [London], 3 (7 March 1846), 219–222, in Higgins and Parker, *Melville: The Contemporary Reviews*, 9. This was the first of two notices to appear in the same journal.

Conclusion

1. On the idea of interpretation, cf. Clifford Geertz, *The Interpretation of Cultures: Selected Essays* (New York: Basic Books, 1973).

2. On the problems of transporting live animals for study in Europe, see Richard W. Burkhardt, "A Man and His Menagerie," *Natural History* 110, no. 1 (February 2001): 62–69.

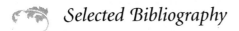 *Selected Bibliography*

All manuscript call numbers cited in the text are listed below. A selection of printed primary sources and secondary sources is provided as a guide for readers unfamiliar with the scholarship on exploration and encounter; scholars with more specialized interests will find additional sources cited in the notes.

MANUSCRIPTS

Archives Nationales, Paris
AJ15/127: Meetings of the professors of the Museum of Natural History.

Bibliothèque Centrale du Muséum National d'Histoire Naturelle, Paris
Nr. 1986, tome 3, 355, Louis Choris to Georges Cuvier, 28 December 1827.
Ms. 1904, dossier 3. Philippe Commerson, "Academia politica, sive universalis, aliter Respublica academica seu litteraria."

Bibliothèque Nationale de France, Département des Cartes et Plans, Paris
Société de Géographie
—carton Du-Ey, microfilm 14.
—carton Gu-Gr (494), Girard, Jules.
—colis 3 bis (1628), Edme-François Jomard, "Questions de Mr Jomard sur l'Amérique pour Mr. Choris."

—colis nr. 18 (2921), Séance de la commission centrale, 6 September 1822.

—colis nr. 19 bis (3186), Minister of the Marine and the Colonies, to Jomard, President of the Central Commission of the Geographic Society, 27 August 1827.

—colis nr. 19 bis (3211), John P. Gosy, Secretary for Foreign Affairs, Medico-Botanical Society of London, to Edme-François Jomard, 14 November 1827.

Geheimes Staatsarchiv Preussischer Kulturbesitz, Berlin-Dahlem

I./109.2508, Geschichte des Seehandels.

I.HA Rep. 89 (2.2.1) Nr. 21361, Wissenschaftliche Reisen des Dr. Meyen 1832.

Rep. V f. Litt.C. Nr. 2, Uhden to Friedrich Wilhelm III, 30 December 1822.

Rep. 76 Vc. Sekt.1. Tit.XI. 6. Abteilung XI, Teil I. Die Gesellschaft für Erdkunde, Bd. I, 1822–1878.

Houghton Library, Harvard University, Cambridge, Massachusetts

The American Board of Commissioners of Foreign Missions, 19.1: Hawaiian Island Missions, vols. 1 and 2.

Mission Houses Museum Library, Honolulu

Hawaiian Historical Society: Cornwall Foreign Mission School.

National Archives, Tartu, Estonia

Stock 1414, series 3, item 23, "Familie von Krusenstern," letters from Nicholas Rumiantsev to Adam von Krusenstern, 1815–1825.

National Library of Australia, Canberra

Ms. 4222, documents by Charles-François Beautemps-Beaupré regarding Jules Dumont-d'Urville.

Niedersächsische Staats- und Universitätsbibliothek, Göttingen

J. F. Blumenbach Nachlass, Part 3 (correspondence).

Phillips Library, Peabody-Essex Museum, Salem

MH-100, J. R. Forster, letters to Thomas Pennant, 1768–1786.

William Clark, Journal, Kept in the U.S. Ship (Vincennes, crossed out), Relief, Charles Wilkes Esq. Commander on a Voyage of Discovery & Survey in the Years 1838–1839–1840–1841–1842. [The journal shifts from the *Relief* to the *Vincennes*.]

Royal Botanic Gardens, Kew, England

Joseph Banks Letters
—1:222, Sigismund Bacstrom to Banks, 28 June 1786.
—2:287–288, G. A. Pollen to Banks, 23 February 1804.
—2:290, Banks to Pollen, 29 March 1804.

Staatsbibliothek zu Berlin

Adelbert von Chamisso Nachlass
—K.17 N.15, Adelbert von Chamisso to Hippolyte de Chamisso, 21 May 1816.
—K.18 N.13, Chamisso to Nicholas Rumiantsev, 3 September 1819.
—K.26 N.52, Conrad Malte-Brun, offprint of "Zu 'Voyage pittoresque' . . . ," *Journal des Débats*, 6 November 1821.
—K.26 N.69, Jules Dumont d'Urville to Adelbert von Chamisso, 15 December 1825.
—K.28 N.38, Wilhelm von Humboldt to Chamisso, 13 May 1829.
—K.28 N.67, Adam von Krusenstern to Chamisso, 2–14 June 1815; Krusenstern to Chamisso, 27 January 1820.
—K.30 N.22 Rumiantsev to Chamisso, 29 January 1820.

State Library of New South Wales, Sydney

C 175, Dumont d'Urville, Collection of holograph letters, etc., regarding the *Astrolabe*, 1826–1846, Letters to King.

Sutro Library, California State Library, San Francisco

Joseph Banks papers
—Botanical Gardens
  I:16, Copy of a letter from James Bowie and Alan Cunningham to William Aiton, 29 March 1815.
  I:39, Joseph Banks to Alan Cunningham, 13 February 1817.
  I:45, Alan Macquarie to Joseph Banks, 18 December 1817.
  I:48, Banks to [Macquarie], July 1818.
  I:64, Banks to James Bowie, undated.
—Russia
  I:17, Sergius Plescheyeff to Joseph Banks, 30 July 1795.

—London Missionary Society

    I:2, Thomas Haweis to Joseph Banks, n.d.

    I:3, Haweis to Banks, 14 June 1796.

    I:7, Haweis to Banks, 22 November 1798.

    I:19, Haweis to Banks, 3 March 1800.

    I:50, Joseph Hardcastle to Joseph Banks, 7 March 1799.

PRINTED SOURCES

Allen, John Logan. *Lewis and Clark and the Image of the American Northwest.* New York: Dover, 1991.

Ballantyne, Tony. *Orientalism and Race: Aryanism in the British Empire.* Basingstoke: Palgrave, 2002.

Banks, Joseph. *The Letters of Sir Joseph Banks: A Selection, 1768–1820.* Edited by Neil Chambers with introduction by Harold Carter. London: Imperial College Press, 2000.

Barratt, Glynn. *Russia in Pacific Waters, 1715–1825: A Survey of the Origins of Russia's Naval Presence in the North and South Pacific.* Vancouver: University of British Columbia Press, 1981.

Bayly, C. A. *Empire and Information: Intelligence Gathering and Social Communication in India, 1780–1870.* Cambridge: Cambridge University Press, 1996.

Beaglehole, J. C. *The Life of Captain James Cook.* Stanford, Calif.: Stanford University Press, 1974.

Boon, James A. *Affinities and Extremes: Crisscrossing the Bittersweet Ethnology of East Indies History, Hindu-Balinese Culture, and Indo-European Allure.* Chicago: University of Chicago Press, 1990.

Browne, Janet. *Charles Darwin: A Biography.* Vol. 1: *Voyaging.* Princeton, N.J.: Princeton University Press, 1995.

Bunzl, Matti, and H. Glenn Penny, eds. *Worldly Provincialism: German Anthropology in the Age of Empire.* Ann Arbor: University of Michigan Press, 2003.

Burkhardt, Richard W., Jr. "Naturalists' Practices and Nature's Empire: Paris and the Platypus, 1815–1833." *Pacific Science* 55 (2001): 327–341.

Buzard, James. *The Beaten Track: European Tourism, Literature, and the Ways to 'Culture,' 1800–1918.* Oxford: Oxford University Press, 1993.

Calder, Alex, Jonathan Lamb, and Bridget Orr. *Voyages and Beaches: Pacific Encounters, 1769–1840.* Honolulu: University of Hawaii Press, 1999.

Cañizares-Esguerra, Jorge. *How to Write the History of the New World: Histories, Epistemologies, and Identities in the Eighteenth-Century Atlantic World.* Stanford, Calif.: Stanford University Press, 2001.

Chamisso, Adelbert von. *A Voyage around the World with the Romanzov Exploring Expedition in the Years 1815–1818 in the Brig Rurik, Captain Otto von Kotzebue.* Translated and edited by Henry Kratz. Honolulu: University of Hawaii Press, 1986.

Cheah, Pheng, and Bruce Robbins, eds. *Cosmopolitics: Thinking and Feeling beyond the Nation.* Minneapolis: University of Minnesota Press, 1998.

Choris, Louis. *Journal des Malers Ludwig York Choris.* Edited with commentary by Niklaus R. Schweizer. Bern: Peter Lang, 1999.

Cook, James. *The Journals of Captain James Cook on His Voyages of Discovery.* 3 vols. Edited by J. C. Beaglehole. [Hakluyt Society, extra series, vols. 34–36.] Cambridge: Cambridge University Press, 1955–1967.

Darwin, Charles. *The Correspondence of Charles Darwin.* Vol. 1: *1821–1836.* Edited by Frederick Burkhardt and Sydney Smith. Cambridge: Cambridge University Press, 1985.

——— *Voyage of the Beagle: Charles Darwin's Journal of Researches.* Edited by Janet Browne and Michael Neve. London: Penguin, 1989.

Davidson, J. W. *Samoa Mo Samoa: The Emergence of the Independent State of Western Samoa.* Melbourne: Oxford University Press, 1967.

Dawson, Warren R., ed. *The Banks Letters: A Calendar of the Manuscript Correspondence of Sir Joseph Banks, Preserved in the British Museum, The British Museum (Natural History), and Other Collections in Great Britain.* London: British Museum, 1958.

Dening, Greg. *Beach Crossings: Voyaging across Times, Cultures, and Self.* Philadelphia: University of Pennsylvania Press, 2004.

——— *Mr. Bligh's Bad Language: Passion, Power, and Theatre on the Bounty.* Cambridge: Cambridge University Press, 1992.

Diderot, Denis. *Political Writings.* Translated and edited by John Hope Mason and Robert Wokler. Cambridge: Cambridge University Press, 1992.

Drayton, Richard. *Nature's Government: Science, Imperial Britain, and the 'Improvement' of the World.* New Haven, Conn.: Yale University Press, 2000.

Duchet, Michèle. *Anthropologie et histoire au siècle des lumières: Buffon, Voltaire, Rousseau, Helvétius, Diderot.* Paris: Maspero, 1971.

Dumont d'Urville, Jules. *An Account in Two Volumes of Two Voyages to the South Seas by Captain (later Rear-Admiral) Jules S-C Dumont d'Urville of* the French Navy to Australia, New Zealand, Oceania, 1826–1829 in the Corvette Astrolabe and to the Straits of Magellan, Chile, Oceania, South East Asia, Australia, Antarctica, New Zealand, and Torres Strait, 1837–1840 in the Corvettes Astrolabe and Zélée. 2 vols. Translated and edited by Helen Rosenman. Hawaii: University of Hawaii Press, 1988.

Dunmore, John. *Who's Who in Pacific Navigation*. Honolulu: University of Hawaii Press, 1991.

Eisler, William. *The Furthest Shore: Images of Terra Australis from the Middle Ages to Captain Cook*. Cambridge: Cambridge University Press, 1995.

Elliott, J. H. *The Old World and the New, 1492–1650*. Cambridge: Cambridge University Press, 1970.

Enzensberger, Ulrich. *Georg Forster: Ein Leben in Scherben*. Frankfurt am Main: Eichborn, 1996.

Faivre, Jean-Paul. *L'Expansion française dans le pacifique de 1800 à 1842*. Paris: Nouvelles Éditions Latines, 1953.

Forbes, David W. *Encounters with Paradise: Views of Hawaii and Its People, 1778–1941*. Honolulu: University of Hawaii Press and Honolulu Academy of Arts, 1992.

Forbes, David W., ed. *Hawaiian National Bibliography 1780–1900*. Vol. 1: *1780–1830*. Honolulu: University of Hawaii Press, 1999.

Forster, George. *A Voyage round the World*. Edited by Nicholas Thomas and Oliver Berghof, assisted by Jennifer Newell. 2 vols. Honolulu: University of Hawaii Press, 2002.

——— *Werke: Sämtliche Schriften, Tagebücher, Briefe*. Edited by Gerhard Steiner. Berlin: Akademie-Verlag, 1958–1982.

Forster, Johann Reinhold. *Observations Made during a Voyage round the World*. Edited by Nicholas Thomas, Harriet Guest, and Michael Dettelbach, with a linguistics appendix by Karl H. Rensch. Honolulu: University of Hawaii Press, 1996.

Forsyth, James. *A History of the Peoples of Siberia: Russia's North Asian Colony, 1581–1990*. Cambridge: Cambridge University Press, 1992.

Gascoigne, John. *Science in the Service of Empire: Joseph Banks, the British State, and the Uses of Science in the Age of Revolution*. Cambridge: Cambridge University Press, 1998.

Geertz, Clifford. *The Interpretation of Cultures: Selected Essays*. New York: Basic, 1973.

Geyer, Michael, and Charles Bright. "World History in a Global Age." *American Historical Review* 100 (1995): 1034–60.

Goetzmann, William H. *Exploration and Empire: The Explorer and the Scientist in the Winning of the American West.* New York: Knopf, 1966.

Grove, Richard H. *Green Imperialism: Colonial Expansion, Tropical Island Edens, and the Origins of Environmentalism, 1600–1860.* Cambridge: Cambridge University Press, 1995.

Gunson, Neil. *Messengers of Grace: Evangelical Missionaries in the South Seas, 1797–1860.* Melbourne: Oxford University Press, 1978.

Herbert, T. Walter, Jr. *Marquesan Encounters: Melville and the Meaning of Civilization.* Cambridge, Mass.: Harvard University Press, 1980.

Hoare, Michael E. *The Tactless Philosopher: Johann Reinhold Forster (1729–98).* Melbourne: Hawthorn Press, 1976.

Howard, Alan, and Robert Borofsky. *Developments in Polynesian Ethnology.* Honolulu: University of Hawaii Press, 1989.

Jardine, Nicholas, James A. Secord, and E. C. Spary, eds. *Cultures of Natural History.* Cambridge: Cambridge University Press, 1996.

Joppien, Rüdiger, and Bernard Smith. *The Art of Captain Cook's Voyages.* 3 vols. New Haven, Conn.: Yale University Press, 1985–1988.

Kirch, Patrick V., and Roger C. Green, *Hawaiki, Ancestral Polynesia: An Essay in Historical Anthropology.* Cambridge: Cambridge University Press, 2001.

Kirch, Patrick V., and Marshall Sahlins. *Anahulu: The Anthropology of History in the Kingdom of Hawaii.* Vol. 1: Marshall Sahlins, with the assistance of Dorothy B. Barrère, *Historical Ethnography.* Chicago: University of Chicago Press, 1992.

Koerner, Lisbet. *Linnaeus: Nature and Nation.* Cambridge, Mass.: Harvard University Press, 1999.

Kuykendall, Ralph S. *The Hawaiian Kingdom, 1778–1854: Foundation and Transformation.* Honolulu: University of Hawaii Press, 1938.

Lal, Brij V., and Kate Fortune, eds. *The Pacific Islands: An Encyclopedia.* Honolulu: University of Hawaii Press, 2000.

Lamb, Jonathan. *Preserving the Self in the South Seas, 1680–1840.* Chicago: University of Chicago Press, 2001.

Lamb, Jonathan, Vanessa Smith, and Nicholas Thomas, eds. *Exploration and Exchange: A South Seas Anthology, 1680–1900.* Chicago: University of Chicago Press, 2000.

La Pérouse, Jean-François de. *The Journal of Jean-François de Galaup de la Pérouse, 1785–1788.* 2 vols. Translated and edited by John Dunmore. 2nd ser., nos. 179–180. London: Hakluyt Society, 1994.

Larson, James L. *Interpreting Nature: The Science of Living Form from Linnaeus to Kant.* Baltimore: Johns Hopkins University Press, 1994.

Lavery, Brian ed. *Shipboard Life and Organisation, 1731–1815.* Aldershot: Ashgate, 1998.

Liebersohn, Harry. *Aristocratic Encounters: European Travelers and North American Indians.* Cambridge: Cambridge University Press, 1998.

——— "Discovering Indigenous Nobility: Tocqueville, Chamisso, and Romantic Travel Writing." *American Historical Review* 99 (1994): 746–766.

Linnekin, Jocelyn. *Sacred Queens and Women of Consequence: Rank, Gender, and Colonialism in the Hawaiian Islands.* Ann Arbor: University of Michigan Press, 1990.

Lovejoy, Arthur O. *Essays in the History of Ideas.* 1948; reprint, New York: George Braziller, 1955.

Mackay, David. *In the Wake of Cook: Exploration, Science, and Empire, 1780–1801.* London: Croom Helm, 1985.

Malaspina, Alejandro. *The Malaspina Expedition, 1789–1794: Journal of the Voyage by Alejandro Malaspina.* Vol. 1: *Cadiz to Panama.* Edited by Andrew David et al., with an introduction by Donald C. Cutter. 3rd ser., no. 8. London: Hakluyt Society, in association with Museo Naval, Madrid, 2001.

Miller, David P., and Peter Hanns Reill, eds. *Visions of Empire: Voyages, Botany, and Representations of Nature.* Cambridge: Cambridge University Press, 1996.

Mills, Peter R. *Hawai'i's Russian Adventure: A New Look at Old History.* Honolulu: University of Hawai'i Press, 2002.

Morris, Nancy J. "Hawaiian Missionaries Abroad, 1852–1909." Ph.D. diss., University of Hawaii, 1987.

Mühlmann, Wilhelm E. *Geschichte der Anthropologie.* 2nd ed. Frankfurt am Main: Athenäum Verlag, 1968.

Newbury, Colin. *Tahiti Nui: Change and Survival in French Polynesia, 1767–1945.* Honolulu: University of Hawaii Press, 1980.

Oliver, Douglas L. *Ancient Tahitian Society.* 3 vols. Honolulu: University of Hawaii Press, 1974.

Pagden, Anthony. *The Fall of Natural Man: The American Indian and the Origins of Comparative Ethnology.* Cambridge: Cambridge University Press, 1982.

Penny, H. Glenn. *Objects of Culture: Ethnology and Ethnographic Museums in Imperial Germany.* Chapel Hill: University of North Carolina Press, 2002.

Plischke, Hans. *Johann Friedrich Blumenbachs Einfluss auf die Entdeckungs-reisenden seiner Zeit.* Abhandlungen der Gesellschaft der Wissenschaften zu Göttingen, Philologisch-Historische Klasse, Dritte Folge, Nr. 20. Göttingen: Vandenhoeck & Ruprecht, 1937.

Pratt, Mary Louise, *Imperial Eyes: Travel Writing and Transculturation.* London: Routledge, 1992.

Riedl-Dorn, Christa. *Das Haus der Wunder. Zur Geschichte des Naturhis-torischen Museums in Wien.* Mit einem Beitrag von Bernd Lötsch. Wien: Verlag Holzhausen, 1998.

Rodger, N. A. M. *The Wooden World: An Anatomy of the Georgian Navy.* London: Collins, 1986.

Rousseau, Jean-Jacques. *A Discourse on Inequality.* Translated and edited by Maurice Cranston. London: Penguin, 1984.

Salmond, Anne. *Two Worlds: First Meetings between Maori and European, 1642–1772.* Auckland: Viking, 1991.

Smith, Bernard. *European Vision and the South Pacific.* 2nd ed. New Haven, Conn.: Yale University Press, 1985.

——— *Imagining the Pacific: In the Wake of the Cook Voyages.* New Haven, Conn.: Yale University Press, 1992.

Smith, Vanessa. *Literary Culture and the Pacific: Nineteenth-Century Textual Encounters.* Cambridge: Cambridge University Press, 1998.

Spary, E. C. *Utopia's Garden: French Natural History from Old Regime to Rev-olution.* Chicago: University of Chicago, 2000.

Starobinski, Jean. *Jean-Jacques Rousseau: Transparency and Obstruction.* Translated by Arthur Goldhammer, with an introduction by Robert J. Morrissey. Chicago: University of Chicago Press, 1988.

Stocking, George W., Jr. *Victorian Anthropology.* New York: Free Press, 1987.

Taillemite, Étienne, ed. *Bougainville et ses compagnons autour du monde 1766–1769. Journaux de navigation.* 2 vols. Paris: Imprimerie Nationale, 1977.

Thomas, Nicholas. *Cook: The Extraordinary Voyages of Captain James Cook.* New York: Walker, 2003.

———. *In Oceania: Visions, Artifacts, Histories.* Durham, N.C.: Duke University Press, 1997.

Thomas, Nicholas, and Diane Losche, eds. *Double Vision: Art Histories and Colonial Histories in the Pacific.* Cambridge: Cambridge University Press, 1999.

Valeri, Valerio. *Kingship and Sacrifice: Ritual and Society in Ancient Hawaii.* Translated by Paula Wissing. Chicago: University of Chicago, 1985.

Vancouver, George. *A Voyage of Discovery to the North Pacific Ocean and round the World, 1791–1795.* 4 vols. Edited by W. K. Lamb. Hakluyt Society, 2nd ser., nos. 163–166. London: Hakluyt Society, 1984.

Wallace, Lee. *Sexual Encounters: Pacific Texts, Modern Sexualities.* Ithaca, N.Y.: Cornell University Press, 2003.

Withey, Lynne. *Voyages of Discovery: Captain Cook and the Exploration of the Pacific.* Berkeley: University of California Press, 1989.

Illustration Credits

Page

xiv   Maps drawn by Philip Schwartzberg.

3   *Insulaires et monumens de l'isle de Pâque,* engraved by Godefroy af-
     ter a drawing by Duché de Vancy. Jean-François de La Pérouse, *Voy-
     age de La Pérouse autour du monde, Atlas* (Paris: Imprimerie de la
     République, 1797), plate 11. Courtesy of the John Carter Brown Li-
     brary at Brown University.

16   *Flora attired by the elements.* Engraved by Anker Smith after a design
      by H. Fuseli. Erasmus Darwin, *The Botanic Garden: A Poem, in Two
      Parts* (London: Johnson, 1791), frontispiece. Courtesy of Rare Book
      and Special Collections Library, University of Illinois at Urbana-
      Champaign.

47   Untitled painting by John Francis Rigaud (1780). Courtesy of Hans-
      Jörg Rheinberger.

65   Louis Choris. Artist unknown, lithographed by Langlumé. Courtesy of
      the Donald Angus Collection, Bishop Museum, Honolulu.

89   Title page, Jean-François de La Pérouse, *Voyage de La Pérouse autour
      du monde, Atlas* (Paris: Imprimerie de la République, 1797). En-
      graved by Ph. Triere after a drawing by Moreau le Jeune. Courtesy of
      the John Carter Brown Library at Brown University.

102   *Sir Joseph Banks.* Painting by Thomas Phillips (1810). By courtesy of the National Portrait Gallery, London.

117   Bust of Count Nicolas de Romanzoff (Nikolai P. Rumiantsev). Sculptor unknown. Courtesy of the American Philosophical Society, Philadelphia.

143   *Mr. Mariner in the Costume of the Tonga Islands.* Engraved by Bragg after a painting by Mouchet. John Martin, *An Account of the Natives of the Tonga Islands in the South Pacific Ocean* . . . (London: John Murray, 1818), frontispiece. Courtesy of Rare Book and Special Collections Library, University of Illinois at Urbana-Champaign.

159   *Cadu.* Drawing by Choris. Otto von Kotzebue, *Entdeckungs-Reise in die Süd-See und nach der Berings-Strasse* . . . , 3 vols. (Weimar: Hoffmann, 1821), 3: frontispiece. Courtesy of the Beinecke Rare Book and Manuscript Library, Yale University.

179   *Habitans des îles Aléoutiennes.* Lithographed by Choris and Langlumé after a drawing by Choris. Louis Choris, *Voyage pittoresque autour du monde* . . . (Paris: Didot, 1822), Îles Aléoutiennes, plate 4. Courtesy of the Beinecke Rare Book and Manuscript Library, Yale University.

184   *Camméaméa, Roi des îles Sandwich.* Lithographed by Martes after a drawing by Choris. Louis Choris, *Voyage pittoresque autour du monde* . . . (Paris: Didot, 1822), Îles Sandwich, plate 2. Courtesy of the Beinecke Rare Book and Manuscript Library, Yale University. With permission of the Honolulu Academy of Arts.

187   *Robeing [sic] royalty, a treat for the Sandwichers, at the sign of the Hog in Armour.* Print by Samuel W. Fores (1824). By permission of the National Library of Australia (Rex Nan Kivell Collection), Canberra.

210   *Crânes des habitans des îles Aléoutiennes.* Lithographed by Choris and Langlumé after a drawing by Choris. Louis Choris, *Voyage pittoresque autour du monde* . . . (Paris: Didot, 1822), Îles Aléoutiennes, plate 6. Courtesy of the Beinecke Rare Book and Manuscript Library, Yale University.

229   *Rangui, L'un des chefs de Shouraki. (Nouvelle Zélande).* Lithographed by Maurin and De Lemercier after a drawing by de Sainson. Jules Dumont d'Urville, *Voyage de la corvette L'Astrolabe, exécuté pendant les années 1826–1827–1828–1829, Atlas* (Paris: Tastu, 1833), plate 71. Courtesy of Rare Book and Special Collections Library, University of Illinois at Urbana-Champaign.

250   *Obookiah. A Native of Owhyhee.* Print by P. Maverick Durand & Co. Edwin W. Dwight, *Memoirs of Henry Obookiah* . . . (Elizabeth, N.J.: Hart, 1819), frontispiece. By permission of Houghton Library, Harvard University.

255   *Reine Cahoumanou.* Lithographed by Norblin and Langlumé after a drawing by Choris. Louis Choris, *Voyage pittoresque autour du monde* . . . (Paris: Didot, 1822), Îles Sandwich, plate 3. Courtesy of the Beinecke Rare Book and Manuscript Library, Yale University.

278   *Fuegian (Yapoo Takeenica) at Portrait Cove.* Artwork by T. Landseer and C. Martens. Robert FitzRoy, *Narrative of the surveying voyages of his Majesty's ships Adventure and Beagle, between the years 1826 and 1836* . . . , 3 vols. (London: H. Colburn, 1839), 2: frontispiece. Courtesy of Rare Book and Special Collections Library, University of Illinois at Urbana-Champaign.

 *Index*

Academy of Sciences, Paris, 15, 88, 298; voyage patronage, 82; abolished, 90; prepares voyage instructions, 90

Academy of Sciences, Prussian, 138, 216, 223

Academy of Sciences, Russian, 67

Admiralty, British, 11, 32, 33, 34; appointment of Cook, 80. *See also* Banks, Sir Joseph; Barrow, Sir John

African Association: founding, 112; aided by Blumenbach, 129

Ahutoru, 144, 147. *See also* Bachaumont, Louis Petit de; Bougainville, Louis de; La Condamine, Charles-Marie de; Pereire, Jacob-Rodrigue; Swieten, Godefroy van

Alembert, Jean Le Rond d', 145

Aleuts, 69, 115

Ali'i (Hawaiian elite), 70, 73; defined, 162–163; power under Kamehameha I, 177, 178; situation after Kamehameha I's death, 255

Altenstein, Karl von Stein zum, patronizes F. J. F. Meyen, 130–131

American Board of Commissioners for Foreign Missions (ABCFM), 246–247;

recruitment of Hawaiians, 247–249; missionary school, 249–252; financial support, 252–253; leadership, 253–254. *See also* Missionaries, Hawaiian

Anson, George, 79

Araucanians, 68

Ari'i (Tahitian elite), 162, 169

Austria, voyage patronage by, 125–126

Bachaumont, Louis Petit de, impressions of Ahutoru, 146

Bacstrom, Sidney, 104

Banks, Sir Joseph, 15; joins first Cook voyage, 98; dismissed from second voyage, 98–99; as expedition patron, 100–111; becomes president of the Royal Society, 101; leadership of Kew Gardens, 102–103; correspondence, 103–104; idealization of Tahitians, 166; advises London Missionary Society, 232–233

Baranov, Alexander, 178

Barret, Jeanne, 191; relationship with Commerson, 21–22; on Bougainville voyage, 23; stays on Mauritius and Madagascar, 25–26; inheritance, 28

Barrow, Sir John, 111–114

Basques. *See* Humboldt, Wilhelm von

Bayly, C. A., 231, 236

Beechey, Frederick W., 263–264, 279, 280, 295

Bennet, George, 268–269

Berlin, University of, 61, 127, 129–130

Berlin Geographic Society, 131–132

Bernstorff, J. H. von, 125

Bicknell, Henry, 236

Bildung, 222–297

Billardière, Jacques de la, 106

Bligh, William, 101; Tahiti voyages, 171–172; relations with Pomares, 172–175

Blumenbach, Johann Friedrich, 132, 286; as expedition patron, 127–128; skull collecting, 128, 129; career, 128–129; friendship with Joseph Banks, 129; views on race, 200

Boas, Franz, 224

Bombay, 103

Bonpland, Aimé, 132

Bora Bora, 151

Bougainville, Louis de: world voyage, 1–2; patronage, 85–87; relations with Ahutoru, 144–146; use of Ahutoru as informant, 147–149. *See also* Diderot, Denis

Bowie, James, 105

Brazil, 126, 132. *See also* Bowie, James

Brosses, Charles de, 32, 33

Broughton, William Robert, 170

Broussonet, Pierre, 106–107

Buenos Aires, 23

Buffon, Georges-Louis Leclerc, comte de, 15, 26, 88, 145; patronage, 82–83

Canzler, Friedrich Gottlieb, 123

Captivity: "native" in Europe, 142 (*see also* Ahutoru); Europeans nativized, 144

Caroline Islands, 157. *See also* Kadu

Cartier, Jacques, 142

Catherine II (the Great) (empress of Russia), 99; tries to patronize George Forster, 136

Catlin, George, 142

Chamisso, Adelbert von, 2, 58–76; family, 58; early years in Berlin, 58–59; and Romanticism, 59–60, 76; with Mme de Staël, 60–61; joins Kotzebue voyage, 62; "The Amazing Story of Peter Schlemihl," 62–63; relations with Otto von Kotzebue, 63, 75, 121–122; ship life, 63–64; naturalist work, 66–67; political views, 67–70; "Notes and Opinions," 67–71; views on Hawaii, 70–71; *Tagebuch,* 71–76; on aristocracy, 73–74; populism, 74; on communication, 74–75; relations with *Rurik* voyage planners, 120–121; patronized by Friedrich Wilhelm IV, 137; relations with Alexander von Humboldt, 137–138; use of informants, 155–161; impressions of Kamehameha I, 182–183; criticism of Malte-Brun, 186; Hawaiian studies, 223, 261; and missionaries, 261–262, 270. *See also* Dumont d'Urville, Jules; Humboldt, Wilhelm von

Chamisso, Hippolyte de, 62

Chamisso, Louis Marie de, 58

Choiseul, Étienne François, Duc de, 86–87, 145

Choiseul-Chevigny, César Gabriel de, Duc de Praslin, 87, 145

Choris, Louis, 64; post-*Rurik* career, 94–97; visited by Alexander von Humboldt, 94; *Voyage pittoresque autour du monde,* 94–96, 186; portrait of Kamehameha I, 183–185. *See also* Jomard, Edme-François; Navy, French Ministry of the

Christian, Fletcher, 172

Chuchkis, 69

Clerke, Charles, 152

Cock, John, 236

Columbus Quincentennial, 7

Commerson, Philibert, 1–2, 20–32; and Linnaeus, 21, 83; early years, 21–22; joins Bougainville voyage, 22–23; on ship life, 23–24; on Tahiti, 24–25; stay on Mauritius and Madagascar, 25–26; natural history collections, 26; letter on Tahiti, 27–32; influence of Rousseau, 31; ideal of fraternity, 31; dedication to empirical veracity, 32; patronage, 83–85. *See also* Barret, Jeanne; More, Thomas

Concepción, 66, 67, 75

Condorcet, Nicholas de, 88

Cook, James: first world voyage, impact on contemporaries, 11; second world voyage, 2; voyage aims, 32–33; places visited, 33; uses Mahine as informant, 154–155; relations with Pomare family, 166

Cosmopolitans, travelers' identity as, 2, 17

Cranston, Maurice, 16

Cunningham, Allan, 105–106

Cuvier, Georges, 26, 91, 93, 94, 97

Darwin, Charles, 226; *Journal of Researches*, 273–274, 284; *Beagle* voyage, conditions of, 274–275; Alexander Humboldt and, 274, 276; views on Fuegians, 275–277, 286–287; views on Tahitians, 279–280; views on Maoris, 280–284; *Descent of Man*, 284–288; monogenism, 286; views on Hawaiian islanders, 287

Davis, Isaac, 141

Denmark, voyage patronage, 124–125

Diderot, Denis, 4, 145, 198; views on tribal societies, 188–189; involvement in *History of the Two Indies*, 189–190; review of Bougainville's voyage account, 190–192; *Supplement to Bougainville's Voyage*, 192–197, 239

Dolomieu, Déodat de, 107

Dorpat (Tartu), University of, 62, 64

Duff (ship), 231

Dumont d'Urville, Jules-Sébastien-César: first world voyage, 91; discovers Venus de Milo, 226–227; relations with Adelbert von Chamisso, 227; racial division of Oceania, 227–230. *See also* Geographic Society of Paris

Durkheim, Émile, 29

Dwight, Edwin Welles, 249–251

Earle, Augustus, 280–283

Easter Island, 153

Elliot de Castro, John, 155–156

Ellis, William, 279; defense of missionaries, 262–263, 270–272

Empirical veracity. *See* Commerson, Philibert; Rousseau, Jean-Jacques

Enlightenment, 6, 27, 31; on human nature, 39; enlightened monarchs, 164

Erlangen, University of, 123

Eschscholtz, Friedrich, 64, 73, 160, 183

Eyriès, Jean-Baptiste-Benoît, helps found Geographic Society of Paris, 93, 94

Falkland Islands, 86

Faust (Goethe), 62–63

Ferdinand, Duke of Braunschweig-Wolfenbüttel, patronizes J. R. Forster, 134–135

Finau 'Ulukálala II, 144

FitzRoy, Robert, 79, 274–275

Flinders, Matthew, 101, 102, 104, 107

Forster, George, 2, 32–57; joins Cook voyage, 33; "Cook the Discoverer," 54–57; revolutionary career, 57; writes voyage narrative, 100; relations with Joseph II, 135–136; moves to Mainz, 136; "Another Word about Human Races," 204–205. *See also* Heyne, Christian Gottlob; Humboldt, Wilhelm von; Kant, Immanuel; Soemmerring, Samuel Thomas; *Voyage round the World, A* (George Forster)

Forster, Johann Reinhold: joins Cook voyage, 32, 33; voyage experiences, 33; early years, 99; German patronage, 134–135. *See also* Sandwich, John Montagu, Fourth Earl of

Forster, Therese. *See* Huber-Forster, Therese

Fort-Royal (Fort-de-France), 96–97

Francis I (Habsburg emperor), 125
Fraternity, European–native friendship as, 4, 13. *See also* Commerson, Philibert; *Voyage round the World, A* (George Forster)
Frederick the Great. *See* Friedrich II
Frederik V (king of Denmark), 125
French Revolution, impact on European social hierarchies, 163
Freycinet, Louis de, 255
Friedrich II (Frederick the Great) (king of Prussia), patronizes J. R. Forster, 135
Friedrich Wilhelm III (king of Prussia), 130, 133. *See also* Humboldt, Alexander von
Friedrich Wilhelm IV (king of Prussia), 137
Fuegians. *See* Darwin, Charles

Gall, Franz, 209; analyzes skull for Choris, 94
General Association of Massachusetts Proper, 246
Geographic Society of Paris: founding, 92–93; aims, 93–94; patronizes Louis Choris, 94–96; patronizes Jules Dumont d'Urville, 227
George I (Tāufa'āhau, king of Tonga), 165
George III (king of England and Hannover), 128, 175, 177
Gillispie, Charles, 82
Glasgow, University of, 110
Goethe, Johann Wolfgang von, 211; *Faust*, 62–63
Göttingen, University of, 10, 132, 136; as center for scientific travel, 127–128
Grimm, Jacob, 220
Grimm, Melchior, 190, 192
Grimm, Wilhelm, 220
Guam, 158, 161
Gunson, Neil, 237

Haggerstein, Peter ("Peter the Swede"), 235–237, 244
Halle, University of, 99, 127, 135

Haller, Albrecht von, 83
Hardcastle, Joseph, 233
Hawaiian Islands. *See Ali'i;* American Board of Commissioners for Foreign Missions; Chamisso, Adelbert von; Darwin, Charles; Kamehameha I; Kamehameha II; Kotzebue, Otto von; Missionaries, Hawaiian; Vancouver, George
Haweis, Thomas, 232–233
Hawkesworth, John, 34, 36, 169
Hegel, Georg Wilhelm Friedrich, 215–216
Henslow, John Stevens, 276, 279
Herder, Johann Gottfried von, 131, 204; compared with Wilhelm von Humboldt, 219–220
Herschel, John Frederick William, 226
Herschel, William, 101
Herz, Henriette, 209
Heyne, Christian Gottlob, 211; patronizes J. F. Blumenbach, 128–129; patronizes George Forster, 136
Hirsching, F. C. G., 123
Hitzig, Julius Eduard, 62
Hoffmann, E. T. A., 62
Holbach, Paul Thierry d', 145
Holy Alliance, 67, 70
Hooker, Joseph Dalton, 111
Hooker, William Jackson, 110–111
Hopo, Thomas, 248
Hove, Anton, 103
Huber-Forster, Therese, 210, 211
Humboldt, Alexander von: role in Geographic Society of Paris, 93; visited by William J. Hooker, 110; career, 132–133; patronized by Friedrich Wilhelm III, 133–134. *See also* Chamisso, Adelbert von; Darwin, Charles
Humboldt, Wilhelm von, 133, 138; classical romanticism, 208–209; relations with Jews, 209–210; relations with George Forster, 210–211; relations with August von Schlegel, 211–212; influenced by Friedrich von Schlegel, 212, 218; Basque

studies, 212–214; state service, 214–215; philosophy of language, 216–222; monograph on Kawi language, 216, 219, 220–222; "On the Origins of Grammatical Forms, and Their Influence on the Development of Ideas," 218–219; relations with Adelbert von Chamisso, 222–223. *See also* Herder, Johann Gottfried von

Iceland, 110
Indians, North American, 202, 218, 235–236
Indonesia, 144, 220–221
Institut National (Paris), 106

Jacquin, Joseph Franz von, 126
Jacquin, Nicolaus Joseph von, 125–126
Jefferson, Thomas, 10, 225
Jomard, Edme-François, helps found Geographic Society of Paris, 93; expedition instructions for Choris, 95–96
Joseph II (Habsburg emperor), 126. *See also* Forster, George
Jussieu, Antoine-Laurent de, 26
Jussieu, Bernard de, 21, 84

Ka'ahumanu, 176, 259–260. *See also* Missionaries, Hawaiian
Kadu, 157–161, 186
Kalanimoku, 75
Kamchatka, 64, 66, 118. *See also* Petropavlovsk
Kamehameha I (king of Hawaiian Islands), 70; European aides, 141, 156. *See also* Ali'i; Chamisso, Adelbert von; Choris, Louis; Vancouver, George
Kamehameha II (Liholiho), 186, 254, 257
Kamehameha III, 291
Kant, Immanuel: on travelers' empirical veracity, 197; views on race, 198–200; views on "savage" freedom, 200–203; anticolonialism, 203; dispute with George Forster, 203–207
Kauai, 109, 179
Kaumuali'i, 179

Kealakekua, 177, 180
Kew Gardens, 111. *See also* Banks, Sir Joseph
King, James, 141
Kingship, 164; on Tongan Islands, 164–165
Kotzebue, August von, 62, 63, 67; relations with Krusenstern family, 119
Kotzebue, Otto von: first world voyage, 2, 62, 279, 280; instructions, 64–65; itinerary, 65–66; patronage, 119–120; planning, 120; second world voyage, 122; relations with Kamehameha I, 179–182; visit to Tahiti, 264–270. *See also* Chamisso, Adelbert von
Krusenstern, Adam von, 62; world voyage, 116–118; postvoyage career, 118–119; world voyage as model for others, 119; role in *Rurik* voyage, 119–120; relations with Adelbert von Chamisso, 120–121
Kuykendall, Ralph S., 141

La Condamine, Charles-Marie de, and Ahutoru, 145–146, 149
Lafitau, Jean-François de, 4
Lahontan, Louis-Armand de, 4
Lalande, Joseph de, 21, 27, 31, 83, 145
La Pérouse, Jean-François de, 10, 26; world voyage, 87–90
Lappland, 15
Ledebour, Friedrich, 62
Lewis, Thomas, 236, 237–238
Lewis and Clark expedition, 10, 225
Liholiho. *See* Kamehameha II
Linnaeus, Carl: influence on travelers, 15; as model for Joseph Banks, 100. *See also* Commerson, Philibert
London Missionary Society (LMS), 266, 268; expectations of Tahiti, 231–234. *See also* Missionaries, Tahitian
Louis XVI, as patron of La Pérouse, 88

Mahine (O-Hedeedee, Odiddy), 149, 151–155. *See also* Cook, James; *Voyage round the World, A* (George Forster)

Mai (Omai), 52, 149, 150–151
Mainz. See Forster, George
Malaspina, Alejandro, 80–81
Malte-Brun, Conrad, 95, 230; helps found
  Geographic Society of Paris, 93. See also
  Chamisso, Adelbert von
Maoris, 152–153, 228, 281–282. See also Dar-
  win, Charles
Marin, Don Francisco de Paula: as infor-
  mant for Chamisso, 156–157; conflict
  with missionaries, 256–257
Mariner, William, 144
Marquesan Islands, 75; invaded by David
  Porter, 289–290. See also Voyage round
  the World, A (George Forster)
Marshall Islands, 75, 157–158
Märter, Franz Josef, 126
Mauritius, 25–26, 27, 84, 104, 147
Mauss, Marcel, 78
McCormick, Robert, 275
Melville, Herman, 144; Pacific voyage, 288–
  289; Typee, 289–292, 296–297; views on
  missionaries, 291; Omoo, 292–295
Menzies, Archibald, 101; voyage prepara-
  tion, 107–108; conflict with Vancouver,
  108–110, 178
Metternich, Klemens von, 126
Meyen, F. J. F., 130–131, 132
Michaelis, Johann David, 125
Mills, Samuel J., 245, 248
Missionaries, conflict with scientists, 14,
  262–272. See also Ellis, William; Melville,
  Herman
Missionaries, Hawaiian: relations with
  Ka'ahumanu, 256; view of Hawaiian cul-
  ture, 257–260; moral legislation, 260–
  261. See also American Board of Com-
  missioners for Foreign Missions;
  Chamisso, Adelbert von; Marin, Don
  Francisco de Paula
Missionaries, Tahitian: arrival of first mis-
  sionaries, 231–232; social background,
  232; initial experiences, 234–235; sexual
  relations with Tahitians, 237–239; reli-

gious relations with Tahitians, 238–241.
  See also London Missionary Society;
  Pomare I; Pomare II; Pomare family
Moluccas, 144
Montaigne, Michel de, 4, 142
Montevideo, 23
Moorea, 167, 170, 244, 262, 289, 294
More, Thomas, 28, 31
Museum of Natural History, Paris: school
  for naturalists, 91–92; patronizes
  Choris's American expedition, 96–97.
  See also Royal Garden, Paris

Napoleon, 60–61, 67
Native Americans. See Indians, North
  American
Naturalists: aims, 2; coworkers, 7. See also
  Travelers, scientific
Natural man. See State of nature
Navy, French Ministry of the: approves
  voyage proposals, 90; instructions for
  Dumont d'Urville, 91; facilitates Choris's
  American expedition, 96
Nepean, Sir Evan, 101, 102, 108
Networks, 8–9
Niebuhr, Carsten, 124–125
Nott, Henry, 241, 243, 267, 269
Nouvelles Annales des Voyages, 93
Nukuhiva, 289–290. See also Marquesan Is-
  lands

Obookiah, Henry. See Opukahaia, Henry
Oceania, as laboratory, 44
Omai. See Mai
Opukahaia, Henry, 248–249, 251, 252
Orbigny, Alcide d', 92

Patagonians, 191
Patronage, defined, 77–79
Paul Wilhelm of Württemberg, Duke, 132
Pereire, Jacob-Rodrigue, meets Ahutoru,
  146
Peter the Swede. See Haggerstein, Peter
Petropavlovsk, 88

Philippines, 69
Pickersgill, Richard, 152
Poivre, Pierre, 25–26, 84
Pollen, George Augustus, 104
Polynesia, impact on Europe, 5–6
Pomare I (king of Tahiti), 166–171, 174–175; relations with missionaries, 243–244. *See also* Vancouver, George
Pomare II (king of Tahiti): relations with William Bligh, 172–173, 174–175; relations with missionaries, 243–245
Pomare family, royal family of Tahiti, 46, 195; patronizes missionaries, 241–245. *See also* Cook, James; *Voyage round the World, A* (George Forster)
Porter, David, 289–290
Praslin, Duc de. *See* Choiseul-Chevigny, César
Prichard, James, 226
Prostitution, 41, 70, 260
Prussia, as sponsor of scientific travel, 129–131

Radak island group, 157, 160
Republic of letters, 93, 107
Restoration era, 69–70, 72, 81, 215
Revolution of 1830, 72
Ritter, Carl, leads Berlin Geographic Society, 131
Rother, Christian von, 130
Rousseau, Jean-Jacques: influence on travelers, 16; *Discourse on Inequality* (Second Discourse), 16–18, 28, 31, 50, 202, 299; on travelers' empirical veracity, 17–18, 146, 148. *See also* Commerson, Philibert; *Voyage round the World, A* (George Forster)
Royal Botanical Garden, Berlin, 66
Royal Botanic Gardens. *See* Kew Gardens
Royal Garden, Paris, 15. *See also* Museum of Natural History
Royal Geographical Society (London), 112–114
Royal Prussian Sea Company, 130
Royal Society, London, 79–80; recommends Joseph Banks's appointment to first Cook voyage, 98
Rumiantsev, Count Nikolai P., 62, 117–118, 120, 121, 122
Rurik voyage. *See* Kotzebue, Otto von, first world voyage
Russian-American Company, 115–116, 119, 178

Sahlins, Marshall, 7
St. Helena, 67
Sandwich, John Montagu, fourth Earl of: relations with Joseph Banks 99, 101; quarrel with J. R. Forster, 99–100, 134
Sandwich Islands. *See* Hawaiian Islands
San Francisco, 68, 155
Sanskrit, 212, 219, 302
Sapir, Edward, 224
Schäffer, Georg Anton, 178–179
Schiller, Friedrich von, 211
Schlechtendal, Diederich Franz Leonhard von, 66
Schlegel, August Wilhelm von, 60–61, 212, 302. *See also* Humboldt, Wilhelm von
Schlegel, Friedrich von, 59–60, 211, 218, 297. *See also* Humboldt, Wilhelm von
Scholl, Georg, 126
Second Discourse. *See* Rousseau, Jean-Jacques
Ship life, 18–20
Sitka, 178
Smithsonian Institute, 142
Soemmerring, Samuel Thomas: views on race, 200; influence on George Forster, 203–204, 206
Solander, Daniel, 15, 100, 135
Sparrman, Anders, 42, 100
Staël, Germaine de, 60–61, 67
State of nature: literary discourse, 3–4; in North America, 4; in Oceania, 44, 148; Darwin's views on, 277, 286
Stewart, Charles, 258–260
Swieten, Godefroy van, impressions of Ahutoru, 146

Tahiti, as New Cythera, 25, 28, 149. *See also* Tahitians

Tahitians. *See* Banks, Sir Joseph; Bligh, William; London Missionary Society; Melville, Herman; Missionaries, Tahitian; *Voyage round the World, A* (George Forster)

Tanna. *See* Vanuatu

Tartu. *See* Dorpat

Thouin, André, 92

Thouin, Jean-André, 92

Tongan Islands, 51. *See also* Kingship

Torres, Don Luis de, 161

Travel, scientific: era defined, 1, 4, 12–13; ethnography in, 3–4; Enlightenment and, 6; historiography, 6–7; state sponsorship, 6, 9; German prominence, 10–11; Danish sponsorship, 12; popularization, 12; German sponsorship, 124, 134. *See also* Travelers, scientific

Travelers, scientific: mediating role, 7; hardiness, 20; relations with patrons, 76, 80–81

Travel writing: reception, 1, 2, 11–12; early modern, 12

Tupaia, 149–150

Tyerman, Daniel, 268–270

University of. *See location*

Vancouver, George: voyage aims, 107; political judgment, 109; relations with Pomare I, 170–171; relations with Kamehameha I, 176–178

Vanuatu, 36, 42

Venereal disease, 40–41, 194, 238, 239, 267, 288, 295

Vilna, University of, 135, 203

Vivez, François, 144, 147

Voltaire, 4, 39, 198

Voyage round the World, A (George Forster): justification for writing, 34; dedication to empirical veracity, 34; criticism of Rousseau, 34–35; providentialism, 35–36, 54; natives' humanity praised, 36; on indigenous women, 37; on sailors, 37–39; superiority of Europeans, 39–40; colonialism, 40, 55; anticolonialism, 40–41; ideal of fraternity, 42–44; charmed by Tahiti, 44–46; collecting activities, 45; Marquesan Islands admired, 52; language-learning, 45; critique of Tahitian decadence, 48–50; republicanism, 50–51; native egalitarianism, 51–52; uses Mahine as informant, 153–154; impressions of Pomare family, 168–169; methodology, 206

Voyages, world, 9. *See also individual travelers*

Waimea, 179

Weber, Carl Maria von, 276

Weber, Max, 77–78

Wesley, John, 232

Whitman, Walt, 291

Wied-Neuwied, Maximilian von, 61, 132

Wilkes, Charles, world voyage, 225, 226

Williams, Henry, 282

Williams, William, 282

Wilson, Charles, 265–266, 269

Wormskiold, Morton, 64

Young, John, 75, 141, 176, 179

Harvard University Press is a member of Green Press Initiative (greenpressinitiative.org), a nonprofit organization working to help publishers and printers increase their use of recycled paper and decrease their use of fiber derived from endangered forests. This book was printed on 100% recycled paper containing 50% post-consumer waste and processed chlorine free.